Maritime Law in China

T0313188

The Chinese maritime and shipping market has been expanding enormously in recent times as its commercial capacity to perform shipping, ship building, banking and insurance activities grows and the role of the State as guarantor of commerce is gradually reduced.

This book provides a detailed guide to current Chinese maritime law, written by an expert team of contributors and systematically covering key areas such as carriage of goods by sea, international trade, vessels and seafarers and maritime liabilities. The authors explore cutting-edge issues within each topic, and analyse current trends in law reform.

The book will be of interest to academics researching commercial and maritime law, as well as maritime law practitioners and shipping industry professionals working with aspects of Chinese maritime practice.

Johanna Hjalmarsson is the Informa Associate Professor in Maritime and Commercial Law at the University of Southampton.

Jingbo Zhang is a Lecturer in Maritime and Commercial Law at the University of Southampton.

Contemporary Commercial Law

Maritime Law in China: Emerging Issues and Future Developments
by
Johanna Hjalmarsson and Jingbo Zhang
(2016)

Insurance Law in China
by
Johanna Hjalmarsson and Dingjing Huang
(2015)

Causation in Insurance Contract Law
by
Meixian Song
(2014)

Maritime Law in China

Emerging Issues and Future Developments

Edited by
Johanna Hjalmarsson and Jingbo Zhang

Routledge
Taylor & Francis Group

LONDON AND NEW YORK

First published in paperback 2024

First published 2017
by Routledge
4 Park Square, Milton Park, Abingdon, Oxon, OX14 4RN

and by Routledge
605 Third Avenue, New York, NY 10158

*Routledge is an imprint of the Taylor & Francis Group,
an informa business*

British Library Cataloguing in Publication Data
A catalogue record for this book is available from the British Library

Library of Congress Cataloging-in-Publication Data
Names: Hjalmarsson, Johanna, editor. | Zhang, Jingbo (Law
teacher), editor.Title: Maritime law in China / Johanna Hjalmarsson
and Jingbo Zhang.Description: Abingdon, Oxon ; New York,
NY : Routledge, 2016. | Series: Contemporary commercial law |
Includes bibliographical references and index.Identifiers: LCCN
2015050861| ISBN 9781138666139 (hbk) | ISBN 9781315618296
(ebk)Subjects: LCSH: Maritime law--China.Classification: LCC
KNQ970 .M37 2016 | DDC 343.5109/6--dc23LC record available
at http://lccn.loc.gov/2015050861

ISBN: 978-1-138-66613-9 (hbk)
ISBN: 978-1-138-61437-6 (pbk)
ISBN: 978-1-315-61829-6 (ebk)

DOI: 10.4324/9781315618296

Typeset in Plantin by
Servis Filmsetting Ltd, Stockport, Cheshire

Contents

Foreword

On behalf of the University of Southampton Confucius Institute, I am pleased to offer a short foreword to these proceedings. Our key mission as a Confucius Institute is to deliver Chinese language learning and cultural events at the university, schools, colleges and in the wider community. However, we also take great pleasure in supporting the academic work undertaken by our colleagues in partnership with Chinese Universities. We have funded conferences and symposiums in various subject areas and this was our second joint activity with Southampton Law School.

Our first conference in 2013 on UK-China Insurance Law was an outstanding success, bringing together a diverse audience of scholars and practitioners from China and the UK for two days of presentations and debate at Lloyd's of London and the University of Southampton respectively. This rare opportunity for inter-cultural communication and knowledge exchange was very well received and the feedback strongly positive.

Inspired by this success, we were very keen to support a follow-on initiative in maritime law. China's growing importance as an economic power on the world stage and a major UK partner in international trade makes a comparative discourse in this field an essential element in the future development of trading relations between our two countries.

The event was ambitious with three full days of discussion featuring eminent academics and leading practitioners from China and the UK. Delivered in three different locations, the University of Southampton, Norton Rose Fulbright and the China Maritime Centre, Greenwich, the conference attracted a mixed audience of academics, legal practitioners and representatives from the shipping industry.

The quality of the presentations is best appreciated in the proceedings.

Mark Cranshaw
Director, University of Southampton Confucius Institute

Preface

The collection of papers presented here arose out of the Chinese and English Maritime Law Conference held in April 2014 at three venues in Southampton and London. The vision for the book has been to present particularly significant issues in contemporary Chinese maritime and commercial law to an audience familiar with English law, the common law or international law, but largely unfamiliar with Chinese law. The chapters all take a critical approach to the current state of the law, explaining the direction in which the law needs to develop. We hope that the book gives some indication not just of what China's maritime law is today, but of what is to come.

The papers of Professor Yvonne Baatz, Professor Jason Chuah, Professor Tingzhong Fu, Johanna Hjalmarsson, Professor James Zhengliang Hu, Dr Meixian Song and Dr Jenny Jingbo Zhang were all presented in some form at the conference. The remaining papers have been sourced after the conference and complete a rounded view of Chinese commercial and maritime law. Meanwhile, some papers presented at the conference have been published elsewhere, including 'Delivery of Goods Under a Straight Bill of Lading: Chinese Judicial Practice and Perspective' by Professor Lixin Han in (2015) 7 *Journal of Business Law* 573–586 and Pengfei Zhang's presentation, for which see Zhang, P. and Phillips, E., 'Safety first: Reconstructing the concept of seaworthiness under the maritime labour convention 2006' (2016) *Marine Policy*, 67, pp. 54–59.

Professor Hu's initial chapter foreshadows much of what follows. He discusses the state of modern Chinese maritime law and identifies where the reform needs are greatest. Professor Fu's chapter addresses the core issue of carrier's liability and the concept of the actual carrier as implemented in Chinese law. Dr Song then discusses the rules surrounding crew liability and protection in carriage cases. Dr Zhang focuses on examining bills of lading and the subsequent effects to bank's security. Mr Peng considers the P3 merger, now a historical endeavour but one that permits interesting conclusions to be drawn about Chinese competition law. Dr Huang clarifies the position of maritime liens in the context of insolvency under Chinese law, noting that the law may need to evolve further. Professor

Zhang explains the law and commonly used contract terms applicable to sea towage. Mr Wu and Professor Han tackle the law on direct action for oil pollution damage, making recommendations on the reform of the law. The chapter by Ms Hjalmarsson and Ms Wu deals with the treatment of spot market contracts under Chinese law. Professor Chuah's chapter addresses the philosophy and approach of Chinese private international law, and the chapter is immediately followed by Professor Baatz's chapter which reflects on issues raised by a case where Chinese and English courts both asserted jurisdiction over a dispute based on bills of lading.

Although maritime law is traditionally taken to include marine insurance, we have opted not to cover that subject here. We refer interested readers to Hjalmarsson and Huang (eds), *Insurance Law in China* (Informa, 2014), which contains several chapters on marine insurance; not least by some of the authors contributing to the present volume.

We owe thanks to the speakers, chairs and audience who contributed to the conference and made it an exciting event: Dr Minghua Zhao and our hosts the China Maritime Centre at the University of Greenwich; and Dr Wenhao Han and Norton Rose Fulbright. Gratitude is owed to the Confucius Institute at the University of Southampton, without whose generous funding and confidence the event would not have taken place. Last but by no means least, we thank the team of postgraduate researchers, especially Dingjing Huang and Haihua Song as well as administrative colleagues at all three venues and at the Institute of Maritime Law and wider University of Southampton who helped make the three events happen. We would also like to thank our publishers and others who have contributed to the editing process.

The law is mostly stated as it was in June 2015.

Johanna Hjalmarsson
Informa Associate Professor
in Maritime and Commercial Law

Dr Jingbo Zhang
Lecturer in Maritime
and Commercial Law

Institute of Maritime Law
Southampton Law School
University of Southampton

Notes on contributors

EDITORS

Ms Johanna Hjalmarsson
Juris kandidat (LLM) (Stockholm) 1995; LLM in maritime law (Soton) 2004; Cert HE: languages (Soton), 2008.

Johanna is the Informa Associate Professor in Maritime and Commercial Law at Southampton Law School, University of Southampton. She is a Member of the Institute of Maritime Law and a Co-director of the Insurance Law Research Group. Having served as a Junior Judge in her native Sweden, she worked for many years for the United Nations and the Office of the High Representative in Bosnia and Herzegovina, specialising in law reform. She has published several books and articles in the field of maritime, insurance and commercial law, and is the editor of *Shipping and Trade Law* and *Lloyd's Law Reporter* as well as the IML publication *The Ratification of Maritime Conventions*. She is a founder and general editor of the free web resource AviationLaw.EU and teaches insurance and marine insurance law.

Dr Jenny Jingbo Zhang
Jingbo is a Lecturer in Maritime and Commercial Law at the School of Law, University of Southampton. She is also a member with the Institute of Maritime Law. She completed both her LLB in law and BA in economics at the Southwest University of Political Science and Law (China). She then read an LLM in maritime law and obtained her PhD in international trade law at the University of Southampton. She was conferred the outstanding overseas PhD researcher award by the China Scholarship Council. She coordinated the Chinese-English Insurance Law Conference in 2013 and the Chinese-English Maritime Law Conference in 2014 sponsored by the University of Southampton Confucius Institute.

Jingbo's research interests lie in international trade law; carriage of goods by sea; marine insurance; and WTO law. Her research outcomes have been successfully presented at both international and national conferences and subsequently turned into academic articles, such as 'Bank's

Post-notice Obligations in the Documentary Credits under UCP600' in the *International Journal of Private Law.*

CONTRIBUTORS (following the order of chapters)

Professor James Zhengliang Hu

BSc in nautical science, LLM and PhD in maritime and shipping law at Dalian Maritime University; visiting scholar to the University of Antwerp from 1994 to 1995; senior visiting scholar to the Catholic University of Leuven in 2001.

Zhengliang Hu is a Professor of Maritime Law and Director of the Institute of Maritime Law of Shanghai Maritime University. He is also a visiting professor to the Dalian Maritime University and Swansea University. He is a lawyer with the law firm, Wintell & Co Law, based in Shanghai. He is an arbitrator for the China Maritime Arbitration Commission and the Shanghai International Shipping Arbitration Chamber. He works as a member of the Standing Committee of China Maritime Law Association and is a member of Standing Committee of China Maritime Experts Commission. He is also a draftsman of the Chinese Maritime Code, the Chinese Port Law, the draft Chinese Shipping Law and the revision of the Chinese Maritime Traffic Safety Law as well as various shipping regulations. He was a member of the Chinese delegation to UNCITRAL Working Group III when the Rotterdam Rules were negotiated.

Professor Tingzhong Fu

Professor Fu taught at Dalian Maritime University prior to 2000 and he was the Dean of the DMU Law School. From 2001, he has been a professor of Tsinghua University, China. In 2002, he successively visited Oxford University and Cambridge University as a visiting professor. During his teaching career, he has published more than 90 papers as well as the standard works: 'The Theory of Maritime Law', 'The Theory of Insurance Law', and his recent book *Maritime Law: Concepts, Principles and System* published in 2015.

Professor Fu is also an arbitrator of the China Maritime Arbitration Commission, Managing Director of the China Maritime Law Association, Managing Director of the China Institute of Insurance law and Managing Director of the China Institute of the WTO Rules.

Dr Meixian Song

Dr Meixian Song's main research interest is maritime law, primarily the commercial sector, not least marine insurance law, carriage of goods by sea and contract law. Meixian gained her LLB specialising in maritime law at Dalian Maritime University (China). Later she studied maritime law at University College London for an LLM and completed her PhD at Southampton Law School in 2012. Thereafter, Meixian joined the

University of Exeter, first as a research fellow, then as a lecturer since 2013. Her first monograph, *Causation in Insurance Contract Law*, was published in 2014 by Informa Law from Routledge. She is a qualified lawyer in China where she worked on marine insurance and carriage cases.

Philip Peng (Peng Xianwei)

Deputy-Chair of the Maritime Law Committee of Beijing; the Lawyers' Association; LMAA Supporting Member (since 2014); PhD Candidate of Dalian Maritime University Law School (since 2014); lawyer with Hai Tong & Partners (since 2006).

Mr Peng mainly handles shipping cases for shipowners and P&I Clubs, and also provides legal solutions regarding international trade, arbitration, antitrust, and foreign direct investment. Mr Peng was involved in handling three of the Top Ten Important Cases from China's 30 Years of Maritime Trials published by the Chinese Supreme Court in September 2014. He has authored the chapter 'Movement of Goods (Transport and Shipping)' in *Doing Business in Asia* (Thomson Reuters, 2014), and is the owner of the Chinese Maritime and Commercial Law Group on Linkedin (URL: http://www.linkedin.com/grp/home?gid=4354380). Mr Peng's past cases include the *Conoco Philips 'Penglai 19-3'* oilfield pollution case; the *P3 Network (Maersk, MSC, CMA CGM)* antitrust review case; and several international, high-value disputes.

Dr Dingjing Huang

PhD in maritime law; LLM, University of Southampton.

Dr Huang finished his PhD in maritime law in May 2015. His research focuses on the enforcement of maritime claims. During his PhD study, Dr Huang was involved in various academic activities, including organising the Chinese-English Maritime Law Conference held in April 2014. Dr Huang also worked as a tutor in admiralty law at the University of Southampton.

Professor Lina Zhang

Lina Zhang is a professor and doctoral supervisor in the Law School at Hainan University, China. She is the director of the international law department of the Law School. She is also a Director of the China International Economic Law Association. She worked as a postdoctoral scholar in the Law School of Tsinghua University, China between April 2010 and March 2012. She was a visiting professor in the Law School of Nagoya University, Japan from October 2008 to March 2009 and also a visiting professor in the Law and Business School of Charles Darwin University, Australia from May to August 2010. Between September 2013 and September 2014 she worked as a visiting scholar in the School of Law at Southampton University, UK. Professor Lina Zhang's research interests involve IP law, maritime law and the law of the sea. During the past 15 years she has published more than 50 academic papers and six academic books.

Hongyu Wu

Master student major in international commercial law at the University of Nottingham School of Law; BA (Dalian Maritime University); major in maritime law. Exchange student at the University of Nottingham during the 2014–2015 academic year.

Professor Lixin Han

PhD and Professor of Maritime Law; doctoral supervisor; Vice Dean of the Law School of DMU; Arbitrator for CMAC and CIETAC; Vice Chief Editor of *Journal of Chinese Maritime Law*

Lixin Han was a senior visiting professor at the Institute of Maritime Law, Tulane University from August to November 2006. She is also a visiting professor at the School of Law, University of Hong Kong, a visiting professor at the International Shipping Law School, East China University of Political Science and Law and a distinguished overseas research fellow at the Institute of Maritime Law, Waseda University.

Professor Lixin Han has published nearly 90 papers and more than 10 books during the past 25 years. Her key publications include: *Private International Maritime Laws*, *Study of the Legal System of Compensation for Oil Pollutions Damage Caused by Ships*, *Study of Torts at Sea*, *New Development Regarding the Liability of Classification Society* and various works on bills of lading and admiralty law.

Keren Wu

LLB maritime law, Shanghai Maritime University, China; LLM maritime law, University of Southampton. She is currently a postgraduate research student in insurance law at the University of Southampton. Her research topic is the interpretation of clauses in treaty reinsurance. Since 2015, Keren Wu is also a part-time tutor in marine insurance law.

Professor Jason C. T. Chuah

Jason is Professor of Commercial and Maritime Law and Head of Department at the City Law School, City University London. He has held scholarships from Barclays Bank and the UK Overseas Development Authority at Cambridge University. He is grateful to the Centre for Maritime Law at the National University of Singapore for enabling him to carry out research on PRC maritime law during his time there as Visiting Research Professor. He has authoured several key legal texts and well over 200 articles in reputable law journals. His works have been cited by courts and institutions in the UK, the USA, Asia and the EU. He is the editor of several peer reviewed journals, including the *Journal of International Maritime Law*. He is appointed to the UK Arts and Humanities Research Council. He has also been nominated several times by his students for the Oxford University Press Law Teacher of the Year Award.

Professor Yvonne Baatz

Yvonne Baatz is a Professor in the Law School at the University of Southampton. She qualified as a solicitor in 1981 and practised with two leading firms of solicitors in the City of London, specialising in shipping litigation, until 1991 when she became a lecturer at the University of Southampton. Yvonne has published numerous articles and chapters on carriage of goods by sea; conflicts of law in maritime and insurance disputes; and marine insurance. She is a Member of the Institute of Maritime Law and served as Institute Director for three years from 2003. She has edited the third edition of *Maritime Law*, published in August 2014, contributing two chapters on conflict of laws and charterparties.

Table of cases

European Union

Hong Kong

Singapore

Table of legislation

Chinese Legislation

European Union

France

Italy

Russian Federation

United Kingdom

United States

1 A study on the revision of the Chinese Maritime Code

Professor James Zhengliang Hu

1. Introduction

The Maritime Code of the People's Republic of China[1] (hereinafter referred to as 'the Maritime Code') was adopted on 7 November 1992 by the Standing Committee of the National People's Congress and came into force as of 1 July 1993. It contains in separate chapters the general provisions and the specific provisions on ships, master and crew, contracts of carriage of goods or passengers by sea, charterparties, contracts of towage by sea, ship's collision, salvage at sea, general average, limitation of liability for maritime claims, contracts of marine insurance, time-bars and application of law in relations with foreign elements. The Maritime Code is the main source of maritime law in China and is deemed as one of the four principal laws in support of the maritime and shipping industry in China.[2]

In its implementation for more than 20 years, the Maritime Code has played a role as a milestone in regulating the relations arising from maritime transport and those pertaining to ships, in securing and protecting the legitimate rights and interests of the parties concerned, and in promoting the development of maritime transport, the economy and trade. It has also provided the legal basis for courts of law in the trial of tens of thousands of cases per year in China. As a whole, the implementation of the Maritime Code for more than 20 years proves that the making of the Maritime Code followed the guiding ideology and legislative principles, had the advantages of moderate forward-thinking ideas, an advanced nature, system integrity, clear contents and enforceability and thus received good appraisal from the community. At the same time, the maritime and trading situation in China and in the world, the contents of the principles followed in the making of the Maritime Code and the relevant domestic basic laws have undergone significant development. The Maritime Code does not apply to domestic carriage of goods by sea and lacks a legal regime governing compensation

---

1 In this chapter, 'the People's Republic of China' or 'China' refers to Mainland China unless otherwise expressly indicated.
2 The other three principal laws are the Maritime Traffic Safety Law of 1983, the Port Law of 2003 and the Shipping Law which has not yet been adopted.

for marine pollution damage from ships. Admiralty judicial practice has demonstrated the existence of ambiguities, uncertainties and gaps in some aspects of the Maritime Code. All these serve to prove the necessity of updating the Maritime Code by way of revision thereof.

In this chapter, the author analyses the necessity for the revision, discusses the main contents of revision and anticipates the future of the revision of the Maritime Code.

2. Why is a revision of the Maritime Code needed?

In the opinion of the author, the necessity for revision of the Maritime Code is based on the following main reasons.

2.1 Significant developments in the maritime economy and trade and related areas since the adoption of the Maritime Code in 1992

In the past 20 years or more, the maritime trade and related areas have developed significantly along with global economic growth, especially the economic globalisation and freedom of trade in the world. At the same time, maritime trade in China has also developed significantly along with the implementation of reforms and open policy. In addition, advanced technology in shipbuilding, navigation and communication has been widely accepted. These developments will be analysed in detail as follows.

First, as a result of global economic growth, especially the economic globalisation and freedom of trade in the world, the volume of maritime trade has increased greatly. According to the statistics issued by the United Nations Conference on Trade and Development (UNCTAD), the volume of world seaborne trade in 2013 was about 2.3 times greater than in 1992.[3] It is quite understandable that the economic globalisation and freedom of trade in the world requires uniform rules and practice in economic and trade transactions. In particular, the growth in international maritime transport requires more uniform commercial and technical rules.

Secondly, according to statistics issued by the National Bureau of Statistics of China, the total import and export commodity trade volume of China in 1992 was US$165.53 billion and ranked eleventh in the world. Along with the constant rapid growth of the Chinese economy, China's total import and export commodity trade volume in 2014 reached US$4,160 billion[4] which is 25 times greater than in 1992 and ranked first in the world. About 90% of the imported and exported commodities to or from China are carried by

---

3 The volume of world seaborne trade in 2013 was nearly 9.6 billion tons. UNCTAD, *Review of Maritime Transport 2014*, <http://unctad.org/en/PublicationChapters/rmt2014ch1_en.pdf> accessed 23 May 2015. The volume of world seaborne trade in 1992 was nearly 4.2 billion tons. UNCTAD, *Review of Maritime Transport 1992*, <http://unctad.org/en/PublicationsLibrary/rmt1992_en.pdf> accessed 23 May 2015.

4 See <http://data.stats.gov.cn/workspace/index?m=hgnd> accessed 23 May 2015.

sea. Such developments together with the growing domestic commodity trade greatly enhanced the maritime transport in China. In 2014, the total turnover of cargo in the scaled ports in China reached 11.16 billion metric tons and ranked first in the world for 12 years and the turnover of containers reached 200.938 million TEUs.[5] According to UNCTAD, the number of vessels owned by companies in Mainland China was 5,405 with a total DWT of 200,179,000 tons being 11.94% of the world merchant fleet and ranking third in the world, while the number of vessels owned by companies in Hong Kong was 610 with a total DWT of 26,603,000 tons being 1.59% of the world merchant fleet and ranking fifteenth in the world.[6]

Thirdly, along with rapid developments in containerisation and multimodal transport of goods, most of the general cargoes and even some solid or liquid bulk cargoes are carried in containers. Containerisation makes multimodal transport and even door-to-door service practicable to meet the requirements of modern cargo trade. At the same time, the requirements of cargo traders for timely arrival and delivery of cargo are higher than ever besides their traditional requirement for the safe arrival of cargo, while the slow movement of traditional transport documents (bills of lading) impedes such a purpose.

Fourthly, the application of advanced technology of shipbuilding, navigation and communication makes ships larger, more specialised and more modernised. Along with such technical developments, maritime transport becomes quicker and safer; not to mention that the ability of human beings in overcoming maritime perils has been enhanced.

Fifthly, the above developments have also brought about developments in related industries or sectors besides the shipping industry, the cargo trading industry and port terminal operators, such as marine insurance, seafarers, ship management, logistics, ship finance, freight forwarding and other maritime auxiliary services, shipbuilding and even dispute resolution.

As a result of the significant developments in the maritime economy and trade and related fields in China and in the world since the adoption of the Maritime Code in 1992, modernisation of the Maritime Code is required to reflect those developments. In particular, a modern Code should take into account the prevalent trend of international uniformity of maritime law; be suitable for continued reform in modes of transport (containerisation, multimodal transport) and rapid growth in logistics; should promote maritime transactions and secure their efficiency; and should carefully calibrate the interests of shipowners, cargo interests and other stakeholders under the law.

---

5 The National Bureau of Statistics of China, *Statistical Communiqué of the People's Republic of China on National Economic and Social Development in 2014*, <http://www.stats.gov.cn/tjsj/zxfb/201502/t20150226_685799.html> accessed 23 May 2015.

6 UNCTAD, *Review of Maritime Transport 2014*, <http://unctad.org/en/PublicationsLibrary/rmt2014_en.pdf> accessed 23 May 2015. Several big ship-owning companies in Hong Kong benefit from investment by the companies in Mainland China such as COSCO Hong Kong.

2.2   Changes in the basic principles of the Maritime Code

The making of the Maritime Code followed five basic principles, namely: (a) starting from the current maritime and trading situation in China; (b) being based on the international maritime treaties prevailing in the world; (c) absorbing non-governmental rules reflecting international maritime customs and usages; (d) using the standard maritime contract forms with wide influence for reference; and (e) taking into consideration current trends in international maritime legislation. It has proved correct to follow these basic principles in the making of the Maritime Code. In the past 20 years or more, however, the contents of these basic principles have gone through significant changes.

First, following the principle of starting from the current maritime and trading situation in China prevailing at the time of 1992, the limits of liability adopted in respect of domestic maritime transport are very low. That is, the limit of liability of the carrier for death of, or personal injury to, passengers in domestic maritime transport is as low as RMB40,000 or currently about US$6,500 per person per carriage.[7] The limits of global limitation for maritime claims applicable to domestic ships are 50% of those applicable to international ships;[8] the same as the limits of liability provided for in the 1976 LLMC Convention.[9] These low limits of liability may have been appropriate in the prevailing economic situation in 1992, but have subsequently proven to be too low in practice as a result of economic developments in the last 20 years or more. This may be illustrated by the fact that the per capita disposable income of urban residents was RMB1,826 in 1992,[10] but had increased to RMB28,844 in 2014;[11] an increase of 15.8 times. Due to the quick growth in passenger transport by high-speed railway, highways and air, especially the construction of long bridges, the volume of

7 Article 3 of the Provisions on Limits of Liability in the Carriage of Passengers by Sea between the Ports of the People's Republic of China, promulgated by the former Ministry of Communications and approved by the State Council in 1993. Article 4 provides: 'The limit of liability for death of, or personal injury to, passengers of a ship in the carriage of passengers by sea shall be an amount of RMB40,000 multiplied by the number of passengers which the ship is authorised to carry according to the ship's certificate, but not exceeding RMB21 million.'

8 Article 4 of the Provisions on Limits of Liability Regarding Vessels with Gross Tonnage of Less than 300 Tons and Vessels Engaged in Coastal Carriage or Operations, promulgated by the former Ministry of Communications and approved by the State Council in 1993.

9 Convention on Limitation of Liability for Maritime Claims (LLMC), promulgated by the International Maritime Organization (IMO) and first adopted in 1976, subsequently amended in 1996 and 2012.

10 The National Bureau of Statistics of China, *Statistical Communiqué of the People's Republic of China on National Economic and Social Development in 1992*, <http://www.stats.gov.cn/tjsj/tjgb/ndtjgb/qgndtjgb/200203/t20020331_30006.html> accessed 23 May 2015.

11 The National Bureau of Statistics of China, *Statistical Communiqué of the People's Republic of China on National Economic and Social Development in 2014*, <http://www.stats.gov.cn/tjsj/zxfb/201502/t20150226_685799.html> accessed 28 February 2016.

traditional passenger transport remains stable or is even declining. On the other hand, however, passenger transport by luxury cruise ships is growing rapidly and it is reasonable to apply higher standards of compensation for death of, or injury to, passengers carried by cruise ships.

Another example is that Chapter IV 'Contracts of Carriage of Goods by Sea' of the Maritime Code, arguably the most important part of the Code, does not apply to domestic carriage of goods by sea,[12] due to the existence of differences between the legal regimes applicable to international carriage of goods by sea and to domestic carriage of goods by sea.[13] Domestic carriage of goods by sea is currently mainly regulated by the Contract Law of 1999, causing significant differences in the carrier's liability regime between international carriage of goods by sea and domestic carriage of goods by sea. Such a situation is inappropriate to large-scale domestic carriage of goods by sea,[14] and also does not facilitate the rapid development of the ocean through carriage or multimodal transport of goods.

Secondly, following the principle of being based on the international maritime treaties prevailing in the world, the Maritime Code has the following features: (a) Chapter IV 'Contracts of Carriage of Goods by Sea' is based on the Hague-Visby Rules as amended by its 1979 SDR Protocol in relation to the carrier's liability regime, while also adopting in whole or in part some provisions of the Hamburg Rules[15] regarding the definitions of shipper and actual carrier, shipper's obligations and liabilities, transport documents, etc; (b) Chapter V 'Contracts of Carriage of Passengers by Sea' is essentially a reproduction of the 1974 Athens Convention as amended by its 1976 SDR Protocol to which China is a party; (c) Chapter VIII 'Ship Collision' is a carbon copy of the 1910 Collision Convention to which China is a party; (d) Chapter XI 'Limitation of Liability for Maritime

---

12 Chapter I, Article 2 of the Maritime Code.

13 The differences between the international carriage of goods by sea and the domestic carriage of goods by sea were: (a) the state transport plans should be followed in the domestic carriage, whereas there were no such plans in the international carriage; (b) the carrier's liability was fault liability in the domestic carriage, whereas the carrier's liability based on the Hague-Visby Rules with exemption of nautical fault was followed in the international carriage; (c) the carrier could not avail of any limitation of liability for loss of, or damage to, goods in the domestic carriage, whereas the limit of carrier's liability was based on the Hague-Visby Rules in the international carriage; (d) the transport documents used in the domestic carriage were sea waybills, whereas bills of lading were used in the international carriage.

14 By the end of 2014, there were 11,048 coastal ships with a total carrying capacity of 69.21 million tons. In 2014, the total quantity of cargo carried in coastal trade was 1.89 billion metric tons. The Ministry of Transport, *Statistical Communiqué of Development in Transport and Communication Industry in 2014*, <http://www.moc.gov.cn/zfxxgk/bnssj/zhghs/201504/t20150430_1810598.html> accessed 23 May 2015.

15 China is not a party to the Hague Rules (International Convention for the Unification of Certain Rules of Law Relating to Bills of Lading, Brussels, 25 August 1924), Hague-Visby Rules (The Hague Rules as Amended by the Brussels Protocol 1968), or the Hamburg Rules (United Nations Convention on the Carriage of Goods by Sea, 1978).

Claims' reproduces the 1976 LLMC Convention.[16] In the past 20 years or more, these international maritime treaties have developed greatly. For example, the 2002 Athens Convention came into force on 23 April 2014, significantly increasing the carrier's liability in terms of the basis of liability, limits of liability and liability insurance, and the 1996 Protocol to amend the 1976 LLMC Convention came into force on 13 May 2004,[17] significantly increasing the global limits of liability for maritime claims.

Thirdly, following the principle of absorbing non-governmental rules reflecting international maritime custom and usage, the provisions of Chapter X 'General Average' are essentially extracted from the 1974 York-Antwerp Rules. However, the 1994 or 2004 version of the York-Antwerp Rules is now widely used in general average adjustment in the world.

Fourthly, following the principle of using standard maritime contract forms with wide influence for reference, Section 7 'Special Provisions Regarding Voyage Charterparties' of Chapter IV is based on GENCON 1976; Section 2 'Time Charterparties' of Chapter VI 'Charterparties' is based on NYPE 1946 and BALTIME 1974; and Section 3 'Bareboat Charterparties' of Chapter VI is based on BARECON 1974. However, GENCON 1994, NYPE 1993, BALTIME 2001 and BARECON 2001 are now widely used in the shipping world.

Fifthly, following the principle of taking into consideration general trends in international maritime legislation, Chapter IX 'Salvage at Sea' essentially reproduces the 1989 Salvage Convention.[18] The draftsmen of the Maritime Code realised that this Convention represented the prevailing trend in international legislation on salvage at sea, although this Convention had not yet come into force in 1992.[19] The 1989 Salvage Convention is now widely adopted globally. On the other hand, several new international conventions which represent, or may hopefully represent, the future of international maritime legislation have since been adopted, although they have not yet

16 China is a party to the 1974 Athens Convention (Athens Convention relating to the Carriage of Passengers and their Luggage by Sea, IMO 1974) as amended by its 1976 SDR Protocol, and the 1910 Collision Convention (Convention for the Unification of Certain Rules of Law with respect to Collisions between Vessels, Brussels, 23 September 1910). China is also a party to the 1976 LLMC Convention, but this Convention is applicable to Hong Kong only.

17 According to the statistics of Comité Maritime International (CMI), the 1996 Protocol has now been ratified by 23 countries and the 1976 LLMC Convention has 50 member states, <http://www.comitemaritime.org/Uploads/Publications/CMI_YBK_Part_III.pdf> accessed 23 May 2015. The total DWT of the merchant fleets of the member states of the 1996 Protocol represents about 23% of the world fleet tonnage, and that of the member states of the 1976 LLMC Convention represents about 50% of the world fleet tonnage. The 1996 Protocol increases the limits of liability for maritime claims to the extent of about 2.6 times of those provided for in the 1976 LLMC Convention.

18 International Convention on Salvage, 1989.

19 The 1989 Salvage Convention came into force on 14 July 1996. China is a party to this Convention.

come into force. A typical example is the adoption of the Rotterdam Rules[20] which, although intensely debated in China and even in the international community, perhaps more or less represent current trends in international legislation on the carriage of goods by sea. Another example is the 1996 HNS Convention.[21]

As a result of these significant changes in basic principles in the past 20 years or more, much of the content of the Maritime Code which was enacted in pursuance of international treaties and other documents now needs to be updated.

2.3 Lack of a legal regime in the Maritime Code governing marine pollution from ships

China became a net oil importing country in 1993 and has become the second largest oil importing country after the United States. In 2014, China imported 310 million metric tons of crude oil from 48 countries, of which nearly 170 million metric tons were imported from the member states of OPEC representing 57% of the total imported volume.[22] Most of the imported crude oil was carried by sea. Hundreds of oil tankers carrying crude oil or oil products sail through Chinese coastal waters every day. Fortunately, no very serious incident of oil pollution from a ship has so far occurred in Chinese coastal waters, but the occurrence of such an accident seems inevitable in the future. However, many minor incidents of oil pollution from ships have occurred in the coastal waters in China over the past several years.

Currently, the law applicable in China governing compensation for marine pollution damage from ships includes: (a) international conventions, i.e. the 1992 CLC,[23] the 2001 Bunker Convention[24] and the 1992 Fund Convention[25] which is applicable to Hong Kong only; (b) regulations, i.e. the Regulations on the Prevention and Control of Vessel-induced Pollution to the Marine Environment of 2009[26] and the Administrative Measures Regarding the Levy and Use of Compensation Fund for Oil Pollution from Ships of 2012;[27] (c) judicial interpretations promulgated by the Supreme

---

20 The United Nations Convention on Contracts for the International Carriage of Goods Wholly or Partly by Sea, 2008.

21 The International Convention on Liability and Compensation for Damage in Connection with the Carriage of Hazardous and Noxious Substances by Sea, 1996 as revised by the Protocol of 2010 (2010 HNS Convention). This Convention has not yet come into force.

22 See <http://finance.ifeng.com/a/20150205/13484730_0.shtml> accessed 23 May 2015.

23 IMO Protocol of 1992 to Amend the International Convention on Civil Liability for Oil Pollution Damage 1969, IMO 1992.

24 International Convention on Civil Liability for Bunker Oil Pollution Damage, IMO 2001.

25 IMO Protocol of 1992 to Amend the International Convention on the Establishment of an International Fund for Compensation for Oil Pollution Damage 1971, IMO 1992.

26 The Regulation on the Prevention and Control of Vessel-induced Pollution to the Marine Environment, Order of the State Council No.561, 9 September 2009.

27 The Administrative Measures Regarding the Levy and Use of Compensation Fund for

People's Court in 1991, i.e. the Provisions on Certain Issues in the Trial of Cases of Disputes over Compensation for Oil Pollution Damage from Ships; (d) basic law,[28] i.e. the Marine Environmental Protection Law of 1982 as amended in 1999 and 2013.[29]

However, a sound legal regime governing compensation for marine pollution damage from ships has so far not been established. This is mainly due to the fact that the application of the 1992 CLC and the 2001 Bunker Convention are limited to cases of marine pollution damage from ships with foreign elements,[30] and that the Marine Environmental Protection Law as a basic law and the Regulations on the Prevention and Control of Vessel-induced

Oil Pollution from Ships of 2012 was adopted jointly by the Ministry of Finance and the Ministry of Transport, by virtue of which the Chinese domestic oil pollution compensation fund was established in 2012.

28 In China, a special law such as the Maritime Code shall be applied with priority over a basic law in case of repugnancy; where the special law does not contain any provision, the provisions of the basic law apply.

29 Marine Environmental Protection Law of the People's Republic of China, adopted at the 24th Session of the Standing Committee of the Fifth National People's Congress on 23 August 1982; revised at the 13th Session of the Standing Committee of the Ninth National People's Congress on 25 December 1999 and amended in accordance with the Decision on Amending Seven Laws Including the Marine Environment Protection Law of the People's Republic of China at the 6th Session of the Standing Committee of the Twentieth National People's Congress on 28 December 2013.

30 Article 268 of Chapter XIV 'Application of Law in Relation to Foreign-related Matters' of the Maritime Code provides: 'If any international treaty concluded or acceded to by the People's Republic of China contains provisions differing from those contained in this Code, the provisions of the relevant international treaty shall apply, unless the provisions are those on which the People's Republic of China has announced reservations.' However, a breakthrough is made in the Provisions on Certain Issues in the Trial of Cases of Disputes over Compensation for Oil Pollution Damage from Ships promulgated by the Supreme People's Court in 1991, because paragraph 1 of Article 5 thereof provides: 'where oil pollution damage is caused by an oil tanker carrying persistent oil, the limits of liability shall be determined in accordance with the Administrative Regulations Governing Prevention and Treatment of Pollution to Marine Environment from Ships or the International Convention on Civil Liability for Oil Pollution Damage, 1992'. This means that where oil pollution damage is caused by an oil tanker carrying persistent oil as cargo in bulk, the limit of liability shall be determined in accordance with the 1992 CLC, whether any foreign element is involved or not, i.e. even if the oil pollution is caused by an oil tanker engaged in the Chinese domestic trade. The real reason why this breakthrough is made by the Supreme People's Court is that the limits of liability for oil pollution damage caused by an oil tanker engaged in the domestic trade which would be applicable were 50% of the limits provided for in Chapter XI 'Limitation of Liability for Maritime Claims' and the same as those provided for in the 1976 LLMC Convention, and that such limits proved too low in the admiralty practice. Strictly speaking, however, the validity of this breakthrough is arguable because the Supreme People's Court has the power in interpreting law in the application of law to cases, but has no power to make a law under the Organic Law of the People's Courts of 1979 as amended in 1979, 1986 and 2006. To make the limits of liability provided for in the 1992 CLC applicable to oil pollution damage caused by an oil tanker engaged in the domestic trade without any foreign element is arguably repugnant to Chapter XIV of the Maritime Code, although it may satisfy the need in practice.

Pollution to the Marine Environment of 2009 essentially form part of administrative law rather than civil law. Thus, the Marine Environmental Protection Law contains only two articles governing civil liability for marine pollution damage[31] and proves far from sufficient to govern the compensation for marine pollution damage from ships. It is well recognised in China that there is an urgent need for establishment of such a legal regime.

2.4 The Maritime Code not in harmony with the basic laws

The Maritime Code as a special law must be in harmony with the related basic laws. This is because, theoretically, the main statutory provisions contained in the Maritime Code should be those specially required for regulating the relations arising from maritime transport and those pertaining to ships, while the related basic matters should be governed by the basic laws, and other provisions which are necessitated by the integrity of legal regimes established in the Maritime Code. However, many provisions of the Maritime Code are not in harmony with the related basic laws which were adopted after the coming into effect of the Maritime Code such as the Contract Law of 1999,[32] the Insurance Law of 2014,[33] the Law on Property Rights of 2007[34] and the Law on Tort Liability of 2009.[35] The main reason

---

31 Article 90 the Marine Environmental Protection Law provides: 'Those who cause pollution damage to the marine environment shall eliminate the damage and compensate for the losses; in case of pollution damage to the marine environment resulting entirely from the intentional act or fault of a third party, the third party shall eliminate the damage and be liable for the compensation. If the State suffers heavy losses from the damage to marine ecosystems, marine aquatic resources and marine nature reserves, the departments vested by this Law with the power of marine environmental supervision and administration shall, on behalf of the State, put forward compensation demand to those who are responsible for the damage.' Article 92 provides: 'Those who cause pollution damage may be exempted from the liability if the pollution damage to the marine environment cannot be avoided by any of the following circumstances, in spite of prompt and reasonable measures taken: (1) war; (2) natural calamities of force majeure; (3) negligence or other wrongful acts in the exercise of functions of competent authorities responsible for light houses or other navigational aids.'

32 Contract Law of the People's Republic of China, adopted at the 2nd Session of the Ninth National People's Congress on 15 March 1999.

33 Insurance Law of the People's Republic of China, adopted at the 14th Session of the Standing Committee of the Eighth National People's Congress on 30 June 1995, amended for the first time at the 30th Session of the Standing Committee of the Ninth National People's Congress on 28 October 2002 and amended for the second time at the 10th Session of the Standing Committee of the Twelfth National People's Congress on 31 August 2014.

34 Law on Property Rights of the People's Republic of China, adopted at the 5th Session of the Tenth National People's Congress on 16 March 2007. The author believes the translation of 'Law on Property Rights' can better reflect the content of the law, although the law is commonly referred as the 'Property Law', such as in Chapter 7.

35 Tort Law of the People's Republic of China, adopted at the 12th Session of the Standing Committee of the Eleventh National People's Congress on 26 December 2009.

why the Maritime Code is lacking harmony with the related basic laws is precisely that the related basic laws have been adopted after the adoption of the Maritime Code.

By way of example, some provisions of Chapter XII 'Contracts of Marine Insurance' of the Maritime Code are not in line with the provisions of the Insurance Law of 2014. In particular, the parties to a marine insurance contract under the Maritime Code are the insurer and the insured,[36] whereas the parties thereto under the Insurance Law of 2014 are the applicant and the insurer;[37] the insured has the duty of unlimited disclosure under the Maritime Code, i.e. voluntary disclosure,[38] whereas the applicant has the duty of limited disclosure under the Insurance Law of 2014, i.e. disclosure upon inquiry;[39] the Maritime Code contains provisions for warranties laid down by reference to the provisions of the UK Marine Insurance Act 1906,[40] whereas the Insurance Law of 2014 contains provisions of alteration of risks.[41] It seems unnecessary and unacceptable for the Maritime Code to contain such significant differences and, as a result, harmonisation with sections 1 and 3 of Chapter II of the Insurance Law of 2014 is needed.

2.5 The existence of ambiguities, uncertainties and gaps in the Maritime Code

Admiralty practice in the 10 maritime courts in China in the past 20 years or more has demonstrated that the Maritime Code contains significant ambiguities and uncertainties and lacks sufficiently detailed provisions in some respects. A typical example of provisions lacking in detail is Article 14

---

36 See, for example, Article 216 of the Maritime Code.
37 See, for example, Article 2 of the Insurance Law 2014.
38 Article 222 of the Maritime Code provides: 'Before the contract is concluded, the insured shall truthfully inform the insurer of the material circumstances which the insured has knowledge of or ought to have knowledge of in his ordinary business practice and which may have a bearing on the insurer in deciding the premium or whether he agrees to insure or not. The insured need not inform the insurer of the facts which the insurer has known of or the insurer ought to have knowledge of in his ordinary business practice if the insurer made no inquiry about it.'
39 Article 16 of the Insurance Law 2014.
40 Article 235 of the Maritime Code.
41 Article 52 of the Insurance Law provides: 'Where the degree of peril of the subject-matter insured greatly increases during the term of validity of the contract, the insurant shall notify the insurer in a timely manner as agreed upon in the contract, and the insurer may increase the insurance premium or terminate the contract as agreed upon in the contract. If the insurer terminates the contract, it shall refund the insurance premium to the insurance applicant after deducting the receivable part from the day of commencement of insurance liability to the day of contract rescission as agreed upon in the contract'; 'Where the insurant fails to perform the notification obligation prescribed in the preceding paragraph and an insured incident occurs because the degree of peril of the subject matter insured greatly increases, the insurer shall not be liable for paying insurance indemnity.'

of the Maritime Code, which provides that mortgages may be established on a ship under construction as analysed in section 3.6.3 below.

3. What revision of the Maritime Code is needed?

The primary object of the revision of the Maritime Code is to modernise the Code. Based on the above analysis, the revision must reflect developments in the maritime economy and trade and international maritime legislation; yet should follow the five basic principles adopted in the making of the Maritime Code. The general maritime judicial interpretations adopted by the Supreme People's Court[42] may be abstracted to form supplemental provisions of the Maritime Code. International maritime treaties and advanced maritime legislation in other jurisdictions adopted after the adoption of the Maritime Code in 1992 should (or may) be referred to.

In the author's view, the revision of the Maritime Code should have the effect of extending its application to domestic carriage of goods by sea, should establish a legal regime governing compensation for marine pollution damage from ships, should harmonise with the related basic laws, should remove ambiguities and uncertainties and should fill in the gaps to enhance its enforceability. More specifically, the Maritime Code needs revision mainly in the following aspects.

3.1 Modernisation of Chapter IV regarding contracts of carriage of goods by sea

The need for revision of Chapter IV 'Contracts of Carriage of Goods by Sea' of the Maritime Code is not only because it is the most important chapter in the Maritime Code, but also because it does not apply to domestic carriage of goods by sea as analysed in section 2.2 above, and further because of the adoption of the Rotterdam Rules as well as the ambiguities and uncertainties existing in admiralty practice. Thus, Chapter IV of the Maritime Code should be revised as follows.

First, the revised Chapter IV of the Maritime Code is to be applicable to contracts of domestic carriage of goods as a whole, but will contain necessary specific provisions applicable to contracts of domestic carriage of goods by sea due to the differences between international carriage and domestic carriage which still exist and cannot be unified at this stage. For example, special consideration needs to be given to the issues regarding the carrier's strict liability regime and the absence of limitation of liability for loss or

---

42 So far, the Supreme People's Court has promulgated maritime judicial interpretations of general application in the following aspects: ship's collision in 1995 and 2008; marine insurance in 2006; delivery of goods without production of bills of lading in 2009; limitation fund for maritime claims in 2010; compensation for oil pollution damage from ships in 2011; and freight forwarders in 2012.

damage to goods in domestic carriage. Provisions concerning the latter must be in line with the Contract Law of 1999,[43] which currently governs contracts of domestic carriage and water-borne waybills[44] as the main transport document in domestic carriage. The carrier's strict liability regime and the absence of provisions on limitation of liability for loss or damage to goods as well as water-borne waybills in domestic carriage should be maintained after revision of the Maritime Code.

Secondly, the hybrid regime should be improved mainly by reference to the desirable provisions of the Rotterdam Rules. As analysed in section 2.2 above, a hybrid regime is adopted in Chapter IV 'Contracts of Carriage of Goods by Sea' of the Maritime Code which is based on the Hague-Visby Rules as amended by its 1979 SDR Protocol in relation to the carrier's liability regime, while some provisions of the Hamburg Rules regarding the definitions of shipper, actual carrier, shipper's obligations and liabilities, transport documents, etc are adopted in full or in part. This hybrid regime should be improved mainly by adopting appropriate and reasonable provisions of the Rotterdam Rules. It appears that following lengthy discussions, the Chinese government has decided not to sign and ratify the Rotterdam Rules and to take a 'wait and see' approach at this stage and in the near future, although discussions within academic circles and shipping-related industries remain ongoing. This is because the ratification of the Rotterdam Rules at this stage will not be beneficial to the overall economic interests of China, considering the fact that China is a shipping and trading power in the world in terms of the tonnage of the Chinese merchant fleet and the total volume of imported and exported goods respectively,[45] but most of

43 Article 311 of the Contract Law 1999 provides: 'A carrier shall be liable for damage to or destruction of goods during the period of carriage unless the carrier proves that the damage to or destruction of goods is caused by force majeure, by natural characters of the goods or reasonable loss, or by the fault on the part of the shipper or consignee.' Article 312 of the Contract Law provides: 'The amount of damage to or loss of the goods shall be the amount as agreed upon in the contract by the parties where there is such an agreement. Where there is no such agreement or such an agreement is not nuclear, nor can it be determined according to the provisions of Article 61 of this Law, the market price at the place where the goods are delivered at the time of delivery or at the time when the goods should be delivered shall be applied. Where law or administrative regulations stipulate otherwise on the method of calculation of damages and on the limit of liability, those provisions shall be followed.'

44 A water-borne waybill is defined as evidence of contract of domestic water-borne carriage of goods and a receipt of goods by the carrier in Article 58 of the Regulations on the Domestic Water-borne Carriage of Goods promulgated by the former Ministry of Communications in 2000.

45 See note 6 above. The total volume of imported and exported goods in 2014 ranked first in the world. According to the *Statistical Communiqué of the People's Republic of China on National Economic and Social Development in 2014* issued by the National Bureau of Statistics of China, the total volume of imported and exported goods in 2014 amounted to Chinese currency RMB26,433.4 billion or US$4,303.2 billon in which the total volume of imported goods amounted to RMB12,042.3 billion or US$1,960.4 billon and the total

the shipping companies and trading companies are small or medium-sized ones and do not possess the competitive advantage in the international shipping and trading market implied by the Rotterdam Rules. As a whole, China is in favour of the purposes and underlying principles adopted in the Rotterdam Rules, the regime regarding transport documents and electronic transport records, the provisions regarding the identification of the carrier, the rights and obligations of carrier, performing party and shipper, the provisions regarding burden of proof in cargo claims and those relating to multimodal transport, right of control, etc. In particular, adoption of the provisions regarding electronic transport records and multimodal transport are recognised as helpful to improve the hybrid regime in the Maritime Code in order to meet the rapid use of electronic commerce in the maritime transport and the rapid development of multimodal transport of containerised goods. At the same time, it seems that China is not in favour of the provisions relating to the documentary shipper, volume contracts, delivery of goods without production of transport documents and jurisdiction and arbitration,[46] among others. It is arguable whether deletion of the exemption of nautical faults and the increase of the limits of carrier's liability are beneficial. In addition, the Rotterdam Rules are deemed too complicated and consequently it is not advisable to fully copy even the complicated favourable provisions into the revised Maritime Code.

Thirdly, there is a need for resolution of certain matters which often give rise to disputes in shipping practice. In this regard, examples are the FOB seller's legal position and its rights and obligations, the legal position of a freight forwarder and delivery of goods without production of bills of lading. China has become the largest commodity export country in the world and most of the commodities are exported on FOB terms by small or medium-sized companies and, as a result, protection of FOB sellers' interests is of particular importance by way of expressly stipulating the FOB seller's legal position and its rights and obligations. Delivery of goods without production of bills of lading is quite common, especially in tanker transport, container transport and short sea transport. The use of electronic transport documents may in future reduce related disputes, but it is advisable to adopt explicit provisions to govern the interests of the shipper

---

volume of imported goods amounted to RMB14,391.2 billion or US$2,342.8 billon, <http://www.stats.gov.cn/tjsj/zxfb/201502/t20150226_685799.html> accessed 23 May 2015.

46 The provisions of the Rotterdam Rules relating to the documentary shipper or delivery of goods without production of transport documents seem not to be beneficial to the many small or medium-sized FOB (Free on Board) sellers in China. The provisions relating to volume contract seem not to be beneficial to the many small or medium-sized shipping companies and trading companies because their bargaining power may be much weaker than the big shipping companies or trading companies. The provisions relating to jurisdiction and arbitration may compel the small shipping companies and trading companies to be involved in foreign litigations or arbitrations and thus not beneficial to them.

(including the FOB seller), the carrier or actual carrier, the consignee who is entitled to take delivery of goods and the actual cargo receiver who has taken delivery of goods.[47] Freight forwarders as active intermediaries in the maritime transport of goods act either as a carrier (NVOCC),[48] shipper, consignee or an agent of the shipper or consignee, as the case may be. There are tens of thousands of freight forwarders in China of which many act as NVOCC.[49] Many disputes arise between a freight forwarder and a shipper/consignee or between a freight forwarder and a carrier/actual carrier in practice due to lack of detailed contracts among the parties, irregularities of business operations of the freight forwarders and lack of explicit statutory provisions regarding the legal position of a freight forwarder and its rights and obligations in the Maritime Code or otherwise.[50]

3.2 Establishment of a legal regime governing compensation for marine pollution damage from ships

The regime governing compensation for marine pollution damage from ships to be established in the revised Maritime Code as a separate chapter thereof should be based on or by reference to the 1992 CLC, the Bunker Convention 2001, the 1996 HNS Convention, the 1992 Fund Convention and also possibly by reference to the US Oil Pollution Act of 1990 (OPA). The contents of the regime must include the scope of application, responsible parties, liability and exemptions, limits of liability, recoverable damages, compulsory liability insurance or other financial security and the domestic compensation fund for oil pollution damage from ships, etc.

3.3 Improving provisions regarding masters and crew

China has a very large and complex market for ship's masters and crew. According to statistics from the Maritime Safety Administration (MSA)

---

47 Currently, besides Article 71 of the Maritime Code containing the definition of a bill of lading and requiring carrier's delivery of goods against production of a bill of lading, the statutory provisions regarding delivery of goods without bills of lading are the Provisions Regarding Certain Issues in the Trial of Cases of Delivery of Goods without Original Bills of Lading promulgated by the Supreme People's Court in 2012.

48 The concept of non-vessel carrying operator which is similar to non-vessel operating common carrier (NVOCC) contained in the US Ocean Shipping Reform Act of 1998 is adopted in the Regulations on International Maritime Transport of 2001.

49 According to the statistics provided by the Ministry of Transport, there are more than 5,000 registered NVOCCs, <http://www.moc.gov.cn/zfxxgk/bnssj/syj/201505/t20150529_1826662.html> accessed 23 July 2015.

50 Currently, the statutory provisions regarding the freight forwarders are the Provisions Regarding Certain Issues in the Trial of Cases of Disputes over Freight Forwarders promulgated by the Supreme People's Court in 2012 and the Administrative Provisions Regarding the International Freight Forwarding Industry approved by the State Council in 1995.

under the Ministry of Transport, there were 574,117 registered seafarers including 419,029 international seafarers and 155,088 costal seafarers by the end of 2013.[51] In addition, there are more than 1 million ship's masters and crew in inland navigation. China is thereby the country in the world with the largest number of ship's masters and crew. Besides, there are many companies providing intermediary services to the masters and crew and shipowners or other companies which use the service of the masters and crew, and nearly 100 crew training institutions. The governmental authorities in this sector include the MSA under the Ministry of Transport and its branches responsible for qualifications of the master and crew and crew training institutions, the Ministry of Human Resources and Social Security or corresponding local governmental departments responsible for the social security for masters and crew, and the Ministry of Commence or corresponding local governmental departments responsible for the dispatch of Chinese seafarers to serve on board ships flying foreign flags.[52]

Issues in relation to masters and crew are governed by: (a) Chapter III 'Master and Crew' of the Maritime Code which contains the definition of crew,[53] certificates of competency, the Seaman's Book and other relevant certificates in Section 1 'Basic Principles', the provisions regarding the functions and duties of a master in Section 2 'The Master'; (b) the Regulations on Ship's Crewmembers approved by the State Council in 2007 stipulating the registration and qualifications for crewmembers, crewmembers' duties, crewmembers' professional security, crewmembers' training and services for crewmembers, etc. The issues of crewmembers' training, competency and certification are also governed by the 1995 STCW Convention[54] and various domestic provisions promulgated by the Ministry of Transport or the MSA under it.

A particular issue in the Chinese law on ship's crew relates to social security and other protection available to them. This issue has become more evident as, unlike in the times of the planned economy more than 10 years ago, most ship's crewmembers are not subordinated to specific ship-owning companies, but are employed on board ships based on short-term articles of employment concluded with shipowners or other employers. However, due to the lack of detailed statutory provisions, the low bargaining power of individual ship's crewmembers, and the complexity, irregularities or ambiguities of articles of employment, the protection that is in fact available

---

51 See <http://www.crewcn.com/news/news778.html> accessed 23 May 2015.

52 According to the statistics provided by the MSA, 119,316 Chinese seafarers were dispatched to serve onboard ships flying foreign flags in 2014, <http://www.crewcn.com/news/news778.html> accessed 23 May 2015. This number is less than that in the Philippines, Ukraine or India.

53 Article 31 of the Maritime Code provides: 'The term "crew" means the entire complement of the ship, including the Master.'

54 The International Convention on Standards of Training, Certification and Watchkeeping for Seafarers 1995 as amended in 2010 by 'The Manila Amendments'.

to ship's crewmembers is insufficient. With respect to statutory provisions, Article 34 of the Maritime Code provides: 'In the absence of specific stipulations in this Code as regards the employment of the crew as well as their labour-related rights and obligations, the provisions of the relevant laws and administrative rules and regulations shall apply.' The relevant laws referred to in this Article are the Law on Labour Contract of 2007 as amended in 2012[55] and the Social Insurance Law of 2010[56] covering endowment insurance, medical insurance, industrial injury insurance, unemployment insurance and maternity insurance. However, these basic laws do not reflect the professional features of ship's crewmembers, but contain provisions of general employment protection. More recently, the implementation of the Maritime Labour Convention of 2006[57] requires overall protections of rights and interests to be available to ship's crewmembers. At the time of writing, China has only very recently ratified this Convention.

Thus, besides improvement of provisions regarding the functions and duties of a shipmaster, such as his overriding authority and responsibility in relation to safety and prevention in the marine environment,[58] Chapter III 'Master and Crew' of the Maritime Code requires improvement by stipulating that specific protections of rights and interests are available to ship's masters and crewmembers and specific requirements for the articles of employment, etc.

3.4 Increase of global limits of liability, limit of liability of carrier for personal injuries of passengers, especially in domestic trade

As noted in section 2.2 above, the limit of liability of the carrier for death of, or personal injury to, passengers in the domestic transport is as low as RMB40,000 or currently about US$6,500 per person per carriage, and the limits of global limitation for maritime claims applicable to domestic vessels are 50% of those applicable to international vessels which are the same as the limits of liability provided for in the 1976 LLMC Convention. These limits have in admiralty practice proven to be too low. In addition, due to economic and social developments, the limits of global limitation for maritime claims applicable to ships engaged in international trade have also in

---

55 Labor Contract Law of the People's Republic of China, first adopted at the 28th Session of Standing Committee of the Tenth National People's Congress on 29 June 2007 and subsequently amended at the 30th Session of the Standing Committee of the Eleventh National People's Congress on 28 December 2012.

56 Social Insurance Law of the People's Republic of China, adopted at the 17th meeting of the Standing Committee of the Eleventh National People's Congress on 28 October 2010.

57 Maritime Labour Convention, adopted at 94th International Law Commission session in Geneva on 23 February 2006 and came into force on 20 August 2013.

58 Such an authority and responsibility is stipulated in the ISM (International Safety Management) Code and the Regulations on Ship's Crewmembers of 2007 (adopted at the 172nd executive meeting of the State Council on 28 March 2007 and came into force on 1 September 2007) etc.

practice proven to be too low on many occasions, especially where loss of, or damage to, property is concerned. At least theoretically, the limit of liability of the carrier for death of, or personal injury to, passengers in international transport, that is 46,666 SDR (Special Drawing Rights) per person per carriage is also low, although there is no practice-based evidence in this regard due to the rare occurrence of loss of life or personal injury to passengers. Therefore, the various limits of liability should be increased. In particular, the limit of liability of the carrier for death of, or personal injury to, passengers in domestic transport and the limits of global limitation for maritime claims applicable to domestic vessels should be significantly increased.

There appears to be little doubt that, due to the rapid economic and social developments in China in the past 20 years or more, the limit of liability of the carrier for death of, or personal injury to, passengers in domestic transport should be increased to that applicable in international transport, and the limits of global limitation for maritime claims applicable to domestic vessels should be increased to those applicable to ships engaged in international trade as provided for in the Maritime Code.

However, it is difficult to determine whether the limit of liability of the carrier for death of, or personal injury to, passengers in international transport ought to be increased to the extent provided for in the 2002 Athens Convention, that is 250,000 SDR per passenger on each distinct occasion based on strict liability where the death of, or personal injury to, a passenger is caused by a shipping incident or 400,000 SDR per passenger on each distinct occasion based on fault liability where the death of, or personal injury to, a passenger caused by a shipping incident exceeds 250,000 SDR per passenger or where the death or personal injury is not caused by a shipping incident.[59] Also worth considering is whether the limits of global limitation for maritime claims applicable to ships engaged in the international trade should be increased to the extent of those provided for in the 1996 Protocol amending the 1976 LLMC Convention. Following the principle adopted in the 1976 LLMC Convention, that the level of liability for personal claims remaining subject to global limitation should be sufficient to ensure full compensation in most cases and that the level of liability for property claims

---

59 Paragraph 1 of Article 3 'Liability of the carrier' of the 2002 Athens Convention provides: 'For the loss suffered as a result of the death of or personal injury to a passenger caused by a shipping incident, the carrier shall be liable to the extent that such loss in respect of that passenger on each distinct occasion does not exceed 250,000 units of account, unless the carrier proves that the incident: (a) resulted from an act of war, hostilities, civil war, insurrection or a natural phenomenon of an exceptional, inevitable and irresistible character; or (b) was wholly caused by an act or omission done with the intent to cause the incident by a third party. If and to the extent that the loss exceeds the above limit, the carrier shall be further liable unless the carrier proves that the incident which caused the loss occurred without the fault or neglect of the carrier.' Paragraph 1 of Article 7 'Limit of liability for death and personal injury' provides: 'The liability of the carrier for the death of or personal injury to a passenger under Article 3 shall in no case exceed 400,000 units of account per passenger on each distinct occasion.'

should be moderate and take into account that the property involved is usually covered by insurance,[60] it seems clear that at this stage such high limits of liability are beyond the requirements of domestic carriage of passengers in consideration of the extent of economic and social development in China now and even in the near future.

3.5 Extension of application of the Maritime Code to transport and vessels in inland navigable waters adjacent to the sea

China has a very large inland transport market. The inland waterways are as long as 126,300 km mainly in the Yangtze River located in the centre from west to east, the Pearl River located in the south from west to east, the Heilongjiang River located in the north from west to east and the Beijing-Hangzhou Grand Canal located in the east from north to south. By the end of 2014, there were 158,300 inland vessels with a total DWT of 112.75 million and 25,871 operating berths. In 2014, the total turnover of principal inland ports was 323 million metric tons and 20.66 million TEUs, and the volume of passenger transport reached 102 million person-times.[61] It is noteworthy that the main inland waterways in the Yangtze River and the Pearl River are accessible by seagoing vessels and even large seagoing vessels.

The Maritime Code is in principle not applicable to inland navigation or inland vessels.[62] Currently, inland transport and inland vessels are governed by the basic laws such as the Contract Law of 1999 relating to the contracts of carriage of goods or passengers, the Law on Property Rights of 2007 relating to ship ownership and ship mortgage, the Insurance Law of 2014 relating to hull and cargo transport insurance and the Law on Tort Liability of 2009 relating to ship collisions. No maritime liens, salvage, general average and global limitation of liability for maritime claims are applicable in inland navigation and to inland vessels. This demonstrates that the application of these basic laws is not fully suitable to inland transport and especially to inland vessels. In addition, it is advisable to adopt and apply the legal regimes of maritime liens, salvage, general average and global limitation of liability for maritime claims in inland navigation and to

---

60 Erling Selvig, 'An Introduction to the 1976 Convention', in Institute of Maritime Law *The Limitation of Shipowners' Liability: The New Law*, Sweet & Maxwell, 1986, p.14.

61 See the Ministry of Transport, *Statistical Communiqué of Development in Transport and Communication Industry in 2014*, <http://www.moc.gov.cn/zfxxgk/bnssj/zhghs/201504/t20150430_1810598.html> accessed 23 May 2015.

62 The Maritime Code is applicable in inland navigation and to inland vessels only in four situations, i.e.: (a) Chapter IV 'Contract of Carriage of Goods by Sea' is applicable to the sea-river international direct carriage of goods; (b) Chapter V 'Contract of Carriage of Passengers' is applicable to the sea-river direct carriage of passengers; (c) Chapter VIII 'Ship's Collision' is applicable to a collision between a seagoing vessel and an inland vessel; (d) Chapter IX 'Salvage at Sea' is applicable to salvage between a seagoing vessel and an inland vessel.

inland vessels. An example of such advisability is where a collision occurs between a large seagoing vessel and a small inland vessel. If the seagoing vessel is to blame, her owner is entitled to avail itself of limitation of liability for maritime claims provided for in Chapter XI of the Maritime Code and needs to bear limited liability only; if the inland vessel is to blame, her owner cannot avail itself of any limitation of liability and has to compensate for all the damage arising therefrom. An unreasonable result may occur if the owner of a small inland vessel will have to bear a larger liability than that of a large seagoing vessel.

It is advisable to extend the scope of application of the Maritime Code to inland navigation and inland vessels. However, some necessary restrictions must be made on such extension of application. First, the application of the Maritime Code must be geographically limited to inland navigable waters adjacent to the sea. Secondly, the Maritime Code should not be applicable to very small inland vessels, the legal relations of which are simple and do not need the complex legal regimes of the Maritime Code, considering costs and efficiency.[63] In addition, special provisions may be required due to the features of inland navigation and inland vessels.

3.6 Other issues

3.6.1 Two other objects of revision

The revision of the Maritime Code will have two other objects, namely: (a) to remove ambiguities and uncertainties and to fill in gaps which have been identified in admiralty practice in order to enhance its enforceability; (b) to harmonise with the basic laws mainly the Contract Law of 1999, the Law on Property Rights of 2007, the Insurance Law of 2014 and the Law on Tort Liability of 2009; always to the extent that the required specialised provisions in the Maritime Code regulating maritime transport and ships are not prejudiced.

3.6.2 Non-mandatory provisions

The provisions on charterparties, namely Chapter VI of the Maritime Code regarding time charterparties and bareboat charterparties, and Section 7 of Chapter IV regarding voyage charterparties, are essentially non-mandatory. During the drafting of the Maritime Code, the dominant thought was that, given that they were non-mandatory, the provisions did not need to be very detailed, resulting in very simple provisions on charterparties compared with the complicated contents of actual charterparty contracts. The same

---

63 The Maritime Code does not apply to small vessels of less than 20 tons gross tonnage, unless such a small vessel is involved in a collision or salvage with a seagoing vessel with a gross tonnage of 20 tons or more.

applies to Chapter X 'General Average', which contains only 11 articles compared to the lengthy 1974 or 2004 York-Antwerp Rules. The provisions of this Chapter are non-mandatory by virtue of Article 203 of the Maritime Code.[64]

There is a need to reassess the functions of these non-mandatory provisions. The non-mandatory provisions are not applicable where a contract contains provisions to the contrary. However, detailed non-mandatory provisions regarding complicated contractual regimes such as charterparties may save time and costs in negotiating a contract by the parties and thus promote the efficiency of transactions. This being so, the philosophy behind the Maritime Code of simple non-mandatory provisions regulating complicated issues should be adjusted.

3.6.3 Summary of main points of revision in various chapters of the Maritime Code

In the author's view, the main points of revision in various chapters of the Maritime Code may be summarised as follows.

(1) CHAPTER I 'GENERAL PROVISIONS'

In order to extend the scope of application the Maritime Code, the definition of 'Maritime transport' defined in Article 2 thereof[65] should be extended to encompass the carriage of goods or passengers by sea, in the sea-river direct transport or inland navigable waters adjacent to the sea. Further, the definition of 'ship' in Article 3 of the Code[66] should be extended to include sea-going ships, ships in inland navigable waters adjacent to the sea and other mobile units; while the exclusion of ships or craft to be used for military or public service purposes or small ships of less than 20 tons gross tonnage should remain unchanged.

---

64 Article 203 of the Maritime Code provides: 'The adjustment of general average shall be governed by the average adjustment rules agreed upon in the relevant contract. In the absence of such an agreement in the contract, the relevant provisions contained in this Chapter shall apply.'

65 Article 2 of the Maritime Code provides: '"Maritime transport" as referred to in this Code means the carriage of goods and passengers by sea, including the sea-river and river-sea direct transport. The provisions concerning contracts of carriage of goods by sea as contained in Chapter IV of this Code shall not be applicable to the maritime transport of goods between the ports of the People's Republic of China.'

66 Paragraph 1 of Article 3 of the Maritime Code provides: '"Ship" as referred to in this Code means sea-going ships and other mobile units, but does not include ships or craft to be used for military or public service purposes, nor small ships of less than 20 tons gross tonnage.'

(2) CHAPTER II 'SHIPS'

Article 14 of the Maritime Code provides for the principle that 'mortgages may be established on a ship under construction'. However, this provision has proven difficult to apply effectively in practice, as the following issues are not made explicitly and clear in the Maritime Code: (a) from when can a ship be deemed to be under construction, i.e. at what point in time can a mortgage be established on a ship under construction? (b) what is the scope of a ship under construction, i.e. what is the scope of the subject-matter of mortgage? (c) who can be a mortgagor, i.e. the ship builder or the company who ordered the ship? Resolving these issues is essential, given that China is now the largest shipbuilding country in the world[67] and that many small or medium-sized shipbuilders are in a poor financial situation due to the lasting influence of the financial crisis. Moreover, shipbuilders or the companies that ordered the ships need significant cash flow for the construction of ships by way of mortgage on ships under construction. Based on these reasons, all the elements mentioned above and the other related issues regarding registration of mortgages on a ship under construction need be made specifically and clearly in the revised Maritime Code. It seems advisable to adopt the regime of floating mortgages contained in the Law on Property Rights of 2007 into the Maritime Code to help determine the scope of the subject-matter of a mortgage on a ship under construction.

Besides, it appears to be necessary to extend the priority that the mortgagee enjoys in the insurance indemnity over other creditors in case of loss of the mortgaged ship in the event of damage thereto.[68] With respect to maritime liens, as provided for in Articles 26 and 29 of the Maritime Code, the causes of extinction thereof include: (a) maritime liens have not been enforced within 60 days of a public notice on the transfer of the ownership of the ship made by a court at the request of the transferee when the transfer was effected; (b) the maritime claim attached by a maritime lien has not been enforced within one year of the existence of such maritime lien; (c) the ship in question has been the subject of a forced sale by the court; and (d) the ship has been lost. It seems advisable that the causes of extinction be extended to cover for instance confiscation of a ship by a public authority according to law. In some respects, the provisions regarding ship ownership

---

67 In 2014, the whole Chinese shipbuilding industry completed construction of ships of 39.05 million DWT, received new orders of 59.95 million DWT representing 50.5% in the world market, and held orders of 148.9 million DWT. See China Association of National Shipbuilding Industry, *Report on the Situation of Development in the Shipbuilding Industry in 2014*, <http://www.cansi.org.cn/index.php/Information/detail/id/57> accessed 23 May 2015.

68 Article 20 of the Maritime Code provides: 'The mortgages shall be extinguished when the mortgaged ship is lost. With respect to the compensation paid from the insurance coverage on account of the loss of the ship, the mortgagee shall be entitled to enjoy priority in compensation over other creditors.'

and ship mortgage should be in harmony with those contained in the Law on Property Rights of 2007.

(3) CHAPTER III 'CREW'

As noted in section 3.4 above, the powers and functions of a shipmaster need to be examined. It is necessary to specify the shipmasters' overriding authority and responsibility in relation to safety and prevention of marine environment. To provide enhanced protection of the rights and interests of masters and crew, specific stipulation regarding the requirements upon articles of employment and social security, etc are needed.

(4) CHAPTER IV 'CONTRACTS OF CARRIAGE OF GOODS BY SEA'

This Chapter is one of the greatest concerns in the revision of the Maritime Code. Points of revision should include: (a) extension of its application to the contracts of domestic carriage of goods by sea and the contracts of carriage of goods in inland waters adjacent to the sea with necessary special provisions regarding the domestic carriage of goods by sea and carriage of goods in inland waters adjacent to the sea regarding carrier's liability regime to be in harmony with the Contract Law of 1999 and transport documents; (b) as analysed in section 3.1 above, some reasonable and appropriate provisions of the Rotterdam Rules should be incorporated into this Chapter to improve the hybrid regime contained therein; (c) the provisions regarding voyage charters contained in Section 7 'Special Provisions Regarding Voyage Charterparties' should be updated by reference to GENCON 1994 or any subsequent modification; (d) the provisions regarding multimodal transport in Section 8 'Special Provisions Regarding Multimodal Transport Contract' should be updated by reference to those contained in the Rotterdam Rules; and (e) the provisions regarding cancellation of contracts or other aspects should be harmonised with those contained in the Contract Law of 1999.

(5) CHAPTER V 'CONTRACTS OF CARRIAGE OF PASSENGERS BY SEA'

There are three key points in the revision of this Chapter.

First, to be identical to the revision of Article 2 of the Maritime Code, the scope of application of this Chapter should be extended to the contracts of carriage of passengers in the inland navigable waters adjacent to the sea.

Secondly, the carrier's liability regime should be revised by reference to the 2002 Athens Convention to the effect that the carrier's liability is significantly increased in terms of the limits of liability, in particular the limit of liability of the carrier for death of, or personal injury to, passengers in domestic maritime transport which is currently as low as RMB40,000 or about US$6,500 per person per carriage.[69] There appear to be three options with respect to the limits of liability and the basis of liability:

(a) The current limits of liability and the single basis of liability of the carrier for death of, or personal injury to, passengers remain those provided for in the 1974 Athens Convention, i.e. 46,666 SDR per passenger based on fault liability provided for in Article 117 of the Maritime Code, but are to apply also to the carriage of passengers in domestic coastal waters and in inland navigable waters adjacent to the sea;

(b) The adoption of the same basis of liability, but different limits of liability in relation to passengers in international and domestic carriage. The limits and dual basis of liability provided for in the 2002 Athens Convention, i.e. 250,000 SDR per passenger on each distinct occasion based on strict liability where the death of, or personal injury to, a passenger is caused by a shipping incident or 400,000 SDR per passenger on each distinct occasion with fault-based liability where the death of, or personal injury to, a passenger caused by a shipping incident exceeds 250,000 SDR per passenger or where the death of, or personal injury to, a passenger is not caused by a shipping accident would then be applicable to the international carriage of passengers, while the limits provided for in the 1974 Athens Convention or other modified lower limits could apply to domestic carriage of passengers in both coastal waters and inland navigation. It seems clear that at this stage the limits provided for in the 2002 Athens Convention are beyond the needs of domestic carriage of passengers in consideration of the extent of economic and social developments in China now and even in the near future.

(c) The adoption of the aforesaid dual basis of liability provided for in the 2002 Athens Convention, but the limits of liability provided for in the 1974 Athens Convention, i.e. 46,666 SDR per passenger.

It does not appear advisable to adopt different bases of liability for international carriage and domestic carriage. Therefore, the realistic options are either the single basis of fault liability currently provided for in Articles 114 and 115 of the Maritime Code which is the same as provided for in the 1974 Athens Convention or the dual basis of liability contained in the 2002 Athens Convention.

Thirdly, while the volume of traditional domestic carriage of passengers by sea and in inland navigation has declined due to the development of air, railway and highway transport, the carriage of passengers by cruise ships has increased rapidly in recent years, especially in international transport.[70] The

---

69 See note 7 above.
70 According to the statistics contained in *The Report on the Development of Cruise Ships in China in 2014*, there were 466 calls of cruise ships at the ports in the Mainland China and the number of passengers amounted to 1.72 million in 2014 with an increase of more

relations between those involved, the passenger, the travel agency and the cruise ship operator are unclear in current Chinese law. Normally, in practice, the travel agency and the passenger agree a travel contract by which the travel agency arranges a travel package on board the cruise ship and on land, sightseeing on land and accommodations at sea and on land, etc for the passenger and the passenger pays a lump sum fare to the travel agency. The travel agency also delivers to the passenger a cruise ship ticket by which the passenger may board and travel on board the cruise ship. Unresolved issues include: (a) whether the Maritime Code should regulate the relations among the passenger, the travel agency and the cruise operator and issues arising in the period between embarkation and disembarkation of the passenger; (b) whether the travel agency should be deemed the carrier of the passenger by sea and, if so, the cruise ship operator is deemed to be the actual carrier defined in the Maritime Code or the performing carrier defined in the 1974 or 2002 Athens Conventions, or the cruise operator is the carrier having concluded a contract of carriage with the passenger through the travel agency acting as an agent of the cruise operator; and (c) whether the cruise ship operator and the travel agency may be held jointly and severally liable for the death of, or personal injury to, the passengers that occurs or the cause thereof during the period between embarkation and disembarkation of the passenger. These issues should be resolved in the revision of this Chapter.

(6) CHAPTER VI 'CHARTERPARTIES'

Section 2 'Time Charterparty' should be updated by reference to NYPE 1993 and BALTIME 2001 and any modification thereof. Section 3 'Bareboat Charterparty' should be updated by reference to BARECON 2001 and any modification thereof.

In addition, special provisions regarding financial leasing contracts in respect of ships should be added. Ship financing has recently developed very rapidly in China. A financial leasing contract is defined in Article 237 of the Contract Law of 1999 as 'a contract whereby the lessor, upon the choice of the lease item and seller made by the lessee, purchases and provides the lease item to the lessee for its use, and the lessee pays the rent'. A ship financial leasing contract includes in essence a contract of purchase and sale of a ship or a shipbuilding contract between the lessor and the third party seller of the ship or shipbuilder and a bareboat charter between the lessor and the lessee. However, the bareboat charter included therein has its special characteristics; thus the shipowner as lessor should not be responsible for any defect in the ship. Therefore, provisions reflecting special characteristics must be provided for in this Chapter.

than 40% of those in 2013. In particular, Shanghai is becoming an important home port of cruise ships in Asia, <http://ocean.china.com.cn/2014-12/24/content_34400845.htm> accessed 23 May 2015.

(7) CHAPTER VII 'CONTRACTS OF SEA TOWAGE'

The provisions in this Chapter must be updated by reference to the modern forms of towage contract, for example TOWCON 2008 and TOWHIRE 2008.

(8) CHAPTER VIII 'COLLISION OF SHIPS'

It is important to note that, unlike in the common law jurisdictions, there is no *in rem* action in China. Therefore, the 'ship' at fault in a collision as the liable party provided for in Articles 168 and 169 of the Maritime Code or in the 1910 Collision Convention to which China is a party should be personalised to mean the owner or, in case of bareboat charter of the ship, the bareboat charterer.[71]

In admiralty practice, the scope and assessment of recoverable damages arising from a ship's collision are often in dispute. While it is not advisable for this Chapter to stipulate the recoverable damages in detail because this would require many lengthy provisions, it would appear helpful to lay down the principles in determining the scope and assessment of recoverable damages by reference to the judicial interpretations promulgated by the Supreme People's Court, i.e. *restitutio in integrum*, direct causation and obligation to mitigate loss.[72]

(9) CHAPTER IX 'SALVAGE AT SEA'

The provisions of this Chapter are essentially a reproduction of the 1989 Salvage Convention. Article 182 of the Maritime Code addresses situations

---

71 By virtue of Article 25 of the Regulations of the People's Republic of China Governing the Registration of Ships (issued by the State Council on 6 February 1994 and amended on 29 July 2014), a bareboat charter shall be registered where a Chinese ship is bareboat chartered out to a Chinese company, or a Chinese company bareboat chartered in a foreign ship, or a Chinese ship is bareboat chartered out to a foreign company. Article 4 of the Provisions on Certain Issues Regarding Trial of Cases of Disputes Arising from Ship's Collisions promulgated by the Supreme People's Court on 19 May 2008 provides: 'The liability for ship's collision shall be borne by the shipowners; where a ship is in the charter period of a bareboat charter and the bareboat charter is registered, it shall be borne by the bareboat charterer.' In some other jurisdictions, such as South Korea, a bareboat charter is not required by law to be registered. It is not decided yet whether the bareboat charterer shall be liable for the ship's collision where the bareboat charter of a foreign a ship is not registered in other jurisdictions.
72 The Provisions on the Trial of Cases of Compensation for Property Damage Arising from Ship's Collisions or Allisions promulgated by the Supreme People's Court on 18 August 1995 contains these principles, detailed provisions of the scope and assessment of recoverable property damage. These principles are also provided for in the Law on Tort Liability of 2009.

giving rise to special compensation, i.e. where the salvor has carried out salvage operations in respect of a ship which by itself or its goods threatened pollution damage to the environment, without a definition of 'pollution damage to the environment'. In contrast, Article 14 of the 1989 Salvage Convention does not limit the situation giving rise to special compensation to pollution damage to the environment, but embodies all situations of 'damage to the environment' as defined in Article 1(d).[73] It seems necessary to amend 'pollution damage to the environment' in Article 182 of the Maritime Code so as to be identical to 'damage to the environment' as defined in Article 1(d) of the 1989 Salvage Convention.

A gap exists in Article 192 of the Maritime Code which provides: 'With respect to the salvage operations performed or controlled by the relevant competent authorities of the State, the salvors shall be entitled to avail themselves of the rights and remedies provided for in this Chapter in respect of salvage operations.' Disputes have arisen as to whether a competent authority such as a branch of the MSA which performs or controls a salvage operation is entitled to avail itself of the rights and remedies available to the salvor. In this regard, paragraph 1 of Article 5 of the 1989 Salvage Convention provides that the Convention shall not affect any provisions of national law relating to salvage operations by, or under, the control of public authorities. Paragraph 3 of this Article further provides that the extent to which a public authority under a duty to perform salvage operations may avail itself of the rights and remedies provided for in this Convention shall be determined by the law of the state where such authority is situated. However, current Chinese law lacks provisions addressing this issue, creating a gap to be filled in the revision of the Maritime Code. Quite probably, public authorities will not be entitled to such rights and remedies, unless it is proven that the public authority has no duty to perform salvage operations or the salvage operations performed are beyond its statutory duties.

In addition, employed salvage services in which the salvage reward is based on the time of use of the salvage vessels, equipment and labour appear to be more common in practice, not least due to the high and uncertain salvage reward based on the principle of 'no cure, no pay' for property salvage or special compensation. This kind of salvage is not excluded from the application of the Chapter, but the Chapter does not contain specific provisions to regulate this kind of salvage. Hopefully, such specific provisions will be contained in the revised Chapter.

---

73 'Damage to the environment' means substantial physical damage to human health or to marine life or resources in coastal or inland waters or areas adjacent thereto, caused by pollution, contamination, fire, explosion or similar major incidents.

(10) CHAPTER IX 'GENERAL AVERAGE'

The provisions of this Chapter were formulated by reference to the 1974 York-Antwerp Rules and the 1975 Beijing Adjustment Rules[74] and, as noted above, are too simple. The provisions need be updated by reference to the 2004 York-Antwerp Rules.

(11) CHAPTER XI 'LIMITATION OF LIABILITY FOR MARITIME CLAIMS'

As noted in section 3.4 above, the focus on the revision of this Chapter is to increase the global limits of liability, especially those applicable to the ships engaged in domestic trade, i.e. 50% of those which are the same as the limits provided for in the 1976 LLMC Convention and applicable to ships engaged in international trade, based on the situation of economic and social development in China and following the principle that the level of liability for personal claims remaining subject to global limitation should be sufficient to ensure full compensation in most cases and that the level of liability for property claims should be moderate and take into account that the property involved is usually covered by insurance. It seems unnecessarily complicated to apply different global limits of liability to ships engaged in international trade and those engaged in domestic trade.

Besides, unlike the 1976 LLMC Convention which includes the manager of a seagoing ship in the term of 'shipowner', the manager of a ship is not included in the term 'shipowners' in paragraph 2 of Article 204 of the Maritime Code because there was no concept of ship manager in China in 1992 when the Maritime Code was adopted. Currently, however, there is a large industry of professional ship management companies mainly due to the implementation of the ISM Code and the NSM Code.[75] As a result, the manager of a ship should be included in the term of 'shipowner' to entitle it to avail itself of the global limitation of liability for maritime claims. Similar to Article 3 of the 1976 LLMC Convention, Article 208

---

74 The 1975 Beijing Adjustment Rules or the so-called 1975 Beijing Rules were made by the China Council for the Promotion of International Trade in 1975. The Rules contain provisions of scope of general average, principles of adjustment, calculation of general average and contributory values, general average security, time-bar, etc. It has been proven that the provisions of the Rules are too simple. The Rules are seldom applied because on most occasions the York-Antwerp Rules are agreed upon between the parties to a contract.

75 National Safety Management Code, i.e. the Administrative Regulations on Safe Operation of Ships and Pollution Prevention, made according to the principles of the ISM Code and the actual situations in China, adopted by the former Ministry of Communications on 12 July 2001. The NSM Code contains provisions similar to those contained in the ISM Code and is applicable to domestic vessels. As required by the ISM Code or the NSM Code, ship safety management systems shall be established and approved by the maritime authority, i.e. MSA in China. A Document of Compliance shall be obtained for the company responsible for the safety management of ships and a Safety Management Certificate shall be obtained for and carried onboard a ship.

of the Maritime Code excluded from global limitation the claims for oil pollution damage under the 1992 CLC to which China is a party. It is noteworthy that the 2010 HNS Convention sets up limits of liability higher than those provided for in the 1992 CLC for damage from hazardous and noxious substances carried by ships. There may be further international conventions in future, setting limitations of liability for special damage arising from ships or maritime transport which should also be excluded from global limitation. Thus, Article 208 of the Maritime Code should be extended to exclude from global limitation any claims for damage arising from hazardous and noxious substances carried by ships as well as other damage arising from ships or maritime transport which are subject to the limitations of liability provided for in other international conventions to which China is a party.

(12) CHAPTER XII 'CONTRACT OF MARINE INSURANCE'

As noted in section 2.4 above, this Chapter is not in harmony with the Insurance Law of 2014 in some basic respects. Thus, one task of the revision of this Chapter is harmonisation with the Insurance Law of 2014.

Admiralty practice has demonstrated the existence of ambiguities, uncertainties and gaps in this Chapter. Such ambiguities and uncertainties should be removed and gaps be filled in via revision of the Maritime Code, mainly by reference to the Provisions on Certain Issues in the Trial of Cases of Disputes Arising from Marine Insurance promulgated by the Supreme People's Court on 23 November 2006.

To be consistent with the trend of development of marine insurance law in some other jurisdictions, it seems necessary to provide improved protection to the insured in the revision of this Chapter.

(13) CHAPTER XIII 'LIMITATION OF TIME'

Admiralty practice has demonstrated the existence of ambiguities, uncertainties and gaps in this Chapter. Such ambiguities and uncertainties should be removed and gaps be filled in via revision of the Maritime Code.

(14) CHAPTER XIV 'APPLICATION OF LAW IN RELATION TO FOREIGN-RELATED MATTERS'

Consideration should be given to harmonisation with the Law of the Application of Law for Foreign-related Civil Relations of 2010.[76]

Unlike the law on the carriage of goods by sea of some other jurisdictions,

76 Law of the People's Republic of China on Application of Law for Foreign-related Civil Relations has been adopted at the 17th Session of the Standing Committee of the Eleventh National People's Congress on 28 October 2010.

notably the US Carriage of Goods by Sea Act of 1936 or the Hague or Hague-Visby Rules, Chapter IV 'Contracts of Carriage of Goods by Sea' of the Maritime Code does not have any scope of mandatory application by virtue of Article 269 thereof.[77] However, it is commonly recognised in academic circles in China that Chapter IV of the Code should have some scope of mandatory application to carriage from China or to China, or both. This issue must be carefully considered in the revision of the Maritime Code.

4. Expectations of revision of the Maritime Code

Under the Chinese legislative system, as a principle, the making or revision of a law should first be listed in the national legislation plan which is made every five years. The revision of the Maritime Code has not yet been listed in the national legislation plan, mainly due to the limited resources of national legislation. However, the need for revision of the Maritime Code is well recognised in academic circles, the relevant industries and judicial circles. The Ministry of Transport which was responsible for the drafting of the Maritime Code strongly proposes the revision and has designated maritime law experts to carry out the requisite research in preparation for a revision in the near future.

Hopefully, the revision of the Maritime Code will be listed in the national legislation plan in the coming years and the work on revision will officially start by virtue of such a plan.

5. Conclusions

From the above analysis, the following conclusions may be drawn.

(a) The revision of the Maritime Code is necessitated by significant developments in the maritime economy and trade and the related areas in China and in the world since the adoption thereof in 1992, significant changes in the content of basic principles followed in the making of the Code, the lack of a legal regime governing compensation for marine pollution from ships and of harmony with the related basic laws, the existence of ambiguities, uncertainties and gaps in the Code.
(b) The main objects and contents of the revision of the Maritime Code should be the modernisation of the law on the carriage of goods by sea, establishment of a legal regime governing compensation for marine pollution from ships, an increase of the global limits of liability and the

---

77 Article 269 of the Maritime Code provides: 'The parties to a contract may choose the law applicable to such contract, unless the law provides otherwise. Where the parties to a contract have not made a choice, the law of the country having the closest connection with the contract shall apply.'

limit of liability of carrier for death of, or personal injuries to, passengers especially in the domestic trade, extension of the application of the Code to the transport and vessels in inland navigable waters adjacent to the sea, removal of ambiguities and uncertainties and filling in the gaps to enhance its enforceability, and harmonisation with the basic laws.

(c) Hopefully, the revision of the Maritime Code will be listed in the national legislation plan in the coming years by virtue of which the revision will start, based on the academic research on the revision thereof carried out by maritime law experts.

2 The legal framework surrounding the 'actual carrier' in the Chinese Maritime Code

Professor Tingzhong Fu

1. Introduction

The so-called actual carrier as a concept is contrasted with that of carrier (or contracting carrier). The concept first appeared in Article 1(c) of the Guadalajara Convention,[1] and was then introduced into the Hamburg Rules.[2] In the Chinese Maritime Code, the legal rules on the actual carrier were also established with the Hamburg Rules as a point of reference. The reasoning behind the introduction of the concept into Chinese maritime legislation was that there are several stages in the process of the carriage and the relationship between the parties is very complicated. Persons who are not parties to the contract of carriage but who have been entrusted by the carrier with the performance of the carriage should have a defined place within the legal framework of the law of carriage, so as to expand the body of responsibility and to protect the lawful interests of the parties concerned in international trade.

As regards the relationship between the carrier and the actual carrier, the Maritime Code contains only one Article, in which it is provided that 'the provisions with respect to the responsibility of the carrier contained in this Chapter shall be applicable to the actual carrier'.[3] This provision is deceptively simple on its face, but is rich in content. A correct interpretation of the law requires deep analysis of both legal theory and practice.

2. Defining the concept of actual carrier

In the Chinese Maritime Code, the actual carrier is defined as 'the person to whom the performance of carriage of goods, or of part of the carriage, has been entrusted by the carrier, and includes any other person to whom

---

1 Convention Supplementary to the Warsaw Convention for the Unification of Certain Rules Relating to International Carriage by Air Performed by a Person other than the Contracting Carrier, signed in Guadalajara on 18 September 1961.
2 United Nations Convention on the Carriage of Goods by Sea (Hamburg Rules), adopted in Hamburg on 30 March 1978.
3 Article 61 of the Maritime Code.

such performance has been entrusted under a sub-contract'.[4] Starting from this definition, in order to qualify as an actual carrier, an entity should meet two criteria: the first is to be entrusted with the carriage by the carrier. This concept of being entrusted in the context of commercial law is different from that of contract law under which the principal should conclude a commission contract with the agent, while there is no need to especially conclude such a commission contract in carriage by sea. The carriage of goods under a sub-contract of carriage has *per se* the 'entrusting' character. The second criterion is that the carriage has actually been performed. In shipping practice, it is a common phenomenon to entrust the sub-carrier with the performance of the carriage, however, whether the entrustment is direct or indirect, only the person who has actually performed the carriage is in the legal position of an actual carrier. In other words, a person who has handed the goods over to other persons for carriage after accepting the shipment of the goods should not be regarded as an actual carrier.

In view of current shipping practice, the carriage of goods under a bill of lading can be classified into the carriage of containerised goods and that of non-containerised goods. In the context of carriage of containerised goods, the responsibility of the carrier covers the entire period during which the carrier is in charge of the goods, starting from the time the carrier takes over the goods at the port of loading, until the goods are delivered at the port of discharge. As for the carriage of non-containerised goods, it covers the period during which the carrier is in charge of the goods, starting from the time of loading of the goods onto the ship until the time the goods are discharged therefrom.[5] In either set of circumstances, there is no doubt that the persons who have been entrusted by the carrier with performing the carriage must be regarded as the actual carrier. However, a theoretical argument may arise over questions regarding the legal position of a person who has only performed obligations at some specific stage of the carriage. Taking the operator of a transport terminal as an example, although the conduct of loading and discharging is encompassed within the concept of the carriage by sea, it should not be regarded as an actual carrier.

Some within the judiciary have interpreted the concept of carriage as a 'process', thus deeming that as long as a person has been entrusted by the carrier with participation in the carriage, he should be considered as an actual carrier even if only involved at some specific stage as opposed to the whole process of carriage. Others are inclined to interpret the concept of carriage in a narrow sense, and in their opinion only a person who actually performs the carriage with a ship as conveyance will fall within the definition of actual carrier.

Comparing the different viewpoints mentioned above, it can be seen that the doctrine of 'performance' of carriage is more accurate than the doctrine

---

4 Article 42 of the Maritime Code.
5 Article 46 of the Maritime Code.

of 'process' of carriage. The reasons can be discussed from two aspects as follows.

Starting with the point of view of principle, the carriage of goods by sea should meet two conditions: the first is the operation of the ship, and the second is to move the goods from one place to another at sea.[6] The persons who are in charge only of loading and discharging in the harbour district do not meet this condition since the instrument of production used by them are pieces of port machinery instead of ships, and their purpose of production is only to load the cargo on board and discharge the goods from the ship. Though it is provided in the Maritime Code that the person to whom the performance of 'part of the carriage' is entrusted should be regarded as an actual carrier, the provision refers only to the performance of carriage of part of cargo or performance of a particular stage of the carriage at sea. It by no means refers to the performance of connecting stages of the carriage.

Moreover, from the legal perspective, it is provided in the Maritime Code that 'a contract of carriage of goods by sea is a contract under which the carrier, against payment of freight, undertakes to carry by sea the goods contracted for shipment by the shipper from one port to another'.[7] It is obvious that the operator of a transport terminal does not fall within this definition since the place of performance of his activity is confined to the harbour district; its productive activity is performed against the payment of stevedoring charges rather than freight. Considering the above legal elements, the definition of actual carrier should not be construed in a broad sense. Those who regard the operators of transport terminals as actual carriers are arguably muddying the demarcation line between the 'process' of carriage and the 'performance' of carriage.

3. Precondition for actual carrier's liability

In view of the fact that under the Chinese Maritime Code the provisions in respect of the responsibility of the carrier apply to the actual carrier, the primary task is to determine the scope of the carrier's responsibility. In fact, the responsibility of the carrier is a broader concept which includes not only the obligations of the carrier but also the legal responsibility for breach of contract. With reference to the obligations of the carrier, these consist of the obligation to exercise due diligence to make the ship seaworthy before, or at the beginning of, the voyage, the obligation to care for the goods during the whole voyage and the obligation of reasonable dispatch without unreasonable deviation. As regards the legal responsibility for breach of contract, it refers to the liability for loss of, or damage to, or delay in delivery of, the goods due to the wrongful conduct of the carrier. Given that the true position of the actual carrier is different from that of the carrier (the carrier is

---

6 John Wilson, *Carriage of Goods by Sea* (6th edn, Pearson Longman, 2008), p.1.
7 Article 41 of the Maritime Code.

a party to the contract, while the actual carrier has no contractual relationship with the shipper), there should be some differences in the application of the law regarding the responsibilities of the carrier.

Viewed from the angle of the carrier, its obligations as set out in the Maritime Code are mandatory. Accordingly, the following rules apply with binding force: (a) the carrier is not entitled to reduce his legal obligations or mitigate the responsibility for loss of, or damage to, or delay in delivery of, the goods other than when assuming obligations not provided for in the Code; (b) the carrier is not allowed to increase his rights in addition to the basic rights conferred by law (however waiving or diminishing his conferred rights is permitted); (c) the carrier is not allowed to insert a clause in the bill of lading under which the benefit of insurance is in favour of the carrier.

From the standpoint of the actual carrier, on the other hand, though it is provided in the Maritime Code that the provisions regarding the responsibility of the carrier are applicable to the actual carrier, this does not mean that the three mandatory obligations provided for the carrier apply directly to the actual carrier without any restrictions. Since the actual carrier is not a party to the contract, he is not aware of what rights have been waived or what obligations have been assumed by the carrier. The following two elements should therefore be taken into consideration in judicial practice in determining the responsibility of the actual carrier.

3.1 Whether or not the actual carrier has agreed in writing to the special agreements concluded between carrier and shipper

As stated above, the minimum obligations and maximum rights of the carrier are set out in the Maritime Code; meanwhile, the carrier is entitled to waive rights conferred by law or to assume obligations not provided for in the Code. However, such special agreement is not binding upon the actual carrier unless confirmed in writing by that actual carrier.[8]

3.2 Is the loss of, or damage to, or delay in delivery of the goods connected to the conduct of the actual carrier?

Though it is provided in the Maritime Code that the provisions with respect to the responsibility of the carrier shall be applicable to the actual carrier, it is also provided that where both the carrier and the actual carrier are liable for compensation, they shall be jointly liable within the scope of such liability.[9] In maritime judicial practice, this precondition is usually neglected. Some consider that the carrier and actual carrier are to be jointly liable for compensation in any event. This doctrine leads to the misconceived view that the actual carriers are usually liable for compensation incurred

8 Article 62 of the Maritime Code.
9 Article 63 of the Maritime Code.

at stages of the transport in which they are not involved. It goes without saying that judgments issued under the guidance of this doctrine benefit the cargo claimant, but it may damage the lawful interests of the innocent actual carrier. For this reason, in determining the joint liability of the carrier and actual carrier, two elements should be taken into consideration: first, whether or not the actual carrier has been involved in the specific stage concerned in the dispute. The concept of carriage by sea includes several stages (loading, handling, stowage, keeping, care for and discharging), and even if the actual carrier is entrusted by the carrier, it does not mean that it should be liable for a claim arising from any stage of the carriage. For instance, there may be a special agreement in the contract which provides that the actual carrier is in charge only of the carriage at sea, while the delivery of the goods is to be performed by the carrier itself. In such circumstances, if the carrier delivered the goods otherwise than against a bill of lading to a person who is not entitled to receive the goods so that the lawful interests of the holder of bill of lading are infringed, the actual carrier will not be liable for compensation arising from the wrongful delivery of goods. The second element is to see whether or not there are causal connections between the loss and the conduct of the actual carrier. In some circumstances, the carrier and the actual carrier are both at fault in the carriage; however, if there is sufficient evidence to suggest that the loss of, or damage to, or delay in delivery of, the goods is the result of conduct by the carrier rather than that of the actual carrier, then there should be no joint liability at all. For instance, if an incompetent crewmember joins the ship before the voyage, this falls within the meaning of unseaworthiness of the ship. However, if there is sufficient evidence to support that the loss is not the result of improper crewing but due to the fact that the carrier accepted the shipment of dangerous goods from a shipper, there are no reasons to consider joint liability for the carrier and the actual carrier.

4. Application of the rules on the actual carrier in judicial practice

The concept of the actual carrier is derived from the concept of the carrier, while the carrier is a special concept under the bill of lading. For this reason, in shipping and judicial practice, the application of the rules on the actual carrier should be considered at two levels as outlined below.

4.1 Direct application under the bill of lading

4.1.1 Marine bill of lading

The bill of lading, as evidence of the contract of carriage by sea, is a shipping document which is unilaterally printed and signed by the carrier. The shipper has no opportunity to negotiate the clauses of a bill of lading with the carrier, so that the shipper is in fact in a weak bargaining position. In order to protect the lawful interests of the shipper and the consignee, the conduct of the carrier should be governed by mandatory provisions in the Maritime Code so that its rights do not go beyond the bounds of the law, its obligations are not reduced below the legal standards and its liability for compensation is not lower than the test determined in legislation. Due to the fact that the parties to the bill of lading are the carrier and the shipper, and that the concept of actual carrier is derived from the concept of carrier, if the carrier has entrusted the performance of the carriage to a third party, that third party will naturally fall within the definition of the actual carrier, and the rules regarding the actual carrier will automatically apply.

4.1.2 Multimodal transport bill of lading

The multimodal transport bill of lading is evidence of the multimodal transport contract. As defined by the Chinese Maritime Code, a multimodal transport contract means a contract under which the multimodal transport operator undertakes to transport the goods, against payment of freight for the entire transport, from the place where the goods were received in his charge to the destination and to deliver them to the consignee by two or more different modes of transport, one of which being sea carriage.[10] Starting from this definition, the multimodal transport to which the Maritime Code applies is essentially combined transport by rail-sea, sea-air and sea-rail-air. However, the Maritime Code does not apply to combined transport without sea carriage. In multimodal transport, the person who issued the bill of lading is in the legal position of a multimodal transport operator, while the persons who actually performed the transport at different stages are referred to as carriers for individual stages. Among such carriers for a stage, the person in charge of the carriage by sea falls within the definition of the actual carrier in the sense of the Maritime Code. Subject to the contract terms, the multimodal transport operator is liable for the entire carriage, while carriers who are in charge of the various stages of the transport will only be responsible for the particular carriage they have performed and their responsibility will be determined under the law applicable to that section. Since this system of allocating responsibility is similar to a network, it is referred to as a network liability system.[11] Accordingly, no matter at what stage the loss of, or damage to, the goods occurs, a claim may be brought against either the multimodal transport operator or the specific carrier who actually caused the loss, and the responsibility of the specific carrier will be determined in accordance with the law applicable to that stage. If the location at which the loss of, or damage to, the goods occurred cannot be

---

10 Article 102 of the Maritime Code.
11 Si Yuzhuo (ed), *The Dictionary of Maritime Law* (People's Communication Press, Beijing, 1998), p.267.

ascertained (concealed loss), then the multimodal transport operator will be liable for compensation in accordance with the law of carriage by sea for the reason that the perils of the sea in general are greater than those of other sections of transport.[12]

As per the above, the precondition for application of the Maritime Code to multimodal transport contracts is that the mode of sea carriage is included in the transport. The party in charge of the sea carriage element of the multimodal transport might be a shipping company or a legal person registered as a non-vessel owning operator under the Regulations of the People's Republic of China on International Maritime Transportation,[13] since the legal status of a shipping company is different from that of a no-vessel operator under administrative law, they are protected by law to different degrees.[14] By way of example, a multimodal transport is procured by a non-vessel operator, while the stage of the carriage by sea is actually performed by a shipowner. During the period of navigation, damage is caused to the goods due to the fault of the crew. In such circumstances, the shipowner, who is also the carrier, is entitled to invoke the right of exemption provided in the Code. Even if he should be liable for compensation, he still has the right to assert limitation of liability. However, if the claim is brought against the multimodal transport operator who is a non-vessel owning operator, since it is not in the position of the carrier under the contract of carriage by sea, it has neither the right of exemption nor that of limitation.

4.2 Indirect application of the rules under the voyage charterparty

4.2.1 Identification of legal nature of voyage charterparty

In the Chinese Maritime Code,[15] the voyage charterparty is defined as a contract under which the shipowner charters out and the charterer charters in the whole or part of the ship's space for the carriage by sea of the intended goods from one port to another and the charterer pays the agreed amount of freight. The voyage charterparty appears on the surface to be a leasing contract, yet it is in fact a contract of carriage. This conclusion can be demonstrated either from the starting point of legislation or that

---

12 Article 106 of the Maritime Code.

13 Regulations of the People's Republic of China on International Maritime Transportation, adopted at the 49th Executive Meeting of the State Council on 5 December 2001, came into force on 1 January 2002 and further amended on 18 July 2013. In the Regulation, the NVOCC was referred to as the 'non-vessel owning operator'.

14 According to Article 7 of the Regulations on International Maritime Transportation, the concept of non-vessel owning operator refers to the legal person which is neither a shipowner nor a ship operator, but it is entitled as a carrier to accept the consignment from the shipper against payment of freight and issue its bill of lading and then perform the carriage of goods through the international shipowner or operator.

15 See Article 92 in Chapter IV Section 7 of the Maritime Code.

of principle. From the perspective of legislation, the charterparty, which is concluded for a single voyage where the fundamental purpose of the parties to the contract is to carry the goods, should be regarded as a contract of carriage by sea.[16] In the maritime legislation of China, the special provisions regarding voyage charterparties are accordingly placed within Chapter IV entitled 'Contracts of Carriage of Goods by Sea'.

From the academic perspective, most scholars are inclined to interpret the voyage charterparty as a contract of carriage by sea. The late Professor William Tetley, a well-known Canadian specialist of maritime law, asserted that the voyage charterparty possesses many characteristics of a contract of carriage by sea since the voyage charterparty under normal circumstances is for carriage of agreed goods from one place to another.[17] It has also been directly identified by a Chinese scholar that the legal nature of a voyage charterparty is that of a contract of carriage.[18]

Accordingly, there is no real doubt that the voyage charterparty should be considered a contract of carriage by sea.

4.2.2 Academic arguments as to whether or not the legal framework of the actual carrier should be applied to the voyage charterparty

Although the charterparty is considered a contract of carriage by sea under the Chinese Maritime Code, there is ambiguity as to the applicable scope of the rules regarding the actual carrier, giving rise to divergent judicial practice. Some judges have considered that since the concept of actual carrier is provided in Section 1 (Basic Principles) of Chapter IV (Contracts of Carriage of Goods by Sea), and voyage charterparties as well as contracts evidenced by a bill of lading are all precisely in the nature of contracts of carriage by sea, the rules on the actual carrier should be applicable to voyage charterparties just as to bills of lading. By way of example, in March 2009, the China Marine Shipping Company concluded a voyage charterparty with the Hao Sheng Shipping Company (Hao Sheng). Under this voyage charterparty, the shipping company entrusted Hao Sheng with the carriage of goods accepted by them from a shipper. Hao Sheng concluded another voyage charterparty with the Heng Rong Shipping Company (Heng Rong) on back-to-back terms for the consignment of the same goods. In the process of carriage performed by Heng Rong. While the carriage performed by Heng Rong was in progress, a dispute arose as to the payment of freight so that the goods could not be duly discharged from the ship. In this case, though there were three parties involved in the carriage, while Heng Rong

---

16 See Article 4(4) of the Convention on the Law Applicable to Contractual Obligations, opened for signature in Rome on 19 June 1980.
17 William Tetley, *International Maritime and Admiralty Law* (Editions Yvon Blais Inc, Quebec, 2002), p.127. Mandarin translation by Zhang Yongjian (Law Press, Beijing, 2005), p.101.
18 Si Yuzhuo (ed), *Maritime Law* (Law Press, Beijing, 2012), p.198.

was the carrier that actually performed the carriage, Heng Rong was held to be an actual carrier although the carriage had been performed under a charterparty rather than a bill of lading.[19]

Conversely, in a case from January 2009, the China Forwarding Company, a subsidiary of the China Ocean Shipping (Group) Company (COSCO) concluded a voyage charterparty with the Tong Ping Shipping Company (Tong Ping). It was provided in the contract that Tong Ping would be in charge of the carriage. Tong Ping concluded another voyage charterparty with the Lin Wei Shipping Company (Lin Wei), which actually performed the carriage with the ship *Asian Star* under the charterparty which was in the nature of a sub-entrustment. During the voyage, a navigational accident occurred causing damage to the goods. Therefore, the plaintiff, the China Forwarding Company, brought an action to the maritime court asserting that Tong Ping and Lin Wei should be jointly liable for the damage to the goods. It was held by the court that the actual carrier was a concept pertaining to the definition of 'carrier', while the carrier should be regarded as a concept specific to the bill of lading rather than to the charterparty. Since the litigants in the action were all parties to the charterparty, their legal position should not be interpreted within the framework of the rules regarding the bill of lading. In other words, the plaintiff's claim for compensation could only be made against the shipowner under the charterparty, not against the carrier or actual carrier under the bill of lading.[20]

These cases demonstrate that there are different points of view about the question of applicability of the rules regarding the actual carrier to the charterparty. The cause of controversy can be summarised as follows.

(1) AMBIGUITY OF THE DEFINITION OF PARTIES TO DIFFERENT TYPES OF CONTRACTS

In the structure adopted by the Chinese Maritime Code, the special provisions of the charterparty and those regarding bills of lading are placed in the same chapter, showing that the voyage charterparty and bill of lading are all in the nature of a contract of carriage; yet the parties to the bill of lading are defined as carrier and shipper, while the parties of the voyage charterparty are defined as shipowner and charterer. From a perspective of principle, there are no mistakes with these definitions in the legislation; however, since the linguistic milieu of China is different from that of the UK, such specific descriptions may mislead people into perceiving that there is no connection

19 *China Marine Shipping Co Hainan v Hao Sheng Shipping Co Nanjing* (2009) Maritime Judgment No.50 by the Haikou Maritime Court, <http://pkulaw.cn/case/pfnl_117632439. html> accessed 3 August 2015.
20 *COSCO Wenzhou Branch v Topping Enterprises Ltd and Linkway Shipping Inc* (2011) Final Judgment No.156 by the Fourth Civil Adjudication Tribunal of the Higher People's Court of Shanghai, <http://www.lsbar.com/assistant/caseContent/10473/26383> accessed 3 August 2015.

between the concept of carrier or actual carrier under the bill of lading and the concept of shipowner or charterer under the charterparty. Those holding this viewpoint ignore the important phenomenon whereby the parties of the charterparty may become a carrier or actual carrier by issuing a bill of lading.

(2) INCOMPLETE UNDERSTANDING OF THE APPLICABLE SCOPE OF THE RELEVANT CONVENTION

It is provided in Article 1(b) of the Hague Rules[21] that the contract of carriage applies only to contracts of carriage covered by a bill of lading or any similar document of title, in so far as such document relates to the carriage of goods by sea. This provision is closely followed by a supplementary clause that the bill of lading includes 'any bill of lading or any similar document as aforesaid issued under or pursuant to a charterparty from the moment at which such bill of lading or similar document of title regulates the relations between a carrier and a holder of the same'.[22] However, in shipping practice, attention is only paid to the first part of the provision, neglecting the supplementary provision that the 'contract of carriage' also includes a bill of lading issued under the charterparty as long as such a bill of lading has been transferred to a third person and regulates the relations between the carrier and the third party. The mistake is akin to looking only at one tree instead of seeing the whole forest.

(3) AN INCORRECT ASSUMPTION ABOUT THE LEGAL OUTCOME OF APPLICATION OF THE RULES

In shipping practice, a carrier may be classified as a common carrier or a private carrier, and the legal obligations entrusted to each are different.[23] In

---

21 International Convention for the Unification of Certain Rules of Law Relating to Bills of Lading, Brussels, 25 August 1924 (Hague Rules).
22 Though the contracting parties of the voyage charterparty are named as the shipowner and the charterer, when the goods have been loaded on board, the charterer, who is under normal circumstances the buyer or seller under a contract for sale of the goods, may ask the shipowner to issue a bill of lading. Under such condition, if the charterer keeps the bill of lading in his hands rather than transferring it to the third party, the relationship between the shipowner and the charterer shall be governed by the charterparty, the bill of lading then only becoming a cargo receipt. Conversely speaking, if the bill of lading has been transferred to the third party, including the consignee, since there is no relation between the shipowner and the consignee, then the consignee shall not be bound by the charterparty, the relationship between both shall be governed only by the bill of lading. In such circumstances, the status of the shipowner in relation to the consignee is instead that of carrier under the bill of lading, so that the consignee is entitled to ask the shipowner to fulfill the obligations under the bill of lading. Accordingly, it is provided in the Hague Rules that those Rules shall not apply to the charterparty; but they are applicable to the bill of lading issued under the charterparty.
23 Bryan A. Garner (ed), *Black's Law Dictionary* (8th edn, Thomson West, 2004) p.226.

Coggs v Bernard,[24] the House of Lords confirmed the strict liability of the common carrier, and the carrier under a bill of lading falls within the scope of a common carrier. However, where carriage is performed by chartering a ship, that is done for a specific person under a specific contract, there is no doubt that such a carrier is in the nature of a private carrier.

In common carriage, the document to be issued is a formatted document, a bill of lading, and the shipper has no opportunity to negotiate the clauses of the contract with the shipowner. Carriers, in a favourable bargaining position, are therefore inclined to insert some clauses which are beneficial to themselves. In view of this, it is necessary to regulate the conduct of the carrier through legislation so as to protect the lawful interests of the public. For this reason, there has been concern that if the rules on the actual carrier are applied to the bill of lading under the charterparty, it may lead to bad results in that compulsory provisions which are only applicable to the common carrier are applied to private carriers, reducing the freedom of contract applicable to the charterparty. In fact, the mistake in this viewpoint is to take a dogmatic approach to the relation between different types of contract, and in overlooking an important fact that a bottom line has been fixed in legislation for differentiating the liabilities of the carrier under different contracts.

4.2.3 An ideal state as regards the application of the rules on the actual carrier under the charterparty?

With reference to the question of the relation between the rules on the actual carrier and the voyage charterparty, the analysis can be performed at the levels of legislation and of shipping practice.

(1) INTERPRETATION AT THE LEVEL OF LEGISLATION

The purpose of the rules on the actual carrier in the legislation is simply to break through the relativity of the contract so as to protect the lawful interests of the parties concerned in international trade. With the modernisation of international trade, traditional modes of operation have become a thing of the past and the division of labour in shipping is highly specific. Viewed from the perspective of the mode of transport, shipping can be classified into liner shipping, tramp services and international multimodal transport. As regards the bill of lading, it can be divided into bills of lading under liner shipping, bills of lading under charterparties and bills of lading under multimodal transport contracts. In shipping practice, the different kinds of contracts are frequently used, and it is quite common that the carrier entrusts a third party with the carriage of goods after accepting the shipment from the shipper. In such complex circumstances, the person who

---

24 (1703) 2 Ld Raym 909.

has finally fulfilled the carriage is often not one of the original contracting parties. If the legal position of that person cannot be recognised within the framework of the legislation, claims brought by a shipper or consignee will be faced with an impassable obstacle deriving from contract law. Similarly, standing in the position of the actual carrier, if his vessel is damaged by the goods of the shipper, there will be no legal basis for compensation. It is for this very reason that the rules on the actual carrier were established in the Hamburg Rules, giving the actual carrier the same position as the carrier.[25]

As regards the Hamburg Rules, special attention should be paid to two significant changes: the first is the title of the convention. The full name of the Hamburg Rules is 'United Nations Convention on the Carriage of Goods by Sea'; whereas the full title of the Hague Rules has a much narrower scope: the 'International Convention for the Unification of Certain Rules of Law Relating to Bills of Lading'. The second significant change is the definition of the contract of carriage by sea which is defined as 'any contract whereby the carrier undertakes against payment of freight to carry goods by sea from one port to another; however a contract which involves carriage by sea and also carriage by some other means is deemed to be a contract of carriage by sea for the purpose of this Convention only in so far as it relates to the carriage by sea'.[26] Considering these significant changes, it becomes apparent that within the framework of the Hamburg Rules the scope of application of the Hamburg Rules is enlarged from the bill of lading to encompass also other contracts involving carriage by sea. Similarly, in the Chinese Maritime Code, the definition of the contract of carriage by sea is defined with that of the Hamburg Rules as a point of reference. However, the so-called expansion of the scope of application is by no means without restrictions. The bill of lading is issued under the charterparty and regulates the relation between the carrier and the holder of the bill of lading, whereas the voyage charterparty is concluded between the shipowner and the charterer. The consignee is only a party to the bill of lading rather than the voyage charterparty, so that the consignee or other holder of the bill of lading should not be bound by the terms of the charterparty. If the shipowner has issued a bill of lading pursuant to a charterparty and the bill of lading has been transferred to a consignee, then the consignee is of course entitled to assert his rights by virtue of the bill of lading. Accordingly, if the bill of lading is issued by the shipowner but the goods have been carried by another person, then the person entrusted with fulfilling the carriage is in the position of an actual carrier under the bill of lading. For this reason, it can be deemed that though the position of the carrier is not automatically produced under the charterparty, it can be established as arising from the act of issuing the bill lading under the charterparty.

Within professional legal circles in China, some consider that the

25 Article 10(2) of the Hamburg Rules.
26 Article 1(6) of the Hamburg Rules.

significance of the rules regarding the actual carrier is merely to harmonise the relationship between the rules of action *in rem* applicable in common law jurisdictions and the rules of action *in personam* applicable in civil law systems. In other words, the concept of 'actual carrier' is only designed to correspond to the concept of 'ship' in civil actions. Accordingly, the actual carrier is merely a new concept rather than a new legal framework or rule. It goes without saying that this interpretation is not in conformity with the fundamental purpose of establishing the rules.

In fact, the contradiction between the rules of action *in rem* adopted in common law jurisdictions and the rules of action *in personam* adopted in the civil law system had been properly coordinated as early as in the age of the Hague Rules. In the Hague Rules, the concepts of 'carrier' and 'ship' are concurrently used, and it is provided in Article IV rule 2 that 'Neither the carrier nor the ship shall be liable for . . .'. There is no doubt that the concept of 'carrier' is used for actions *in personam*, while the concept of 'ship' can be used for the action *in rem*, so that there is no need to harmonise the contradictions of two concepts within the framework of the Hamburg Rules. Based on the above reasons, the expression of actual carrier in the context of the Hamburg Rules is not merely a simple concept but a legal framework, the fundamental function of which is to break through the privity of contract rather than merely harmonising the relationship between the civil law system and common law system. The legal basis for this viewpoint can be summarised as follows.

First of all, under the legal structure of the Hamburg Rules, all persons who are entrusted with performing the carriage, including any other persons who are in charge of this work, are all put into the framework of the contract of carriage by sea.

Secondly, in the Hamburg Rules, there is no concept of 'independent contractor' such as that adopted in the Hague-Visby Rules.[27] Accordingly, unlike the Hague-Visby Rules, the Hamburg Rules do not prevent an independent contractor from availing itself of the carrier's defences or limits of liability.[28] Thus the Hamburg Rules tend to expand the scope of application of defences and limitation and brush aside the restrictions set out before it. Looking back at the framework on the actual carrier established in the Maritime Code of China, its fundamental function is entirely the same as that of the Hamburg Rules. The concept of the actual carrier is provided in Section 1 on the General Principles of the Contract of Carriage by Sea rather than in Section 4 (the Bill of Lading).[29] It can therefore be concluded that the legislature had no intention of precluding the rules regarding the actual carrier from being applied to the voyage charterparty. In other words,

---

27 Article IV *bis* rule 2 of the Hague-Visby Rules.
28 Ibid.
29 See Chapter IV Section 1 Article 42(2) of the Maritime Code.

the rules on the actual carrier apply not only to bills of lading but also to bills of lading issued under a charterparty.[30]

As regards an expansion of the scope of application of the rules on the actual carrier, some people have expressed concern that if these rules are applied to bills of lading under a charterparty, the compulsory obligations and liabilities of common carriers will be placed on the shoulders of private carriers, infringing the parties' freedom of contract. However, there are good reasons why this will not occur in shipping practice, which can be summarised as follows. First, a 'bottom line' has been determined for the actual carrier's obligations. Among the obligations of the carrier under the bill of lading, only two rules (the obligations of seaworthiness and reasonable dispatch) are compulsorily applied to the voyage charterparty. As regards the obligations in relation to the management of cargo, the rules on the actual carrier can only be applied when there are no special provisions or contrary provisions provided in the voyage charterparty.[31] Secondly, in order to prevent the actual carrier from being improperly compensated, a legal 'fire wall' is set up in the Maritime Code. As has been described above, any special agreement under which the carrier assumes obligations not provided for in the Code or waives rights conferred by the Code is binding upon the actual carrier when the actual carrier has agreed in writing to the contents thereof.[32] For this reason, the idea that the application of the rules on the actual carrier to the voyage charterparty will impact the freedom of contract is only a theoretical assumption.

(2) EXAMINATION OF SHIPPING PRACTICE

With reference to international shipping practice, the voyage charterparty and the contract evidenced by the bill of lading are all within the meaning of the contract of carriage by sea. By comparison of the two, carriage performed in liner shipping possesses distinct characteristics which can be termed fixed line, fixed sailing schedule, fixed port of call and fixed vessel. Under this mode of shipping, the carrier performs a regular transport service according to a timetable and with the terms and conditions provided in advance, and the liner shipping company may not entrust other persons with the performance of the carriage on its behalf. In contrast, the actual carrier will usually emerge in shipping by chartering. The mistake of those who argue against the application of the rules regarding the actual carrier to the voyage charterparty is to consider only the surface of the phenomenon,

30 In this chapter, the applicable scope of the rules of actual carrier is expressed as 'under' instead of 'in' the voyage charterparty. The author's purpose in doing so is to highlight that although the rules on the actual carrier are not directly applicable to the voyage charter, they are applicable to the bill of lading issued under the charterparty. In other words, the rules on the actual carrier are to be indirectly applied to the voyage charterparty.
31 See Article 94 of the Maritime Code.
32 See Article 62 of the Maritime Code.

rather than taking into account the underlying purpose of the legislation. In shipping practice, there are three sets of circumstances in which the actual carrier may operate.

The first is that the charterer performs the carriage of goods using a chartered ship and issues the bill of lading as a carrier. In such circumstances, the charterer is a carrier under the bill of lading, while the shipowner who actually performs the carriage is identified as an actual carrier.

The second set of circumstances is that after concluding the voyage charterparty, the charterer has concluded a further contract with another person on back-to-back terms. Once the goods have been loaded on board, the charterer asks the shipowner to issue the bill of lading. In such circumstances, once the bill of lading has been transferred to the consignee, the shipowner becomes not only the carrier but also an actual carrier. As regards the charterer in this case, although he was involved in two contracts (in the first contract, he is a charterer and in the second contract he is in the position of shipowner), he did not issue the bill of lading, and is therefore neither the carrier nor the actual carrier under the bill of lading.

The third set of circumstances is that the shipowner entrusts the carriage to another person, but the person who has accepted the entrustment concludes a contract of sub-entrustment under which the carriage of goods is entrusted to a third party. The bill of lading is issued by the third party. In such circumstances, the person who is in charge of the carriage under the sub-contract is in the position of carrier. However, since the carriage of goods has been actually performed by the shipowner, the shipowner is naturally in the position of actual carrier. As regards the sub-entruster, he neither actually performed the carriage nor issued the bill of lading, and is therefore neither the carrier nor the actual carrier under the bill of lading, but only obliged to perform the obligations under the two voyage charterparties.

In the context of the true state of shipping practice, it can be concluded that though the concepts of carrier and actual carrier are not directly embodied in the voyage charterparty, they are in fact hidden behind it. Those who reject the relation between the concept of actual carrier and the voyage charterparty by virtue only of the fact that there is no concept of carrier or actual carrier in the charterparty have misinterpreted the concept of actual carrier. As a matter of fact, it has been clearly provided in the Hague Rules that the concept of 'carrier' includes the shipowner as well as a charterer who enters into a contract of carriage with a shipper. In this sense, the liability of the actual carrier has already been taken into consideration as early as in the Hague Rules; there is merely no explicit concept of actual carrier in the Rules. In this aspect, scholars at home and abroad have reached consensus. The well-known specialist of maritime law, the late Professor John Wilson pointed out in his monograph *Carriage of Goods by Sea* that when goods are shipped on a chartered vessel by a party other than the charterer, two problems face the shipper in the event of the cargo being lost or damaged during transit, the first of which is that he has to identify the carrier against whom the cargo claim can be pursued. The second problem facing the shipper is to establish the precise terms of the contract of carriage.[33] Another well-known scholar, Professor Yang Renshou of Taiwan, has directly attributed the charterer into the scope of the definition of carrier, thus it can be seen that the concept of carrier or actual carrier by no means lacks a relation to the voyage charterparty, the only question being that of how to identify their status through the issue of the bill of lading.[34]

5. Consideration of the relevant rules in the Chinese Maritime Code

All in all, some reasonable elements have been introduced into the Maritime Code which have the virtue of being forward-looking. Nevertheless, from a technical legislative perspective, there are some drawbacks which are worthy of consideration.

5.1 Unclear relation between the general and specific concepts of contract

The bill of lading, the voyage charterparty and the multimodal transport bill of lading are all attributed to the legal framework of the contract of carriage of goods by sea. As regards the concept of the contract of carriage by sea, it is generally defined in Article 41 of the Maritime Code as a contract under which the carrier, against payment of freight, undertakes to carry by sea the goods contracted for shipment by the shipper from one port to another. However, because the designations of the parties in each of the contracts is not the same (the parties to the bill of lading are defined as carrier and shipper, the parties under the voyage charterparty are referred to as shipowner and charterer, while the parties of the multimodal transport bill of lading are referred to as operator and shipper), it is difficult to link the general contractual concept to the particular concepts. This will give people a false impression that the contract of carriage by sea means only the bill of lading to the exclusion of the voyage charterparty; this being the fundamental cause of confusion in judicial practice.

5.2 Provisions regarding limitation of time affecting the application of the rules regarding the actual carrier

In the Chinese Maritime Code, two separate rules regarding limitation of time are provided for claims under bills of lading and voyage charterparties.[35]

---

33 John Wilson, *Carriage of Goods by Sea* (6th edn, Pearson Longman, 2008), p.237.
34 Yang Renshou, *The Latest Theory of Maritime Law* (San Min Book Co Ltd, Taiwan, 1999), p.194.
35 See Article 257 of the Maritime Code.

The limitation period for claims against the 'carrier' with regard to 'carriage of goods by sea' is one year, counting from the day on which the goods were delivered or should have been delivered by the carrier. The limitation period for claims with regard to 'voyage charterparties' is two years counting from the day on which the claimant knew, or should have known, of a breach of contract.[36] Such provisions may contribute to a false impression that a voyage charterparty is not a contract of carriage by sea and that the concept of carrier or actual carrier has no relation to the voyage charterparty. According to such interpretations, the voyage charterparty has been excluded from the application of the rules regarding the actual carrier. Those who hold this viewpoint neglect the important point that although no concepts of carrier and actual carrier appear in the voyage charterparty itself, the process of transfer of the bill lading will cause a carrier and actual carrier to emerge. Therefore, the effect of the rules regarding the actual carrier has been reduced by the rules on limitation of time, reducing the scope of application of the concept of actual carrier.

6. Conclusion

In accordance with the current framework of the maritime code, the key element of the actual carrier is to be entrusted with and to perform the carriage. As a result, a person who has only taken part at specific stages of the carriage (such as an operator in multimodal transport) should not be regarded as an actual carrier. In international maritime transport, although the shipper or consignee is entitled to claim against the actual carrier and the carrier for joint liability, it should be emphasised that the precedent condition must be followed. This condition is expressed as 'both the carrier and the actual carrier are liable for compensation'.

It should be noted that along with the development of international trade, the rule of privity of contract is being broken through so as to protect the lawful interests of the parties concerned. From the Himalaya Clause of the Hague-Visby Rules[37] and the rules on the actual carrier established in the Hamburg Rules, up to the rules on the performing party in the Rotterdam Rules,[38] it can be clearly seen that this trend is being strengthened. Against this historical background, excluding the person who actually performed the carriage from the scope of application of the rules on the actual carrier, goes against the trend. Nevertheless, the author is by no means an advocate of the application of the rules on the actual carrier to the charterparty without

---

36 See Article 257 of the Maritime Code.
37 See Article III rule 2 of the Hague-Visby Rules.
38 See Article 1(6) of the Rotterdam Rules (United Nations Convention on Contracts for the International Carriage of Goods Wholly or Partly by Sea, adopted by the United Nations on 11 December 2008).

any conditions; the condition precedent is that the bill of lading under the charterparty has been issued and then transferred to the third party.

The maritime legislation of China arguably displays three defects which will affect the application of the rules on the actual carrier. These defects can be described as: (i) the relation between the basic principles and the particular rules is unclear; (ii) the general and specific concepts of contract are incompatible; and (iii) claims under voyage charterparties are isolated from claims under bills of lading, and the ambiguity of the concepts used in enshrining the rules in legislation gives rise to misunderstandings. In order to improve the function of the legal framework with respect to the actual carrier, the following measures can be adopted.

First, in order to prevent the actual carrier from eschewing its responsibility, a supplementary provision should be made for the 'Basic Principle' to the effect that the responsibility of the carrier applies to the contract evidenced by the bill of lading and the bill of lading issued under the voyage charterparty, if the bill of lading or any similar document of title regulates the relation between the carrier and the holder of the bill of lading. The party which is actually in charge of the carriage according to the voyage charterparty should also assume the liability of the actual carrier.

Secondly, in order to keep the coherence of the relevant concept in the legal system, the current provisions regarding the limitation of time should be modified to the effect that 'the limitation period for claims under the bill of lading is one year, counting from the day on which the goods were delivered, or should have been delivered, by the carrier. The limitation period for claims under the voyage charterparty is two years, counting from the day on which the claimant knew, or should have known, that his rights had been infringed. If the bill of lading under the charterparty has been transferred to the third party, including the consignee, the limitation period for claims under such bill of lading is one year as stipulated above.

In the author's opinion, such modifications may not only coordinate the general concept of contract of carriage by sea and the specific concept of the particular contract, but may also ensure that the effect of the substantive system will not be distorted by the rules on time-bars.

3 Crew negligence and 'civil' liabilities in carriage by sea: a comparative analysis

Dr Meixian Song

1. Introduction

The maritime system is operated by people, and human errors figure dramatically in casualty situations. About 75–96% of marine casualties are caused, at least in part, by some form of human error.[1] Human error can be described as an incorrect decision by the managing team, including the master, or an improperly performed action by the crew.

When casualties occur in the course of carriage due to master or crew negligence, the results may involve losses of goods, damage to the vessel, loss of freight and sometimes public liability in the case of oil pollution, and even loss of life. Some extreme cases from the last few years are concerned with human error in forms of negligence and even deliberateness. For instance, the *MV Rena* incident is one of New Zealand's most significant and worst maritime environmental disasters. On 5 October 2011, the vessel was running behind schedule and the master decided to shorten the route. The ship grounded, causing huge losses both environmentally and economically. The ship was carrying containers, eight of which contained hazardous materials, as well as heavy fuel oil and marine diesel. Bad weather subsequently caused the ship to shift on the reef. The shifting of the ship caused further damage, resulting in further oil leaking. Due to increased pressure to her hull, in early January 2012 it was reported that the *Rena* had broken in two.

The *Costa Concordia* in January 2012 is another overwhelming and costly example. Its protection and indemnity (P&I) claim including wreck removal ran to US$1.5 billion, and along with hull and machinery insurance rocketed to nearly US$2 billion. The huge vessel which had more than 4,000 passengers and crew on board, in calm weather, struck rocks and then lost power, drifted and partially capsized. The evacuation was slow and chaotic and took over six hours, with conflicting information passed between the captain, the ship's crew and the coastguard authorities. The captain was

---

1 Dr Anita M. Rothblum, 'Human Error and Marine Safety', p.1, <http://bowles-langley. com/wp-content/files_mf/humanerrorandmarinesafety26.pdf> accessed 5 May 2015.

subsequently personally charged with manslaughter, causing a shipwreck and abandoning ship. Similarly, the sinking of the *MV Sewol*, a South Korean ferry, in April 2014 also received widespread social and political reaction to the fact that the operations of the ferry became out of control due to overloading of cargo and other causes. The captain and crew abandoned ship with passengers still on board and were subsequently arrested on suspicion of dereliction of duty and violation of maritime law, and some crew were found guilty of murder.

The key question in this chapter is who, in the context of carriage by sea, should bear the contractual or tortious liabilities arising from crew negligence. It will be answered based on a comparative study of English law and Chinese law.

Actions may be brought against a number of parties besides the master and crew: the shipowner or demise charterer, also known as the disponent shipowner, as the employer of the crew, as they are under the duty to man the ship. The shipowner is sometimes the actual carrier in relation to the cargo carriage, as well as the contractual carrier.[2] In contrast, if the vessel has been chartered under a voyage charterparty or a time charterparty, the charterers are very likely to be the contractual carrier. This is especially so under a time charterparty, and the crew are also obliged to follow instructions given by the charterers, as though they are the charterer's employees under the employment clause.

In addition, assorted marine insurance covers are provided by the insurance companies and P&I Clubs.[3] The cargo owner will place the marine cargo policy, the ship's managers will find hull and machinery insurance for the ship, freight insurance and liability insurance from P&I cover if needed, for instance where the ship is arrested by judicial order or due to alleged environmental liability.

All in all, the aim of this chapter is to scrutinise the current law regarding the civil liabilities that may be imposed on the crew and the ship, and any defences or limitation of liability that avails to the crew under both jurisdictions at issue. The chapter also aims to analyse the impact of crew negligence on the allocation of risks of losses between the carrier and the cargo owner and the trends in law on this matter. In this chapter, the word 'crew' connotes a broad meaning which includes the master as well as other crew members; however, where required, the master may be discussed separately from the crew in some contexts.

---

2 English shipping law does not recognise the concept of actual carrier when ascertaining duties and liabilities. See *The Starsin* [2003] UKHL 12.
3 Regarding the issue of crew negligence under marine insurance law, see Dr Meixian Song, 'Is Negligence a Cause of Loss in Marine Insurance?' [2014] *British Insurance Law Association Journal* (BILA), pp.57–69.

2. The scope of crew negligence

The master and crew play important roles in ensuring that the carriage can be completed safe and sound, since the master has the right to make decisions relating to the navigation and the crew is charged with the execution of the decisions made by the competent or authorised parties. Negligence is conceived as the failure to exercise a duty of care, thus crew negligence is based upon the prerequisite that a duty of care is recognised by contracts of affreightment and law.

Article 35 of the Chinese Maritime Code 1992 (CMC) clearly states that the master shall be responsible for *the management and navigation of the ship*. Orders given by the master within the scope of his functions and powers must be carried out by other members of the crew, the passengers and all persons on board.

In English law, in *The Hill Harmony*,[4] the master failed to follow the charterer's instructions as to the route to be taken by the vessel in respect of two journeys from Canada to Japan. The ship had previously encountered adverse weather on the route chosen by the time charterer, so the master decided to take a longer but safer route, causing the two voyages to be delayed. The main issue was whether the choice of route is a matter of navigation to be decided by the master, or a matter of employment up to the time charterer. It was held that the master was entitled to make decisions in respect of navigation involving matters of seamanship, whereas decisions as to the employment of a vessel involving economic aspects of its operation should be made by the charterer and such orders should be followed by the master. The House of Lords found that it is a mistake to use the word 'navigation' as though it included everything which involved the vessel proceeding through the water; thus, the choice of route was, but for some overriding considerations, a matter relating to the employment of a vessel, her scheduling and her trading. The navigation or seamanship is referring to the operations of the master or crew pertaining to the physical safety of the vessel along with the people and cargo on board, as opposed to the economic exploitation of the service of the vessel. The decision sets up a fine line of the master and the crew's duty of care when coping with navigational matters.

As to the employment of the ship, the issue especially under a time charterparty is largely resolved by the 'Employment and Indemnity' clause,[5] which clearly stipulates that the charterer will be liable for reimbursement

---

4 [2001] 1 Lloyd's Rep. 147.
5 For example, Cl. 9 of BALTIME states: '. . . The Master to be under the orders of the Charterers as regards employment, agency or other arrangements. The Charterers to indemnify the Owners against all consequences or liabilities arising from the Master, Officers or Agents signing Bills of Lading or other documents . . .'

of loss suffered due to the master following the order given by the charterer in the course of the employment of the ship.

The master and crew's duty of taking care of *the vessel* is further explained in *The Glenochil*.[6] After the arrival of the vessel at her port of destination, and during the discharge of the cargo, it became necessary to stiffen the ship. For this purpose, the engineer ran water into a ballast tank, but negligently failed to ascertain the condition of the pipe and casing, which had, owing to heavy weather during the voyage, become broken. The goods were damaged by the water. The point clearly made in the judgment was that the master and crew undertook the duty of navigation and management of the ship, and that most of the time the two words meant the same thing. However, strictly speaking, it is clear that the word 'management' goes somewhat beyond navigation, far enough to take in this very class of acts which do not affect the sailing or movement of the vessel, but do affect the vessel herself. That is to say, the 'management' was not limited to the period during which the vessel was at sea, but extended to the period during which the cargo was being discharged.

Secondly, the management of the ship as to want of care of vessel indirectly affecting the cargo is distinct from want of care of cargo. Management of the ship is one which is necessarily done in the proper handling of the vessel for the safety of the ship herself, but is not primarily done at all in connection with the cargo. It should be emphasised here that the ship's management is under legal duties to take care of both the ship and the goods, however the distinction lies in the legal consequences, which are discussed in further detail in section 3 below.

3. Legal basis of the shipowner's/employer's liabilities

The question as to the liability between crew and shipowner/employer is not peculiar to maritime law. This is essentially a question pertaining to the legal relationship of employment or agency. The main concern is to what extent the crew members can be 'covered' or protected under the wings of their employer when claims are made by third parties.

3.1 English law

From the perspective of contract law, masters and crew are employees under contract with the shipowners or demise charterers. The nature of the employment contract is based upon the doctrine of agency; the crew are rendered as the agents of the employer equipped with actual authority or apparent authority under certain circumstances. A principal will be bound by the acts of his authorised agent within the scope of the actual authority, whereas if the agent is acting beyond the scope of authorisation, the

6 [1896] P. 10.

principal may still be estopped from denying the effect of the agent's act on him with a third party due to apparent authority[7] or usual authority.[8] There is an actual but somewhat slim chance that the employee/agents will be directly liable for the third party's loss on the ground of breach of warranty, where the principal is not capable of undertaking the liability and the agent has negligently broken the warranty made by himself to the third party, where he is clothed with legitimate authority to act.[9]

Furthermore, vicarious liability in tort recognised in English law is a strict liability through which one entity A is made liable for the torts of another, even though A is not at fault. It is trite law that employers may be vicariously liable for the torts of their employees. The doctrine enshrines an early twentieth-century notion of employment and industry for assuring that the employer is to be liable for the employee's wrongful act authorised by the employer, or an unauthorised mode of performing some act authorised by the employer.

There are two exceptions to such vicarious liability where the employee may be faced with direct claims. First, the servant[10] may have committed acts of wilful misconduct falling outside the ambit of their employment; their act/omission must constitute a 'frolic of their own'. In *The Druid*,[11] the master intentionally ambushed a sloop to claim a GBP5 towage fee owed by the sloop. The rejection caused the master to drag the sloop up and down the river. The court defined the behaviour of the master as utterly unlawful and not authorised under the employment contract, so that the master was personally liable for the losses of the injured party.

Secondly, the crew is personally liable for tortious liability such as a passenger's physical injury.[12] Under the contract of carriage of passengers, if a passenger was injured while disembarking due to the negligence of the

---

7 *Rama Corp Ltd v Proved Tin & General Investments Ltd* [1952] 2 QB 147. It was addressed in the case that in nature, apparent authority is a form of estoppel, for instance when a good faith third party reasonably relies upon the representation, either express or implied, by the principal, the contract concluded with the agent is binding to the principal.

8 *Watteau v Fenwick* [1893] 1 QB 346. It was held that the principal was liable for all acts of their agent which were within the authority usually conferred upon an agent of his particular character, although he had never been held out by the defendants as their agent, and although the authority actually given to him by them had been exceeded.

9 *Hedley Byrne & Co v Heller Partners Ltd* [1964] AC 465; *Yonge v Toynbee* [1910] 1 KB 215.

10 The old-fashioned term 'servants' has been replaced in modern English law by the term 'employee', but will occasionally be used here in the discussion of older case law.

11 *The Druid* (1842) 1 W Rob 391.

12 *Adler v Dickson* [1955] 1 QB 158. This case is the basis for the term 'Himalaya clause'. The clause states that 'The company will not be responsible for and shall be exempt from all liability in respect of any . . . injury whatsoever of or to the person of any passenger . . . whether the same shall arise from or be occasioned by the negligence of the company's servants . . . in the discharge of their duties, or whether by the negligence of other persons directly or indirectly in the employment or service of the company . . . under any circumstances whatsoever . . .' The court held that such clause, albeit clearly and well worded, could not preclude the master from being sued for personal claims.

master and crew, the passenger is entitled to sue the master for tortious liability, regardless of the exclusion clause within the carriage contract with the employer. A direct claim in tort against the crew due to negligence in the carriage of passengers is distinguished from the case where the owner of a chartered vessel is vicariously responsible for the tortious acts of the master and crew while acting under the orders of the charterers, such as damage to cargo due to bad stowage.[13]

3.2 Chinese law

Under Chinese law, 'civil liability' is recognised to be undertaken by the employer arising either from contracts or tort, due to the employee's breach or negligence. This is similar to the concept of vicarious liability in English law. There is some relevant judicial practice, for example a decision of Guangzhou Maritime Court (in Canton) where the shipowner sued the master asserting civil liability due to the master's nautical negligence in causing the ship to run aground. The court held that there was no legitimate ground in law or in the pertinent contracts and that it was even unfair to find that the master should bear civil liability to the cargo owner and the shipowner for the losses in the course of the navigation, which required special skills and expertise.[14]

As a matter of law, however, legislation has provided adequate grounds in principle for precluding the crew from responding for direct civil liabilities. The apex provision is Article 43 of the General Principles of the Civil Law of the People's Republic of China 1986[15] providing that 'an enterprise as legal person shall bear civil liability for the operational activities of its legal representatives and other working personnel'.

Section 58 of the Interpretation of the Supreme People's Court of Some Issues on Implementation of the General Principles of Civil Law (1988) interprets the phrase 'operational activities' of Article 43 such that where the employee is acting *in the name of the employer/company* and causes economic loss to a third party, the employer/company must bear liability accordingly. However, pertaining to tortious liability, Article 35 of the Tort Liability Law 2009 reaffirms that the employer assumes liability for physical losses and injuries in place of the employees *as a result of the employed services*. Moreover, section 8 of the Interpretation of the Supreme People's

---

13 Per Jenkins LJ in *Adler v Dickson* at p.196, distinguished from the case of bad stowage of *Elder, Dempster & Co v Paterson Zochonis & Co Ltd* [1924] AC 522.

14 See <http://seafarers.msa.gov.cn/Applications/Information/NewsView.aspx?infoid=a4c0fa 04-49b3-45df-be27-16053981e299&MenuCode=201311017> accessed 28 May 2015.

15 This Law ranks at the top of the Chinese legal system, having been adopted by the National People's Congress, and therefore provides the overriding principles determining the application of other civil law statutes. The Chinese law has not yet consolidated its civil law into a single code. The National People's Congress has so far promulgated, inter alia, The Contract Law, The Law of Tort Liability.

Court of Some Issues concerning the Application of Law for the Trial of Cases on Compensation for Personal Injury (2004) defines 'operational activities' as *activities out of employment* or under the employment, in order to find the employer's vicarious liability for the employee's negligence.

It will be observed that the two constructions, both provided by the Supreme Court, are not exactly identical as a matter of practice. This divergence has been widely identified by academia and practitioners. When the employee is acting under the employment relationship, the employee is normally acting in the name of the employer, or sometimes not (undisclosed agency). In contrast, where the employee is acting in the name of the employer, it does not necessarily follow that his activities are fully within the scope of the employed service. Therefore, 'in the name of the employer' and 'as a result of the employed services' do not bear the same meaning. However, it cannot be said that one interpretation is more precise than the other. By way of reconciling explanation, 'operational activities' will result in liability for the employer if the employee as agent is attempting to conclude contractual relationships with a third party, by analogy with apparent authority or usual authority; while for tortious liabilities, 'operational activities' must be within the scope of the employment or else the employer will not be burdened with vicarious liability.

This essentially amounts to recognition of a concept of vicarious liability of the employer for the acts of its employees in Chinese law. The overriding effect of this principle means that legislative documents at lower levels, such as administrative laws and regulations by the State Council and local laws, must not contain any rules or regulations which are contradictory to such principle. Nonetheless, an exception to the principle can be found in legislation which is to some extent comparable to English law. According to section 9 of the Interpretation of the Supreme People's Court of Some Issues concerning the Application of Law for the Trial of Cases on Compensation for Personal Injury (2004):

> 'Where the employee causes physical harm to a third party while under employment, the employer undertakes the liability. If due to wilful misconduct or gross negligence of the employee, then the employer and employees are jointly liable to the injured party. The employer is entitled to recover the compensation from the employee, if the employer assumes the liability primarily.'[16]

The construction of the concept 'operational activities' thus confines the employee's negligence within the ambit of the employment, which is consistent throughout Chinese legislation. This is similar to the decision in *The Druid*: if the employee's act is beyond the description and authorisation of the labour contract, the employer is jointly liable to the injured

16 Translated by the author.

party for the purpose of favouring the innocent and injured party, however the employer may not ultimately bear the liability in this regard because of the opportunity for recourse against the employee. The joint liability recognised in Chinese law clearly and only copes with the internal legal relationship between the employer and employee against the external liability to an injured third party. As to personal claims such as tortious liability arising from the employment, vicarious liability is only excepted in the case of wilful misconduct or gross negligence; a mere lack of reasonable care cannot preclude the vicarious liability of the employer in Chinese law. This is not the same decision as in *Adler v Dickson* in English law. Under Chinese law, the question whether a personal claim is an exception to the principle depends also upon the severity of the negligence.

4. Crew negligence as an exclusion of the carrier's liability to the cargo damage

The conventional exceptions recognised in common law include an act of God or enemies of the Queen, and the inherent vice of the goods and the shipper's own fault. Nevertheless, in the good old times of the nineteenth century, carriers were able to abuse a superior bargaining position with the support of the freedom of contract, and escaped liability even resulting from own their negligence, such as providing an unseaworthy ship. Against such a background, measures began to be taken through domestic legislation to adjust the balance of interests between the interests of the ship and the goods, and finally model laws at the international level were achieved, substantially in the twentieth century.[17] One of the common aims of the international conventions including the Hague-Visby Rules (and its predecessor the Hague Rules), the Hamburg Rules and the Rotterdam Rules, is to set up and specify the carrier's obligations at certain levels; as a result, the carrier will not freely be exempted from liability in the case of his own fault or negligence. However, it is very interesting that the attitude towards crew negligence, as being an exclusion from the carrier's liability, gradually varies as time goes by.

The common law exceptions are set out in Article IV rule 2 of the Hague-Visby Rules, which provides for the immunities available to the carrier or the ship against liability to the cargo owner or the lawful holder of the bill of lading. More importantly, Article IV rule 2(a) provides exemptions from liability in circumstances of nautical negligence of the carriers' employees; whereas none of the exceptions protect the carrier in case he is personally negligent.[18]

---

17 Lord Justice Aikens, Richard Lord QC and Michael Bools, *Bills of Lading* (Informa, 2006), Chapter 1, para.1.46.

18 Article 2: 'Neither the carrier nor the ship shall be responsible for loss or damage arising or resulting from: (a) Act, neglect, or default of the master, mariner, pilot, or the servants of

A different tone in modern transport law in this regard is set by the Hamburg Rules and subsequently the Rotterdam Rules. Article 5 of the Hamburg Rules sets out the basis of the carrier's liability: the carrier is liable for loss resulting from loss of, or damage to, the goods unless the carrier proves that he, his servants or agents took all measures that could reasonably be required to avoid the occurrence and its consequences.[19] Article 5(7) clarifies that if fault or neglect on the part of the carrier, his servants or agents is one of the concurrent causes of the loss of the cargo, the carrier is liable only to the extent that the loss, damage or delay in delivery is attributable to such fault or neglect and the carrier is to bear the burden of proof.

More recently, the Rotterdam Rules demonstrate the same tendency of removing crew negligence from the list of the exemptions of the carrier's liability. Article 17(2) states that the carrier is relieved of all or part of its liability if it proves that the cause or one of the causes of the loss, damage or delay is not attributable to its fault or to the fault of any performing party; the master or crew of the ship; the employees of the carrier or a performing party and others under the carrier's order or control. Furthermore, nautical negligence is deleted from the listed exemptions of the carrier's liability in Article 17(3).

4.1 English law

Section 1 of the English Carriage of Goods by Sea Act 1971 gives the force of law to the Hague-Visby Rules, incorporating the Rules as part of English Law. That is to say, so long as the contractual parties choose English law as the applicable law or governing law of the contract, the Hague-Visby Rules are automatically applicable. Although as is well known, English common law is a case-based legal system, legislative instruments are also primary legal sources.

The Hague-Visby Rules, as aforementioned, clearly recognise crew negligence in terms of navigation and the management of the ship to exempt the carrier from the liability for cargo losses. On the contrary, should losses of the goods on board result from the lack of care of the goods, this is a breach of duty of the carrier under Article III, rule 2 of the Hague-Visby Rules such that the carrier will be liable for the losses. For instance, in *Gosse Millerd*,[20] while the ship was being repaired in dry dock by workmen regarded as the servants of the carrier, the workers frequently had to be in and out of the hold where the goods were stored, and the hatches in consequence were often left open. Owing to the negligence of the shipowner's servants,

---

the carrier in the navigation or in the management of the ship. The interpretation in details is addressed later under English Law. (b) . . .'

19 Article 5(1) and (4)(a)(ii).
20 *Gosse Millerd Ltd v Canadian Government Merchant Marine Ltd* (1928) 32 Ll LR 91; and followed by *The Iron Gippsland* [1994] 1 Lloyd's Rep. 335.

the hatches were not protected when rain was falling, and the rain water entered the hold and damaged the goods.

The court has drawn a fine line between the management of the goods through the operation of parts of the ship and the management of the ship on its own. It was held that the negligence in the management of the hatches was not negligence 'in the management of the ship' within the meaning of Article IV rule 2(a). The hatch covers did not affect the ship herself, as the operation was not a necessary action to properly handle the vessel, thus the exception could not be relied upon in this context. Instead, the correct use of the hatch covers was considered in relation to the requirement of taking care of the goods and pertained to the sole interest of the goods. Therefore, since the servants of the carrier failed properly and carefully to keep and care for the goods, as required by Article III rule 2, the carrier was liable for the damage. In contrast, Chinese law has been confronted with more difficulty in judicial practice in terms of distinguishing nautical fault from lack of care of cargo, as the test set up by the individual cases, albeit leading and typical, is not effectively binding.

Although the ship or the carrier will be responsible for crew negligence pertaining to the care of the goods, the benchmark of due diligence is set at a level reasonable to the crew and carrier. The obligation imposed on the carrier and his crew is to adopt a sound system in light of all knowledge which the carrier had or ought to have had about the nature of the goods; the carrier is not expected in law to be able to suspect special risks of carrying goods of a particular kind.[21] Subsequent case law has provided further clarification as to the application of the Hague-Visby Rules and achieved the primary goal of certainty in the twentieth century.

4.2 Chinese law

In the context of the carriage contract between the carrier and the shipper, the Contract Law 1999 provides the basis of strict liability in the case of breach.[22] This is the same starting point as English law at the contract law level, which indicates that except for legitimate exceptions, so long as the facts show that the contractual duty not to deliver the goods in the condition as agreed, without reference to the negligence of the carrier or his employees, the contractual carrier will be liable for the loss of the shipper or the lawful holder of the bill of lading under this particular carriage contract. However, Article 311 regarding contracts for the carriage of goods states that the carrier is to be liable for any damage or loss of goods occurring in the course of transport, unless the carrier proves that the damage or the loss of the goods is

---

21 Per Lord Pearson, *Albacora SRL v Westcott & Laurance Line Ltd* [1966] 2 Lloyd's Rep. 53.
22 Article 107: 'Either party that fails to perform its obligations under the contract or fails to perform them as contracted shall bear the liability for breach of contract by continuing to perform the obligations, taking remedial measures, or compensating for losses.'

caused by *force majeure*, the natural property of the goods or reasonable wear and tear, or is caused by the negligence of the consignor or the consignee.

Article 311 of the Contract Law 1999 has been followed by lower tier instruments of domestic transport law. The Rules Relating to the Domestic Carriage by Water 2000 promulgated by the Ministry of Transport affirms the strict liability of the carrier in Article 44, and the nautical fault of the crew is not included in the exhaustive list of exclusions of the carrier's liability in Article 48. Moreover, the Civil Aviation Law of the PRC 1995[23] and the Railway Law of the PRC 1990,[24] respectively, also adopt a strict liability approach.

The CMC is *lex specialis* in relation to the Contract Law, providing more specific and concrete rules pertaining to international shipping affairs. The provisions of the CMC cannot be contradictory to the content of the Contract Law; however, the CMC has priority in legal application due to its specificity. Article 51 is worded identically to Article IV rule 2 of the Hague-Visby Rules, such that the carrier is immune from losses caused by crew's nautical fault.

4.3 Ready for absolute liability?

It is evident that both jurisdictions follow the Hague-Visby Rules in that the shipper or holder of the bill of lading shall bear the loss of the goods due to the usual meaning of crew negligence in navigation and the management of the ship. The rationale of the protection afforded to the carrier's side is due to the historical and adventurous marine risks arising in the course of the voyage, compared with the other modes of transport. Such a protective regime may appear obsolete, as the business of carriage of goods by sea has been developed in the direction intended by the law. Therefore, following the somewhat proactive approach of the Hamburg Rules in shifting the liability to the side of the ship, attention has subsequently been paid to the necessity of retaining such exemption, and the balance of liabilities has been reconsidered in the context of the Rotterdam Rules. The prevailing view of the Working Group was that the strict liability of the carrier was an important step towards modernising and harmonising international transport law; essential in the context of establishing international rules for door-to-door transport.[25] Nevertheless, strict liability may lead to some unintended consequences.[26] Obviously, once the liability is shifted, not

---

23 Liability of the Carrier of Chapter IX Section 3.
24 Article 17.
25 Report on the Working Group's 10th session, A/CN.9/525, para.35.
26 Report on the Working Group's 13th session, A/CN.9/552, para.89. Voices for retaining this exception is repeatedly proposed in the 13th and 19th sessions, however the Working Group strongly insisted on the necessity of removing nautical fault from the listed exemptions, <http://www.uncitral.org/uncitral/en/commission/working_groups/3Transport.html> accessed 27 May 2015.

only will the shipowner or the carrier's legal burden be increased, but significant impact will be cast on the P&I Clubs as well as the marine insurance market.

However, the question of whether the Rotterdam Rules should be ratified is a different and entirely technical issue, as what is to be 'sold' here is a bundle of rules, some of which present a striking challenge to some long and well-established rules and will lead to much uncertainty. This is a conundrum far more complex, particularly to English law, than the specific question whether English law or Chinese law is ready to impose on the carrier liability for crew negligence in navigation and management of the ship by removing the risk from the excepted risks list. For example, the basis of the carrier's liability as provided in Article 17 implies several rounds of the game of burden of proof between the carrier and the cargo owner in ascertaining liability.[27] Moreover, Article 17(2) and (6) recognises the room for concurrent causes of loss when determining the apportionment of liability; both concurrent causes and apportionment of liabilities are traditionally not welcomed by the judges in English commercial contract disputes.

On the other hand, Chinese law has the requisite flexibility to simply remove the crew's nautical fault from the exemptions, as the Chinese law has not formally ratified any conventions but elected to incorporate certain parts or rules into the CMC when it was made. The current reform process is likely to adopt the same approach in amending the CMC. The applicability of the Rotterdam Rules extends to inland carriage, with the potential benefit that Chinese law can be more consistent and coherent in the liability regime applicable to the multi-modal transport. Nevertheless, generally speaking, academia in China discreetly observes and considers the consequences of changes to the law in this regard.[28]

The Rotterdam Rules thus put several issues under the spotlight and also compel the global shipping law world to move to a crossroads, where the current regime has not yet fully collapsed, and indeed remains functioning and very much certain in some jurisdictions such as under English law; however, a change will increase the burden of the carrier and the ship, which might in turn benefit nautical safety in carriage by sea. Cargo interests will still be able to obtain their indemnity from the marine underwriters, normally on the ground of perils of sea; what is actually affected here is the right of subrogation of the insurers against the carrier or the ship. More decisions and interpretation will be required to adequately address the distinction between perils of the sea and crew negligence in the context of carriage by sea and marine insurance.

---

27 Julian Clark and Jeffery Thomson, 'Exclusions of Liability' in Professor D. Rhidian Thomas (ed.), *Carriage of Goods under the Rotterdam Rules* (Informa, 2010), para.8.11.
28 Si. Yuzhuo, 'Evaluation and Prospects of the Rotterdam Rules' [2009] *Annual of China Maritime Law*, Vol. 20, Nos 1–2.

5. Limitation of liability

5.1 English law

Article IV rule 5(a) of the Hague-Visby Rules entitles the carrier to limit the amount of damages for which it is liable in respect of cargo damage or losses. The application of the Hague-Visby Rules has been construed by case law to signify that quite literally 'in any event' the carrier may enjoy the limitation of liabilities,[29] except for Article IV rule 5(e) where the carrier may lose the right if it is proved that the damage resulted from an act or omission of the carrier done deliberately or recklessly. However, this test was *not* introduced in order to enable the cargo interests to break the limit, but, on the contrary, to establish a very difficult test so as to ensure, in all but the most exceptional cases, that limits of liability applied for the benefit of the carrier.

Regarding the question whether the crew can enjoy the same limitation of liabilities as the shipowner or carrier, English law was initially confronted with some difficulty due to the doctrine of privity. The privity of contract, also known as 'the third party rule', precludes a third party from interfering in a contract: a contract cannot confer rights or impose duties arising under it on any person except the contractual parties. As is generally agreed, the doctrine of privity was conclusively established in *Tweddle v Atkinson*.[30] A fairly clear lesson is taught by this decision: a third party to the contract may not be a stranger to the contractual parties, but he is definitely a stranger to the consideration or the contract itself so that the privity of contract will stand in the way of allowing the third party to enforce the contract. Essentially, the law of agency can be viewed as an exception to the privity doctrine in that the principal will be able to exercise the rights and duties under the contract instead of the agent.[31] However, in reverse, when a crewmember attempts to rely upon the terms of a contract to which he is not a party, the crewmember will be regarded a third party, despite the fact that the crew as such is working for the carrier or shipowner with a view to performing precisely the service of the carriage contract concluded with the carrier and shipper.

In the landmark case *Adler v Dickson (The Himalaya)*, the Court of Appeal rejected on the particular facts the case of the master and crew in seeking protection from personal tortious liability by relying upon an exclusion clause in the contract of carriage of passengers by sea. The majority led by Denning LJ recognised in principle that should the crew,

---

29 *The Happy Ranger* [2002] EWCA Civ 694; *The Kapitan Petko Voivoda* [2003] EWCA Civ 451.
30 (1861) 1 B & S 393.
31 Law Commission, *Privity of Contract: Contracts for the Benefit of Third Parties* (LC242, 1996), p.14.

the agents and even the stevedores be negligent when participating in the contractual performance, they would be protected by an exception clause made for their benefit while they were performing their duties in carriage of goods cases. If the exclusion clause was not drafted expressly to that effect, the same result could be obtained by necessary implication, and the crew would have sufficient interest to entitle them to enforce it.[32] However, according to Denning LJ's judgment, it was *not* acceptable to confer the benefit of the clause upon the crew in a personal tort case such as that at hand. Jenkins LJ further found that even if these provisions had contained words purporting to exclude the liability of the company's servants, they could hardly rely on them, for they were not parties to the contract.[33]

A similar ratio can be found in *The European Enterprise*,[34] a case of carriage of goods by sea, in terms of construing the definition of 'the carrier' who is entitled to enjoy the limitation of liability under the Hague-Visby Rules. A narrow and restrictive approach was adopted by Steyn J who held that, for commercial reasons, the word 'carrier' refers to the carrier himself and does not naturally include his servants or agents except in so far as employees are regarded as constituting part of the alter ego of the carrier.

Nevertheless, in the context of carriage of goods by sea, either in contract or in tort, the crew can rely upon the same defences and limitation of liability under the Rules as the carrier in accordance with Article IV *bis*.[35] The substance of the rule is often inserted in the carriage contract in the form of a 'Himalaya Clause'. The function of the Himalaya Clause, as explained by the House of Lords, is to prevent cargo owners from avoiding the effect of contractual defences available to the carrier (typically the exceptions and limitations in the Hague-Visby Rules) by suing in tort persons who perform the contractual services on the carrier's behalf.[36]

---

32 Per Denning LJ at p.183. It is worth mentioning that the Contract (Rights of Third Party) Act 1999 appears to follow the ratio of Denning LJ for breaking the limit of privity and conferring rights upon a third party to enforce a contract according to section 1, although it does not apply to contracts of employment, agency or carriage of goods by sea under section 6.

33 Per Jenkins LJ, at p.186.

34 [1989] 2 Lloyd's Rep. 185, p.191.

35 Article IV *bis*: '1. The defences and limits of liability provided for in these Rules shall apply in any action against the carrier in respect of loss or damage to goods covered by a contract of carriage whether the action be founded in contract or in tort.

2. If such an action is brought against a servant or agent of the carrier (such servant or agent not being an independent contractor), such servant or agent shall be entitled to avail himself of the defences and limits of liability which the carrier is entitled to invoke under these Rules . . .'

36 *The Mahkutai* [1996] AC 650.

5.2 *Chinese law*

Privity of contract is a highly specific concept of common law; however, the privity of the debt is a norm essentially equivalent to the privity of contract recognised in civil law systems, including Chinese law. Article 8 of the Contract Law 1999 affirms that the contractual parties are legally bound by a legally executed contract, although statutory exceptions can be found here and there, such as the assignment of debt in Article 64 of the Contract Law.

Another potential hurdle impeding the application of the Himalaya Clause is the validity of the term, that is to say, whether the exclusion of liability clause or the limitation of liability clause to the carrier and his employees are to be rendered void on the ground of unfair terms. Article 40 of the Contract Law regarding the validity of standard clauses clarifies that such unfair terms may be at hand if the party that provides the standard clauses exempts itself from liability, imposes heavier liability on the other party, or precludes the other party from its main rights. In particular, according to Article 53(2), exclusion clauses which exempt the party who causes losses to property to the other party by intention or due to gross negligence are invalid.

Article 58 of the CMC recognises that the carrier's servant or agent is entitled to enjoy the defence and limitation of liability, whether in contract or in tort, provided in the CMC, if he can prove that his activity was within the scope of his employment or agency. Furthermore, Article 59 stresses that the servant or agent of the carrier shall not be entitled to the benefit of limitation of liability, if it is proved that the loss, damage or delay in delivery resulted from an act or omission of the servant or agent of the carrier done with intent to cause such loss, damage or delay or recklessly and with knowledge that such loss, damage or delay would probably result. This means that the crew may be entitled to rely upon the statutory defences and the limitation of liability subject to the condition that the level of negligence is not above gross negligence (recklessness and deliberateness), in line with Article IV *bis* (4) as well as English law.

It should be emphasised that the scope of application of Articles 58 and 59 of the CMC is also confined within the actions arising under contracts of carriage of goods by sea, without reference to the carriage of passengers by sea.

In addition, the majority of cases arising in judicial practice are concerned with independent contractors including stevedores, and some important lessons have been learnt from English case law.[37]

---

37 The legal position of stevedores has been resolved under English law, see *Scruttons v Midland Silicones* [1962] AC 446; *The Eurymedon* [1975] AC 154; *The New York Star* [1980] 2 Lloyd's Rep. 317.

6. Conclusions

Ship's crews are faced with various kinds of liabilities such as administrative liabilities, criminal liabilities, tortious and contractual liabilities, when performing their duties negligently in the course of employment. This chapter has dealt with civil liabilities including contractual and tortious liability in carriage by sea. It is clear that both jurisdictions discussed provide sufficient legal protections to the employees/crew within the scope of the employment in contract as well as in tort. Nevertheless, the crew is exposed to direct and personal liabilities beyond the regime of agency and vicarious liability, and it seems that Chinese law recognises a comparatively wider scope of vicarious liability in tort when the crew commits mere negligence, as opposed to gross negligence. Moreover, it appears that in both jurisdictions, the crew is exposed to greater potential personal liability in relation to contracts of the carriage of passengers by sea than under the carriage of goods by sea.

   With respect to actions against the crew due to their negligence under carriage of goods by sea contracts, both jurisdictions are currently following the Hague-Visby Rules approach. Both jurisdictions appear to be cautious and not quite ready to eliminate the nautical fault of the crew from among the carrier's exclusions of liability. Moreover, the crew is entitled to enjoy the defences and limitation of liability, either in tort or in contract against the crew, unless the crewmember commits gross negligence or causes losses with the requisite intent.

4   Bills of lading in bankers hands: Does Chinese legislation offer sufficient security?

Dr Jenny Jingbo Zhang

1. Introduction

Payment through letters of credit is regarded as a secure means for the seller to get paid under an international trade contract, since the payment is guaranteed by the bank as long as conforming documents are presented. The bank thus takes over the risk of the buyer's insolvency and failure of payment. Apart from getting funds in advance or making an alternative financial arrangement to secure the repayment,[1] the bank has to rely on the collateral security derived from the documents stuck in its hands.[2] The transport document, as one of the documents invariably required to be presented under a commercial letter of credit, 'serves as an objective and apparently enforceable assurance by a third party carrier that there are goods and that they have been shipped as indicated'.[3] A bill of lading can not only demonstrate the status of the shipped goods, but also evidence the terms of the carriage contract and control the delivery. Furthermore, as a 'document of title',[4] it can transfer constructive possession to its holder.

---

1 Sometimes the bank may release the presented documents to its customer (the buyer) and rely on alternative financial arrangements to secure its right of reimbursement, such as using a trust receipt, which is beyond the scope of this chapter. Regarding arrangement of trust receipt, see Richard King, *Guttidge and Megrah's Law of Bankers' Commercial Credit* (8th edn, Europa Publications, 2001), para.8.20 and Ali Malek and David Quest, *Jack: Documentary Credits* (4th edn, Tottel Publishing, 2009), para.11.11.

2 The documents most commonly required under a letter of credit are transport documents and insurance documents. For the legal position regarding insurance documents under letters of credit, see Jingbo Zhang, 'Chapter 12 Cargo Insurance Documents in Letters of Credit' in Johanna Hjalmarsson and Dingjing Huang (eds), *Insurance Law in China* (Informa from Routledge, 2014), pp.235–254.

3 James Byrne, *The Comparison of UCP600 & UCP500* (ICC, 2007), p.171. It should be noted that 'transport document' is a broader concept than 'shipping document'. Shipping documents in this chapter are specifically tailored for the carriage which is wholly or partly involved by sea, including bills of lading, sea waybills and multimodal transport documents involving a sea journey. Transport documents might also include carriage by air, road, rail or inland waterway.

4 It has been referred as a 'document of title' under common law and in global shipping practice. However, the Chinese legislation did not use this expression directly.

It has been suggested that few banks nowadays would rely solely on the security of a shipping document; and deposits are generally requested by banks in order to cope with applicants' insolvency.[5] However, bank deposits cannot remedy a situation when the bank has wrongly paid on discrepant documents. In other words, in circumstances of a bank's default, the bank which is left without reimbursement has to turn back to seeking security offered by the retained documents, as any deposits would be returned to the applicant. Therefore, from the bankers' perspective, not only do they need to be concerned with the issue of whether the tendered documents would fulfil the requirements set out in the credit, but also, more importantly, they have to consider what actions can enhance the level of security brought by the shipping documents.

Although traditional bills of lading are gradually being superseded by alternative forms of shipping documentation,[6] bills of lading are still dominant in the maritime world and their features provide the point of reference of developing forms of transport document. Two main questions will be addressed in this chapter. First, how should a bank examine a bill of lading presented under a letter of credit? Secondly, if a bank was stuck with the documents, what level of security might different forms of bills of lading offer? As a background to answer these questions, the chapter will first briefly review the features of letters of credit transactions and the corresponding legal framework including the Uniform Customs and Practice for Documentary Credits (UCP)[7] adopted by Chinese law. Rather than reiterating the general criteria for document examination, the chapter will focus closely on the special requirements in the UCP regarding bills of lading. As will be seen, the UCP has touched upon the issue of security but has left plenty of issues to local law governing letters of credit. Particular attention will be placed on the interaction between the UCP and Chinese maritime law which has heavily influenced the bank's position as holder of a bill of lading. It will be noted that, on some points, neither the UCP nor Chinese law provide a clear and sufficient answer, giving rise to a need for some areas of law to be considered and readdressed.

---

5 Richard King, *Guttidge and Megrah's Law of Bankers' Commercial Credit* (8th edn, Europa Publications, 2001), para.8-01.
6 Such as sea waybills, straight bills of lading and multimodal transport documents which involve more than one mode of carriage.
7 UCP is a set international standard banking practice for regulating letters of credit transactions published by the International Chamber of Commerce in Paris. Details are in section 2.1 below.

2. Letters of credit and bills of lading under the Chinese legal framework

2.1 Letters of credit and the UCP under Chinese law

Letters of credit, also referred to as documentary credits, are a primary instrument of payment in international trade transactions. In the context of international trade, a documentary credit stands for an unconditional payment promise made by an issuing bank to the beneficiary (normally the seller) according to the applicant's (normally the buyer's) instructions. As long as the beneficiary presents satisfactory documents specified by a letter of credit, the bank will be obliged to provide an appointed payment without hesitation.

There are two fundamental principles in the operation of documentary credits, namely the principle of autonomy and the principle of strict compliance.[8] The principle of autonomy is designed to ensure that disputes extraneous to the credit do not impair the realisation of the credit. Once a letter of credit is opened, it will be independent from the sale contract, and any defences arising from the underlying sale contract will not affect the realisation of payment. Hence, the bank only needs to consider whether the documents constitute a complying presentation. To constitute a complying presentation, the presented documents must be on their face in compliance with the terms of the letter of credit and consistent with one another. These two cardinal principles, being precedent conditions for the operation of documentary credits, are not only established in international standard banking practice, but also reiterated in relevant Chinese legislation.[9]

With the increasing importance of letters of credit in international trade, the International Chamber of Commerce (ICC) has spared no effort to summarise and unify international practices and usages in relation to letter of credit transactions since 1920. Although these ICC products are not mandatory regulations, they have been used in about 95% of letter of credit transactions. The most recently published version of *Uniform Customs and Practice for Documentary Credits* (UCP600[10]), along with its supplementary *International Standard Banking Practice for the Examination of Documents*

---

8 It should be noted that the principle of strict compliance is the traditional way for a bank to examine presented documents under a letter of credit. As discussed below, in order to be in conformity with the provisions in the UCP, the expression of 'strict compliance' was not used in the Chinese legislation regarding letters of credit.

9 See Articles 4, 5 and 14 of the UCP600, Articles 4, 5, 14 and Articles 5–7 of the Chinese LC Judicial Interpretations as discussed in the following.

10 ICC Publication No.600, also referred to as UCP600. The UCP was revised in 1951, 1962, 1974 (UCP 290), 1983 (UCP 400), 1993 (UCP 500) and most recently in 2006 (UCP 600).

under UCP600, Publication No.745 in 2013 (ISBP745[11]), have provided a new comprehensive framework for document examination under letters of credit. It is clear that the applicability of the UCP is not in the nature of a legal or regulatory measure. As the UCP itself states, the rules apply to any documentary credit when the credit expressly indicates that it is subject to these rules. Where it does, the rules will bind all parties unless expressly modified or excluded by the credit.[12]

China, as a civil law jurisdiction, had neither enacted any statutes nor adopted any unified judicial interpretations concerning letter of credit transactions until 2006.[13] In fact, Chinese courts had to deal with letter of credit disputes by applying international practices directly.[14] With the significant growth of letter of credit disputes and the pressure resulting from uncertainty, the Fourth Civil Division of the Supreme People's Court, which hears numerous foreign-related commercial cases, has taken the initiative of drafting a set of Chinese Letter of Credit Rules: The Provisions on Several Issues Concerning the Trial of Disputes over Letters of Credit (the LC Judicial Interpretations).[15] As the first Chinese statute on letters of credit, it provided a legal basis for letter of credit business in China.[16]

The LC Judicial Interpretations is to the greatest extent possible harmonised with international standard banking practices, especially the UCP. In Article 2 of the LC Judicial Interpretations, it is stated that in the adjudication of letter of credit related cases before a Chinese court, where the parties have agreed on the application of any international customs, usages and practices, such agreement shall prevail. Absent such an agreement, the

---

11 ICC Publication No.745, also referred to as ISBP745. The previous versions include ISBP No.645 under UCP500 and ISBP No.681 under UCP600. The practices described in the ISBP aim to highlight how the UCP600 provisions are to be interpreted and applied. Although the ISBP is not formally referred by the main content of UCP600, it is intended to be integrated with the UCP600 as a set of authoritative statements. See Preliminary Consideration, para.ii of the ISBP745.

12 See Article 1 of the UCP600, and Article 1 of the UCP500.

13 Unlike the UK, court judgments and arbitral awards are not considered as legal sources since China adheres to the civil law system, but they may be quite persuasive when no specific rule in relation to the disputable issue of concern can be referred to.

14 Chinese courts can apply international practices directly pursuant to Article 142(3) of the General Principles of the Civil Law of the People's Republic of China (adopted at the 4th session of the Sixth National People's Congress and promulgated on 12 April 1986, further amended on 27 August 2009), which states: 'international practices may be applied on matters for which neither the law of the People's Republic of China nor any international treaty concluded or acceded to by the People's Republic of China has any provisions'.

15 No.13 [2005] of the Supreme People's Court, adopted at the 1368th Meeting of the Trial Committee of the Supreme People's Court on 24 October 2005 and effective from 1 January 2006.

16 According to Article 5 of the Provisions of the Supreme People's Court on the Judicial Interpretation Work (No.12 [2007] of the Supreme People's Court 23 March 2007), the judicial interpretations issued by the Supreme People's Court shall have full legal force.

UCP and other relevant international customs formulated by the ICC are to be applied.[17] It is evident that the UCP is used as a set of default rules in the Chinese courts, even without express or implied agreement from parties, as long as there is no contrary agreement reached by the parties.[18] However, certain issues, especially those which are not provided for in the UCP or other international practice, should still be governed by PRC law.[19]

2.2 References for examining a bill of lading

The general requirements for document examination can be found in Article 6 of the LC Judicial Interpretations, which stipulates that the relevant international customs, usages and practices or any other rules as agreed by the parties are to be applied in the process of examination. It follows that 'absent such standards as agreed, determination shall be made as to whether the documents are on the face in compliance with the terms and conditions of the letter of credit and consistent with one another according to the UCP and other relevant standards as formulated by the International Chamber of Commerce'.[20] It is clear that the LC Judicial Interpretations endeavour to maximise the conformity with the standards used in the UCP.[21]

Nevertheless, apart from laying down the general rule of document examination, the LC Judicial Interpretations did not further specify the requirements in checking transport documents. Therefore, it means that without an agreement to the contrary reached by the parties, the UCP rules and relevant practices will be applied in the Chinese courts in terms of deciding the compliance of shipping documents under letters of credit. Due to the importance of shipping documents, special consideration has been given to them by the UCP.[22] Specific requirements for examining the bills of lading can be found in the current Article 20 of the UCP600 and the recent Section E of the ISBP745.

In respect of shipping documents, the subject-matter discussed in this

---

17 Article 2 of the LC Judicial Interpretations has laid down a general rule for letter of credit disputes; while Article 6 is especially concerned with the standards of document examination. The Supreme Court insists on the same principle, namely, absent an agreement from parties, the UCP and other relevant ICC standards should be applied.

18 It should be noted that in the UK the UCP will not have the force of law unless the parties have expressly incorporated it into their contract. As a common law jurisdiction country, the English courts have established and developed case law to regulate letters of credit cases which do not incorporate the UCP.

19 Such as presentation of bills of lading, recognition of letters of credit fraud, and legal remedies. See Jin Saibo, *The Law of Letters of Credit in China* (ICC, 2013), p.52.

20 Translated by the author.

21 The general standards for document examination are stipulated in Article 14 of the UCP600.

22 See Article 19-22 of the UCP600, Article 23-26 of the UCP500 and Article 25-34 of the UCP400. All the corresponding ISBP revisions also specifically addressed the requirements for shipping documents.

chapter, the Chinese Maritime Code (CMC)[23] as *lex specialis* has provided detailed provisions to regulate the issues arising from the contract of carriage of goods by sea and those evidenced on the shipping documents. Other general legislation, such as the General Principles of the Civil Law,[24] the Contract Law[25] and the Law on Property Rights,[26] will always apply if there are no provisions in the CMC for a specific issue. As we will see later, the whole system can effectively supplement the gaps left by the UCP requirements and the CMC would largely affect the bank's security in holding the bills of lading.

3. Examining bills of lading under documentary credits

According to Article 71 of the CMC, a bill of lading is a document which serves as evidence of the contract of carriage of goods by sea and the taking over or loading of the goods by the carrier, and based on which the carrier undertakes to deliver the goods. It follows from the definition that a bill of lading must have three functions: receipt of cargo, evidence of the carriage contract and proof of delivery.

Article 73 of the CMC stipulates the particulars a bill of lading must contain including a description of the goods, the name of the carrier and the vessel, the name of the shipper and the consignee, the ports of loading and discharge, the date of receiving the cargo and of issuing the bill, and the signature of the carrier or its agent. It goes on to state that the absence of one or more of these particulars does not affect the functioning of a bill of lading, provided that it meets the three functions laid down in Article 71 of the CMC.

The UCP600, in comparison, directs a bank to check the particulars recorded in a bill of lading and stipulates that the absence of any particulars listed under Article 20 of the UCP600 will lead to document rejection. However, the UCP is not particularly concerned with the functions of a bill of lading and the possible security interest provided by the bills of lading to the bank. In the following, the author aims to match the requirements under Article 20 of the UCP600 with the three functions stipulated in the CMC and examine what level of security a bill of lading can offer to the bank, provided that it has met all the UCP requirements. However, it is

---

23 Adopted at the 28th Meeting of the Standing Committee of the Seventh National People's Congress on 7 November 1992, promulgated by Order No.64 of the President of the People's Republic of China and became effective as of 1 July 1993.

24 Adopted at the 4th session of the Sixth National People's Congress, and promulgated on 12 April 1986, amended on 27 August 2009.

25 Contract Law of the People's Republic of China, adopted at the 2nd session of the Ninth National People's Congress on 15 March 1999.

26 Law on Property Rights of the People's Republic of China, adopted at the 5th session of the Tenth National People's Congress on 16 March 2007.

appropriate first to address two conceptually preceding questions: what kinds of bills of lading are at issue, and who can issue such bills of lading?

3.1 Scope of the bills of lading under Article 20 of the UCP600

Article 71 of the CMC stipulates that according to the consignee in the bill of lading, the goods might be delivered to a named person, to order, or to bearer. Therefore, the concept 'bill of lading' employed in the CMC includes a straight bill of lading,[27] an order bill of lading and a bearer bill of lading. Although a straight bill of lading cannot be transferred to another person by endorsement or delivery, the CMC is still applicable according to its general rules.

Similar to the CMC, the UCP does not attempt to distinguish the bills of lading in terms of their transferability. Article 20 of the UCP600 addresses its application to a general bill of lading, *however named*,[28] without specifying more details.[29] Nevertheless, Section E12 of the ISBP745 stipulates that when a credit requires a bill of lading to evidence that goods are consigned to a named entity, i.e. a straight bill of lading, the bill of lading should not contain the expression 'to order' preceding or following the named entity, whether typed or pre-printed.[30] Furthermore, Section E13 (b) provides, when a credit requires a bill of lading to evidence that goods are consigned to 'order of (named entity)', a bill of lading which is only consigned to a named entity will not be acceptable. It is submitted that these ISBP provisions strongly indicate that Article 20 of the UCP600 covers both negotiable[31] and straight bills of lading.

Charterparty bills of lading, however, are excluded by Article 20.[32] Article 20(a)(vi) of the UCP600 stipulates that a bill of lading under this article should not contain any indication that it is subject to a charterparty. A transport document stipulating 'freight payable as per charterparty', will

---

27 For a general introduction to straight bills, see Guenter Treitel, 'The Legal Status of Straight Bills of Lading' (2003) 119 LQR 608.
28 A bill of lading can be named as 'marine bill of lading', 'ocean bill of lading', 'port bill of lading' or words of similar effect. Section E2 of the ISBP745 emphasises that even when the credit so names the required document, it is not necessary for the bill of lading to bear the same title.
29 Section E1 of the ISBP745 further explains that Article 20 is to be applied only if a credit is calling for a transport document merely covering a 'port-to-port shipment', i.e. 'a credit that contains no reference to a place of receipt or taking in charge or place of final destination'. The port here should mean an ocean port, rather than an inland waterway port, since an inland waterway bill will fall within Article 25 of the UCP600.
30 The same provision is shown in para.101 of the ISBP681.
31 For achieving both academic and practical consistency, the author uses the word 'negotiable' to describe transferable bills of lading, although the real meaning is 'transferable' rather than 'negotiable' in law, since a transferor cannot transfer a better title than he has.
32 The issue concerning charterparty bills is also specifically clarified in Article 95 of the CMC under the section of 'Special Provisions Regarding Voyage Charterparty'.

be treated as a charterparty bill of lading under Article 22, since it is subject to or makes reference to a charterparty. By contrast, it is suggested that a bill of lading with an associated charterparty heading, such as 'Congenbill' or 'Tanker Bill of Lading', will not necessarily fall outside the domain of Article 20 as long as there is no further reference to that charterparty.[33] Substance rather than title determines whether a transport document will fall under Article 20.

3.2 Who can issue the bills of lading under Article 20 of the UCP600?

Article 20(a)(i) of the UCP600 requires a bill of lading to indicate the name of the carrier. It is suggested that the name of the carrier not only needs to appear on a bill of lading, but that the name must also be identified as the carrier's.[34] In other words, the capacity of 'carrier' must be linked to the name of the company shown on the bill of lading. Article 20(a)(i) further stipulates that a bill of lading must be signed by the carrier, the master or a named agent on behalf of the carrier or the master, and the signature must demonstrate for which capacity it is signing. However, it should be noted that a bank is not obliged to investigate the legal status or the authenticity of the signing party. A bill of lading may be issued by any party other than an actual carrier or master provided that the transport document meets the requirements of Article 20.[35]

It is common in international trade to engage a freight forwarder in the process of arranging for carriage of goods by sea and it may issue a bill of lading in its own capacity rather than as the carrier's agent. It is, however, very difficult to tell from the appearance of the bill of lading in whose capacity a freight forwarder has signed it, since it depends entirely on the facts of each case and the arrangements between the parties. Therefore, Section E4 of the ISBP745 stipulates that the term 'freight forwarder's bills of lading are not acceptable' or words of similar effect 'has no meaning in the context of the title, format, content or signing of a bill of lading unless the credit provides specific requirements detailing how the bill of lading is to be issued and signed'.[36] It is clear that as long as a bill of lading can pass

---

33 Section G3 of the ISBP745. A Congenbill with the heading 'Bill of Lading to be used with Charter Parties' will be considered as a charterparty bill; however, if a Congenbill is presented without this reference, it will be examined under Article 20. See G. Collyer and R. Katz (eds), *ICC Banking Commission Opinions 2005–2008*, ICC Publication No.697 (ICC, 2008), R648.

34 See para.94 of the ISBP681, and Section E5 of the ISBP745.

35 Section E3 of the ISBP745; also cf. Article 14(1) of the UCP600.

36 On the other hand, Section E3 (b) of the ISBP745 states that if a credit contains 'freight forwarder's bill of lading is acceptable' or words of similar effect, a bill of lading may be signed by a freight forwarder in its own capacity, without the need to identify the capacity in which it has been signed or the name of the carrier.

through the two tests under Article 20(a)(i), i.e. identifying the carrier and following the rule of signature, it would be accepted by the banks in respect of the issuing party.

Apart from the carrier itself, Article 72 of the CMC permits a person who has the carrier's authorisation and the shipmaster to sign the bill of lading.[37] Hence, the situation only becomes tricky if the freight forwarder signs a bill of lading without the carrier's authorisation. The bank's acceptance of a freight forwarder's bill of lading, however, does not necessarily leave the cargo interest without remedies under Chinese law. According to Article 4 of the Provisions of the Supreme People's Court Regarding Certain Issues in the Trial of Cases of Disputes over Freight Forwarders,[38] if a freight forwarder issues a bill of lading in its own name or in the capacity of the carrier's agent but without carrier's authorisation, it needs to undertake the same responsibilities as a carrier. Although a freight forwarder who issues a bill of lading without the qualification as a non-vessel operating common carrier will violate the Regulations of the People's Republic of China on International Maritime Transportation[39] and be subject to a penalty from the transport administrative department,[40] the bill of lading itself as a transport document remains valid.[41]

3.3 Cargo receipt function

Article 20(a)(ii) of the UCP600 stipulates that a bill of lading must 'indicate that the goods have been shipped on board a named vessel at the port of loading stated in the credit'.[42] In the absence of a statement to the contrary in the credit, a received-for-shipment bill of lading will accordingly not be accepted by the bank, since it cannot evidence that the cargo has actually been shipped on board.

Article 27 of the UCP600 mandates a bank to accept only a clean

---

37 Article 72 of the CMC further stipulates that a bill of lading signed by the shipmaster is deemed to have been signed on behalf of the carrier.

38 Adopted at the 1538th Meeting of the Judicial Committee of the Supreme People's Court on 9 January 2012, and came into force as of 1 May 2012.

39 Adopted at the 49th Executive Meeting of the State Council on 5 December 2001, came into force on 1 January 2002, and further amended on 18 July 2013.

40 See Article 14 of the Provisions of the Supreme People's Court Regarding Certain Issues in the Trial of Cases of Disputes over Freight Forwarders.

41 See the Reply from the Supreme People's Court Regarding the Validation of the Carriage of Goods by Sea Contract Made Between the Freight Forwarder without Qualification as A Non-vessel Operating Common Carrier and the Shipper and the Validation of the Bill of Lading Issued under Such Carriage Contract, No.19 [2007] of the Supreme People's Court, 28 November 2007, <http://shlx.chinalawinfo.com/newlaw2002/slc/slc.asp?db=chl&gid=105782> accessed 15 September 2015.

42 There are two ways to satisfy the requirement for a shipped bill of lading, i.e. by pre-printed wording or by an on board notation indicating the date of shipment and the name of the vessel. See Article 74 of the CMC.

transport document unless otherwise indicated in the credit. 'A clean transport document is one bearing no clause or notation *expressly* declaring a defective condition of the goods or their packaging'.[43] Since Article 27 focuses only on the condition and packaging of the goods, clauses concerning the weight and quantity of goods will not make the bill unclean.[44] Clauses such as 'weight and quantity unknown', 'shipper's load and count' and 'said by shipper to contain' are still acceptable.[45]

The UCP transport provisions, however, do not mention any particular requirements for the description of the goods recorded on a bill of lading. For a generic document other than the commercial invoice, the description of the goods, *if stated*, may be recorded in general terms not conflicting with their description in the credit.[46] Clearly, the UCP has adopted a relaxed attitude towards document examination. The standard of compliance has been relaxed to the level of non-conflict. Use of the expression 'if stated' serves to indicate that in the most extreme cases the bank may accept a bill of lading even without any description of the goods.[47]

By contrast, the CMC endeavours to offer protection to the cargo interest against the carrier. Article 77 of the CMC explicitly stipulates that the description of the cargo recorded in the bill of lading is the *prima facie* evidence between the carrier and the shipper, and furthermore, the description becomes conclusive evidence between the carrier and the consignee or a *bona fide* third party.[48] Therefore, the bank, which is stuck with the bill of lading in its hands, can rely on the description of goods recorded on the bill of lading to sue the carrier for any loss or damage of the goods. Nevertheless, an unfortunate situation will arise where the bank has

---

43 Article 27 of the UCP600. Article 76 of the CMC holds the same position.
44 The quantity and weight of the goods as a part of data on the transport document is still restricted by Article 14(d) of the UCP600, which must not conflict with data on the other documents or the credit.
45 See Article 26(b) of the UCP600. In comparison with Article 75 of the CMC, it is possible for a bill of lading with 'unknown clause' to be counted as an unclean bill of lading. Under the provision of unclean bills of lading, it states: '. . . if he [the carrier or the other person issuing the bill of lading on his behalf] has had no reasonable means of checking, the carrier or such other person may make a note in the bill of lading specifying . . . the lack of reasonable means of checking'.
46 Article 14(e) of the UCP600.
47 The relaxation in the UCP does not cause conflict with the CMC. As stated above, Article 73 of the CMC permits one or more elements missing in a bill of lading provided that they will not affect the nature of a bill of lading.
48 Article 77 of the CMC states: 'Except for the note made in accordance with the provisions of Article 75 [unclean bill of lading] of this Code, the bill of lading issued by the carrier or the other person acting on his behalf is *prima facie* evidence of the taking over or loading by the carrier of the goods as described therein. Proof to the contrary by the carrier shall not be admissible if the bill of lading has been transferred to a third party, including a consignee, who has acted in good faith in reliance on the description of the goods contained therein.'

accepted a bill of lading containing an insufficient description of the goods and cannot avail itself of the protection conferred by the CMC.

3.4 Contract of carriage function

Article 78 of the CMC stipulates that the relationship between the carrier and the holder of the bill of lading with respect to their rights and obligations shall be pursuant to the clauses of the bill of lading. The bill of lading accordingly plays a crucial role in the hands of a third party[49] given that it can be construed as the contract of carriage between the carrier and the bill of lading holder. In the following, we consider the bank as bill of lading holder, with the silent assumption that the bill of lading is the only carriage contract between the bank and the carrier. The UCP600 has realised the function of a bill of lading as evidence of the carriage contract by inserting Article 20(a)(v), which requires that a bill of lading must contain terms and conditions of carriage or make reference to another source containing the terms and conditions of carriage (for short form or blank back bills of lading). Article 20(a)(v) further underlines that the terms and conditions of carriage will not be examined by the bank, whether or not they are contained in the bill of lading.

3.4.1 Should carriage terms and conditions be truly ignored?

Clearly, the intention behind the last part of Article 20(a)(v) is to release the bank from the onerous task of reading the small print on the back of the bill of lading and also to deter the bank from calling for the incorporated documents which contain the carriage terms and conditions. Unfortunately, as we will see below, Article 20(a)(v) cannot achieve these aims by failing to define the scope of the carriage terms and conditions. The UCP has divided carriage terms into two categories, namely 'special terms' required to be checked by the UCP and 'general terms' left out by the UCP.[50] 'Special terms' stipulated in the UCP include, notably, shipment and transhipment clauses[51] and on deck cargo clause[52] among others. Broadly speaking, 'general terms' falling into the scope of Article 20(a)(v) are terms which are customarily stated on the back of a bill of lading or by reference to another document.

However, confusion is added to the situation if the general carriage terms appear on the face of the bill of lading.[53] Since there is no clear borderline between special terms and general terms, unless general terms have been

---

49 Third party means the bill of lading holder is neither the charterer nor the shipper.
50 James Byrne, *UCP600: An Analytical Commentary* (IIBLP, 2010), p.895.
51 See Article 20(b)–(c) of the UCP600.
52 See Article 26(a) of the UCP600.
53 G. Collyer and R. Katz (eds), *Unpublished Opinions of the ICC Banking Commission 1995–2004*, ICC Publication No.660 (ICC, 2005), R576.

specifically indicated within the layout of the text, it would be extremely difficult for the bank to extract those carriage terms under Article 20(a)(v) in the process of reviewing the front of a bill of lading, especially when those terms are linked with the letter of credit requirements.[54] The tension is enhanced when the general carriage terms contradict the letter of credit terms, or render the required terms in the bill of lading meaningless.

In ICC Opinion R646,[55] the credit required presentation of a bill of lading marked 'freight pre-paid'. The presented bill of lading was so marked, but contained pre-printed wording which qualified the 'freight pre-paid' statement. The qualification, though stated on the face of the bill of lading, was still classified as one of the general carriage terms and conditions by the ICC Banking Commission. Accordingly, the qualification term was not to be examined and the bill of lading was not discrepant. Another example can be found in ICC Opinion R758.[56] The credit stipulated that 'bills of lading that on their face indicate that goods may be released without presentation of an original bill of lading are not acceptable'. However, the tendered bill of lading contained a delivery clause which distinguished between the negotiable form and the non-negotiable form. It stated the same presentation rule as the credit did for the negotiable form, but contained an inconsistent rule for the non-negotiable form, where the carrier might give delivery of goods to the named consignee upon reasonable proof of identity. The Banking Commission considered the delivery clause on the face of the bill of lading to constitute terms and conditions of carriage so that it would not be examined according to Article 20(a)(v).[57]

Although the conclusion reached by the ICC Banking Commission seemed reasonable for the above cases, the analysis leading to the conclusion was vague and difficult to extrapolate into a general rule. First, nothing in the UCP has attempted to grant Article 20(a)(v) paramount status over the bespoke terms in the credit. When there is a conflict between a bespoke term and an incorporated term from the UCP, the bespoke term in the credit should prevail. Secondly, as stated above, in order to constitute a compliant presentation, data in a document must not conflict with data coming from the same document, data in any other stipulated document or the credit.[58] If the credit explicitly requires one thing, the term in the transport document must not conflict with it and state another. Thirdly, it

---

54 For example, R758 in G. Collyer and R. Katz (eds), *ICC Banking Commission Opinions 2009–2011*, ICC Publication No.732 (ICC, 2012) concerned whether or not the bank should examine the 'delivery clause' shown above the carrier's signature on the front of the bill of lading, which was also linked with the letter of credit requirement in respect of delivery.

55 *ICC Opinions 2005–2008*, R646.

56 *ICC Opinions 2009–2011*, R758.

57 Since the bill of lading in the case was issued in a negotiable form, there was no discrepancy for that specific bill of lading.

58 Article 14(d) of the UCP600.

sounds rather arbitrary that the bank is only entitled to examine particular carriage terms mentioned within the UCP regime rather than any other terms, especially when both types of terms are written in the same pre-printed paragraph.[59]

It is true that the bank is not intended to take on the onerous task of examining all the carriage terms and conditions on the bill of lading; however, it is not sensible to ignore all the terms and conditions, especially those required by the credit and vital to the parties' security.[60] Generally, the bank never intends to receive the goods. The paramount interest of the bank is having the right to take delivery of the goods and the right to claim damages against the carrier for misdelivery. At the same time, the bank does not wish to become liable to pay freight, demurrage and other costs generated under the carriage contract.[61] Without keeping an eye on the carriage terms and conditions, the bank can neither satisfy its customer's mandate nor realise its position against the carrier. Although it is unrealistic to suggest that the bank should scrutinise all the small print on a bill of lading, the application of Article 20(a)(v) does urgently need to be clarified. It is this author's opinion that Article 20(a)(v) should be taken only to cover the general carriage terms and conditions which have not been specifically requested by the credit. It should be incumbent upon the bank, which is highly dependent on the bill of lading as security, to ensure that the necessary carriage terms, such as carriage costs, delivery rights and carrier's liabilities, have been clearly stipulated in the letter of credit.

3.4.2 Transhipment and carrier's liability

It is common in practice for bills of lading to contain a clause conferring on the carrier a right of transhipment. Transhipment is routinely performed in the container trade where containers are often transferred between different vessels. In recognition of current practice, Article 20(b)–(d) of UCP600 specifically address transhipment issues. Article 20(b) defines transhipment as 'unloading from one vessel and reloading to another vessel during the carriage from the port of loading to the port of discharge stated in the credit'.[62] Article 20(c)(i) stipulates that banks should accept bills of lading

---

59 See *ICC Opinions 2009–2011*, R758, in which the delivery clause was stated in the same pre-printed paragraph with the status of shipment and the number of bills of lading. The statement for the latter two elements was examined by the bank without doubt.

60 For example, as stated in Section E6(d) of the ISBP745, the bank needs to examine whether the on-board statement on the bill of lading is for the pre-carriage from the place of receipt to the port of loading.

61 Article 78(2) of the CMC stipulates that neither the consignee nor the holder of the bill of lading shall be liable for the demurrage, dead freight and all other expenses in respect of loading occurred at the loading port unless the bill of lading clearly states that such expenses shall be borne by the consignee and the holder of the bill of lading.

62 Transhipment may have another meaning in the context of Article 19 regarding multi-modal transhipment. As Section E17 of the ISBP745 provides, when a bill of lading does

which 'indicate that the goods *will or may* be transhipped provided that the *entire carriage* is covered by one and the same bill of lading'. Article 20(c)(ii) further states that even if transhipment is expressly prohibited by the credit, where the goods evidenced in the bill of lading have been shipped in a container, trailer or LASH barge, a bill of lading indicating that transhipment *will or may* take place is still acceptable. Lastly, Article 20(d) stipulates that clauses in a bill of lading stating that the carrier *reserves the right* to tranship will be disregarded.[63]

The UCP600 is evidently intended to accommodate the nature of modern transportation in which containerised shipment frequently involves transhipment. The default position of the UCP600 is that transhipment is permitted unless expressly prohibited by the letter of credit. Even where the credit has prohibited transhipment, it is still entirely possible for the goods to be transhipped. The main problem for the UCP600 transhipment rules is that they have failed to achieve harmony either within the section itself or with other sections. First, both Article 20(c) and (d) cover the situation when the transhipment *may* happen, either by express words indicating that the transhipment may take place or by a liberty of transhipment clause in the bill of lading. The overlap causes unnecessary confusion here: should the bank disregard the possibility of transhipment according to Article 20(d), or examine it pursuant to Article 20(c)? It unfortunately leaves the risk of construction to the bank.

The other major problem is the implication behind the words '*entire carriage* covered by one and the same bill of lading' in Article 20(c)(i).[64] Does this requirement simply mean that the bill of lading must literally cover the entire carriage route, despite the fact that the goods will or may be transhipped? If this is the case, the requirement of complete coverage in Article 20(c) seems to add nothing to what has already been stipulated under Article 20(a)(iii), i.e. that the bill of lading must indicate shipment from the port of loading to the port of discharge as stated in the credit. Alternatively, the requirement of complete coverage may indicate that the issuing carrier must accept liability for the whole voyage, even if several carriers have been involved on different legs of the route. If this is the case, the bank needs to make sure that there is no clause disclaiming the carrier's liability before or after transhipment. However, this process will inevitably involve examination for the general carriage terms and conditions contained in the bill of lading, which are supposed to be avoided by Article 20(a)(v).

---

not indicate unloading and reloading between loading port and discharge port, it is not transhipment in the context of the credit and Article 20 of the UCP600.

63 The UCP, however, does not provide the meaning of 'disregard'. It may signify that no attention should be paid to what is being disregarded and liberty of transhipment clause may not be a basis for refusal of a presentation.

64 A full discussion for this point can be found in Charles Debattista, 'The New UCP 600 – Changes to the Tender of the Sellers' Shipping Documents under Letters of Credit' [2007] JBL 329, pp.344–350.

This author considers that it is inappropriate to give a literal interpretation to the requirement of 'covering the entire carriage' as 'showing the complete physical route on a bill of lading', since a bill of lading which does not provide continuous documentary cover will inevitably impair the quality of the bank's security against the carrier. The bank, which is stuck with the documents, may find that it has no recourse against the issuing carrier if the damage or loss occurred on a leg of the journey not performed by the issuing carrier. Therefore, it is submitted that the alternative interpretation of 'entire liability coverage' is better adapted to practice as well as being consistent with sound legal analysis.[65] Article 46 of the CMC sets out the carrier's responsibilities with regard to the goods starting from the time that the carrier takes over or loads the goods at the port of loading, until the goods are delivered or discharged at the port of discharge.[66] For the situation where the performance of the carriage or part thereof has been entrusted to an actual carrier, Article 60 states that the contractual carrier is nevertheless to remain responsible for the entire carriage.[67] However, Article 60 continues to permit an exception to the default position; thus the contractual carrier and the shipper can agree in writing in the contract of carriage that the contractual carrier is not to be liable for loss or damage occurring while the goods are under the control of the specified actual carrier.

One should therefore be slow to conclude that a bill of lading containing a transhipment clause which exempts the carrier's liability for part of the voyage will violate Chinese law. The bank will seek to protect its security by becoming the holder of a bill of lading which evidences entire liability coverage. The issue then again becomes how to construe the requirement of 'entire liability coverage' under Article 20(c) of the UCP600. If the concept is construed in line with the default position, a bill of lading seeking to disclaim the carrier's responsibility after transhipment should be rejected;[68]

65 Under English law, a sound bill of lading must provide a continuous documentary cover during the whole journey. The principle was stated in *Hansson v Hamel and Horley Ltd* [1922] 2 AC 36, where the House of Lords decided that the bill of lading issued by the subsequent carrier who only undertook liability regarding the second part of journey, without any complementary promises to bind the prior carriers, was a bad tender under a CIF (Cost, Insurance and Freight) contract.

66 Article 46 of the CMC distinguishes container shipping from bulk carriage, so different words have been used in describing the period of carrier's liability.

67 Article 313 of the PRC Contract Law reflects the same position: 'Where two or more carriers jointly carry the goods by the same means of transportation, the contractual carrier who has made a contract of carriage with the shipper shall be responsible for the whole course of carriage. Where the losses occurred at a particular segment, the contractual carrier and the actual carrier for such segment are jointly liable for the loss' (translated by the author).

68 *Jack* suggests that a bank should reject a bill of lading indicating that the goods will be transhipped but the carrier will cease being liable after transhipment. See Ali Malek and David Quest, *Jack: Documentary Credits* (4th edn, Tottel Publishing, 2009), para.8.101; also see Peter Ellinger and Dora Neo, *The Law and Practice of Documentary Letters of Credit* (Hart Publishing, 2010), p.254, which also tends to give the meaning of entire liability coverage.

but how can a bank assess the coverage of carrier's liability without scrutiny of carriage terms and conditions? The tension between the requirement of continuous liability coverage and a liberty not to read and assess carriage terms under Article 20(a)(v) can never be quite eradicated, since in nature the transhipment terms are carriage terms *per se*.

3.5 *The proof of delivery function*

Article 71 of the CMC stipulates that the carrier undertakes to deliver the goods according to the bill of lading. It follows that a clause on a bill of lading indicating that the goods should be delivered to a nominated consignee, to the order of a nominated person, or to the holder of the bill of lading, constitutes the carrier's undertaking to deliver the goods. This links with Article 79, which divides bills of lading into three types in terms of their transferability: non-transferable straight bills of lading; order bills of lading which can be transferred by way of endorsement to order or endorsement in blank; and bearer bills of lading which can be transferred without endorsement. As mentioned in section 3.1 above, Article 20 of the UCP600 does not attempt to exclude from its scope of application to bills of lading in terms of transferability. As stipulated by Section E12 of the ISBP745, the bank should not accept a 'to order' bill of lading if the letter of credit requires a straight bill of lading, or *vice versa*.[69] Article 20 of the UCP600 is designed as inclusive to cover all the three types of bill of lading.

3.5.1 *Presentation rule and delivery*

The language of Article 71 of the CMC may appear at first sight to focus on designating the person who has the right to obtain delivery from the carrier under a bill of lading, rather than on how to achieve delivery. In order to resolve lasting disputes arising from deliveries of goods without production of an original bill of lading, the Fourth Civil Division of the Supreme People's Court drafted the Provisions of the Supreme People's Court on Certain Issues concerning the Application of Law to the Trial of Cases Involving Delivery of Goods without Production of an Original Bill of Lading (in the following referred to as the Bill of Lading Judicial Interpretations).[70] Article 2 provides that when the carrier delivers the goods without production of an original bill of lading (including a straight bill of lading[71]), he will incur civil liability[72] to the bill of lading holder who suffers loss as a result of his actions. Accordingly, the carrier would be deprived of the right to limit liability under

69 Sections E12 and E13(b) of the ISPB745.
70 It has been adopted at the 1463rd Meeting of the Judicial Committee of the Supreme People's Court on 16 February 2009 and came into force on 5 March 2009.
71 Article 1 of the Bill of Lading Judicial Interpretations defines bills of lading as including straight bills of lading, order bills of lading and bearer bills of lading.
72 Article 3 of the Bill of Lading Judicial Interpretations provides that the bill of lading holder

Article 56 of the CMC in such circumstances.[73] However, when the bills of lading have been issued in multiple copies, the carrier's liability arising from the cargo delivery would be exempted as long as he has delivered the cargo to the first person who surrenders an original bill of lading.[74]

The UCP600 does not directly mention the delivery issue. Instead, Article 20(a)(iv) of the UCP600 requires the beneficiary to present the full set of original bills of lading as issued or the sole original bill of lading if only one was issued.[75] It is clear that the condition precedent for obtaining delivery from the carrier under Chinese law is to surrender an original bill of lading. This follows the common law rule that 'the one being accomplished, the others to stand void'.[76] It appears therefore that by holding the entire set of bills of lading, the bank can effectively control the delivery of the goods and reduce the risk of fraud under letter of credit transactions. It is submitted that the above conclusions apply to straight bills of lading as well, given that they are covered both by Article 20 of the UCP600 and the Bill of Lading Judicial Interpretations.

3.5.2 Delivery clause in a bill of lading

Apart from the full set requirement in Article 20(a)(iv) of the UCP600, Section E28 of the ISBP745 further enhances the bank's control over delivery by providing that, unless all of the referenced bills of lading form part of the same presentation under the same credit, a bill of lading should not expressly state that goods covered by that bill of lading will only be released upon its surrender together with one or more other bills of lading. The intention behind this long-winded sentence is to achieve effective control over the cargo through the presented bills of lading alone. However, the ISBP does not specify whether the bank is entitled to reject such a bill of lading, and if so, how the delivery clause in the bill of lading can be detected without careful consideration of the carriage terms and conditions.

As mentioned under 3.4.1 above, in the ICC Opinion R758, the Banking Commission considered the 'delivery without production' clause on the face of the bill of lading to constitute terms and conditions of carriage so that it would not be examined according to Article 20(a)(v). According to

---

may require the carrier to accept liability for breach of contract or liability in conversion if the holder is in possession of the property.

73 Article 4 of the Bill of Lading Judicial Interpretations.
74 Article 10 of the Bill of Lading Judicial Interpretations.
75 Section E11 of the ISBP745 even requires a bill of lading to indicate the number of originals that have been issued. It is suggested that if a bill of lading is not an original document, it will not be regarded as a transport document under the UCP600 at all.
76 Under common law, the carrier need not await all original bills before delivery, nor need he take further steps to ensure that the presenter is in fact the person entitled. See *Glyn Mills & Co v East and West India Dock Co* (1882) 7 App Cas 591.

the Banking Commission, a bill of lading containing a clause giving the carrier liberty to deliver the goods to the named consignee upon reasonable proof of identity would be acceptable to the bank, even though the letter of credit had expressly prohibited bills of lading containing a 'delivery without production' clause. Since a negotiable bill of lading was issued in this case, the presentation rule was still followed and no real conflict with the letter of credit requirement was triggered by the bill of lading delivery clause. Nevertheless, the fundamental issue remains: should the bank accept a bill of lading containing the 'delivery without production' clause? The answer should be no, as such a clause will make the requirement of Article 20(a)(iv) regarding full sets of bills of lading ineffective and, more importantly, it will undermine the bank's security generated by the bills of lading. The ICC Banking Commission, which was eager to relieve the bank's burden in documentary examination, presumably overlooked the fundamental damage caused by enlarging the scope of Article 20(a)(v) in terms of the bank's security.

According to Article 44 of the CMC, any stipulation in a bill of lading derogating from the provisions of Chapter IV[77] is to be null and void, but such nullity will not affect the validity of other provisions of the bill of lading. As the Bill of Lading Judicial Interpretations are intended to specify the position of transport documents under Chapter IV, it is suggested that the delivery clause in a bill of lading would violate the CMC and become null and void. It was held by the Supreme People's Court in an earlier judicial interpretation[78] that the carrier will be exempted from liability for delivery without production of an original bill of lading if the carrier can sufficiently prove that the bill of lading holder has accepted such delivery.[79] A delivery clause in the bill of lading may be thought to constitute conclusive proof that the bill of lading holder has permitted delivery without the bill of lading. However, this provision has not been listed in the Bill of Lading Judicial Interpretations as a qualified exception[80] and therefore, in the author's opinion, the legal status of such a delivery clause is uncertain.

---

77 That is, Chapter IV Contract of Carriage of Goods by Sea of the CMC.

78 Notification by the Supreme People's Court regarding Distribution of the Second National Foreign Commercial and Maritime Related Judicial Committee Meeting Summary (referred as the Notification), No.26 [2005] of the Supreme People's Court on 26 December 2005.

79 Article 110 of the Notification.

80 The Bill of Lading Judicial Interpretations have listed three exceptions of carrier's liability in Articles 7–9. Article 7 refers to delivery without a bill of lading according to the local law of discharge port and Article 8 is for disposal by customs or courts after the lapse of period. Article 9 provides that the carrier's liability to the consignee under a straight bill of lading will be exempted, if the carrier has suspended carriage, returned cargo, changed the destination, or delivered to other person according to shipper's instructions. In the author's view, this article is quite problematic here, since it will undermine the presentation rule for straight bills.

3.5.3 Title to claim delivery

With the full set of bills of lading in its hand, the bank can effectively control the physical delivery of the goods to the buyer. This does not necessarily mean that the bank can take delivery of the goods by itself or be entitled to claim against the carrier for misdelivery. With reference to Article 71 of the CMC, the carrier only undertakes to deliver to a qualified bill of lading holder, including the consignee under a straight bill of lading, the endorsee of an order bill of lading and the holder of a bearer bill of lading. Hence, unless the bank ensures that it is named as one of the persons above, it would not be entitled to delivery and the title to sue against the carrier for misdelivery.[81] Since there is no requirement as to the form of the bill of lading in the UCP600,[82] the bank needs to consider the issue at the application stage and include express stipulation in the letter of credit.

4. Document of title and bank's security interest

Banks in most circumstances are not interested in taking delivery of the goods and instead prefer to obtain title under the documents and realise the documents by resale. Among the types of shipping documents, negotiable bills of lading regarded as 'documents of title'[83] are best suited to the banks' needs. As documents of title, negotiable bills of lading function as 'a key to the warehouse'[84] under common law and can transfer constructive possession of the goods to their holder.[85] However, the function of 'document of title' has not been explicitly adopted by the CMC, as the CMC almost exclusively approaches bills of lading from the perspective of the contract of carriage of goods by sea, leaving the legal nature of the bills of lading undefined. It has long been argued in academia whether a transferable bill of lading can confer proprietary rights on its holder, as implied by the concept of 'document of title'.[86] Admittedly, the transfer of bills of lading

---

81 According to Article 11 of the Bill of Lading Judicial Interpretations, the original bill of lading holder can request the carrier who delivers goods without the original bill of lading and the person who collects goods without the original bill of lading to undertake the joint liability for the compensation.

82 For example, whether a bill of lading should be made out to bearer or to order, and if the latter, to whose order.

83 However, there is no authoritative definition of 'document of title' at common law. See Michael Bridge (ed.), *Benjamin's Sale of Goods* (8th edn, Sweet & Maxwell, 2010), para.18-007.

84 *Sanders Brothers v Maclean & Co* (1883) 11 QBD 327.

85 It was established in *Sewell v Burdick* (1884) 10 App Cas 74 that transfer of a bill of lading is not necessary to transfer the property of the goods, because the property could only be passed when the parties intended to do so.

86 See Si Yuzhuo and Chu Beiping, 'A Review on the Controversy about Character of Right in Rem of Bill of Lading from the Aspect of Delivery of Cargo Without Production of Bill of Lading' (2006) 16 (1) *Annual of China Maritime Law* 1.

can reasonably indicate an intention to transfer the property; however, it would be a mistake to conclude that property always passes together with the transfer of bills of lading, given that passing of property depends on the intention of the parties, rather than being an automatic consequence of the endorsement or delivery of a bill of lading.

Although the bank does not generally obtain property in the goods by holding the bills of lading, it can create a pledge which constitutes a special legal title on the goods. The PRC Law on Property Rights[87] and the Law of Guarantee[88] have now recognised that the security arising from possession of bills of lading operates as a pledge of rights.[89] The bill of lading becomes pledged to the bank when it is delivered in pursuance of the terms of a credit.[90] The pledge gives banks an independent right of sale so as to secure the amount which they have advanced. As pledgee, the bank can retain the documents until it is paid and, if not paid in accordance with the terms agreed, the bank is entitled to take possession of the goods and sell them to reimburse itself from the proceeds.[91]

The pledge would not appear to add anything further to the bank's security when the bank is already qualified as a bill of lading holder under the CMC, namely, where the bills of lading are drawn to order of the bank or indorsed to the bank. Complexity ensues where the bills of lading are drawn to order of the buyer or other consignee. In such a situation, the bank, which can still become a pledgee of documents in principle[92] based on the agreement with the pledger, will be left with an ineffective power of sale. Moreover, given that the bill of lading itself does not designate the bank as the party entitled to take delivery, it is unlikely that the bank will be able to convince the carrier that he is entitled to take possession of the goods under the framework laid down by the CMC.

As the CMC concentrates only on regulating the bills of lading from the

---

87 Adopted at the 5th session of the Tenth National People's Congress on 16 March 2007 and came into force from 1 October 2007.

88 Adopted by the Standing Committee of the Eighth National People's Congress at the 14th session on 30 June 1995.

89 See Article 75 of the Law of Guarantee and Article 223 of the Law on Property Rights. Again, there is no distinction between negotiable bills of lading and straight bills regarding pledge in the Chinese legislation. The straight bills have not been traditionally regarded as documents of title under common law and therefore cannot generate pledge of the goods by constructive delivery.

90 See Article 76 of the Law of Guarantee and Article 224 of the Law on Property Rights. According to Article 64 of the Law of Guarantee and Article 210 of the Law on Property Rights, the parties must conclude the right of pledge in a written contract. The pledge is usually expressly stated in the agreement between the issuing bank and the applicant contained in the application form. However, the written requirement will cause difficulties for the intermediary bank, as a pledge is normally implied by the English law when it pays or negotiates documents presented to it by the seller.

91 See Article 77 of the Law of Guarantee and Article 225 of the Law on Property Rights.

92 There is no clear guidance from the Chinese legislation on whether a bill of lading can still be pledged to the bank if it is not drawn on 'to order of the bank'.

perspective of carriage contracts, the issues generated by the law on pledges have been largely overlooked. In the result, the form of a bill of lading and the person to whose order it must be made out are still decisive of the bank's rights of security. Regrettably, without sufficient legal guidance provided by the Law of Guarantee and the Law on Property Rights, the security generated by a pledge is not as powerful as it might appear. Due to the special nature of bills of lading, it would be necessary to consider them as an independent subject-matter and endeavour to harmonise the possessory elements with the CMC reform.

5. Conclusion

Since the Chinese legal framework concerning letters of credit relies heavily on the UCP, close attention has been paid in this chapter to Article 20 of the UCP600 as well as the recent ISBP745 and the implications of those instruments upon the examination of bills of lading presented under a letter of credit. Most of the requirements of Article 20 focus on the function of a bill of lading as a receipt of the goods. It also incidentally, but controversially, reflects the role of the bill of lading as evidence of the carriage contract. The third classical function of the bill of lading as a document of title, along with the accompanying delivery issue, has only been lightly touched upon by the UCP600.

Regarding the function as a cargo receipt, it is noteworthy that neither the UCP nor the CMC contains compulsory requirements regarding cargo description. If the bank wants to ensure that the bill of lading presented is truly that pertaining to the specific cargo, it has to specify in the letter of credit the requirement of the description of the cargo recorded in the bill of lading. As the cargo description will become conclusive evidence in the hands of the bank as bill of lading holder, this specification will strengthen the bank's security, should the bank become embroiled in litigation against the carrier.

Admittedly, the UCP has not successfully reconciled the tension between the bank's disclaimer and the consideration of the bank's security. On the one hand, the bank is not supposed to examine the carriage terms and conditions contained in a bill of lading. On the other hand, the bill of lading will become the only contract of carriage between the carrier and the bank when the latter becomes the bill of lading holder. The most obvious difficulty can be found in the process of dealing with 'delivery without production clauses' appearing on the bill of lading. The transhipment provisions stipulated in the UCP and the consideration of carrier's liability are further examples of issues that will require a resolution in the next UCP revision.

The delivery issue and the document of title function carried by bills of lading have been largely left by the UCP to the governing law of a documentary credit. For the purpose of the bank's security, the UCP does ask for a full set of bills of lading in document presentations. The CMC with the recent development of judicial interpretations has made the presentation rule clear in terms of cargo delivery. However, the CMC focuses only on regulating bills of lading from the perspective of carriage of goods by sea, rather than approaching bills of lading as an independent subject-matter and addressing the legal issues generated from bills of lading into a whole. Incomplete guidance on the document of title function in Chinese law makes the bank's security uncertain. The forthcoming law reform needs to consider how bank's pledge is going to operate within the contractual framework established by the CMC and whether straight bills of lading should be distinguished in performing the document of title function.

It is true that few modern banks would rely solely on the security provided by the transport documents. However, the reality is that where the bank has inadvertently or by mistake paid against irregular documents that go on to be declined by the buyer, the bank will be left with no recourse apart from enforcing the security provided by the presented documents. There is therefore an urgent need for clarification as to what terms a qualified bill of lading should contain under the imperfect framework provided by the UCP and how the governing law can assist the bank's security in letter of credit transactions.

5 Chinese antitrust law and its application to the liner shipping industry: issues arising from the P3 Network case

Xianwei Peng

1. Introduction

In a review of major events from the global shipping industry, the Chinese antitrust authority's refusal to give the green light to the proposed P3 Network shipping alliance[1] should surely have a place in the 'Top Ten' list. In the P3 Network case, the top three container carriers of the world, i.e. A.P. Moller-Maersk A/S (Maersk),[2] CMA CGM SA (CMA)[3] and MSC Mediterranean Shipping Co SA (MSC)[4] agreed on 18 June 2013 to set up a Network Centre (NC) to jointly share vessels and engage in related cooperative operating activities in the trades between the US and Asia, North Europe, and the Mediterranean. The P3 Network would have operated at a capacity of 2.6 million TEU (initially 255 vessels on 29 loops) on three trade lanes: Asia-Europe, Trans-Pacific and Trans-Atlantic. Maersk was to provide 42%, MSC 34% and CMA the remaining 24% capacity to the network, and it was intended to account for about 14.7% of the world total TEU capacity. The P3 Network was to commence operations in the second quarter of 2014, subject to obtaining the approval of relevant competition and other regulatory authorities.[5] In the event, China's merger control authority, the Ministry of Commerce (MOFCOM), blocked the P3

---

1 Ole Mikkelsen, 'China MOFCOM Shocks with P3 Shipping Alliance Decision' (*Reuters*, 17 June 2014), <http://uk.reuters.com/article/2014/06/17/maersk-network-idUKL5N0OY2VQ20140617> accessed 15 September 2015.
2 The Maersk Group is made up of five core businesses which include Maersk Line, APM Terminals, Maersk Oil, Maersk Drilling and APM Shipping Services. See more at <http://www.maersk.com/en> accessed 15 September 2015.
3 Founded in Marseille in 1978 by Jacques Saadé, the CMA CGM Group is a leading worldwide shipping group. See more at <https://www.cma-cgm.com/> accessed 15 September 2015.
4 Mediterranean Shipping Company, a world leader in global container shipping. See more at <https://www.msc.com/gbr> accessed 15 September 2015.
5 'Maersk Line, MSC Mediterranean Shipping Company SA and CMA CGM have in principle agreed to establish a long-term operational alliance on East–West trades, called the P3 Network. The aim is to improve and optimise operations and service offerings', <http://www.maersk.com/en/the-maersk-group/press-room/press-release-archive/2013/6/maersk-line-msc-and-cma-cgm-to-establish-an-operational-alliance> accessed 29 October 2015.

Network for the reason that it was a notifiable concentration of undertakings and that it was not justified to have it approved due to its negative influence on competition status in the Asia-EU container shipping route.

China does not have a long history of antitrust law and this was only the second blocking decision since the start of merger reviews approximately six years ago, and remarkably it was also the first time that MOFCOM had blocked a transaction between foreign firms.[6] However, close scrutiny is warranted of MOFCOM's interpretation of the P3 Network as a notifiable merger and concentration of undertakings, and whether MOFCOM correctly applied Chinese law to ban the P3 Network, especially considering that US and EU antitrust authorities gave their respective green lights to the P3 Network. As such, comprehensive legal analysis of this landmark case adds meaningful understanding to China's antitrust laws generally, how they will be applied to the shipping sector, and how to engineer legal compliance of similar merger-like transactions.

2. Global antitrust review of the P3 Network shipping alliance

It is generally recognised that China, the EU and the US are the world's three major antitrust law enforcement zones. The pertinent elements of the review process of each can be summarised as follows.

2.1 The US review of the P3 Network

On 24 October 2013, Maersk, CMA and MSC filed the 'P3 Network Vessel Sharing Agreement, FMC Agreement No.012230' with the US Federal Maritime Commission (FMC). On 12 December 2013, the FMC issued a Notice of Request for Additional Information (RFAI) and ordered that interested parties may file comments within 15 days after publication of this notice in the Federal Register.[7] On 7 February 2014, P3 members filed a response to the Commission's RFAI dated 5 December 2013. On 24 March 2014, the P3 Network Vessel Sharing Agreement filed with the FMC became effective under the 1984 US Shipping Act.[8]

As per public comments released by the FMC, 64 companies, persons and organisations submitted written comments regarding the P3 Agreement, including shippers, shippers' associations, ports and terminals, workers, non-vessel operating common carriers (NVOCCs), forwarders and logistics service providers relating to shipping, carriers, government departments

---

6 'MOFCOM's Block of the P3 Network Shipping Alliance', <http://antitrustlawyerblog. com/mofcoms-block-of-the-p3-network-shipping-alliance/> accessed 15 September 2015.

7 Available at <http://www.gpo.gov/fdsys/pkg/FR-2013-12-12/pdf/2013-29599.pdf> accessed 15 September 2015.

8 'P3 Network Vessel Sharing Agreement', <http://www.fmc.gov/news/p3_network_vessel_ sharing_agreement.aspx> accessed 15 September 2015.

and government civil servants, etc. The comments of the same can be summarised as follows:

Table 6.1[9]

No.	Name	Representing	Response
1	Global Shippers' Forum	Shipper's association	No
2	German Shippers Council (DSVK)	Shipper's association	No
3	National Industrial Transportation League	Shipper's association	No
4	Med-America Shippers Association	Shipper's association	No
5	US Shippers Association	Shipper's association	No
6	Fashion Accessories Shippers Association	Shipper's association	No
7	Saramax Apparel Group Inc	Shipper	Yes
8	Mega Shipping and Forwarding Ltd	Shipper	Yes
9	RAB Lighting	Shipper	Yes
10	Barnes Noble	Shipper	Yes
11	Mountaire Farms Inc	Shipper	Yes
12	DHL Global Forwarding	Shipper	Yes
13	QT Plastics Trading Inc	Shipper	Yes
14	Hayday Farms Inc	Shipper	Yes
15	Intertrans Express NY Inc	Shipper	Yes
16	Essex Manufacturing Inc	Shipper	Yes
17	Pexim International	Shipper	Yes
18	Total Cargo Logistics Inc	Shipper	Yes
19	Bassett & Walker International Inc	Shipper	Yes
20	Baillie Lumber Co	Shipper	Yes
21	Tumi Inc	Shipper	Yes
22	Ahlstrom Nonwovens LLC	Shipper	Yes
23	OTS Astracon	Shipper	Yes
24	One Bowerman Drive	Shipper	Yes
25	Terra Nova Trading Inc	Shipper	Yes
26	KCL Logistics Inc	Shipper	Yes
27	BMT Commodity Corporation	Shipper	Yes
28	Mondelēz International	Shipper	Yes
29	Wayne Kaminski	Shipper	Yes
30	BCO GROUP	Shipper	Yes
31	Owens Corning Sales, LLC	Shipper	Yes
32	GA Paper International Inc	Shipper	Yes

9 Source: FMC Public Comments Submitted to the Commission regarding P3 Network
Vessel Sharing Agreement, <http://www.fmc.gov/resources/public_comments.aspx>
accessed 26 February 2016.

Table 6.1 (cont.)

No.	Name	Representing	Response
33	Coaster Company of America Inc	Shipper	Yes
34	Samson Investment Holding	Shipper	Yes
35	Unitcargo Container Line Inc	Shipper	Yes
36	Export Packers Co Ltd	Shipper	Yes
37	Certified International	Shipper	Yes
38	Atlantic Container Line (ACL)	Carrier	No
39	Georgia Ports Authority	Port	Yes
40	Port Miami	Port	Yes
41	Port of Seattle	Port	Yes
42	Port of Baltimore	Port	Yes
43	South Florida Container Terminal	Port	Yes
44	South Carolina Port Authority	Port	No
45	American Maritime Officers	Labour force	Yes
46	International Transport Workers' Federation (ITF)	Labour force	No
47	International Longshoremen's Association	Labour force	No
48	TKR Shipping Inc	Forwarder/logistic provider	No
49	CSX Transportation	Forwarder/logistic provider	Yes
50	MTC Logistics	Forwarder/logistic provider	Yes
51	BNSF Railway Co	Forwarder/logistic provider	Yes
52	Ercument Selamet MSc	Forwarder/logistic provider	No
53	Logistics International Service (LIS)	NVOCC	Yes
54	Intermodal Tank Transport	NVOCC	No
55	TTS Worldwide	NVOCC	Yes
56	Shipco Transport Inc	NVOCC	Yes
57	CEVA Logistics Limited	NVOCC	Yes
58	Committee of Foreign Affairs of US House of Representatives	Government authority/civil servant	No
59	Bob Huff Senator of California State Senate	Government authority/civil servant	Yes
60	Lawrence K Grooms Chairman of the Senate Transportation Committee and Chairman of the Review & Oversight Commission on the South Carolina Ports Authority	Government authority/civil servant	Yes

Table 6.1 (cont.)

No.	Name	Representing	Response
61	New Jersey General Assembly	Government authority/civil servant	Yes
62	Senator Kip Bateman	Government authority/civil servant	Yes
63	John M Bramnick	Government authority/civil servant	Yes
64	Thomas H Kean	Government authority/civil servant	Yes

As can be seen in Table 6.1 above, amongst the 64 written submissions only 14 are not in support of the P3 Network. It should be especially pointed out that although the German Shippers' Council (DSVK), the National Industrial Transportation League, the Global Shippers' Forum, the Med-America Shippers Association, the US Shippers Association and the Fashion Accessories Shippers Association all voiced their 'no' for fear of monopoly, reduction in competition, reduced port call options (elimination of direct calls at side ports), negative influence on existing carriers, increases in transportation cost, etc, none of the individual shippers said 'no' to the P3 Network. Most of the port operators, NVOCCs, government authorities and civil servants are also in support of the same. On the other hand, two of the three labour force organisations expressed a negative opinion. It should also be noted that just one small carrier, Atlantic Container Line (ACL), submitted a written opinion, and its opinion is negative. But it appears that no major carrier such as Evergreen or Hapag-Lloyd submitted written comments to the FMC.

In terms of the FMC Commissioners, Richard A. Lidinsky, Jr. is reportedly the only one who expressed a negative opinion of the P3 Network for the stated reason that:

> 'This agreement will allow the controlling carrier the ability, when coupled with existing discussion agreements, to deploy its assets along with those of the other two carriers, to dominate vessel competition and narrow shipper options at US ports. Other than the publicity machine of the three would be partners to rally support, there is nothing in the record before us of Americans clamoring for this proposal.'[10]

However, the FMC decided to give the green light to the P3 Network for the reason that:

10 'Comments of Commissioner Richard A. Lidinsky, Jr. on Proposed P3 Vessel Sharing Agreement' (24 March 2014), <http://www.fmc.gov/commissioner_lidinsky_comments_on_proposed_p3_agreement/> accessed 15 September 2015.

'The Commission's decision is based on a determination that the agreement is not likely at this time, by a reduction in competition, to produce an unreasonable increase in transportation cost or an unreasonable reduction in transportation service under section 6(g) of the Shipping Act.'[11]

2.2 EU and China reviews of the P3 Network

Under EU law, a block exemption was applicable to liner conferences allowing shipowners to jointly organise services (cooperate in price- and capacity-fixing arrangements) until 2008, when Regulation (EC) 1419/2006 regarding rules for the application of Articles 81 and 82 of the EC Treaty on maritime transport came into effect. Regulation (EC) 906/2009 bans collective pricing through conferences, to enhance price-based competition, but allows vessel-sharing consortia to use common services (e.g. ships) provided that market shares remain below 30%. Larger alliances are not necessarily unlawful, but self-assessment is then required to ensure there is no abuse of dominant positions.[12] The P3 Network then conducted a self-assessment and had been in voluntary discussions with the EU to confirm the P3 members' view of the alliance being in compliance with EU competition law. On 3 June 2014, the European Commission informed the P3 members that the Commission would not open proceedings in connection with the P3 Network, but that the EU would follow the P3 Network to ensure it remained in compliance with EU competition law.[13]

As for China's competition scrutiny, in the final decision issued by MOFCOM, it is noted that on 8 September 2013 MOFCOM received a notification of concentration of undertakings and, following review, MOFCOM required the P3 members to submit supplementary documents. On 29 December 2013, MOFCOM decided to register this case and commenced the review work. On 18 January 2014, MOFCOM decided to extend the time period for review and on 18 April 2014 the period was further extended to 17 June 2014. It is said that MOFCOM listened to opinions of some government departments, enterprise associations and relevant enterprises, and also retained a third party institute to provide a report with legal and economic analysis. However, such materials have not been released to the public. From information in the public domain, it is apparent that on 1 November 2013 the China Ship-owners Association

---

11 'P3 Agreement Clears FMC Regulatory Review' (20 March 2014), <http://www.fmc.gov/NR14-06/> accessed 15 September 2015.

12 Monika Nogaj, 'Cost of Non-Europe in the Single Market in Transport and Tourism' (October 2014), <http://www.europarl.europa.eu/document/activities/cont/201410/2014 1028ATT92090/20141028ATT92090EN.pdf> accessed 15 September 2015, p.39.

13 'Maersk Line and P3 Partners Receive European Commission Affirmation' (4 June 2014), <http://www.maerskline.com/en-us/countries/int/news/news-articles/2014/06/p3-partners> accessed 15 September 2015.

issued a news report that on 28 October 2013 its deputy director had a meeting with Maersk to exchange views regarding the P3 Network and that the China Ship-owners Association was very concerned about the negative influence on competition if the P3 Network were to be established.[14] The China Shipper's Association also expressed negative views of the P3 Network.[15]

Further, it should be noted that although MOFCOM is the statutory government agency empowered to review mergers, this does not mean that it is the only government agency with competency in mergers review. The National Development and Reform Commission (NDRC) and the Ministry of Industry and Information Technology are the other parts of China's government most mentioned by survey respondents as those that have an industrial policy agenda as part of the merger review process.[16] As reported in the 2013 Work Report and 2014 Work Plan of NDRC, the Commission was considering enhancing price regulatory investigations regarding price monopoly activities in international shipping in China.[17] In this case, it is reported that the Ministry of Transportation (MOT) of the PRC cooperated extensively with MOFCOM in the review of the P3 Network.[18] Some scholars also commented at the time that the P3 Network might use its bargaining power to force Chinese ports to reduce the price of services. Due to such concerns on the part of Chinese ports, MOFCOM banned the P3 Network, and it appears that the P3 Network underestimated the lobbying powers of local government with MOFCOM.[19]

3. The prohibition of monopoly agreements and its applicability to liner shipping: what is the position under the law of China?

In China, the sources of competition law regarding prohibition of monopoly agreements (cartel control) applicable to liner shipping can be divided into three categories, namely international conventions, general competition law applicable to all industries and industrial competition law applicable to

14 'China Ship-owners Association Expresses its View on P3 Network for the First Time' (4 November 2014), <http://www.ship.sh/news_detail.php?nid=10696> accessed 15 September 2015.

15 'Denying P3 is in Line with National Interest' (18 June 2014), <http://finance.ifeng.com/a/20140618/12567962_0.shtml> accessed 18 September 2015.

16 D. Daniel Sokol, 'Merger Control Under China's Anti-Monopoly Law' (2013) 10 *NYU Journal of Law and Business*, 1, <http://ssrn.com/abstract=2207690> accessed 18 September 2015, p.10.

17 '2013 Work Report and 2014 Work Plan of NDRC' [2014] 3 *Journal of Chinese Price Supervision and Anti-monopoly* (in Chinese), p.13.

18 'MOT and MOFCOM are Conducting Extensive Review of the P3 Network' (28 April 2014), <http://www.csbulk.com/hykx_detail.asp?id=35790> accessed 18 September 2015.

19 Liu Xu, 'A Comment on the MOFCOM's Ban of the P3 Network' (17 June 2014), <http://zhuanlan.zhihu.com/competitionlaw/19780904> accessed 18 September 2015.

specific industries (which may also be referred to as sector specific competition law).

3.1 UNCTAD Liner Convention

Adoption of the UNCTAD Liner Convention[20] is a milestone event in the world maritime industry, deeply shaping the shipping competition laws of the world. China is no exception. The Liner Convention is the backbone of Chinese maritime competition law, and a proper understanding of the Convention is critical to the evaluation of the Chinese regulator's decision regarding the P3 Network case. An examination thereof is therefore warranted to underpin the analysis of Chinese law.

Until the mid-nineteenth century, the dependence of maritime navigation on the vagaries of wind and weather, and lack of any system of speedy international communications other than by post, meant that the shipping industry was largely organised on an *ad hoc* basis. Due to technical developments in ship building and communications, etc, ship owners then became able to provide regular scheduled shipping services in a real sense.[21] International merchant shipping can be divided into two categories of services, namely liner services and tramp shipping.[22] By way of summary description, liner service is akin to city buses and tramp shipping to taxies.

The replacement of sail by steam, and of wood by iron (later by steel), changed the situation considerably, particularly as steam engines improved. Reliance on trade winds became a thing of the past; without major difficulties, steam ships could keep to a fixed sailing schedule. Between 1860 and 1880 the number and capacity of steam ships grew enormously. In the UK, for example, the registered gross tonnage of steam vessels increased fivefold over that period, from 450,000 tonnes to 2,720,000 tonnes.[23] Finally, the increase in world tonnage – from 7 million tonnes in 1850 to 29 million tonnes in 1900 – was not accompanied by a proportional increase in world trade which, while extraordinary, could not fully employ the available fleet. All these factors meant that the supply of liner transport services exceeded demand.[24]

Due to this excess tonnage problem, fierce rate wars emerged amongst owners. These rate wars were so brutal that some freight rates were even

20 Convention on a Code of Conduct for Liner Conferences 1974 (TD/CODE/13/Add.1), published by UNCTAD in 1974, <http://unctad.org/en/pages/PublicationWebflyer.aspx?publicationid=356> accessed 19 September 2015.
21 Martin Stopford, *Maritime Economics* (1st edn, Harper Collins Academic, 1988), p.176.
22 Lane C. Kendall, *The Business of Shipping* (5th edn, Chapman and Hall, 1986), p.5.
23 Luis Ortiz Blanco, *Shipping Conferences Under EC Antitrust Law: Criticism of a Legal Paradox* (Hart Publishing, 2007), p.3.
24 Ibid, p.4.

lower than the direct voyage costs.[25] As a result, carriers grouped together to establish cartel-like liner conferences to jointly decide freight rates, in response to the rapid increases in shipping tonnage, and a consequent fall in freight rates, caused by the introduction of steamers and a rapid growth of non-British (US and Norwegian) merchant fleets.[26] As early as 1875, the first shipping conference in the modern sense (the UK-Calcutta conference) was established, consisting of five carriers: the P&O (Peninsular and Oriental Steam Navigation Co), the B.I. (British India), and the City, Clan and Anchor Lines. By the beginning of the twentieth century, liner shipping companies had established cartels on nearly all world trade routes.[27]

From an historic point of view, the shipping industry has been in the controlling hand of developed countries causing developing states to feel at a disadvantage. In 1970, although 62.4% by volume of all exports and 16.5% of all imports were generated by developing states, developing states controlled just 7.4% of world tonnage, presenting a major drain of foreign exchange for developing states that did not have sufficient foreign exchange reserves.[28] Generally, developing states observed that the goods they exported to developed states were sold on an FOB basis, while the goods they imported were sold on a CIF basis. Typically, the choice of transporting vessels in both cases was out of the hands of the developing state. Developing states had a strong desire to reverse the situation and take control of shipping. However, when developing states applied to join conferences, their applications were either not approved or they would be allocated only a small quota. Developing states viewed this as neo-colonialism, and as a consequence of such problems they faced for securing their cargo at 'proper' freight levels and in light of the low bargaining power of shipping interests in the developing states, many such states insisted upon government intervention (by way of cargo reservation) in the name of protection of the national economic interest.[29]

Although liner conferences had been under discussion in UNCTAD since 1964, the concept of an international convention to regulate liner conference practices was not actively pursued prior to 1970. Developing countries were strongly in favour of government interventions, but developed

25 Amos Herman, *Shipping Conference* (Lloyd's of London Press, 1983), p.8.
26 Bureau of Transport Economics, *A Study of Liner Shipping Services Into and Out of Australia* (Australian Government Publishing Service, Canberra, 1986), <https://bitre.gov.au/publications/1986/files/report_060_v1.pdf> accessed 19 September 2015, vol.1, p.7.
27 Nikhil Gupta, *Competition Concerns in Shipping Conferences*, <http://www.competition-commission-india.nic.in/advocacy/F2_LatestRevisedFinalReportNikhil32.pdf> accessed 19 September 2015, p.25.
28 Stephen Zamora, 'UNCTAD III: the Question of Shipping' (1973) 7 *Journal of World Trade Law* 92.
29 Lawrence Juda, 'World Shipping, UNCTAD and the New Economic Order' (1982) 35(3) *International Organization* 496.

countries preferred no direct government role.[30] After rounds of negotiations and compromise, the UNCTAD Liner Convention was adopted by a vote of 132 in total; 96 states voting to approve, 28 states abstaining, and eight states voting 'no'.

Liner conferences are generally considered to be hard core cartels,[31] and some EU members including the UK do not approve of such cartels considering them contrary to policy traditions which honour preservation of free competition and prevention of monopolies. The accession of the EU to the Liner Convention and the adoption of the Brussels Package 1979 (EC Regulation 954/79[32]) was motivated by the rationale that if the EU did not join this Convention, developing states might use more unilateral protection measures (such as cargo reservation) to bring control of transportation into their own hands.[33] As a result, as a matter of compromise between the traditional free competition doctrine and national policy regarding prevention of control of shipping by developing countries, the EU adopted Council Regulation 4056/86 allowing liner conferences to set common freight rates, take joint decisions on the limitation of supply and coordinate timetables. The Regulation was subsequently abolished in 2006 when the EU abolished the antitrust exemption by way of Council Regulation (EC) 1419/2006, also denouncing the Liner Convention.

As a developing country, China has skirmished with conferences for a long time, starting when liner conferences were forced to reduce freight rates on the Far-East/European lines by about 30% in 1959, until 1966 when COSCO adopted the 'China Ocean Shipping Tariff' and the first battle of the Chinese government with liner conferences ended.[34] After adoption of the UNCTAD Liner Convention, in 1979 the Ministry of Foreign Trade (now MOFCOM), the Ministry of Communication (now the MOT) and the Ministry of Foreign Affairs submitted the 'Report Regarding China's Accession to UNCTAD Liner Convention' to the

---

30 William J. Bosier, Jr. and William G. Green, 'The Liner Conference Convention Liner Conference Convention Launching an International Regulatory Regime' (1974) 6 *Law & Policy in International Business* 554. See also Stephen Zamora, 'Rate Regulation in Ocean Transport: Developing Countries Confront the Liner Conference System' (1971) 59 *California Law Review* 1299.

31 William Sjostrom, 'Ocean Shipping Cartels: A Survey' (2004) 3(2) *Review of Network Economics* 107.

32 Council Regulation (EEC) 954/79 of 15 May 1979 concerning the ratification by Member States of, or their accession to, the United Nations Convention on a Code of Conduct for Liner Conferences, OJ L 121, 17/05/1979, pp.1–4.

33 Ademuni-Odeke, 'The Brussel Package: The United Kingdom and the EEC response to the Code' (1984) 11(4) *Maritime Policy & Management* 237.

34 Hongyan Liu, *Liner Conferences in Competition Law: A Comparative Analysis of European and Chinese Law* (Springer-Verlag, 2010), p.30.

National People's Congress of China[35] and on 23 September 1980, China decided to accede to this Convention with a reservation as follows:

'The joint shipping services established between the People's Republic of China and any other country through consultations and on a basis that the parties concerned may deem appropriate, are totally different from liner conferences in nature, and the provisions of the United Nations Convention on a Code of Conduct for Liner Conferences shall not be applicable thereto.'[36]

With the development of containerisation, the influence of shipping conferences is in gradual decrease. As reported by Lloyd's List on 19 November 2013, there are thus far only 65 conferences and agreements in the non-European trades, despite the demise of heavyweights such as the Far Eastern Freight Conference and the Trans-Atlantic Conference Agreement when these were outlawed in Europe.[37]

3.2 General competition law in China

The PRC has only a short history since its establishment in 1949 and its economic miracle has taken place only in the last 30 years. However, the regulation of the competitive process is not entirely neglected in Chinese law. Substantive rules go back as far as 1980 when the State Council of China issued regulations that, inter alia, no products should become subject to monopolised control unless authorised by law. In 1993, the Anti-Unfair Competition Law was enacted by the Standing Committee of the National People's Congress.[38] This statute is primarily a consumer protection law rather than a complete competition code.[39]

On 30 August 2007, the Anti-Monopoly Law (AML) was enacted by the Standing Committee of the National People's Congress.[40] This law is the culmination of a drafting process lasting over 13 years.[41] The AML

---

35 CCCPC Literature Research Office (eds), *Chronology of Deng Xiaoping 1975–1997* (CCCPC Literature Publishing House, 2004), p.513.

36 UN Treaty Series, vol.1334 (1983), p.204.

37 Janet Porter, 'P3 Threatens Non-EU Conferences' (*Lloyd's Loading List*, 19 November 2013), <http://www.lloydsloadinglist.com/freight-directory/adviceandinsight/P3-threatens-non-EU-conferences/4940.htm#.Vf8SKfQ31lF> accessed 19 September 2015.

38 It was adopted by the 3rd session of the Standing Committee of the Eighth National People's Congress on 2 September 1993.

39 Mark Williams, *Competition Policy and Law in China, Hong Kong and Taiwan* (Cambridge University Press, 2005), p.166.

40 It was adopted at the 29th meeting of the Standing Committee of the Tenth National People's Congress of the People's Republic of China on 30 August 2007 and became effective from 1 August 2008. Full text translation to this law is available at <http://www.wipo.int/edocs/lexdocs/laws/en/cn/cn099en.pdf> accessed 1 November 2015.

41 Adrian Emch and Qian Hao, 'The New Chinese Anti-Monopoly Law – An Overview'

contains 57 articles divided into the following eight chapters: General Provisions (Chapter I); Monopoly Agreements (Chapter II); Abuse of Dominant Market Position (Chapter III); Concentration of Undertakings (Chapter IV); Abuse of Administrative Authority to Eliminate or Restrict Competition (Chapter V); Investigation of Suspected Monopolistic Practices (Chapter VI); Legal Liabilities (Chapter VII); and Supplementary Provisions (Chapter VIII).[42] The most relevant chapters to the issue under discussion in this chapter are Chapters I, II and IV.

In General Provisions (Chapter I), the relevant rules read as follows:

'Article 3 (monopolistic conducts): For the purposes of this Law, monopolistic conducts include:

(1) monopoly agreements reached between undertakings;

Article 12 (definition of undertakings and relevant market):

For the purposes of this Law, undertakings include natural persons, legal persons, and other organizations that engage in manufacturing, or selling commodities or providing services.

For the purposes of this Law, a relevant market consists of the range of the commodities for which, and the regions where, undertakings compete each other during a given period of time for specific commodities or services.'

In Monopoly Agreements (Chapter II), the relevant rules include that:

'Article 13 (monopoly agreements) Competing undertakings are prohibited from concluding the following monopoly agreements:

(1) on fixing or changing commodity prices;
(2) on restricting the amount of commodities manufactured or marketed;
(3) on splitting the sales market or the purchasing market for raw and semi-finished materials;
(4) on restricting the purchase of new technologies or equipment, or the development of new technologies or products;
(5) on joint boycotting of transactions; and
(6) other monopoly agreements confirmed as such by the authority for enforcement of the Anti-monopoly Law under the State Council.

Article 16 (prohibition of monopoly actions by trade associations): Trade associations may not make arrangements for undertakings

---

(2007) eSapience Center for Competition Policy, <http://papers.ssrn.com/sol3/papers.cfm?abstract_id=1030451> accessed 19 September 2015.

42 Zhenguo Wu, 'Perspectives on the Chinese Anti-Monopoly Law' (2008–2009) 75 *Antitrust Law Journal* 79.

within their respective trades to engage in the monopolistic practices prohibited by the provisions of this Chapter.'

It is noted that there is a general exemption clause in Article 15 of Chapter II that:

'Article 15 (general exemption) The provisions of Articles 13 and 14 of this Law shall not be applicable to the agreements between undertakings which they can prove to be concluded for one of the following purposes:

(1) improving technologies, or engaging in research and development of new products; or
(2) improving product quality, reducing cost, and enhancing efficiency, unifying specifications and standards of products, or implementing specialized division of production;
(3) increasing the efficiency and competitiveness of small and medium-sized undertakings;
(4) serving public interests in energy conservation, environmental protection and disaster relief;
(5) mitigating sharp decrease in sales volumes or obvious overproduction caused by economic depression;
(6) safeguarding legitimate interests in foreign trade and in economic cooperation with foreign counterparts; or
(7) other purposes as prescribed by law or the State Council.'

3.3 Industrial competition law in China's shipping industry: Regulations of the PRC on International Maritime Transportation

As early as 1992, the MOT began to draft administrative regulations for the shipping market. In 1995, the draft of the Regulations of the PRC on International Shipping was submitted to the State Council of China for review. After various discussions and revisions, the Regulations of the PRC on International Maritime Transportation were adopted at the 49th Executive Meeting of the State Council on 5 December 2001.[43]

In terms of rules applicable to liner conferences, operational agreements and freight agreements, the Regulations state that:

'Article 22: Photocopies of liner conference agreements, service operation agreements and freight rate agreements concluded between international shipping operators engaged in international liner services in which Chinese ports are involved shall be submitted to the competent

43 The Regulations came into force from 1 January 2002 and was further amended on 18 July 2013. Full text translation can be seen at <http://app.westlawchina.com/> accessed 2 November 2015.

communications department of the State Council within 15 days from the date of conclusion of such agreements.

Article 35: The competent communications department of the State Council may, upon the request of the interested parties or at its own discretion, conduct investigations into the following cases:

(1) liner conference agreements, operational agreements or freight rate agreements concluded among international shipping operators engaged in international liner services in which Chinese ports are involved and which can be detrimental to fair competition; . . .'

Due to the Regulations of the PRC on International Maritime Transportation, the legality of liner conferences are admitted in China and liner conferences covering the Chinese ports are legitimised by submitting the required documents. This means that the typical restrictive practices of liner conferences, such as freight rate-fixing, capacity management programmes and loyalty arrangements, are to be allowed. This is a general legitimisation of liner conferences. The submission requirements constitute the only condition for this general legitimisation, and no other competition assessment or legal obligations are stipulated.[44] Plainly, although it is disputable that the formalities prescribed for liner conferences etc can be viewed as granting antitrust immunity, if hard core liner conferences can lawfully exist under the regime of the Liner Convention, there is essentially no reason why soft cartels such as freight discussion agreements, vessel sharing agreements and liner alliances, etc cannot also lawfully exist.

3.4 The (draft) Shipping Law of China

As early as 1996, China began to draft a Shipping Law, but the work was suspended in relation to some basic shipping policies, for example the application of competition law to the shipping sector, and there was debate as to the relationship between the Shipping Law and the AML.[45]

The draft Shipping Law submitted to the State Council for review in 2004 addresses competition law in its Chapter VI (Competition Rules regarding Waterways Transportation). Article 65 sets out the antitrust exemption for liner conferences regarding the coordination of schedules, the allocation of capacity and the allocation of freight income, etc. Article 66 addresses the antitrust exemption for joint venture agreements or consortia regarding operation agreements for slot sharing, joint operation of vessels, temporary adjustments of capacity, joint arrangements for freight income, joint market

---

44 Hongyan Liu, *Liner Conferences in Competition Law: A Comparative Analysis of European and Chinese Law* (Springer-Verlag, 2010), p.138.
45 Hu Zhengliang et al., 'On Several Basic Theoretical Issues in the Drafting of Chinese Shipping Law' (2012) 1(1) *Chinese Journal of Maritime Law* 65.

activities and conclusion of freight agreements, etc. Although this draft Shipping Law is still in the process of being drafted and it is not clear when it might be adopted by China, such drafts should at least to some extent be representative of the Chinese government's opinion.

In addition, during the process of drafting the Shipping Law, some leading experts have voiced their support for maintaining antitrust immunity for liner conferences and discussion agreements. For example, Professor Hu Zhengliang of Shanghai Maritime University Law School argued in his PhD thesis that the Shipping Law ought to adopt block exemptions the main rule, supplemented by individual exemption; and should expressly grant exemptions to competition restrictive measures in the shipping sector, including an exemption for liner conference and joint ventures/consortia, royalty agreements and volume contracts.[46] Professor Yu Shicheng of Shanghai Maritime University wrote in his book *Study of American Shipping Law* that, although the EU has abolished its antitrust exemption for liner conferences, China should still maintain the same because: (1) antitrust exemptions are still the core of shipping competition laws in the world and this will be not be changed in the near future; (2) except in the EU, most countries have not abolished the exemption; (3) under Regulations of the PRC on International Maritime Transportation, liner conference and freight discussion agreements are still lawful; (4) the exemption is helpful to achieve the aim of building of making China into a strong force in maritime transportation, and strikes a reasonable balance between the interests of shippers, carriers and the nation.[47]

4. Chinese antitrust laws regarding merger control and their applicability to liner shipping

4.1 Introduction: merger rules before AML

The AML was adopted in 2007, but this does not mean that prior to that there were no merger control laws in China. Before the AML, in light of the increasing number of foreign-backed mergers and acquisitions (M&A), activities following the WTO accession and fear that such activities could lead to distortions of competition in the Chinese market, Chinese policymakers began designing merger review provisions targeted at controlling foreign investments from a competition perspective in the early 2000s.[48] China then set up a merger and acquisition notification and evaluation

---

46 Hu Zhengliang, 'A Comprehensive Study on China Shipping Law' (PhD thesis, Dalian Maritime University, 2003), p.226.

47 Yu Shicheng, *Study of American Shipping Law* (in Chinese) (Peking University Press, 2007), p.195.

48 Tingting Weinreich-Zhao, *Chinese Merger Control Law: An Assessment of its Competition-Policy Orientation after the First Years of Application* (Springer-Verlag, 2015), pp.32–33.

system in March 2003, which was the first of its kind in the country, by promulgating the Interim Provisions on the Mergers and Acquisition of Domestic Enterprises by Foreign Investors.[49] In 2006, MOFCOM and five other government agencies revised the 2003 merger regulations. There were several new features in the 2006 Provisions on Mergers and Acquisitions of Domestic Enterprises by Foreign Investors (2006 M&A Rules).[50] In March 2007, MOFCOM issued the Guidelines on Declarations for Anti-Monopoly Review in Mergers and Acquisitions of Domestic Enterprises by Foreign Investors.[51]

After enactment of AML in 2008, the 2006 M&A Rules were substantially revised in 2009 (2009 M&A Rules). As per Article 2 of the 2009 M&A Rules:

> 'For the purposes of these Provisions, "a foreign investor's merger and acquisition of a domestic enterprise" shall mean a foreign investor's purchase of any equity interests of any shareholder of an enterprise in China other than an FIE (hereinafter, "Domestic Company") or subscribe to any increased capital of a Domestic Company, thus making the Domestic Company converted to and established as an FIE (hereinafter, "M&A of Equity Interests") or making the foreign investor establish an FIE and purchase, through such enterprise, any asset of any Domestic Enterprise by an agreement and operate such asset, or the foreign investor purchase any asset of a Domestic Enterprise by an agreement and invest, with such asset, in the establishment of an FIE to operate such asset (hereinafter, "M&A of Assets").'[52]

However, it should be noted that in the 2006 M&A Rules and 2009 M&A Rules, nothing is mentioned about whether establishing joint ventures will be viewed as a kind of merger. MOFCOM subsequently published in 2014 Guiding Opinion on the Application for Concentration of undertakings Operators, Interim Provisions on the Standards Applicable to Simple Cases of Concentration of undertakings Operators, and the Guiding Opinions of the Anti-monopoly Bureau of the Ministry of Commerce on Declaration

---

49 The Interim Provisions, which were adopted at the first ministerial affairs meeting of the Ministry of Foreign Trade and Economic Cooperation of the People's Republic of China on 2 January 2003 and came into force on 12 April 2003, were substituted by the 2006 M&A Rules and expired from 2006.

50 The Provisions were adopted at the 7th executive meeting of the Ministry of Commerce of the People's Republic of China and came into force as of 8 September 2006, and were further amended on 22 June 2009, referred as 2009 M&A Rules.

51 Order [2006] No.10 of the Ministry of Commerce. See Ping Lin and Jingjing Zhao, 'Merger Control Policy Under China's Anti-Monopoly Law' (2012) 41 (1)–(2) *Review of Industrial Organization* 111.

52 Order [2009] No.6 of the Ministry of Commerce – Releasing the Provisions on Foreign Investors' Merger with and Acquisition of Domestic Enterprises, dated 22 June 2009, full text translation available at <http://app.westlawchina.com/> accessed 2 November 2015.

of Simple Cases of Concentration of undertakings Operators (For Trial Implementation).[53] Amongst these regulations, the Guiding Opinions on the Application for Concentration of undertakings Operators contained detailed rules regarding merger control in AML, which will be considered in the following.

4.2 AML and joint ventures

In February 2004, the Draft Anti-Monopoly Law (Submission Draft or 2004 Draft) developed by the Department of Treaties and Law of MOFCOM, was submitted by MOFCOM to the Legislative Affairs Office of the State Council for further review. Article 27[54] also required notification of transactions creating or transferring control 'by means of delegated operation or joint venture'. However, neither 'delegated operation' nor 'joint venture' was a defined term. It has been commented that the concepts are modelled on the western experience, but that they could embrace almost any kind of concentration (or merger) and were too harsh for merger control review.[55]

In June 2006, the State Council submitted the Draft AML (First Review Draft) to the Standing Committee of the National People's Congress. In this First Review Draft, 'concentration of undertakings' is defined as: a merger of undertakings; acquisition by an undertaking of voting shares or assets in one or more other undertakings to an adequate extent; acquisition of control of other undertakings by contract, technology or other means, or the capability of imposing material effects on competition.[56] The reference to 'joint venture' in the 2004 Draft was deleted and subsequently in June and August 2007 the Draft AML (Second Review Draft) and the Draft AML (Third Review Draft) were reviewed by the Standing Committee of the National People's Congress. After three 'reviews' by the highest Chinese legislative body, the National People's Congress, the final wording of the AML no longer contains any reference to joint ventures.

Information in the public domain provides no explanation for these developments in the course of the legislation process. What did the Chinese legislator think the term 'joint venture' denoted, and why was the legal term employed during the drafting of the AML but subsequently deleted in the

---

53 Susan Ning, 'China – Merger Control 2015', <http://www.iclg.co.uk/practice-areas/merger-control/merger-control-2015/china> accessed 20 September 2015.

54 Stephen Harris, Jr. and Kathy Lijun Yang, 'China: Latest Developments in Anti-Monopoly Law Legislation' (2005) 19 *Antitrust* 89, p.92.

55 Wei Qiong, 'Procedure Rules regarding Merger Control: with a Comment on the Draft Anti-Monopoly Law (Submission Draft or 2004 Draft AML)' (in Chinese) (2004) 11 *Law Science* 101.

56 Maher Dabbah and Paul Lasok QC, *Merger Control Worldwide: First Supplement to the First Edition* (Cambridge University Press, 2006), p.21.

final edition of the AML? An issue for consideration is therefore: if 'joint ventures' are caught by the AML, what is a so-called joint venture?

As explained by Mr Zhang Qiong (Deputy Director of the Legal Office of the State Council of China and the Leader of the Experts Group of State Antitrust Commission) in his book *A Theoretical Study of Anti-Monopoly*,[57] during the drafting process of the AML, mergers, acquisitions, tie-ups and other phrases inadequately reflected the concept of 'concentration of undertakings'. The AML instead came to employ the concept of concentration of undertakings, to describe a situation where undertakings form a legal entity, or obtain control of another undertaking, or exert a decisive influence on other undertakings, resulting in the adoption of concerted measures in competition matters. Concentration of undertakings is distinguished from M&A in the sense of company law or securities law; the concept includes connotations of obtaining control, especially in respect of joint ventures.[58] However, Mr Zhang Qiong does not explain why joint ventures are a kind of concentration of undertakings and why the final edition of the AML omitted them from the 2004 Draft.

5. Legal nature of the P3 Network and comments on China's ban

We can now examine the two key issues, namely, the legal nature of the P3 Network (monopoly agreement or concentration of undertakings?), and whether it is a notifiable concentration of undertakings.

5.1 The P3 Network: monopoly agreement or concentration of undertakings?

Plainly, the first issue in relation to this case concerns the legal nature of the P3 Network. Did the P3 Network as proposed constitute a concentration of undertakings, subjecting it to review by MOFCOM? If the P3 Network was correctly to be considered a monopoly agreement, MOFCOM may not have jurisdiction over the same. This is a very important formal issue, determining whether MOFCOM has jurisdiction over the case in the first place. Before considering this issue, it should be noted that it was the US FMC, rather than the US Federal Trade Commission or the US Department of Justice, that conducted the antitrust review of the P3 Network. Similarly, should this case be subject to the review of the MOT or MOFCOM?

When the AML was enacted in August 2007, the question of which authority would be in charge of its enforcement remained undecided. The

---

57 Zhang Qiong, *A Theoretical Study of Anti-Monopoly* (in Chinese) (China Legal Publishing House, 2007).
58 Ibid, pp.17 and 178.

State Council subsequently issued so-called *san ding*[59] notices giving central government ministries and equivalent organisations instructions on their jurisdiction, staff and internal organisation. As a result, MOFCOM is now in charge of merger control. The NDRC is responsible in relation to monopoly agreements, abuses of dominance and anticompetitive abuses of administrative powers (dubbed 'administrative monopoly') as long as the underlying anticompetitive conduct is related to pricing. If the conduct is not related to pricing, it falls under the jurisdiction of State Administration for Industry and Commerce (SAIC). Although there is an Anti-Monopoly Commission on top of these three antitrust watchdogs, it is just an inter-institution agency for such matters as coordination of antitrust enforcement work and overall competition policy.[60]

However, this does not mean that antitrust enforcement power can be exercised only by the said three government agencies. In this respect, as provided by Article 15(7) of the AML (regarding exceptions to monopoly agreements), 'the provisions of Article 13 and 14 of this Law (monopoly agreements) shall not be applicable to the agreements ... if there are otherwise prescribed by law or the State Council'. Further, as provided by Article 31 of the AML, concentrations involving national security are subject to national security review as well.

In terms of the so-called 'otherwise prescribed by law or the State Council', this mainly involves the relationship between the industrial laws of China, for example the application of competition law to the energy, civil aviation and railway sectors. In this regard, as explained by Mr Zhang Qiong, pursuant to the principle that *lex specialis derogat legi generali*, in terms of the relationship between sector-specific competition rules and the AML, where the sector-specific competition rules have already had related regulation regarding the monopoly activities in a given industry, such competition rules shall be applied in priority against the AML. Where the sector-specific competition rules have no special regulation regarding a matter, then the AML should be applied.[61]

China is a contracting state to the 1974 UNCTAD Liner Convention. In terms of the legal status of international conventions in the legal system of China, in 1997 China acceded to the Vienna Convention on the Law of Treaties 1969.[62] China applies the principle of *pacta sunt servanda* to the effect that if a treaty to which China is a party contains provisions inconsistent with Chinese legislation, treaty provisions should prevail unless China

---

59 San ding represents a tripartite layout.
60 Adrian Emch, 'Chinese Antitrust Institutions – Many Cooks in the Kitchen' (2014) 10(1) *Competition Policy International* 217.
61 Zhang Qiong, *A Theoretical Study of Anti-Monopoly* (in Chinese) (China Legal Publishing House, 2007), pp.17 and 106.
62 Adopted by the United Nations on 22 May 1969 and opened for signature on 23 May 1969. The Convention entered into force on 27 January 1980. China joined the Convention on 3 October 1997 with a reservation of its Article 66.

has made reservations to the relevant provisions.[63] The most cited provision in this regard is Article 142 of the General Principles of the Civil Law of the People's Republic of China (1986),[64] according to which if any international treaty concluded or acceded to by the PRC contains provisions differing from those in the civil laws of the PRC, the provisions of the international treaty shall apply, unless the provisions are ones to which the PRC has made a reservation.

It is noted that MOFCOM concluded in point IV (1) of its Decisions on Anti-monopoly Review of the P3 Network[65] entitled 'competition analysis' that:

> 'The proposed transaction under this Case will result in a close-knit alliance which is substantively different from traditional loose shipping alliances. International container liner transport is a capital-intensive industry that requires large investment and entails high risks. As a result, shipping enterprises often engage in mutual cooperation of varying degrees, mainly in the form of vessel sharing agreements, slot exchange agreements, etc. On such basis, a number of shipping alliances have been formed on the market.'[66]

Generally speaking, liner conferences are deemed to be cartels. In terms of China, so far China has not withdrawn from the Liner Convention and, due to the Regulations of the PRC on International Maritime Transportation (a regulation adopted by the State Council), hard core cartel liner conferences can lawfully exist in China. That being the case, even if assuming that the P3 NC could be viewed as a close-knit alliance, what would be the difference compared to traditional liner conferences? In addition, as observed by the United Nations, the legal status of liner conferences varies from country to country and may also have the characteristics of unincorporated associations or possess corporate legal identity.[67] Even if the P3 Network were deemed to be a corporate legal entity, MOFCOM should have considered the differences between the P3 Network and traditional liner conferences, and why it is a kind of concentration of undertakings in

---

63 Xue Hanqin et al., 'National Treaty Law and Practice: China', in Duncan B. Hollis et al. (eds), *National Treaty Law and Practice: Dedicated to the Memory of Monroe Leigh* (Martinus Nijhoff Publishers, 2005), p.164.

64 Adopted at the 4th session of the Sixth National People's Congress, promulgated on 12 April 1986, and amended on 27 August 2009.

65 MOFCOM Announcement No.46 of 2014 on Decisions of Anti-monopoly Review to Prohibit Concentration of Undertakings by Prohibiting Maersk, MSC and CMA CGM from Establishing a Network Center, published by MOFCOM on 17 June 2015.

66 See <http://english.mofcom.gov.cn/article/policyrelease/buwei/201407/20140700663862. shtml> accessed on 22 September 2015.

67 United Nations Economic and Social Commission for Asia and the Pacific, *Guidelines for Maritime Legislation* (United Nations, 1999), p.27.

the sense of China's merger control rules. The lack of such analysis renders its conclusion incomplete.

5.2 *Is it correct to view the P3 Network as a notifiable concentration of undertakings?*

As seen from the above analysis, the legal analysis underpinning MOFCOM's view of the P3 Network as different from traditional hard core cartels is incomplete. The question which must follow is whether, assuming that the P3 Network cannot benefit from the protection of the Liner Convention, it is proper to view it as a notifiable concentration of undertakings. The Liner Convention does not deal with the issue of concentration of undertakings in the shipping industry. As such, MOFCOM then has *prima facie* jurisdiction over this case.

Before analysing this issue, it should be noted that as per Article 6.1(a) of the P3 Network Agreement as filed with the US FMC, the P3 was to have an NC for the purposes of the joint coordination and management of the P3 Network. The NC as a legal entity was to operate and be governed by its organic corporate documents and applicable corporate law. As per Article 14 of the Law of the People's Republic of China on the Application of Laws to Foreign-Related Civil Relations (2010),[68] the law of the place of registration applies to the capacity for civil rights, capacity for civil conduct, organisational structure, shareholders' rights and obligations and other matters pertaining to a legal person and the branch offices thereof. It appears from news reports that the intention was that the P3 NC should be established in London and, as such, English law instead of Chinese law would have applied to determine the legal nature of the P3 NC, including its nature of alliance, vessel sharing agreement or joint venture.[69]

However, if Chinese law were to be applicable, it would be necessary to determine whether the P3 NC was in the nature of an alliance or a joint venture, and whether such joint venture should be notified to MOFCOM. As per Articles 11 and 20 of the AML, trade associations and mergers are within the scope of AML, but the Act makes no specific reference to alliances or joint ventures. Nor is there any definition of the concept of alliance in other legislation.

As for the reason why China views joint ventures as notifiable, in the book *Anti-monopoly Law of the People's Republic of China: Interpretations and*

---

68 It was adopted at the 17th session of the Standing Committee of the 11th National People's Congress of the People's Republic of China on 28 October 2010 and came into force on 1 April 2011.

69 Jorgen Rudbeck, 'P3 CEO: These are the Challenges for the Alliance' (*Shipping Watch*, 5 September 2013), <http://shippingwatch.com/carriers/article5917350.ece> accessed 22 September 2015.

Applications edited by the Anti-monopoly Bureau of MOFCOM, it is said that:

> 'generally speaking, establishing of joint ventures is just a kind of establishment of a new civil entity and it has nothing to do with concentrations . . . however, the reason justifying capturing of joint ventures by AML is that "control over other undertakings or the ability capable of exerting a decisive influence on the same gained by an undertaking through signing contracts or other means" . . . because once one undertaking put its assets and equity shares into the newly established joint venture enterprise, it may lose control of the same. If the said undertaking is not a controlling shareholder, its control to the said assets and equity shares in the joint venture enterprise will fall into hands of the controlling shareholder of the joint venture enterprise. As such, in many other jurisdictions of the world, establishing of joint ventures is deemed as an important kind of concentration of undertakings.'[70]

It appears that MOFCOM relies largely on the concept of 'full function' joint ventures. By comparison, under EU law a joint venture is deemed not to be full function if it only takes over one specific function within the parent company's business activities without access to the market, for instance research and development or production, and is only auxiliary to its parent company's business activities.[71]

MOFCOM does not refer in its decision to the concept of 'full function'. As for the reasons why MOFCOM deemed it a 'close-knit alliance', in MOFCOM's decision it is said that:

> 'P3 members will jointly set up a network center to conduct routine management of all their vessels and will only retain the right of technical management of such vessels; in terms of operating procedures, the proposed network center will be independently responsible for management and operations according to pre-agreed work procedures; in terms of cost-sharing arrangements, P3 members will be divided into several settlement groups for unified settlement by prescribing voyage costs (including charter rates, fuel costs, port fees and canal fees), and the operating costs of vessels will be shared among P3 members; in terms of the sales of unused containers, the proposed network center shall be responsible for the uniform coordination and handling of the sales of unused containers by the P3 members; and finally, in

---

70 Anti-monopoly Bureau of MOFCOM (eds), *Anti-monopoly Law of the People's Republic of China: Interpretations and Applications* (Peking University Press, 2007), p.175. Translation of this sentence was done by the author.

71 Paragraph 13 of the Commission Notice on the concept of full-function joint ventures under Council Regulation (EEC) 4064/89 on the control of concentrations between undertakings.

terms of blanking, the proposed network center can directly decide on suspension.'[72]

However, other clauses of the P3 Network Agreement may lead to a different conclusion:

'Article 5.6(a): Each Party shall retain its separate identity and shall have fully separate and independent sales, pricing and marketing functions.

Article 5.6(b): Subject to the procedures set forth in this Agreement, the Parties are authorized to obtain, compile, maintain and exchange information related to any aspect of operations in the Trade including, not but limited to, forecasts/projections, records, statistics, studies, compilations, costs, cargo volumes, market share information and other data, whether prepared by a Party or Parties or obtained from outside sources. Notwithstanding the preceding sentence, no information which is commercially sensitive (customers (save as necessary to comply with the terms of a particular contract of carriage), customer pricing and other, similar commercially sensitive information) may be exchanged hereunder directly or indirectly between any of the Parties.'

As provided in Article 5.6(a) and (b) of the P3 Network Agreement, the most important commercial issues, including sales, pricing and marketing functions were to remain in the hands of individual P3 members. In sum, in light of the Separate Identities and Sensitive Information clause in the P3 Network Agreement, it is arguably appropriate to regard the P3 Network as a 'full function' joint venture, instead of an *ad hoc* operational agreement. As such, it needs further explanation why P3 Network will cause control or loss of control of any P3 members of its capacity contributed to the P3 Network. On the other hand, it is hard to see from this Agreement how one party can take control of the other party and then subject the same to merger control rules of the AML.

6. Conclusion

Trust and anti-trust issues in liner shipping date back quite some time, to the days of the emergence of the first shipping conference. The legal debates of related issues continue. However, in light of the Liner Convention acceded to by China, it is difficult to understand when hard core cartel liner conferences (closed or open conferences) can be exempted, why the P3 Network could not be exempted as a species of soft cartel.

---

72 See <http://english.mofcom.gov.cn/article/policyrelease/buwei/201407/20140700663862. shtml> accessed 22 September 2015.

On the other hand, as observed by Professor Pitofsky, the former chairman of the Federal Trade Commission, the concept of 'joint venture' as used in the antitrust field is a vague and protean concept, which, at the extreme, might be taken to include all situations in which two or more persons or independent firms join forces to achieve some common goal.[73] Although China is the only regulatory authority amongst the top three antitrust enforcement agencies (the US, the EU and China) to state reasons regarding its refusal of a green light to the P3 Network, the very same decision leaves many questions unanswered. What is a joint venture? Is a joint venture notifiable under the AML? What type of joint venture should be notified? Was the proposed P3 Network a species of 'full function' joint venture notifiable under the AML? While the decision against the P3 Network came as no real surprise, the process of reasoning of the Chinese antitrust authority gives rise to a need for further detailed considerations and deliberations.

---

73 Robert Pitofsky, 'Joint Ventures under the Antitrust Laws: Some Reflections on the Significance of Penn-Olin' (1969) 82 *Harvard Law Review* 1007.

6 Maritime liens and insolvency under Chinese law

Dr Dingjing Huang

1. Introduction

The law of corporate liquidation and insolvency appears to have developed with little regard to admiralty proceedings. It is difficult to fit admiralty proceedings into the legislative language of the relevant statutes that regulate the winding up of companies and bankruptcy.[1] For instance, a ship may concurrently be the subject of an arrest in the Admiralty Court and an asset capable of liquidation in a company's winding-up process or in a personal bankruptcy. In such a case, it is important for a maritime claimant to be able to ascertain whether it is the jurisdiction of the Admiralty Court or some other court which prevails and which mode of legal process is available for the satisfaction of the claim.[2] A maritime lien gives the claimant an effective and powerful weapon in that the lien is enforceable against other creditors, whether secured or unsecured, and takes precedence over all other creditors whether the claims of those creditors arose before or after the creation of the lien.[3] Therefore, it is vital for a maritime claimant to understand whether his claim is secured by a maritime lien and how to enforce the lien effectively where the defendant shipowner has financial difficulties. This has drawn concerns across the shipping industry, particularly in the recent economic downturn.[4]

The People's Republic of China has a relatively short insolvency practice history. In 1986, the first insolvency law for state-owned enterprises was promulgated. Bankruptcy and insolvency for private companies and foreign-invested companies continued to be governed by separate laws until the Chinese Enterprise Insolvency Law was enacted in 2007. This chapter aims to provide a thorough analysis of the enforcement of maritime liens in insolvency proceedings within the Chinese legal framework. It will investigate the

---

1 D.R. Thomas, *Maritime Liens* (London, Stevens, 1980), p.65.
2 Ibid.
3 This is subject to existing possessory liens, statutory right of detention and other litigation costs.
4 For example, STX Pan Ocean Co, South Korea's biggest commodities shipping line, filed for bankruptcy protection in 2013.

characteristics of a maritime lien under Chinese law and compare it with the concept of security rights under insolvency law, with a view to examining whether a maritime lien has the same function as a security right. This chapter will also look into the current Chinese legislation on enforcing a maritime lien in light of competing insolvency proceedings. In addition, the role of a maritime lien in cross-border insolvency circumstances will be analysed. This is an area drawing little concern from Chinese lawmakers.

2. Maritime lien under Chinese Law

The main scope of maritime liens is set out in Articles 21 to 34 of the Chinese Maritime Code 1992.

2.1 Recognised maritime liens

In respect of provisions on maritime liens, the Chinese Maritime Code was drafted on the basis of a draft version of the International Convention on Maritime Liens and Mortgages which was considered at the diplomatic conference in Geneva in April 1993.[5] The Chinese Maritime Code defines a maritime lien as a right of the claimant to take priority in compensation against shipowners, bareboat charterers or ship operators with respect to the ship which gave rise to the said claim.[6] Payment for wages, other remuneration, crew repatriation and social insurance costs made by the master and crewmembers; claims in respect of loss of life or personal injury occurring in the operation of the ship; payment for ship's tonnage dues, pilotage dues, harbour dues and other port charges; salvage payment; and compensation for loss of, or damages resulting from, tortious acts in the course of the operation of the ship are recognised as maritime liens under Chinese law.[7]

2.2 Enforcement of maritime liens

Article 28 of the Chinese Maritime Code provides that a maritime lien shall be enforced by the court by means of arrest of the ship which gave rise to the said maritime lien.[8] Under Chinese law, an action can only be brought against a person and no action can be brought directly against a vessel or other property. Arrest of ships is established as a part of maritime claims preservation in Chinese law and is regulated by the general rule of maritime claims preservation, which is set out in Chapter III Section 1 of the Special Maritime Procedure Law.

---

5 The 1993 Maritime Liens and Mortgages Convention had not been published officially at that time.
6 Article 21 of the Maritime Code 1992.
7 Article 22 of the Maritime Code 1992.
8 Article 28 of the Maritime Code provides: 'A maritime lien shall be enforced by the court by arresting the ship that gave rise to the said maritime lien.'

The claimant who wishes to apply for the arrest of a ship must file a written application to the competent maritime court. In the application, the particulars of the maritime claim, reasons for the application, the name of the ship and the amount of security required should be specified with relevant evidence attached. When the supporting documents are in another language, a Chinese translation is required. The maritime court, having accepted the application, is to make an order within 48 hours based on its discretion. Where the arrest of the ship is ordered, it will be executed forthwith; where the conditions for the arrest of ship are not met, the court will make an order rejecting the application.

2.3 Characteristics of maritime liens

The maritime lien is said to represent one of the most striking features of maritime law.[9] The characteristics of maritime liens were well illustrated in the classical decision of *The Bold Buccleugh*[10] where a maritime lien was described as a privileged charge on maritime property arising by operation of law.[11] Such a lien does not depend on possession of the property or on agreement; it accrues from the moment of the event which gives rise to a cause of action and travels with the property.[12] Maritime liens are 'secret' in that there is no requirement for registration; thus a maritime lien cannot be lost by the sale of the property to a *bona fide* third party purchaser. A maritime lien also consists partly of the right to have the ship itself seized to provide pre-judgment security if it is not released on bail or in return for the provision of security.[13] More importantly, a maritime lien is also considered as a 'privilege'. This refers to the high priority enjoyed by a maritime lien holder.[14] A maritime lien is enforceable against other creditors, whether secured or unsecured, and takes precedence over all other creditors whether the claims of those creditors arose before or after the creation of the lien.[15] Therefore, such liens give claimants an effective and powerful weapon which secures and prefers a restricted list of maritime claims.

These characteristics are also reflected in the relevant provisions of the Chinese Maritime Code 1992. Article 21 of the Maritime Code 1992 defines a maritime lien as the right of the claimant, subject to the provisions of claims listed in Article 22 of the Code, to take priority in compensation

---

9 D.R. Thomas, *Maritime Liens* (London, Stevens, 1980), p.2. Along with limitation of liability, it is perhaps the most striking feature of maritime law.

10 *The Bold Buccleugh* (1850) 7 Moo PC 267.

11 Ibid, per Sir John Jervis at 285. The judge stated that a maritime lien 'gives a privilege or claim upon the thing, to be carried into effect by legal process'.

12 Ibid.

13 *The Father Thames* [1979] 1 Lloyd's Rep. 364, per Sheen J at 368.

14 D.R. Thomas, *Maritime Liens* (London, Stevens, 1980), p.12.

15 This is subject to existing possessory liens, statutory right of detention and other litigation costs.

against shipowners, bareboat charterers or ship operators with respect to the ship which gave rise to the said claim. The meaning of the word 'priority' is further clarified in Article 25 of the Chinese Maritime Code which provides that a maritime lien is ranked higher than a possessory lien or a mortgage.[16] The fact that a maritime lien can only be enforced by means of ship arrest means that a maritime lien remains inchoate until it is enforced by arrest of the ship.[17] Furthermore, Article 26 of the Chinese Maritime Code, which provides that maritime liens will not be extinguished by the transfer of the ownership of the ship, reflects the characteristic that a maritime lien travels with the vessel surviving its conventional sale.[18]

3. Insolvency and security rights under Chinese law

3.1 General insolvency law principles

The basic scheme of the legislation on insolvency law is that the unsecured creditors of an insolvent company are to rank proportionately subject to statutory provision as to preferential payments.[19] In order to achieve this result, there are provisions restricting the right of a creditor to make use of procedures outside the liquidation. Finch in *Corporate Insolvency Law* submits that the *pari passu* principle is often said to constitute a fundamental rule of corporate insolvency law, which holds that, in a winding up, unsecured creditors are to share rateably in those assets of the insolvent company that are available for residual distribution.[20]

This approach is reflected also in Chinese legislation. The Chinese Enterprise Insolvency Law 2006 and the judicial interpretations of the Enterprise Insolvency Law issued by the Supreme People's Court[21] provide the basic principles in relation to the priorities for creditors' claims, each of which operates in parallel with the other. The general principle is that

16   As a general position of Chinese law, a possessory lien or a mortgage is ranked higher than unsecured debts: see Article 170 of the Property Law of the People's Republic of China.

17   The Maritime Code only applies to sea-going ships and other mobile units, but does not include ships or craft to be used for military or public service purposes, nor small ships of less than 20 tons gross tonnage: see Article 3 of the Maritime Code.

18   Article 26 of the Maritime Code provides: 'Maritime liens shall not be extinguished by virtue of the transfer of the ownership of the ship, except those that have not been enforced within 60 days of a public notice on the transfer of the ownership of the ship made by a court at the request of the transferee when the transfer was effected.'

19   For example, *In re Redman (Builders) Ltd* [1964] 1 W.L.R. 541.

20   Vanessa Finch, *Corporate Insolvency Law: Perspective and Principles* (2nd edn, Cambridge, Cambridge University Press, 2009), p.599.

21   Provisions (I) of the Supreme People's Court on Several Issues concerning the Application of the Enterprise Insolvency Law of the People's Republic of China was issued and came into force in 2011; and Provisions (II) of the Supreme People's Court on Several Issues concerning the Application of the Enterprise Insolvency Law of the People's Republic of China was issued and came into force in 2013.

public interest debts, employees' benefits (including existing employees' benefits), social welfares and taxes should be paid before general unsecured bankruptcy debts; and if the claims within the same rank cannot be fully repaid, they shall be repaid in proportion.[22]

3.2 Security rights in insolvency proceedings

The general rule in bankruptcy or winding up is that all creditors are paid proportionately, sharing in the proceeds of realised assets. The principal reason therefore why a lender prefers to take a security is to avoid the effect of this proportionate rule.[23] In other words, the most compelling reason for the taking of security is that such a device separates secured creditors from unsecured creditors in the event of the debtor's insolvency.

Again, the Chinese Enterprise Insolvency Law 2006 reflects the above consideration. Article 109 of the Chinese Enterprise Insolvency Law provides that a secured creditor, who has security over a specific asset of the debtor, is entitled to obtain payment in priority over the secured asset. Therefore, it is established in Chinese law, a valid security allows the creditor to avoid the general rule of sharing proportionately and to realise the security separately from the general insolvency proceeding.[24] The remaining question is whether a maritime lien should be regarded as a security right.

3.3 Maritime lien and security right

A maritime lien, as a type of maritime claim, has three aspects of enforcement, namely the interim or provisional remedy aspect, the jurisdictional aspect and the security aspect (See D. C. Jackson, *Enforcement of Maritime Claims* (4th edn, Richmond, LLP, 2005) 1.). The security function of a maritime lien has also been pointed out by various writers. When describing the efficacy of maritime liens, Thomas submits that '[t]he material advantage which accrues to a maritime lienee is that from the moment service is rendered to or damage done by an encumbranced *res*, the lienee is provided with a security for his claim to the value of the res'.[25] William Tetley described a maritime lien as 'a secured right peculiar to maritime law'.[26]

---

22 Articles 41 to 43 and 131 of the Chinese Enterprise Insolvency Law 2006.
23 R.M. Goode, *Goode on Commercial Law* (4th edn, London, Penguin, 2010), pp.619–620.
24 Where the value of the secured asset is not sufficient to repay the whole secured claim, the fee related to realisation of security rights shall be repaid prior to the secured principal and interests payments unless otherwise agreed by the security provider and secured creditor. See Article 74 of the Supreme People's Court on Several Issues concerning the Application of the Security Law of People's Republic of China effective as of 13 December 2000.
25 D.R. Thomas, *Maritime Liens* (London, Stevens, 1980), p.4.
26 William Tetley, *Maritime Liens and Claims* (2nd edn, Montreal, International Shipping Publications, 1998), p.59.

With regard to the functions of arrest of ship in civil law countries, D.C. Jackson has commented as follows:

'. . . The questions of jurisdiction and arrest will be dealt with usually in the Code of Procedure and in many cases independently of each other. Often "arrest" is relevant only as an interim remedy and there will usually be provision for security (such as bail or guarantee) which may prevent arrest or cause the property to be released from arrest. Jurisdiction on the merits may be based on a more substantial contact between the country and the issue than the seizure of a ship temporarily there.

Security for the merits claim is based on the classification of claims as preferred claims which give priority over unsecured creditors and, in addition, may confer enforceability of the claim against purchasers from the person against whom the claim is made. These preferred claims are sometimes labelled "liens" and will be set out in the Maritime or Commercial Code.'[27]

As a codified legal system, the above statement also applies to arrest of ships and maritime liens under Chinese law. Those so-called 'preferred claims' are listed in Article 22 of the Chinese Maritime Code 1992 and are labelled as 'maritime liens'. However, the literal meaning of the Chinese expression referring to a 'maritime lien' is actually a 'right of priority upon ship'. In this sense, a maritime lien appears to be regarded as a right of priority rather than a lien under Chinese law. The right of priority is a concept that usually exists in the property law of a codified legal system. Such a concept of priority right may be found in the French Civil Code, the Italian Civil Code, etc.[28] However, there is no such concept of 'right of priority' existing under the Chinese civil law framework although it is a codified system which to some extent reflects a certain impact of French and German law.[29] There are similar rights existing under Chinese law but these rights are provided separately in different statutes. For example, the Chinese Civil Aviation Law 2009[30] provides in Chapter III section 3 that claimants for remuneration for rescuing an aircraft and for necessary expenses incurred for the custody

27 See D.C. Jackson, *Enforcement of Maritime Claims* (4th edn, Richmond LLP, 2005), Chapter 15, para 14.3 and 15.4.
28 See Book III, Title XVIII (Of Privileges and Mortgages), Chapter 2 (Of Privileges) of the French Civil Code, under which it is provided in Article 2095 that a privilege is a right which the quality of his credit confers upon a creditor of being preferred to the others, though mortgage-creditors. The English version of the French Civil Code is available at <http://www.napoleon-series.org/research/government/c_code.html> accessed 12 October 2015. Under Italian law, privileges are provided in Book VI, Chapter III. See the Chinese translation cited in Mingrui Guo, Xiang Zhong and Yanli Si, *A Study on Priority Right* (Beijing, Peking University Press, 2004), pp.233–245.
29 Mingrui Guo, Xiang Zhong and Yanli Si, *A Study on Priority Right* (Beijing, Peking University Press, 2004), pp.171–172.
30 Adopted at the 16th session of the Standing Committee of the Eighth National People's Congress on 30 October 1995. The current version is as revised in 2009.

of the aircraft may enjoy a right to take precedence before other claims in compensation against the owner of the aircraft.[31] Similarly, Article 21 of the Chinese Maritime Code 1992 provides that certain maritime claims may take priority in compensation against shipowners, bareboat charterers or ship operators with respect to the ship which gave rise to the said claim.[32] Both of the above two rights are termed as 'rights of priority' in the Chinese versions of the statutes whereas the word 'lien' is used in the English versions, translated as 'civil aircraft liens' and 'maritime liens', respectively. These facts make a maritime lien as well as a civil aircraft lien unique concepts under the Chinese legal framework and, therefore, the nature of such rights appears to be unclear.

With regard to the security function of a maritime lien, the Chinese Maritime Code provides an answer to some extent. The Chinese Maritime Code provides that a maritime lien is 'the right of the claimant ... to take priority in compensation against shipowners, bareboat charterers or ship operators';[33] a maritime lien shall not be extinguished by virtue of the change of the ownership of the ship;[34] and a maritime lien is enforced by arrest of the particular ship.[35] It would appear that Chinese law provides the maritime lien holder with a right of preference and a high priority in ranking; which travels with the property, namely the ship; and it is enforced by arresting the ship. It is therefore arguable that a maritime lien should properly be regarded as a right of separation entitling the creditor to keep the collateral out of the bankruptcy or liquidation. The fact that ship arrest in China may only be decided by a Maritime Court further supports this proposition.[36]

In addition, various Chinese scholars consider that a maritime lien should be regarded as a special type of security right affiliating to *jus in re aliena* under the Chinese property law framework.[37] This view is further supported by the fact that the section regarding maritime liens is located together with those on ownership and mortgage of ships in Chapter 2 of the

---

31 Articles 18 and 19 of the Chinese Civil Aviation Law 2009. Article 18 of the Civil Aviation Law provides: 'A civil aircraft lien is the right of the claimant, subject to the provisions of Article 19 of this Law, to take priority in compensation against the owner and lessee of the civil aircraft with respect to the civil aircraft which gave rise to the said claim.' Article 19 provides that following obligatory rights shall be entitled to civil aircraft liens: (1) remuneration for rescuing the civil aircraft; and (2) necessary expenses incurred for the custody of the civil aircraft. An inverse order rule is also provided by Article 19 for the ranking of the above claims.

32 Article 21 of the Maritime Code 1992.

33 Article 21 of the Maritime Code 1992.

34 Article 26 of the Maritime Code 1992.

35 Article 28 of the Maritime Code 1992.

36 Article 13 of Maritime Procedure Law of PRC 1999 provides that Article 13 applications for maritime preservation prior to proceedings shall be submitted to the Maritime Court of the place where the property is located. Arrest of a ship is regarded as a special type of maritime preservation so that it shall be also enforced through a Maritime Court.

37 See Yuzhuo Si and Zhiwen Li (eds), *Study on the Theories of Chinese Maritime Law* (Beijing, Peking University Press, 2009), pp.91–102.

Chinese Maritime Code, entitled 'Ships'.[38] It is therefore argued that the intention of the draftsmen of the Maritime Code was to regard the maritime lien as a type of property right.[39] However, the obstacle for this point of view is the applicable law for maritime liens. According to Article 272 of the Chinese Maritime Code, matters concerning maritime liens are governed by the law of the place of the court hearing the case, *lex fori*. In this sense, it would appear that the Chinese Maritime Code has followed the approach of *The Halcyon Isle*[40] and that therefore a maritime lien is regarded as a procedural right under Chinese law. However, the decision in *The Halcyon Isle* is mainly for the purpose of protecting the interests of English shipowners and mortgagees rather than deciding the true nature of a maritime lien.[41] In this regard, Article 272 of the Maritime Code shall not affect the nature and function of the maritime lien. It is further submitted that *lex fori* being the applicable law is not due to the nature of the maritime lien but to the fact that a maritime lien is enforced via a specific procedure and such procedure is subject to *lex fori*.[42]

4. Enforcement of maritime lien in competition with insolvency proceedings

4.1 Ship arrest in insolvency proceedings

Under English law, when the claimant who has a statutory right *in rem* enforces it by arresting the ship before the filing of the petition in a compulsory winding-up[43] or the passing of resolution in a voluntary winding-up,[44] he will not be affected by the subsequent winding-up proceedings.[45] It has been confirmed through a number of decisions that an admiralty writ *in rem*

38 Chapter II of the Chinese Maritime Code 1992.
39 Hai Li, *A Study on Real Rights in Ships* (Beijing, Law Press, 2002), p.149.
40 *Bankers Trust International Ltd v Todd Shipyards Corporation (The Halcyon Isle)* [1980] 2 Lloyd's Rep. 325.
41 As per Lord Diplock, recognition of foreign maritime liens may not only affect the priorities as between classes of creditors but '. . . *may also extend the classes of persons who are entitled to bring an action against a particular ship, i.e., by including among them some who, although they have no claim against the current owner of the ship, have claims against his predecessor in ownership.*' See ibid, at 329. In the dissenting view, Lord Salmon and Lord Scarman were of the view that a maritime lien was a right of property given by way of security for maritime claims; see ibid, at 339. Also, in Reiter Petroleum Inc v The Ship "Sam Hawk" [2015] FCA 1005, the court held that maritime liens should be considered as being of a substantive nature under Australian law.
42 Yuzhuo Si and Zhiwen Li (eds), *Study on the Theories of Chinese Maritime Law* (Beijing, Peking University Press, 2009), p.94.
43 *Re Aro Co* [1980] Ch 196.
44 *John Carlbom & Co Ltd v Zafiro (Owners) (The Zafiro)* [1959] 1 Lloyd's Rep. 359.
45 The claimant must nevertheless ask for leave to continue but such request will almost certainly be granted.

may give rise to a security interest upon the vessel.[46] Such a type of security is described as a procedural security, making the asset in question a security for the claimant to which the plaintiff can have recourse for the satisfaction of his judgment even if the other party has meanwhile become bankrupt or gone into liquidation.[47] On this basis, where a company in court-protected administration (such as winding-up) achieves a moratorium against creditors' claims, the claimant may seek to attach assets of the debtor elsewhere in the world, for example by ship arrest, to achieve secured status, which is regarded as a statutory lien.[48] Nevertheless, where the event giving rise to a statutory right *in rem* occurs after the commencement of the winding-up or the passing of the resolution, the claimant will be unsecured and the court will stay any proceedings commenced in Admiralty.

In terms of the relationship between admiralty proceedings and insolvency proceedings, there are no explicit rules or regulations under Chinese law. Article 109 of the Chinese Enterprise Insolvency Law 2006[49] provides that where a creditor is secured by an encumbrance over the property belonging to the insolvent enterprise, the creditor may enforce such right and be paid prior to other creditors.[50] According to the Special Maritime Procedure Law 1999, the arrest of ships is provided as a special type of 'maritime preservation', which refers to a compulsory measure, upon the request of the claimant, ordered by Maritime Courts against the property of the respondent to ensure that any maritime claims of the claimant can be fulfilled.[51] If the 'maritime preservation' can be interpreted as measure of encumbrance under the Insolvency Law, arrest of ship under Chinese law should have the same security function as it does under English law. Furthermore, whilst there is no action *in rem* under Chinese law, Article 25 of the Special Maritime Procedure Law 1999 provides that the application of a maritime claimant to arrest the involved ship will not be affected, even if the name of the defendant party cannot be ascertained.[52] Such a position potentially supports the proposition that arrest of ships under Chinese law provides true security to the claimant.

46 *John Carlbom & Co Ltd v Zafiro (Owners) (The Zafiro)* [1959] 1 Lloyd's Rep. 359; *Re Aro Co* [1980] Ch 196; and *Cosco Bulk Carrier Co Ltd v Armada Shipping SA & Anor* [2011] EWHC 216 (Ch).

47 *Goode on Commercial Law* (4th edn), p.663.

48 See *The Monica S* [1968] P. 741; and *The James W Elwell* (1921) 8 Ll. L. Rep. 115. See also *Enforcement of Maritime Claim* (4th edn), Chapter 23.

49 The Enterprise Insolvency Law of the People's Republic of China was adopted at the 23rd meeting of the Standing Committee of the Tenth National People's Congress of the People's Republic of China on 27 August 2006 and came into effect as of 1 June 2007.

50 Article 109 of the Chinese Enterprise Insolvency Law 2006.

51 Article 12 of the Special Maritime Procedure Law of China 1999. The provisions on arrest of a ship are contained in section 2 of the second chapter of Maritime Procedure Law entitled 'Maritime Preservation'.

52 Article 25 of the Special Maritime Procedure Law of China 1999.

Having said this, clearer rules under Chinese law are needed in the case where a ship is arrested while the shipowner is insolvent; that is, the issue of whether the ship can be arrested outside the framework of an insolvency proceeding needs to be clarified by the Chinese lawmakers. In November 2013, the Supreme People's Court issued Provisions on Issues Relating to Ship Arrest and Judicial Sale (Draft for comments) which was published for the purpose of collecting public comments and opinions.[53] In the draft Provisions, Article 25 provided that only claims arising from maritime liens, maritime possessory liens and ship mortgages were to be separated from insolvency proceedings with the remaining part of the proceeds of the ship to be returned to the People's Court dealing with the owner's insolvency case. From this proposition, it would appear that, in the view of the Supreme People's Court, an unsecured maritime claim will be included in the insolvency proceedings. In other words, the right of arrest of a ship does not provide the claimant with a security, i.e. a right similar to a statutory lien under English law. The final version of the Provisions was issued by the People's Supreme Court on 28 February 2015 and came in to force on 1 March 2015. However, Article 25 of the Draft Provisions was not included in the final version. The position of maritime liens and arrest of ships under insolvency proceedings is therefore still awaiting clarification under Chinese law.

4.2 Maritime liens in insolvency proceedings

Although the position of ship arrest in relation to insolvency proceedings remains unclear under Chinese law, the position of maritime liens may be a different story. As mentioned earlier, it appears to be widely agreed that a maritime lien should be regarded as a security right under Chinese law, notwithstanding that such a position is not confirmed by the Chinese Maritime Code or indeed other legislation. In the context of the insolvency of a shipowner, it is submitted that a maritime lien should be treated as an encumbrance within the meaning of Article 109 of the Chinese Enterprise Insolvency Law.[54] It is further submitted that analogy may be drawn between a maritime lien and a contractor's lien on a construction project.[55] Pursuant to Article 286 of the Chinese Contract Law 1999, where the contract-offering party fails to pay the contract price, the contractor may apply to a People's Court for the auction of the construction project and the payment for the construction of the project is to be effected, with priority,

---

53 The public consultation was closed on 15 December 2013. However, for the sake of prudence, the Supreme Court has been consulting shipping law practitioners since March 2014.

54 Ying Jiang and Bo Wang, 'Enforcement of Maritime Liens under the Insolvency Proceeding', *Management & Technology of SME*, 2009, vol. 8. Article 109 of the Insolvency Law 2006 provides that 'secured creditor is entitled to obtain payment in priority over debtor's specific asset'.

55 Article 286 of the Contract Law 1999.

out of the proceeds from the conversion into money or auction of the said project.[56] This right of the contractor is deemed to be a security right and to be enforced according to the procedure of realising a security right as provided in the Civil Procedure Law 2012.[57] Following such an approach, a maritime lien should also be regarded as a security right and could be enforced separately from the insolvency proceedings.

Such a position was supported by the Provisions on Issues Relating to Ship Arrest and Judicial Sale (Draft for comments). As mentioned earlier, Article 25 of the Draft Provisions provided explicitly that a maritime lien can be enforced separately from insolvency proceedings. The sale of the ship belonging to the insolvent enterprise may be delegated to a Maritime Court[58] and the Maritime Court will deal with the registration and compensation for maritime liens, possessory liens[59] and ship mortgages. Where the proceeds of the ship are not exhausted, the Maritime Court will hand over the remainder to the court hearing the insolvency case. This article of the Draft Judicial Interpretation would have served to confirm that a maritime lien can be enforced notwithstanding the insolvency of the shipowner. It may be speculated that the primary reason why Article 25 was not included in the final version of the Provision that entered into force in March 2015 may have been that the Supreme People's Court was uncertain about the security function of ship arrest for ordinary maritime claims; and not that the Supreme court was trying to reject the concept of a maritime lien as a security right.

Furthermore, Article 22 of the final version of the Provisions on Issues Relating to Ship Arrest and Judicial Sale provides a list ranking maritime claims in which maritime liens are ranked before maritime possessory liens as well as ship mortgages. This provision is essentially a reproduction of Articles 24[60] and 25 of the Chinese Maritime Code. These provisions suggest that a maritime lien should take priority over a mortgage and therefore that a maritime lien appears to provide the claimants with stronger security than a mortgage.

---

56 Although no express word 'lien' is used in Article 286 of the Contract Law, it is implied that the contractor's right hereunder is in nature a type of 'lien'.

57 Articles 196 and 197 of the Chinese Civil Procedure Law 2012; see Junqiang Xu, 'Issues Regarding Connection of Maritime Proceedings with the Amended Civil Procedure Law of the People's Republic of China' (2013) 24(1) *Chinese Journal of Maritime Law* 85.

58 However, the Draft Provisions do not provide for the situation under which such delegation may be made; nor does it provide that the delegation shall be made by the claimant or the court hearing the insolvency case.

59 Here the possessory lien refers to the ship-repairer's possessory lien. See Article 24 of the Maritime Code 1992.

60 Article 24 of the Maritime Code provides that the legal costs and other expenses for the common interests of the claimants shall be deducted before paying the maritime lien holders. Such a position is also reflected in the list provided in Article 22 of the Provisions on Issues Relating to Ship Arrest and Judicial Sale where such expenses are listed before maritime lien.

4.3 Extinction of a maritime lien

In *The Two Ellens*,[61] Mellish LJ held that a maritime lien accrues and contin-ues to be binding on the ship until it is discharged, either by being satisfied or from the laches of the lien holder, or in any other way by which it may be discharged by law.[62] It is commonly agreed that there are various modes by which maritime liens may be extinguished, either in substance or in effect.[63]

With regard to the modes of extinction of maritime liens under Chinese law, Article 29 of the Chinese Maritime Code 1992 provides:

'A maritime lien shall, except as provided for in Article 26 of this Law, be extinguished under one of the following circumstances:

(1) The maritime claim attached by a maritime lien has not been enforced within one year of the existence of such maritime lien;
(2) The ship in question has been the subject of a forced sale by the court;
(3) The ship has been lost.
(4) The period of one year specified in sub-paragraph (1) of the pre-ceding paragraph shall not be suspended or interrupted.'

The above three circumstances set out in Article 29 are those under which the maritime lien is absolutely extinguished and destroyed. Article 29(1) refers to laches or delay in suit; Article 29(2) refers judicial sale; and Article 29(3) refers to destruction of the property. Besides these three modes, it is submitted by the editors of *Study on the Theories of Chinese Maritime Law* that the maritime lien may also be extinguished by satisfaction of claims and by provision of security under Chinese law.[64]

From the above, it appears that insolvency proceedings do not fall into any of the categories of extinction of a maritime lien as provided in Article 29 of the Chinese Maritime Code. Also, insolvency proceedings can hardly be interpreted as a method of satisfying a maritime claim in full or as a method of providing security. In terms of the provision of security, Chapter 6 of the Special Maritime Procedural Law 1999 provides for rules of maritime secu-rity. According to Article 93 of the Special Maritime Procedural Law, types of maritime security refer to cash, guarantee, mortgage or pledge. In this sense, the insolvency proceedings do not have the function of destroying a maritime lien or preventing a maritime lien from being enforced.

---

61 (1872) LR 4 PC 161.
62 (1872) LR 4 PC 161, at 169.
63 Different writers put forward different summaries on the modes of extinction of maritime liens.
64 Si Yuzhuo and Li Zhiwen (eds), *Study on the Theories of Chinese Maritime Law* (Beijing, Peking University Press, 2009), pp.111–115. The editors of the book list seven circum-stances under which the maritime lien will be extinguished including: satisfaction of claims, loss of the ship, delay in enforcement, delay in suit, judicial sale, confiscation of ship and provision of security.

5. Cross-border insolvency

5.1 Jurisdiction and conflict of law

Shipping is an international industry and ships are highly movable from jurisdiction to jurisdiction. Meanwhile, insolvency may also be international in nature. The financially distressed debtors may have assets or creditors in more than one country. Like traditional conflict of laws rules, cross-border insolvency focuses upon three areas, i.e. choice of law rules, jurisdiction rules and enforcement of judgment rules.[65] However, in relation to insolvency, the principal focus tends to be the recognition of foreign insolvency officials and their powers.

In terms of cross-border insolvency, it appears that the Chinese lawmakers does not pay much attention to this area. The only provision related to cross-border insolvency is Article 5 of the Enterprise Insolvency Law 2006. This Article allows a Chinese party to seek to enforce a Chinese court issued judgment in a foreign country in which the assets are located. The same applies to an overseas liquidator seeking recognition in China of an overseas court judgment or arbitral award relating to insolvency procedures involving assets located in China. The latter is subject to international bilateral or multilateral treaties to which China is a party, as well as public interests and the legitimate rights of creditors in China.[66]

In terms of the applicable law, the Law of the People's Republic of China on Choice of Law for Foreign-related Civil Relationships does not contain any specific provisions regarding the cross-border insolvency issue. It is therefore unclear whether the law of the place where insolvency proceedings have been commenced should be applicable to the merits and procedures of the insolvency. The applicable law issue remains to be clarified by the Chinese lawmakers.

5.2 Foreign maritime liens

As ships travel between jurisdictions all the time, a maritime lien may possibly occur and attach to the ship while she is in foreign waters. This draws the concern whether such a foreign maritime lien should be recognised when the ship is eventually arrested. One example could be the insolvency of O.W. Bunkers in 2014, which led to numerous actual and threatened vessel arrests. In some jurisdictions, such as the US and Canada, a local supplier is secured by a maritime lien for necessities and given priority status.[67] A number of bunker suppliers who incorporated US law into

---

65 Andrew Keay and Peter Walton, *Insolvency Law* (2nd edn, Jordans, 2011), p.385.
66 See Article 5 of the Chinese Enterprise Insolvency Law 2006.
67 For example, see *The Mana* [2006] EWHC 777 (Comm). In this case, O.W. Bunkers was also involved but it was before its bankruptcy.

their supply contracts contended that US law gives rise to a maritime lien permitting the arrest of ships elsewhere in the world. The foreign court was therefore obliged to assess the priority of claims based upon the governing law of the bunker supply contract.[68] The question is therefore what the applicable law is for a given maritime lien.

As mentioned above, Article 272 of the Chinese Maritime Code 1992 provides that matters of maritime liens are to be governed by the law of the place of the court hearing the case. Therefore, if a ship is arrested in China and the claimant relies upon a maritime lien, Chinese law will be applicable to the question of whether the claimant has a legitimate maritime lien. By virtue of the Chinese Maritime Code, only claims arising from seamen's wages, loss of life or personal injury, ship's tonnage dues, pilotage dues, harbour dues and other port charges, salvage payment and compensation for loss of, or damages resulting from, tortious acts in the course of the operation of the ship are recognised as maritime liens. Maritime suppliers' claims for necessities are not secured by maritime liens under Chinese law.

5.3 Foreign insolvency proceedings

Another situation where a maritime lien would interact with cross-border insolvency is where a claimant is trying to realise a maritime lien in one jurisdiction and the shipowner has started insolvency proceedings in another jurisdiction. An example of this situation is provided by the facts of *The Sanko Mineral*.[69] In this case, the defendant owner of the *MV Sanko Mineral* petitioned in Tokyo for the commencement of insolvency proceedings and entered into reorganisation proceedings on 23 July 2012. In May 2014, the Bank of Tokyo-Mitsubishi UFJ Ltd, which held a mortgage on the vessel, arrested the ship in England and the Bank subsequently obtained judgment on its claim, and the sale of the vessel was advertised. Later in July 2014, the claimant, Glencore, became aware of the notice of sale and applied to the court for permission to commence a claim *in rem* on the basis of an alleged maritime lien under US law and/or a statutory lien under Japanese law. The English court held that when a vessel was sold by the Admiralty Court, rights *in rem* were transferred to the sale proceeds and Glencore had not lost its statutory right of action *in rem*, although Glencore's claim for breach of the contract of carriage was found barred on other grounds.[70]

This example well illustrates how effectively a maritime lien can protect the creditor in circumstances where the shipowner is insolvent. The position of Chinese law in relation to maritime liens competing with foreign

---

68 Adrian Moylan, 'Bankruptcy and Unpaid Bunkers – A Global Dilemma for Shipping', *Maritime Risk International*, February 2015.

69 [2015] 1 Lloyd's Rep. 247.

70 The decision has been criticised; Case comment on Bank of Tokyo-Mitsuibishi UFJ Ltd v Owners of the MV Sanko Mineral ('The Sanko Mineral') [2014] EWHC 3927 (Admlty), p.3.

insolvency proceedings remains unclear but it appears that nothing in current Chinese legislation would prevent a Chinese court from enforcing a recognised maritime lien despite the existence of foreign insolvency proceedings. As mentioned above in section 4.1, the Chinese Enterprise Insolvency Law 2006 allows the recognition of foreign insolvency proceedings subject to certain requirements. Where the foreign insolvency proceedings are not recognised, a maritime lien can be enforced as usual; and even if the foreign insolvency proceedings are recognised by the Chinese court, as long as the security function of a maritime lien is admitted under Chinese law, the lien can still be enforced separately from the insolvency proceedings.[71]

6. Conclusion

To conclude, it appears that the security function of maritime liens has been widely recognised, notwithstanding that neither the Chinese Maritime Code nor other legislation confirms such a position. In the context of the insolvency of a shipowner, it is submitted that a maritime lien is to be treated as an encumbrance within the meaning of Article 109 of the Chinese Enterprise Insolvency Law.[72] If a provision similar to Article 25 of the Supreme People's Court's Provisions on Issues Relating to Ship Arrest and Judicial Sale (Draft for comments) is inserted in the Chinese Maritime Procedure Law 1999, the position of a maritime lien in insolvency proceedings would be clarified.

In terms of cross-border insolvency, the Chinese legislation is far from sufficient. As a result, it remains unclear how a maritime lien could operate in the circumstances of cross-border insolvency, although the Chinese Maritime Code 1992 provides that any issues related to maritime liens are to be governed by the law of the forum. There is arguably ample space remaining for Chinese lawmakers to fill up. Reference may here be made to the EC Regulation on insolvency proceedings (EC 1346/2000)[73] and the UNCITRAL Model Law on Cross-Border Insolvency.[74] Under both regimes, creditors' rights in Admiralty proceedings are unaffected by insolvency proceedings.

71 In addition, Article 47 of the Provisions (II) of the Supreme People's Court on Several Issues concerning the Application of the Enterprise Bankruptcy Law provides that where the court entertaining an insolvency case has difficulties in exercising its jurisdiction on maritime-related debts, the court's superior court may assign the relevant claims to a suitable court, namely a maritime court.

72 Ying Jiang and Bo Wang, 'Enforcement of Maritime Liens under the Insolvency Proceeding', (2009) 8 *Management & Technology of SME* 169.

73 See Philip Smart, 'Rights In Rem, Article 5 and the EC Insolvency Regulation: An English Perspective' (2006) 15 *International Insolvency Review* 17–55.

74 UNCITRAL, UNCITRAL Model Law on Cross-Border Insolvency with Guide to Enactment, <http://www.uncitral.org/pdf/english/texts/insolven/insolvency-e.pdf> accessed 9 October 2015.

7 Sea towage under Chinese law

Professor Lina Zhang

1. Introduction

Sea towage is a service by one vessel to another for a fixed remuneration, which is distinguished from marine transportation and salvage. In China towing is often divided into different types according to different standards and each classification has its own implications. In order to perform the towing operation, the tugowner and the tow party usually sign a towage contract. There are several sets of standard towage contracts[1] with different clauses in use in China. The Maritime Code of the People's Republic of China (the Maritime Code)[2] further provides some important clauses of the towage contract and stipulates that the contract of sea towage shall be made in writing.[3] Meanwhile, the towage contract can also be terminated in certain circumstances.[4] In the sea towage contract, both parties' rights and duties are very important and must be set out clearly. During the course of the sea towage, injury, death or property losses are often caused. Liability may arise between the tugowner and the tow party, and sometimes between the parties to the contract and a third party. The former is often deemed a liability in contract and governed by the contract; the latter is often deemed a liability in tort and governed by the law of tort[5] and other

---

1 See Chapter 7 of the Maritime Code, Articles 155–164.
2 Adopted at the 28th meeting of the Standing Committee of the Seventh National People's Congress on 7 November 1992 and effective on 1 July 1993.
3 Article 156 of the Maritime Code, 'A contract of sea towage shall be made in writing'.
4 Article 158 of the Maritime Code, 'If before the commencement of the towage service, due to force majeure or other causes not attributable to the fault of either party, the towage contract could not be performed, either party may cancel the contract and neither shall be liable to the other. In such event, the towage price that had already been paid shall be returned to the tow party by the tugowner, unless otherwise agreed upon in the towage contract . . .' Article 159, 'If after the commencement of the towage service, due to force majeure or other causes not attributable to the fault of either party, the towage contract could not be performed, either party may cancel the towage contract and neither shall be liable to the other.'
5 Tort Law of PRC, adopted at the 12th session of the Standing Committee of the Eleventh National People's Congress on 26 December 2009, came into force on 1 July 2010.

relevant regulations. Compared with other countries' maritime law, the Maritime Code of China contains a large number of provisions concerning sea towage contracts.[6] However, these provisions cannot meet the requirements of current towage practice and some of its provisions need reform to continue to provide a good legal foundation in future.

Sea towage, a category of operations at sea, emerged and has developed with the wide usage of powered vessels. In the early stages, towage was particularly used within the port area, inland waters and rivers and between coastal ports to provide assistance or service to barges, unpowered vessels and large vessels sailing into or out of the port or shifting within the port area. In the past 40 years, the demand for sea towage has gradually increased with the rapid development of marine transportation and marine oil development. The business of towage in connection with large barges, oil-drilling platforms, large oil equipment, salvage and very large and/or super-length floating objects has flourished. Many developed shipping countries have established specialised towing teams and companies which engage in national or international towing business. In the late 1970s, China also founded a specialised institute engaging in the business of sea towage, namely the China Towing Company. Although the business of sea towage is developing rapidly, at present there is not much by way of domestic law or regulatory framework adjusting the relations of towage, and there is also a lack of international treaties. Therefore, the operation of sea towage is mainly governed by the towage contracts provided by specialised towing companies. In China, sea towage is governed by the Maritime Code[7] and the China Towing Company standard terms of sea towage.[8]

2. General introduction to sea towage

2.1 Definition of towage

According to *Black's Law Dictionary*, towage is the act or service of towing a ship or vessel, usually by means of a small vessel called a tug.[9] Some scholars have adopted different definitions. According to Christopher Hill, towage is in essence a service by one vessel to another for a fixed remuneration. Generally speaking, towage is a service rendered by one vessel to another vessel and the most common reason for one vessel to require such service is that for one reason or another it lacks its own motive power.[10] The vessel that supplies the power in such an arrangement is typically called a tug, a term which encompasses many different types of vessels ranging

---

6 See Chapter 7 of the Maritime Code, Articles 155–164.
7 See Chapter 7 of the Maritime Code, Articles 155–164.
8 Xianglan Zhang, *Maritime Law* (Wuhan University Press, 2014), p.178.
9 Bryan A. Garner (editor-in-chief), *Black's Law Dictionary* (8th edn, Thomas, 2004), p.1528.
10 Christopher Hill, *Maritime Law* (LLP Ltd, 1998), p.363.

from large, ocean-going ships, coastal and harbour tugs to river vessels that push or pull a barge or a fleet of barges. Vessels that employ tugs and use their towing services range from barges and scows with no motive power of their own to ocean liners and freighters that use tugs for auxiliary power or to assist them in moving about in harbours and docks. The vessel towed may be manned, but barges and scows are often unmanned.[11] A vessel may emerge from a dockyard without functioning engines. Alternatively, she may be manoeuvring in a restricted area of water where her very size could cause her to be a hazard to other waterway traffic, were she to rely entirely on her own motive power.[12]

2.2 Types of towage

In China, towing is often divided into different types in accordance with different standards. Each classification has its own significance.

2.2.1 Towing astern, towing at side and pushing tow

According to the location of the tug and the tow, the types of towing encompass towing astern, towing at side and pushing tow. Towing astern means that the tug is in front of the barge or string of barges, called a tow, and pulls them. Towing astern is a common method of towage. Towing at side means the tow is secured to one or both sides of the towing vessel and is towed through the water. This method is usually used in the port area or inland waters or rivers and sometimes used in barge freight at sea. Towing by pushing ahead means the tow is secured to the front of the towing vessel and is pushed through the water. This method is often used in rivers or assisting the large ships in or out of dock or to turn them around. This classification is helpful to understand the meaning of towage at sea. Sea towage does not only involve towing astern, but also towing at side(s) and towing by pushing.

2.2.2 Towing within port area, towing between river and sea, towing between coastal ports, international towing

According to the area of the towing operation, the types of towage include towing within a port area, towing between river and sea, towing between coastal ports and international towing. Towing within a port area means that within some ports a tug will assist another vessel to enter or depart the port, shift within the port or provide other services; towing between river and sea means that the departure place and destination place are located respectively in an inland river or sea. Towing between coastal ports means

11 Thomas J. Schoenbaum, *Admiralty and Maritime Law* (4th edn, Thomas, 2004), p.717.
12 Christopher Hill, *Maritime Law* (LLP Ltd, 1998), p.364.

that both the place of departure and that of destination are located in the sea area of the same country. International towing, frequently referred to as 'ocean towing', means that the place of departure and the place of destination are located in the sea area of different countries.

In practice, the operation of towage in different sea areas is not governed by the same laws or regulations. This classification is helpful to inform the application of law to different categories of towage.

2.2.3 Daily hire towage, lump sum towage

According to the method of payment, the types of towing include daily hire towage and lump sum towage. In daily hire towage, the tow party pays the tugowner according to the daily rate of hire. Lump sum towage means that the tow party must pay the tugowner a lump sum fixed by both parties when they sign the towage contract.

3. Sea towage contract

3.1 Form of towage contract

Under the Maritime Code, a contract of sea towage is a contract whereby the tugowner undertakes to tow an object by sea with a tug from one place to another and the tow party pays the towage.[13] The contract of towage is an admiralty contract which is subject to general maritime law standards. In some countries, no written towage contract is required and in fact many towage contracts are verbal agreements. The general rules of contract law apply to the formation of towage contracts.[14] However, in China the situation is different and the Maritime Code stipulates clearly that a contract of sea towage shall be made in written form.[15] Oral towage contracts will not be recognised by the law in China. According to the Contract Law of the People's Republic of China (the Contract Law),[16] 'written form' refers to a form such as a written contractual agreement, letter or electronic data text (including a telegram, telex, fax, electronic data exchange and email) that can tangibly express the contents contained therein.[17]

3.2 Contents of towage contract

While in many countries there are customary standard towing conditions, and some countries permit the parties to negotiate the terms of the contract,

13 Article 155 of the Maritime Code.
14 Thomas J. Schoenbaum, *Admiralty and Maritime Law* (4th edn, Thomas, 2004), p.720.
15 Article 156 of the Maritime Code.
16 Adopted by the National People's Congress on 15 March 1999, and promulgated by the Presidential Order No.15, came into force on 1 October 1999.
17 Article 11 of the Contract Law.

the Maritime Code provides that the towage contract must include the name and address of the tugowner, name and address of the tow party, name and main particulars of the tug and name and main particulars of the object to be towed, the horse power of the tug, the place of commencement of the towage and the destination, the date of commencement of the towage price and the method of payment thereof, as well as other relevant matters.[18]

In China, the standard towage terms in common use are the China Towing Co Towage Contract (Daily Hire) and the China Ocean Engineering Services Ltd Towage Contract (Lump Sum). The former contains notably the following clauses: Tug and Towage Operations, Period of Hire, Port of Delivery, Port of Redelivery, Hire Rate, Charges and Expenses to be borne by Tug Owner, Charges and Expenses to be borne by Charterer, Residues of Fuel Oil, Seaworthiness of Object to be Towed, Infringement, Business beyond the Contract, Weather Conditions and Cast-off, Special Agreement, Cancellation, Responsibility for Damages Sustained by Object to be Towed and Third Parties, Responsibility for Damage Sustained by Tug, Salvage and Arbitration.

The latter terms include two parts. The first part contains the clauses Date and Place of Contract, Tugowner (disponent owner)/place of business, Tow-party/place of business, Tug (Name, Gross tonnage, Dimensions, Main power), Tow (Name, Gross tonnage, Dimensions, Towing draft), Place of departure, Place of destination, Lump sum towage price/each instalment, Payment of lump sum and other amounts, Free time at place of departure, Free time at place of destination, Demurrage rate, Tug's daily rate of hire, Date of departure, Cancelling date, Notice of arrival at destination and additional clauses.[19] The second part covers Object to be Towed, Towage Price and Conditions of Payment, Notice of Expected Arrival, Seaworthiness, Riding Crew, Connecting and Releasing Tow, Cancellation, Delay in Commencement of Voyage, Impossibility of Performance of Towage Service, Delay in Releasing Tug at Destination, Time Lost by Tug during Voyage, Port Charges and Expenses, No Claim for Salvage, Deviation, Immunities, Penalties, Lien, Substitution, General, Claim, Brokerage and Arbitration.

Although the Maritime Code and such standard contracts provide the basis for the contents of towage contracts, the parties are entitled to negotiate the terms of the contract.

3.3 Cancellation of towage contract

Once the towage contract has been agreed, it is binding. The parties must perform their duties according to the terms of the contract. Neither party

18 Article 156 of the Maritime Code.
19 Part I 17 of Towage Contract (Lump Sum) of China Ocean Engineering Service Ltd.

may unilaterally modify or cancel the contract. Otherwise, liability for breach of contract will arise. However, the laws in many countries still stipulate that the parties shall be entitled to cancel the contract when the objective situation has changed significantly so that the towage contract cannot be performed or continue to be performed.

According to Article 94(iv) of the Contract Law, the parties may terminate the contract if the other party delays performance or is otherwise in breach of the contract, thereby frustrating the purpose of the contract. This provision also applies to towage contracts. Therefore, the tow party will be entitled to cancel the towage contract if the tugowner does not supply a tug and make her seaworthy and tow-worthy in accordance with the agreed time and place; meanwhile, the tugowner will be entitled to cancel the towage contract if the tow party cannot make the towed object tow-worthy in accordance with the agreed time and place. The other party will be entitled to cancel the contract and claim compensation if one party breaches the towage contract.

Under the Maritime Code, if before the commencement of the towage service, due to *force majeure* or other causes not attributable to the fault of either party, the towage contract cannot be performed, either party may cancel the contract and neither will be liable to the other.[20] In such an event, any towage price that has already been paid is to be returned to the tow party by the tugowner, unless otherwise agreed in the towage contract.[21] If after the commencement of the towage service, due to *force majeure* or other causes not attributable to the fault of either party, the towage contract cannot be performed, either party may cancel the towage contract and neither shall be liable to the other.[22] Where the object towed is unable to reach its destination due to *force majeure* or other causes not attributable to the fault of either party, unless the towage contract provides otherwise, the tugowner may deliver the object towed to the tow party or its agent at a place near the destination or at a safe port or anchorage chosen by the tugmaster and the contract of towage will be deemed to have been fulfilled.[23]

In practice, many standard contracts also include a cancellation clause. For example, the Towage Contract (Lump Sum) of China Ocean Engineering Service Ltd includes a cancellation clause as follows:

'In the event of war, warlike operations, hostilities, rebellions, riots, civil commotions, acts of terrorism or sabotage, strikes, lockouts, disputes, stoppages or labour disturbances, prohibition of navigation, requisition of ships, blockades and similar events, hindering the performance, the

---

20 Article 158 of the Maritime Code.
21 Ibid.
22 Article 159 of the Maritime Code.
23 Article160 of the Maritime Code.

Tugowner shall be entitled to cancel this contract, or to deliver the Tow to an alternative destination subject to the provision. Should the Tow be unable to commence the voyage at the date specified for any reason other than fault of the Tugowner, the Tugowner shall have the right to cancel this Contract and be released from this obligation under this Contract to perform the towage, in which case, the Tow-party shall compensate the Tugowner hire at the rate provided from the time the Tug sails from her station place to the place of departure until she returns to her original station place. Should the Tug not be ready for the towage service by the date specified, the Tow-party shall be entitled to cancel this Contract or require a substitute tug.'[24]

There are thus detailed provisions in relation to the cancellation of towage contracts in the standard towage contract. Permitted causes for cancellation of the towage contract are generally attributable to either breach of the contract by one of the parties or *force majeure* or other causes not attributable to the fault of either party.

4. Obligations and rights of tugowner and tow party

4.1 Tugowner's rights and obligations

4.1.1 Tugowner's rights

(A) TOWAGE FEE

Under a sea towage contract, the tugowner is entitled to request the tow party to pay the towage price when the obligations have been performed. As mentioned in the above, the sea towage contract may be in the form of a Daily Hire Contract or a Lump Sum Contract and the method of payment under each is very different. Under the Daily Hire Contract, the tow party pays the tugowner a sum on signing the contract, and at the commencement date of hire pays the hire of 30 days in advance according to the daily rate of hire and pays the same in advance each successive month, to be settled within two weeks from the date of termination of the services in conformity with the terms of the contract. Under a Lump Sum Contract, the payment terms usually involve a lump sum towage price paid in instalments. Each instalment will fall due, respectively, upon signing the contract, on sailing from the place of departure, or on sailing from or passing a particular point; and the balance is to be paid on arrival at destination.

It is noteworthy that the tugowner may deliver the towed object to the tow party or its agent at a place near the destination or at a safe port or an anchorage chosen by the tugmaster if the object towed cannot reach

24 Part II 16 of Towage Contract (Lump Sum) of China Ocean Engineering Service Ltd.

its destination due to *force majeure* or other causes not attributable to the fault of either party. If that happens, the tugowner will be deemed to have fulfilled the obligations and be entitled to claim the full towage price.[25]

(B) THE LIEN ON THE OBJECT TOWED

In accordance with Article 161 of the Maritime Code, where the tow party fails to pay the towage price or other reasonable expenses as agreed, the tugowner shall have a lien on the object towed. Standard towage terms in China usually contain a clause providing for such a lien. Under the Towage Contract (Lump Sum) of China Ocean Engineering Services Ltd, the tugowner has a maritime lien on the tow if the tow party fails to pay the towage price or other sums payable under the contract including any costs and expenses incurred in exercising the lien.

The provision concerning the lien under the Maritime Code is in accordance with the Property Law of the People's Republic of China (the Property Law).[26] According to the Property Law,[27] in case an obligor (debtor) fails to pay its due debts, the creditor is entitled to a lien on the obligor's movable properties of which he has lawful possession, and is entitled to seek preferred payments from that movable property.

Therefore, the Maritime Code and the Property Law apply to liens arising from towing operation. That means, after completing the towing operation, the tug party is entitled to convert the towed object under lien into money, or seek preferred payments from the money raised at auction or sell the towed object under lien if the tow party fails to pay the towage price or other reasonable expenses incurred.

(C) DECISION TO SALVAGE

In the course of towage, the object towed is at all times under the management of the tugmaster. Should the object towed be in peril at sea, the tugowner will be obligated to rescue. Therefore the tugmaster is granted the corresponding rights. Once the object towed encounters danger or risk at sea, the tugmaster is entitled, on behalf of the tow party, to seek or receive salvage services from other ships or persons in order to protect the object towed. Any charges thereby incurred will be borne by the tow party.

---

25 Article 160 of the Maritime Code.
26 Adopted at the 5th session of the Tenth National People's Congress of the People's Republic of China on 16 March 2007 and came into effect on 1 October 2007.
27 Article 230 of the Property Law.

4.1.2 Tugowner's obligations

(A) FURNISHING THE TUG AND MAKING THE TUG SEAWORTHY

Under the Maritime Code in China, the tugowner shall, before and at the beginning of the towage, exercise due diligence to make the tug seaworthy and tow-worthy and to properly man the tug and equip it with gears and tow lines and to provide all other necessary supplies and appliances for the intended voyage.[28] Standard towage contracts in use in Japan also provide that the tugowner shall, at the commencement of the towage, exercise due diligence in ensuring that the tug is seaworthy and properly manned, equipped and supplied, and also furnish towing ropes and other towing gear to be used.[29] However, there are no similar provisions in some standard towage contracts in China. For example, the Towage Contract (Daily Hire) of China Towing Co and the Towage Contract Lump Sum of China Ocean Engineering Services Ltd fail to provide the relevant clauses. These clauses are about the obligations of the tugowner and ought to appear in the standard contract; otherwise it is not fair to the tow party. Moreover, under the law of China the standard towage contract should include similar provisions because the obligation of seaworthiness not only binds the tow party, but also the tugowner.

(B) THE TOWING OPERATION

In the course of the sea towage, unless otherwise agreed upon in the towage contract, the tugowner will be generally in charge of directing the towing operation. The operations of connecting and releasing the tow and towing shall be at the absolute direction of the tugmaster. It is a condition of the towage contract that the agreed route or, if none stated, the customary route, is open to the tug and tow and remain navigable; the tugowner is under no obligation to perform or complete the towage by any other route. In the event when the tow disconnects from the tug during the course of the towage, the tug is to make all reasonable endeavours to reconnect the tow, and the tugowner cannot claim payment of salvage from the tow party, unless the tug has rendered services to the tow not contemplated by the towage contract.[30]

(C) REASONABLE DISPATCH

The tugowner must finish the towing operation as quickly as possible and not delay unreasonably. During the course of towage, the tugowner must,

---

28 Article 157 of the Maritime Code.
29 Part III 4 of NIPPONTOW Towage Contract (Lump Sum Basis).
30 Xianglan Zhang, *Maritime Law* (Wuhan University Press, 2014), p.184.

as quickly as possible, tow the object to be towed from the place of departure to the place of destination in the period agreed under the towage contract, or, in the absence of such agreement, by the usual route of operation. Certainly, reasonable delay and deviation will be allowed. The tug may at any time during the course of the towage and until redelivery of the tow at the place of destination render assistance to any vessels in distress for the purpose of saving life or property, i.e. by calling at any place for fuel, medical aid, repairs, supplies or other necessaries or landing disabled seamen.[31]

(D) DELIVERY OF THE OBJECT TOWED

The tugowner is to notify the tow party and deliver the object towed according to the condition agreed by the parties at the place of destination. In the case that the object towed could not reach its destination due to *force majeure* or other causes not attributable to the fault of either party, the tugowner may deliver the object towed to the tow party or its agent at a place near the destination or at a safe port or an anchorage chosen by the tugmaster. It shall be deemed that the tugowner will have performed the obligation of delivery.[32]

4.2 Tow party's right and obligations

4.2.1 Tow party's right

(A) THE RIGHT TO RECLAIM THE TOWAGE PRICE

If the towage contract is cancelled before the commencement of the towage service due to *force majeure* or other causes not attributable to the fault of either party, then neither party will be liable to the other. In such an event, the tow party will be entitled to reclaim the towage price, unless otherwise agreed in the towage contract.[33]

(B) THE RIGHT TO BE TOWED

For the tow party, the aim of the towage contract is to tow the object from one place to another through the services of the tugowner. The tow party obtains the right to be towed by paying the towage price. The tow party has the right to require the tugowner to provide the towage service according to the conditions agreed, finish the towage operation and deliver the object towed at the place of destination.

---

31 Faxiang Yuan, *Bilingual Textbook on Maritime Law* (Peking University Press, 2014), p.257.
32 Article 160 of the Maritime Code.
33 Article 158 of the Maritime Code.

4.2.2 Tow party's obligations

(A) DELIVERY OF A TOW-WORTHY OBJECT

Under the Maritime Code, the tow party must, before and at the beginning of the towage, make all necessary preparations therefore and exercise due diligence to make the object to be towed tow-worthy.[34] It must provide a true account of the object to be towed and provide a certificate of tow-worthiness and other documents issued by the relevant survey and inspection organisations. There are more detailed regulations in standard towage contracts in use in China, usually along the following lines. The tow party will be responsible for the seaworthiness of the object to be towed and must, not later than the date of departure specified in the contract, make the object to be towed ready in all respects (including navigation lights, lashing wires and special towing gear or equipment) for the towage service and to maintain it in such seaworthy condition as will meet the requirements of the underwriter's surveyor or a recognised Classification Society and other relevant documents. The commencement of the towage will not constitute any warranty on the part of the tugowner or tugmaster that the object to be towed is seaworthy for the towage.[35]

(B) FOLLOWING THE COMMAND OF THE TUGMASTER

In the course of towing operations, the crew and other persons on the tow must take reasonable measures to cooperate with the tug's sailing and obey the commands of the tugmaster whenever the towing operation is under the direction of the tug. If it is required by the public authorities or deemed necessary by the tugmaster or the underwriter's surveyor to assign a riding crew on the tow (or on board the tug), the tow party will be responsible for the arrangement of a riding crew at his own expense. If the tow party so wishes, he may place a riding crew on board the tug or the tow at his own expense subject to the agreement of the tugmaster. All riding crew will at all times be under the orders of the tugmaster.

(C) SAFE PORT WARRANTY

The tow party warrants[36] that the place of departure and destination and any intermediate places to call in connection with the towage contract or at the request of the tow party, will in all respects be safe for the tug and tow to enter, lie in and depart from. Standard towage contracts also stipulate that

---

34 Article 157, paragraph 2 of the Maritime Code.
35 Part II 2 of Towage Contract (Lump Sum) of China Ocean Engineering Service Ltd.
36 Part II 4 of Towage Contract (Lump Sum) of China Ocean Engineering Service Ltd.

the tug and tow will remain always afloat at all stages of tide at the place of departure and destination and any intermediate places of call.[37]

(D) PAYMENT OF THE PRICE AND OTHER EXPENSES

The payment of the price and other expenses arising from the adventure is the core obligation of the tow party. The tow party must pay the towage price and other expenses according to the when, where and how under the towage contract. Under the standard towage contracts in China, the towage price specified in the contract is earned and paid in instalments as set forth in the contract. Upon commencement of the towage service, the towage price is deemed fully and irrevocably earned by the tugowner, even if the contract terminates because of any reasons other than those caused by the tugowner before the tow reaches its destination. However, if the contract terminates because of *force majeure*, the tugowner retains payments according to the ratio of the distance from the place of departure to the alternative place of redelivery to the length of the whole towage as originally contemplated. In addition, there may be other charges or expenses arising from the towage operation. Generally, the tug crew's wages and provisions, insurance on the tug, bunkers, agency fees, taxes and dues, pilotages, all port charges, canal tolls and other charges and expenses in connection with the tug are borne by the tugowner. Insurance on the tow, agency fees and dues, pilotage fees, all port charges, canal tolls, survey expenses for the tow and towage arrangements at all ports or places, cost of assisting and escorting tugs and/or boats required owing to narrow fairway, manoeuvring in port and for the purpose of safe navigation and other charges and expenses in connection with the tow are borne by the tow party.

(E) TAKING DELIVERY OF THE TOWED OBJECT

After receiving the notice of readiness tendering the towed object from the tugowner or the tugmaster, the tow party must take reasonable measures and take over the towed object in time at the place of destination. In the event that the towed object has not been able to reach its destination due to *force majeure* or other causes not attributable to the fault of either party, the towed object will be towed to the place near the destination or the safe port chosen. In this situation, the tow party must take over the towed object at this place or safe port and the tugowner is not deemed in breach of the contract, unless the towage contract provides otherwise.[38]

---

37 Part II 4 of Towage Contract (Lump Sum) of China Ocean Engineering Service Ltd.
38 Article 160 of the Maritime Code.

5. Liability for damages arising from sea towage

Injury, death or loss of property often arise in the course of sea towage. Such loss or damage may involve not only the tugowner and the tow party, but also to a third party. Therefore, there are two kinds of liability involved. The first is liability between the tugowner and the tow party; the second is liability to a third party owed by the tugowner and the tow party jointly. The former is often referred to as 'contractual liability' because it is set out clearly in the towage contract; the latter is referred to as 'non-contractual liability' or 'liability in tort'. Although the parties may agree between them who is to be responsible for injury, death and property loss to a third party in the towage contract, the agreement between the tugowner and the tow party is not valid as against a third party.

5.1 Liability for damages between the tugowner and the tow party

In the course of sea towage, liability for damages between the tugowner and the tow party is subsumed under liability for breach of contract, so that the general provisions for the liability of breach of contract are applicable and any issues are determined according to the contract and applicable laws. The liability for damages between the tugowner and the tow party is generally provided by the standard towage contract. Meanwhile, the maritime law of some countries also govern issues of liability for damages between the tugowner and the tow party. However, the provisions of the laws are subject to contract, so that the apportionment of liability between the tugowner and the tow party is mainly governed by the provisions of the towage contract. The law will apply only when or if there are no provisions or no clear provisions in the towage contract.

With regard to the issue of liability and immunities, there are very detailed provisions in the standard towage contract in China. Clause 14 of the Towage Contract (Lump Sum) of China Ocean Engineering Services Ltd is about liability and immunities, which provides:

'(1) The tow party shall bear responsibility for loss or damage of what-soever nature and howsoever caused to the tow or third parties during the course of this towage service, even though such loss or damage is caused by the fault or negligence on the part of the tugowner or person on board the tug (including tug master, crew, pilots, tugower's servants and agents, or anyone else who is on board at the request or with the consent of the tugowner) or by any latent defect, unfitness or breakdown of the tug's machineries and equipment, lack of fuel, stores, speed or otherwise. (2) The tugowner shall not be responsible or liable for the consequences, direct or indirect, of *force majeure*, perils, dangers and accidents of the sea or other navigable waters, fires, war, war-like operations, riots, hostilities, civil commotions, acts of terrorism or sabotage, strikes, lockouts, disputes, stoppages or labour disturbances, prohibition of navigation, requisition of ships, blockades and similar events, delays of any kind, and any other events whatsoever beyond the control of the tugowner in the performance of this contract. (3) The tugowner shall be not liable for any claim for loss and/or damage, or delay, or liability to third parties whatever resulting from the condition of or accident to the tow, and the tow party shall indemnify the tugowner for any sum paid by way of such claim and any costs, charges and expenses which the tugowner may incur in defending such claims. (4) Notwithstanding the provisions of paragraphs (1) and (3) of this Clause, the tow party shall not be responsible or liable for damage to the tug if caused by the defects in the tug or by the fault or negligence of the Master or crew of the tug or for the damage caused to vessels or property of third parties by reason of collision with the tug in so far as the tow party can prove that such damage was not caused by the tow or the tow was not a contributing factor in causing the damage.'[39]

Meanwhile, in China there is also statute law governing this issue. Under the Maritime Code, in the course of sea towage, if the damage suffered by the tugowner or the tow party was caused by the fault of one of the parties, the party at fault will be liable for compensation.[40] If the damage was caused by the fault of both parties, both parties are liable for compensation in proportion to the extent of their respective fault.[41] However, the tugowner is not liable if it is proven that the damage suffered by the tow party is due to one of the following causes: (1) fault of the tugmaster or other crew members of the tug or the pilot or other servants or agents of the tugowner in the navigation and management of the tug; (2) fault of the tug in saving or attempting to save life or property at sea.[42]

The above provisions of the Maritime Code are subject to any contractual provisions to the contrary in the sea towage contract.[43]

5.2 Liability to a third party owed by the tugowner and the tow party

During the course of the towage operation, liabilities arising to third parties are usually in tort and therefore the general provisions concerning such liabilities apply. In China these provisions are stipulated by the Tort Law of the People's Republic of China (the Tort Law).[44]

---

39 Part II 14 of the Towage Contract (Lump Sum) of China Ocean Engineering Services Ltd.
40 Article 162, paragraph 1 of the Maritime Code.
41 Ibid.
42 Article 162, paragraph 2 of the Maritime Code.
43 Article 16, paragraph 3 of the Maritime Code.
44 Adopted at the 12th session of the Standing Committee of the Eleventh National People's Congress on 26 December 2009, entered into force on 1 July 1 2010.

Under the Tort Law, where two or more persons engage in conduct that endangers the personal or property safety of another person, if only the conduct of one or several of them causes harm to another person and the specific tortfeasor can be determined, that tortfeasor shall be liable;[45] or if the specific tortfeasor cannot be determined, all of them shall be liable jointly and severally.[46] Where two or more persons commit torts respectively, causing the same harm, and each tort is sufficient to cause the entire harm, the tortfeasors shall be liable jointly and severally. Where two or more persons commit torts respectively, causing the same harm, if the seriousness of liability of each tortfeasor can be determined, the tortfeasors must assume corresponding liabilities respectively;[47] or if the seriousness of liability of each tortfeasor is difficult to determine, the tortfeasors are equally liable for compensation.[48] Where joint and several liabilities are assumed by the tortfeasors according to law, the victim of torts is entitled to require some or all of the tortfeasors to assume the liability.[49] The compensation amounts in respect of tortfeasors who are jointly and severally liable are determined according to the seriousness of the actions of each tortfeasor; and if the seriousness of the actions of each tortfeasor cannot be determined, the tortfeasors are equally liable for compensation.[50] A tortfeasor who has paid an amount of compensation exceeding his contribution is entitled to recovery from other tortfeasors who are jointly and severally liable.[51]

During a sea towage operation, because the tug and the towed object are connected, it may be very difficult to determine whose fault has caused the damage to a third party. Therefore, the tugowner and the tow party are usually considered as a unit, in order to protect the interests of third parties. The tugowner and the tow party jointly bear the liability to a third party and then the principle of fault liability is used to determine their respective liability.

According to the Maritime Code,[52] if death of, or personal injury to, a third party or damage to their property has occurred during sea towage due to the fault of the tugowner or the tow party, the tugowner and the tow party are liable jointly and severally to that third party. Except where otherwise provided in the towage contract, the party that has paid compensation in an amount exceeding the proportion for which it is liable has the right of recourse against the other party. This provision in the Maritime Code prompts the following reflections.

First, if the third party's injuries or damage is caused by the tugowner or

---

45 Article 10 of the Tort Law.
46 Ibid.
47 Article 12 of the Tort Law.
48 Ibid.
49 Article 13 of the Tort Law.
50 Article 14, paragraph 1 of the Tort Law.
51 Ibid.
52 Article 163 of the Maritime Code.

the tow party separately, the tugowner and the tow party are considered as a unit and liable jointly to the third party. The tugowner and the tow party are liable in accordance with the contract or the fault.

Secondly, if the third party's injuries and damage are caused by the tugowner or the tow party jointly, the tugowner and the tow party undertake the liability to the third party as one unit. The tugowner and the tow party then share the compensation in proportion to the extent of their respective faults or according to the contract. Certainly they can share the compensations in accordance with the contract.

Thirdly, if the tugowner or the tow party has paid compensation in an amount exceeding the proportion for which it is liable, it shall have the right of recourse against the other party. This stipulation applies only in the absence of corresponding provisions in the contract.

Fourthly, while the contractual stipulations have priority to determine and share the internal responsibility between the tugowner and the tow party, they are not binding in the determination of the external responsibility to a third party. Under the Maritime Code, the parties of the towage contract bear joint liability to a third party; this provision is compulsory and they cannot resist or avoid joint liability by means of their contract.

6. Improvement of relevant provisions in the maritime code

Compared with other countries' law, the Maritime Code contains a larger number of provisions governing sea towage. However, these provisions fail to meet the requirements of practice. Some of the provisions of the Maritime Code should be improved by reform.

6.1 The form of towage contract

The Maritime Code stipulates that the towage contract must be made in writing.[53] However, some scholars in China do not agree with this requirement.[54] The following arguments are often advanced in favour of the latter position: (1) There are many verbal contracts in the towing business, especially for towing operations between large fishing boats. If the oral towage contract is deemed invalid, this will have a negative impact in existing legal relations. (2) In addition, this provision of the Maritime Code is not consistent with the Contract Law. Under the Contract Law, the parties may use written, oral or other forms in entering into a contract.[55] Therefore these scholars have argued that the requirement for the written form of towage contracts should be cancelled.

---

53 Article 156 of the Maritime Code; see above.
54 Jinyu Wang, 'A Review on Right of Parties to a Sea Towage Contract on Fairness Principle' [2010] 38 *Journal of Liaoning University (Philosophy and Social Sciences)* 155 at 156.
55 Article 10, paragraph 1 of the Contract Law.

In fact, this issue is related to the compulsory form of the contract. Under certain conditions, the law requires the contract to be concluded in written form. The Contract Law in China permits the parties to use all kinds of forms of contract including written, oral or other forms, but meanwhile the Contract Law also stipulates that a contract must be in written form if the laws or administrative regulations so provide.[56] Why do the laws or regulations so provide? The following reasons are often put forward: (1) The legal form of the contract is a means to upholding the interests of the parties. First, it may prevent the parties from rushing into their agreement, avoiding damage and ensuring that the parties have time to obtain professional advice. Secondly, it can provide evidence for the conclusion and contents of the contract. (2) The legal form of the contract is beneficial to the interests of a third party and the safety of the transaction. The contract is not open to the public, so some further requirements for the form of the contract such as registration can ensure that the contract is published and conveniently available for retrieval by interested persons and ensure that expectations are reasonable. This will reduce transaction costs, as well as the risk of disputes. (3) The legal form of the contract may help to uphold the public interest and to organise reasonably the social economy. The mandatory disclosure of private agreements is an effective means of implementing national economic policies and protecting the public interests of the society and transaction security.[57]

However, the compulsory form of contracts is not always reasonable. As a point of orientation for the development of contract law, freedom of contract is still one of the most basic starting points. Only when injustice may result are some measures necessary. Therefore, some scholars have argued that the law should advocate but not force the parties to use contracts in written form.

Based on the above analysis, the Maritime Code should permit the parties to choose the oral form for their towage contract, and also contain some provisions to support the written form of the towage contract. In addition, according to Article 36 of the Contract Law, where a contract is concluded in written form as required by relevant laws and administrative regulations or as agreed by the parties, and the parties have not concluded their contract in written form, but one party has performed the principal obligation and the other party has accepted it, the contract is established. This situation under the Contract Law should be adopted by the Maritime Code.

---

56 Article 10, paragraph 2 of the Contract Law.
57 Hong Zhang, 'A Legal Evaluation of the Form of Contract' [2004] 22 *Journal of Guizhou University (Social Science)* 47.

6.2 Immunity clauses

In any towage contract, immunity from liability is a primary concern. Should immunity clauses be valid? There is debate on this issue among scholars in China.

Some scholars hold that when the parties conclude the towage contract, the party providing the towing service is in a dominant position and the tow party is limited as to its freedom of choice. Therefore, the tugowner stipulates many clauses concerning immunities in the towage contract which are obviously unfair and an unfair mechanism for allocating liability is formed, according to which the tugowner only enjoys rights and assumes few obligations.[58] In the opinion of those scholars, the Maritime Code should provide that unfair immunity clauses are invalid.

Other scholars have argued that as for the parties to the towage contract, the owner of a barge or the owner of a drilling platform as tow party is not in a weaker position than the tugowner in terms of economic position and strength, and can negotiate the terms of the towage contract with the tugowner. In practice, it is often the case that the tugowner agrees to cancel or modify immunity clauses in accordance with the requirements of the tow party. Therefore, such scholars believe that the provisions of the Maritime Code appropriately balance the interests of the parties and comply with the trends of maritime safety, and that the development of the maritime industry has been sufficiently taken into account. Accordingly, the provisions relating to the immunities under the Maritime Code need not be modified.[59]

For the immunity clauses of the towage contract, we need to examine the following issues: (1) whether or not the immunity clauses in towage contracts are standard terms; (2) whether or not these clauses reflect the genuine intentions of the parties.

Are the immunity clauses in the towage contract standard terms? If yes, the provisions concerning standard terms in the Contract Law will apply. Under the Contract Law, where standard terms are adopted in concluding a contract, the party supplying the standard terms defines the rights and obligations between the parties abiding by the principle of fairness, and must inform the other party of exclusions or restrictions of its liabilities in a reasonable way, and must also explain the standard terms upon request by the other party.[60] When standard terms belong to the circumstances stipulated in Articles 52 and 53 of the Contract Law,[61] or the party which

---

58 Jinyu Wang, 'A Review on Right of Parties to a Sea Towage Contract on Fairness Principle' [2010] 38 *Journal of Liaoning University (Philosophy and Social Sciences)* 155 at 157.

59 Shaochun Yuan, 'On the Exemption Clauses in Contract of Sea Towage' [2001] 12 *Annual of China Maritime Law* 197.

60 Article 39, paragraph 1 of the Contract Law.

61 Article 52 of the Contract Law provides the circumstances under which the contract shall be concerned as invalid, '(i) One party induced conclusion of the contract through fraud

supplies the standard terms exempts itself from its liabilities, increases the liabilities of the other party, and deprives the other party of material rights, the terms will be invalid.[62]

The Contract Law defines standard terms as clauses which are prepared in advance for general and repeated use by one party, and which are not negotiated with the other party when the contract is concluded.[63]

Therefore, if the tow party can negotiate any modification of the immunity clauses in the standard towage contract when the towage contract is concluded, the immunity clauses are not standard terms. Otherwise, they are.

The other important issue is whether or not the immunity clauses reflect the real intentions of the parties. If not, the provisions of the Contract Law will also apply. Under the Contract Law, a party has the right to request the People's Court or an arbitration institution to modify or revoke the following contracts: (1) those concluded as a result of significant misconception; and (2) those that are obviously unfair at the time when concluding the contract. If a contract is concluded by one party against the other party's true intentions through the use of fraud, coercion or exploitation of the other party's unfavourable position, the injured party has the right to request the People's Court or an arbitration institution to modify or revoke it. Where a party requests a modification, the People's Court or the arbitration institution may not revoke the contract.[64]

So if the immunity clauses in the towage contract reflect the real intentions of the tow party, its clauses are valid, or else they can be modified or revoked.

6.3 Limitation of liability

Limitation of liability for maritime claims is a feature unique to maritime law. In order to protect the shipowner, balance the interests of different parties and support the shipping industry, shipping countries have established the legal framework surrounding the limitation of liability. This framework of rules covers also sea towage. In the context of sea towage, the following issues must be considered in connection with the use of

or duress, thereby harming the interests of the state; (ii) The parties colluded in bad faith, thereby harming the interests of the state, the collective or any third party; (iii) The parties intended to conceal an illegal purpose under the guise of a legitimate transaction; (iv) The contract harms public interests; (v) The contract violates a mandatory provision of any law or administrative regulation.' Article 53 of the Contract Law provides the circumstances under which the exception clauses in the contract are invalid, '(i) excluding one party's liability for personal injury caused to the other party; (ii) excluding one party's liability for property loss caused to the other party by its intentional misconduct or gross negligence.'

62 Article 40 of the Contract Law.
63 Article 39, paragraph 2 of the Contract Law.
64 Article 54 of the Contract Law.

limitation of liability: (1) Are the tug and tow considered to be 'ships' as per domestic law or international conventions? Is the definition of ship a sufficient premise for the limitation of liability? (2) Who exactly is entitled to limit their liability? Only shipowners? Or others too? (3) How is the amount to be calculated – by reference to the gross tonnage of the tug or to the gross tonnage of the tow, or by reference to the gross tonnage of both tug and tow?

6.3.1 *The tug, tow and the definition of 'ship' in the context of limitation of liability*

To what kind of vessels is limitation of liability applicable? The regulations are very different from country to country. Generally, the law will define vessels entitled to enjoy the right to limit liability as 'sea-going ships'. However, some countries stipulate that 'sea-going ships' are only ships as defined by maritime law; whereas other countries make further regulations restricting what ships may enjoy the right to limit liability.

At present, the convention most widely used in respect of limitation of liability is the Convention on Limitation of Liability for Maritime Claims 1976 (the Limitation Convention 1976).[65] This convention does not definitively regulate what ships will be entitled to limit limitation. However, the convention does stipulate that it applies to sea-going ships[66] of more than 300 tons[67] but not to air-cushion vehicles[68] or to floating platforms constructed for the purpose of exploring or exploiting the natural resources of the seabed or the subsoil thereof.[69]

Under the Maritime Code, the vessels which enjoy the right to limit liability are only those provided by the Maritime Code. According to Article 3 of the Maritime Code, 'ships' means sea-going ships and other mobile units, but does not include ships or craft to be used for military or public service purposes, nor small ships of less than 20 tons gross tonnage. The definition of 'ship' also includes ship's apparel.

In China, scholars have discussed the issue of drilling platforms and given that they are often towed to their place of operations they are worthy of specific mention here. Both the Maritime Code and the Convention on Limitation of Liability 1976 are silent on the status of drilling platforms and their right to limit liability. But drilling platforms also often cause injury, death or property loss during sailing and operations due to incidents such as

---

65 Signed at London on 19 November 1976. The Convention replaced the International Convention Relating to the Limitation of the Liability of Owners of Seagoing Ships, which was signed in Brussels in 1957, and came into force in 1968. It has been amended by the 1996 Protocol, which was signed at London on 2 May1996.
66 Article 1, paragraph 2 of the Limitation Convention 1976.
67 Article 15, paragraph 2(b) of the Limitation Convention 1976.
68 Article 15, paragraph 5(a) of the Limitation Convention 1976.
69 Article 15, paragraph 5(b) of the Limitation Convention 1976.

collision, fire or and explosion. Meanwhile, the basic idea behind the right to limit liability was that every encouragement should be given to shipowners to carry on their business.[70] Developing oil and gas resources at sea is an adventurous pursuit to be encouraged rather than discouraged in the interests of the promotion of the world economy. Therefore, drilling platforms should be regarded as ships and should enjoy the right to limit liability.

Given the above reflections, both tug and tow, if they meet the requirements of the Maritime Code, can be entitled to enjoy the limitation of liability.

6.3.2 Who can be entitled to the limitation of liability?

The circle of persons entitled to limit liability is another important issue. According to the Convention on Limitation of Liability for Maritime Claims 1976, persons entitled to limit liability involve shipowner and salvors,[71] and 'shipowner' means the owner, charterer, manager and operator of a seagoing ship.[72] 'Salvor' means any person rendering services in direct connection with salvage operations.[73] Moreover, any person for whose act, neglect or default the shipowner or salvor is responsible is entitled to avail itself of limitation of liability.[74] Under the Maritime Code, shipowners and salvors may limit their liability,[75] and shipowners include the charterer and the operator of a ship.[76] Meanwhile, the persons for whose act, neglect or default the shipowners or salvors are responsible may limit their liability.[77]

There are no special provisions in the Maritime Code in respect of the persons entitled to limit liability in connection with towage. Therefore, the general provisions concerning limitation of liability apply equally to sea towage.

6.3.3 How to calculate the amount?

There are no provisions concerning the calculation of the amount of limitation involved in sea towage under the Maritime Code. In judicial practice, there are two distinct calculation methods in use. One is the total sum by adding the tonnage of the tug to the tonnage of the tow; and the other is the total sum by adding the limitation amount of the tug to the limitation amount of the tow. Whichever method is employed, the tug and the tow are

70 Christopher Hill, *Maritime Law* (5th edn, LLP, 1998), p.375.
71 Article 1, paragraph 1 of the Limitation Convention 1976.
72 Article 1, paragraph 2 of the Limitation Convention 1976.
73 Article 1, paragraph 3 of the Limitation Convention 1976.
74 Article 1, paragraph 4 of the Limitation Convention 1976.
75 Article 204, paragraph 1 of the Maritime Code.
76 Article 204, paragraph 2 of the Maritime Code.
77 Article 205 of the Maritime Code.

regarded as one unit and each party is responsible for the whole sum up to the limit of liability.

The first method is based on the fleet theory which seems reasonable in some aspects. However, three problems arise and will be discussed in the following.

First, it violates the principle of one limitation amount per incident. According to the principle of one limitation amount per incident, in each and every incident, the claim, whether deriving from inside the unit of the tug and the tow or from a third party, is limited by a single limit of liability.

Secondly, it violates the principle of establishment of a limit for each ship. In accordance with the law of limitation of liability for maritime claims, the limit amount is calculated on the basis of the tonnage of the ship. The amount of the limit for each ship should be a specified amount.

Thirdly, the amount of the limit of the insurer is not certain. In shipping practice, the shipowner usually procures insurance for its various ships from different insurance companies, or even from the same insurance company, but the insurance company may procure reinsurance. The insurance company for each ship is entitled to benefit from each ship's limitation of liability. However, adding the tonnage of tug and tow together makes it difficult to distinguish the amount of limitation of each individual ship, causing difficulties in the payment of claims by the insurer.

On such grounds, the calculation method of the limitation amount under the fleet theory has been justly questioned by scholars.

The second method of calculation is on the basis of the non-fleet theory. The external liability of each ship within the fleet is limited according to each ship's own tonnage. The total amount of limitation is composed of the limit of limitation of each ship. This second method is arguably more reasonable. For sea towage, the calculation of the amount of limitation of liability under the non-fleet theory matches the principle of liability of sea towage and should be adopted in China.[78]

7. Conclusion

With the development of the maritime industry, sea towage operations are also used more and more widely. Employed in a variety of different situations, the sea towage contract may possess the nature of employment or the nature of services. When the sea towage is controlled and the tug is directed by the tow party, the towage contract has the nature of employment; when the tugowner provides the service and completes the towing operation according to his own capacity and plan, the towage contract has the nature of a service. In addition, there are lots of links and differences between sea towage and marine transportation and salvage.

78 Xianjiang Wu, 'Study on the Limitation of Liability for Maritime Claims', PhD Thesis in Law, Dalian Maritime University, March 2010.

The obligations of the parties are agreed when the towage contract is concluded. However, some primary obligations such as the obligation of seaworthiness prescribed by the Maritime Code are not affected by immunity clauses contained in the towage contract. In some countries, the mutual obligations of the tugowner and the tow party are generally divided according to 'the principle of dominance',[79] which should be adopted by the Maritime Code.

During the sea towage, there are two types of loss or damage to which different principles apply. Claims for loss or damage arising between the tugowner and the tow party may be resolved in accordance with the towage contract. In the absence of relevant provisions in the contract, the Maritime Code applies. However, claims for loss or damage arising between the parties of the towage contract and a third party are governed by the Maritime Code together with the Tort Law.

Limitation of liability for maritime claims applies to sea towage. The tug and the tow are both involved, resulting in a complex legal situation. In practice, the tug and the tow are regarded as one unit and the total amount of limitation is based on the limit of liability of each ship.

While specific provisions regarding sea towage are present in the Maritime Code, they do not fully meet the requirements of current towage practice. The relevant provisions should be improved with the resolution of some of the issues described.

---

79 'The principle of dominance' means that the party who dominates the tow operation will bear the claim.

8 Legal issues arising under the direct action framework in relation to oil pollution damage

Hongyu Wu and Professor Lixin Han

1. Introduction

With the rapid development of the shipping industry and crude oil transportation, there is a growing risk of oil leakage. In such circumstances, there is a risk of increased litigation against liable shipowners for oil pollution damage. The legal framework for direct action against the insurer for oil pollution liability established by the International Convention on Civil Liability for Oil Pollution Damage (CLC 1992)[1] can secure full compensation to the victims of oil pollution damage. China has acceded to the CLC 1992,[2] so that claims which fall within the scope of application[3] of the Convention would be governed by its provisions. However, in Chinese domestic law there is no defined and detailed substantive legislation to regulate the direct action framework. The Special Maritime Procedure Law[4] has translated into Chinese domestic law a provision from the CLC 1992[5] under which the victims of oil pollution damage may bring a direct action against the insurer for oil pollution liability.[6] However, this procedural provision is incomplete

---

1 Ji Luo, 'Research on Marine Compulsory Liability of Oil Pollution Insurance in China' (2010) 1 *Annual of China Maritime Law* 97 at 98. The original convention was signed at Brussels on 29 November 1969 and came into force on 19 June 1975 (hereafter CLC 1969). The CLC 1969 has been updated by a 1976 Protocol and, in some states including China and the UK, by the 1992 Protocol (hereafter CLC 1992).

2 The CLC 1992 came into force on 30 May 1996. China acceded to the CLC 1992 on 5 January 1999.

3 Article II of the CLC 1992.

4 Adopted at the 13th meeting of the Standing Committee of the Ninth National People's Congress on 25 December 1999 and effective as of 1 July 2000.

5 Article VII(8) of the CLC 1992, '[a]ny claim for compensation for pollution damage may be brought directly against the insurer or other person providing financial security for the owner's liability for pollution damage'.

6 Article 97 of the Special Maritime Procedure Law, 'with respect to a claim for indemnity against oil pollution damage caused by a ship, the person suffering for the damage may make the claim to the shipowner causing the oil pollution damage, or directly make the claim to the insurer bearing the liability for oil pollution damage of the shipowner or to other person providing financial security therefor. Where the insurer bearing the liability for oil pollution damage of the shipowner or the other person providing financial security

and enacted using an imperfect legislative technique, resulting in incoherent application of the direct action tool in China.[7]

The aim of this chapter is to analyse legal issues arising from the direct action framework in connection with the oil pollution damage compensation in China. It will be considered whether the insurance of oil pollution damage constitutes mandatory liability insurance in China, followed by a discussion of the existing problems of the direct action framework and analysis of the status quo, including relevant legislation and its significance. The defences available to the insurer against oil pollution liability claims, the litigation status of the shipowner who caused the oil pollution damage and the form of assumed liability between the shipowner and the insurer will be examined. Last but not least, the relationship between direct action and the pay to be paid principle of the P&I Clubs will be discussed. After the analysis of each aspect, some suggestions on the improvement of the direct action regime in China will be provided.

2. Is insurance for oil pollution liability mandatory in China?

2.1 Mandatory liability insurance

Mandatory liability insurance occurs where a particular group of people are required by national law to buy insurance covering their potential liability.[8] Such liability insurance is compulsory for individuals or companies wishing to engage in some particularly risky activity, for instance driving a car on the road. Mandatory liability insurance has two main characteristics. First, it is compulsory, disregarding the intention of the assured when the two parties conclude their insurance contract; secondly, such a rule, while imposed on the commercial insurance industry, is for common, public benefit rather than to enhance commercial profits. The purpose of mandatory liability insurance for shipping oil pollution is to ensure that victims obtain due compensation for the oil pollution damage suffered.

This kind of compulsory insurance system in maritime law was first established in the CLC 1969.[9] This Convention was created on the basis of a serious oil pollution incident, namely the *Torrey Canyon* in 1967. This was a disaster affecting both the shipping industry and the oil industry.

---

therefor against whom an action is filed, he is entitled to require the shipowner causing the oil pollution damage to participate in the proceedings.'

7 Weili Song, 'Comments on the Direct Action by the Claimant against the Insurer for the Owner's Liability for Pollution Damage – Comments on the Legislative Perfection of Article 97 of Special Maritime Procedure Law of the People's Republic of China' (2009) 4 *Annual of China Maritime Law* 69.

8 Wen Yang, 'Direct Litigation System in Marine Compulsory Liability Insurance' (2009) 13 *Chinese and Foreign Entrepreneurs: Economic Analysis* 48.

9 See note 1 above.

As a result of the incident, about 100,000 tons of crude oil spilled into the English Channel and caused severe contamination to the coastlines of the UK, France and Holland. The Convention was established in a short time and embraced a regime of compulsory insurance combined with rights of direct action against the insurer.

2.2 Relevant legislation in China

The legislative approach of mandatory liability insurance for shipping oil pollution in China is the coexistence of international conventions with domestic law.[10]

As for international conventions, China has acceded to the CLC 1992 and the International Convention on Civil Liability for Bunker Oil Pollution Damage 2001 (Bunkers Convention).[11] In the light of the CLC 1992, the owner of a ship carrying more than 2,000 tons of persistent hydrocarbon mineral oil is required to possess compulsory insurance.[12] Under the Bunkers Convention, the shipowner is required to carry compulsory insurance if the vessel has a gross tonnage of more than 1,000 tons.[13] If a foreign ship with a gross tonnage of more than 1,000 tons wants to enter or leave a port or an offshore terminal in the territory of a State Party, it has to carry on board a certificate attesting that its insurance is in force.[14]

However, the liability insurance for Chinese vessels sailing in coastal lines or inland waters should be regulated by Chinese domestic law: in 2011, China's Ministry of Transport issued the Measures of PRC for the Implementation of Civil Liability Insurance for Vessel-induced Oil Pollution Damage (the Implementation Measures). According to the Implementation Measures, shipowners must possess civil liability insurance for vessels navigating within the territorial waters of China carrying oil substances, or carrying non-oil substances but with a gross tonnage of more than 1,000 tons.[15] China's domestic regulation extends the scope of application of the CLC 1992 to a more rigorous level. As long as the vessel navigates within the sea area of China carrying oil substances on board, the shipowner is required to possess liability insurance regardless of the country of registry or gross tonnage. Also, if the ship carries non-oil substances but its gross tonnage exceeds 1,000 tons, the shipowner is required to possess liability insurance when the ship sails in the territorial waters of China.

---

10 Zirui Bao, 'The Analysis of China's Legal System of Mandatory Liability Insurance of Shipping Oil Pollution' (2011) *Ecological Economy* 154.
11 The Bunkers Convention was signed at London on 23 March 2001 and came into force on 21 November 2008. China acceded to the Convention on 9 March 2009.
12 Articles I(5) and VII(1) of the CLC 1992.
13 Article 7.1 of the Bunkers Convention.
14 Article 7.2 of the Bunkers Convention.
15 Article 2 of the Implementation Measures.

2.3 Existing problems

The Implementation Measures demonstrate that a compulsory liability insurance system for oil pollution from shipping is established in China. However, there is an argument on the reasonableness of such regulation in the context of potential expansion of its scope of application.[16] It is said that the expansion will have an impact on vessels engaged in domestic oil transportation in China which are small in size and fall outside the scope of application of the CLC 1992, the owners of which, in the light of the Implementation Measures, will be obliged to buy liability insurance. As a result, some small shipping companies may suffer an undue economic burden. Nevertheless, such regulation is reasonable and crucial to the development of the shipping industry in China for two major reasons.

First, in 2010, the majority of coastal line tankers were smaller than 1,000 gross tons. In particular, 87% of tankers sailing in inland waters were smaller than 500 gross tons.[17] These vessels navigated in the coastal areas where there is high population density and the economy is developed. Collisions resulting in oil pollution would seriously affect the normal economic activities of local residents, causing grave damage to the local or regional economy. As a result, the shipowner liable for the pollution would be confronted with very large compensation claims, far beyond its compensatory ability. In such a context, mandatory liability insurance is a necessary tool to guarantee the complete compensation of the victims.

Secondly, vessels which sail in coastal and inland waters are often old and in poor condition. The seafarers do not receive sufficient training and the communications and navigation systems on board are not advanced. Such vessels are likely to cause accidents; and what is more, these ships are often owned by single ship companies so that there is only one ship registered in the name of the company. Having lost that ship, the company becomes insolvent and the shipowner can circumvent the compensation claims for oil pollution damage. As a result, the victims will receive nothing from the liable shipowner. Again, a mandatory liability insurance regime is needed to secure the right and interests of pollution victims in the event of the insolvency of such small shipping companies.

Mandatory liability insurance for shipping oil pollution does exist in China, by way of domestic extension of the scope of application of the CLC 1992 beyond its immediate scope. This may affect the shipping industry of China; however, in the long run it is beneficial to oil transportation in coastal and inland waters.[18] This will provide the impetus for shipping companies

---

16 Zirui Bao, 'The Analysis of China's Legal System of Mandatory Liability Insurance of Shipping Oil Pollution' (2011) *Ecological Economy* 154 at 155.

17 Ji Luo, 'Research on Marine Compulsory Liability of Oil Pollution Insurance in China' (2010) 1 *Annual of China Maritime Law* 97 at 98.

18 Zirui Bao, 'The Analysis of China's Legal System of Mandatory Liability Insurance of Shipping Oil Pollution' (2011) *Ecological Economy* 154 at 155.

to enhance their management standards, and old vessels will gradually cease to operate. The shipping industry will improve its international competitiveness and aspire to meet international standards in the future.[19]

3. The status quo of direct action in China

While compulsory liability insurance for oil pollution damage is in place in China, traditional liability insurance only permits the victim to claim compensation against the assured who caused the oil pollution incident. In the event that the assured becomes insolvent and is unable to pay the victim, the victim cannot sue the insurer because it is contrary to the principle of privity of contract. As a result, the victim may not be able to recover compensation in full or indeed any compensation at all from the liable assured. In order to fill this gap, the CLC 1969 establishes a rule on direct action against the mandatory liability insurer, under which the victim of oil pollution damage can sue the insurer of the liable shipowner directly, breaking through the privity of contract. The purpose of this special regime is to afford extra protection to victims who have suffered great losses because of an oil pollution incident.

3.1 *The significance of the direct action regime*

First, the direct action rule safeguards the victim's legal right and interests. Under the traditional insurance system, only the assured has the entitlement to claim insurance compensation from his insurer. In such circumstances, the assured can dispose of its right at will, and may be slow to exercise this right which will in turn prejudice the right and interests of the victim.[20] By means of the direct action regime, the victim can sue the insurer directly to avoid being affected by the misconduct of the assured. The legal rights of the victim can thereby receive better protection.

Secondly, the rule simplifies related judicial proceedings. Under the traditional insurance system, the victim would receive compensation either when the assured obtains compensation from his insurer or the assured pays in advance and later claims the sum against the insurer. Either way, the compensation is likely to be affected by the misconduct of the assured. By contrast, direct action is more straightforward: the victim may sue the insurer directly and obtain full compensation. He no longer needs to await the judgment from the claim between the shipowner and insurer. Further,

---

19 Zirui Bao, 'The Analysis of China's Legal System of Mandatory Liability Insurance of Shipping Oil Pollution' (2011) *Ecological Economy* 154 at 155.
20 Haitao Zhou and Tiansheng Li, 'On Direct Action of Marine Compulsory Insurance' (2011) 1 *Law Science Magazine* 98.

it is unnecessary for the shipowner to bring litigation against his insurer. Litigation costs will also be reduced.[21]

3.2 The relevant legislation in China

China is a state party to the CLC 1992.[22] According to that Convention, the victim is entitled to sue the insurer directly if the oil pollution damage is caused by a vessel which falls within the scope of its application[23] and carries persistent hydrocarbon mineral oil as cargo.[24]

In other circumstances, the domestic law of China would apply. Unfortunately, the substantive law of China does not contain defined or detailed provisions on direct action. Chapter XII of the Chinese Maritime Code[25] contains provisions on marine insurance contracts. Nonetheless, there are no specific provisions granting the right of direct action to the victim; nor does the Insurance Law provide for a direct action regime. However, Article 97 of the Special Maritime Procedure Law, for the purposes of procedural law, stipulates that victims of oil pollution damage may claim directly against the insurer.[26] The provision appears to grant a right of direct action to the victim; however, a few difficult issues arise.

First, the entitlement to direct action of the victim is a substantive right, which should not be enshrined in procedural law.[27] Secondly, the lack of substantive law provisions appears to indicate that there is no legal basis for requiring the insurer to assume the oil pollution liability.[28] Thirdly, the direct action framework is arguably incomplete; the existing provision should be combined with other provisions, such as defences for the insurer, litigation status and the forms of assumed liability.[29] The availability of direct action is a compromise, based on balancing the interests of each party. However, Article 97 of the Special Maritime Procedure Law does not set out the defences available to the insurer in the direct action, which will

21 Ibid at 100.
22 See note 2 above.
23 Article VII(8) of the CLC 1992.
24 Articles I(5) and VII(1),(8) of the CLC 1992.
25 Maritime Code of the People's Repulic of China, which was adopted at the 28th meeting of the Standing Committee of the Seventh National People's Congress on 7 November 1992, promulgated by Order No. 64 of the President of the People's Republic of China on 7 November 1992, and effective as of 1 July 1993.
26 See note 6 above.
27 Haitao Zhou and Tiansheng Li, 'On Direct Action of Marine Compulsory Insurance' (2011) 1 *Law Science Magazine* 98 at 101.
28 Wen Yang, 'Direct Litigation System in Marine Compulsory Liability Insurance' (2009) 13 *Chinese and Foreign Entrepreneurs: Economic Analysis* 48 at 51.
29 Weili Song, 'Comments on the Direct Action by the Claimant against the Insurer for the Owner's Liability for Pollution Damage – Comments on the Legislative Perfection of Article 97 of Special Maritime Procedure Law of the People's Republic of China' (2009) 4 *Annual of China Maritime Law* 69 at 72.

affect the legal rights and interests of the liability insurer. Moreover, the legislation of China more generally does not provide support for direct action against liability insurers. In order to improve and perfect the direct action regime, these legal issues require urgent resolution, as will be discussed in the following.

In conclusion, the direct action regime in China needs strengthening. Its legal basis in the substantive law is weak and supporting provisions, such as the defences of the insurer, should be set out in the domestic law to enable direct action to play an efficient role in protecting the legal right and interests of victims and the marine environment.

4. Defences of the insurer under the direct action regime

Well-defined defences are crucial to protect the rights of insurers in direct actions brought by pollution victims. Under mandatory liability insurance, even an innocent assured cannot be exempted from liability because of the application of the strict liability approach.[30] Meanwhile, the victim's rights of direct action are granted with no defences given to the insurer.[31] The insurer undertakes a great risk by assuming only the compensation obligations without specific defences attached. However, the national law of China lacks the relevant provisions to grant defences to the insurer. There is only one article in a judicial interpretation[32] issued by the Supreme People's Court which provides that the insurer or other party acting as guarantor may avail itself of the defences which the owner itself would have been entitled to invoke.[33] Further, unless the oil pollution damage has resulted from the wilful misconduct of the owner, the defences of the insurer or the party acting as guarantor for the vessel owner will not be upheld by the Court.[34] Compared with paragraph 8 of Article VII of the CLC 1992,[35] this article is much simpler and needs to be supplemented in several respects.

---

30 Haitao Zhou and Tiansheng Li, 'On Direct Action of Marine Compulsory Insurance' (2011) 1 *Law Science Magazine* 98 at 100.

31 Ibid.

32 Article 8 of Provisions of the Supreme Court on Several Issues Concerning the Trial of Cases of Disputes over Compensation for Vessel-induced Oil Pollution Damage, which was adopted at the 1509th meeting of the Judicial Committee of the Supreme People's Court on 10 January 2011, and came into force on 1 July 2011.

33 Ibid.

34 Ibid.

35 Article VII(8), of the CLC 1992 '. . . In such case the defendant may, even if the owner is not entitled to limit his liability according to Article V, paragraph 2, avail himself of the limits of liability prescribed in Article V, paragraph 1. He may further avail himself of the defences (other than the bankruptcy or winding up of the owner) which the owner himself would have been entitled to invoke. Furthermore, the defendant may avail himself of the defence that the pollution damage resulted from the wilful misconduct of the owner himself, but the defendant shall not avail himself of any other defence which he might have been entitled to invoke in proceedings brought by the owner against him. The defendant shall in any event have the right to require the owner to be joined in the proceedings.'

4.1 Defences of the insurer under the CLC 1992

4.1.1 Limitation of liability

An insurer is always entitled to limit liability to the same amount as the shipowner, even when the shipowner has lost his right to limitation.[36] This is to protect the insurer from the potential astronomical figure arising from marine pollution incidents. Also, a defined amount of liability is an essential foundation for premium calculation for the insurer; otherwise, the impact of potentially vast underwriting losses may have a financial impact upon the normal operation of insurance companies.[37] Accordingly, the insurer's defence of limitation of liability will not be affected in situations where the shipowner is barred from limiting its liability.

4.1.2 Wilful misconduct of the shipowner

The insurer may avail itself of the defence that the pollution damage was caused by the wilful misconduct of the shipowner.[38] However, the concept of 'wilful misconduct' is construed differently in different countries. In the context of the English Marine Insurance Act 1906, it means a deliberate act by the insured that is designed to cause loss, or which is committed recklessly with a blind eye as to its consequences.[39] This interpretation entails a strong defence for the insurer and is also accepted by China. However, the insurer cannot avail itself of other defences it might have been entitled to invoke against the shipowner under the insurance contract.[40] Such provisions are enforced between contracting parties, but cannot affect the rights of the third party.

4.1.3 Other defences of the shipowner

The insurer may further avail itself of the defences to which the shipowner would have been entitled.[41] Such defences include exemption clauses in favour of the shipowner in conventions and other national laws. For instance, there is no liability for pollution damage attached to the shipowner if the accident has resulted from *force majeure*.[42] Additionally, any applicable

---

36 The second sentence of Article VII(8) of the CLC 1992.
37 Haitao Zhou and Tiansheng Li, 'On Direct Action of Marine Compulsory Insurance' (2011) 1 *Law Science Magazine* 98 at 100.
38 The fourth sentence of Article VII(8) of the CLC 1992.
39 Merkin, Robert et al., *Marine Insurance Legislation* (5th edn, Informa, Abingdon, 2014), p.90.
40 The fourth sentence of Article VII(8) of the CLC 1992.
41 The third sentence of Article VII(8) of the CLC 1992.
42 Article III(2)(a) of the CLC 1992.

time-bar will provide a defence for the insurer.[43] If the claim of the victim arises after the claim has been time barred, the insurer will not accept liability for pollution damage. Nevertheless, defences such as bankruptcy or winding up of the shipowner are not among the defences available to the insurer.[44] The object of liability insurance is the liability of the assured for the damage caused to the victim.[45] If the assured himself can invoke defences negating liability for damage, the insurer is no more under an obligation to compensate the third party than is the shipowner. However, such defences are construed narrowly in the context of mandatory liability insurance.[46] They are restricted to express stipulations in the convention or legislation; otherwise it would be too difficult for the victim to obtain compensation.

4.2 How can the law be improved?

The CLC 1992 arguably provides a sound set of provisions regulating the defences of the insurer under the direct action regime. One of the key points in improving the domestic direct action regime in China is to grant the insurer a complete and workable set of defences. Compared with the CLC 1992, it is especially urgent to provide for the defence of limitation of liability for the insurer under the law of China. Accordingly, the interests of the parties can be balanced; otherwise the balance will be tilted too far, causing excessive protection for the victim.

5. Litigation status of the shipowner

According to Article 97 of the Special Maritime Procedure Law, when the victim initiates a direct action against the insurer, the latter is entitled to join the shipowner that caused the oil pollution damage to the litigation.[47] In such circumstances, is the shipowner a co-defendant or just a third party?

5.1 Co-defendant or third party

This is a controversial issue in China. Some commentators take the view that the shipowner should be given the legal status of a third party in the

43 For example, see Article VIII of the CLC 1992, '[r]ights of compensation under this Convention shall be extinguished unless an action is brought thereunder within three years from the date when the damage occurred. However, in no case shall an action be brought after six years from the date of the incident which caused the damage. Where this incident consists of a series of occurrences, the six years' period shall run from the date of the first such occurrence.'
44 The CLC 1992 expressly excludes 'bankruptcy or winding up of the owner' from the defences available to the insurer, see the third sentence of Article VII(8).
45 Xiao Ma and Hengsi S. Wang, 'The Direct Action with Respect to Oil Pollution Damage in China' (2013) 3 *Chinese Journal of Maritime Law* 68 at 72.
46 Ibid.
47 See note 7 above.

direct action against the insurer.[48] This opinion is upheld by the Supreme People's Court in its Judicial Interpretation.[49] However, the view that the shipowner should be a co-defendant also has its advocates.[50] This opinion is based upon the view that there are unresolved issues with the Judicial Interpretation. If the litigation status of the shipowner is as a third party, he is obliged to cooperate with the court in order to help the court examine the facts of the dispute and discern the responsibilities of each party. Such third parties are rarely required to assume liability for damage in judicial practice in China.[51] If that were right, a negative effect in practice might be that the shipowner would have no incentive to be diligent in preventing the risks of oil pollution. On the other hand, if the shipowner has the litigation status of a co-defendant, he will be expected to assume liability for damage as well. Therefore, it is a better solution for the court to join the shipowner to the litigation as a co-defendant in that it helps prevent the potential moral hazard of the shipowner. A potentially liable shipowner is required to make every effort to prevent oil pollution or mitigate damage after the incident. In addition, the developing trend of the modern mandatory liability insurance is to give victims better means of protecting their legitimate interests.[52] Allowing the insurer to require the shipowner to participate in the direct action as a co-defendant is just a reflection of such tendency.

5.2 Proposals for reform

Neither the CLC 1992 nor other international conventions contain express stipulation as to the litigation status of the shipowner in a direct action. However, the Merchant Shipping Code of the Russian Federation contains a provision indicating that the insurer is entitled to require that the shipowner be joined to the proceedings as a co-defendant in the direct action.[53] It may be inferred that Russian domestic law provides an explicit answer to the question, in considering the insurer and the shipowner as

---

48 Xiao Maand and Hengsi S. Wang, 'The Direct Action with Respect to Oil Pollution Damage in China' (2013) 3 *Chinese Journal of Maritime Law* 68 at 74.
49 Interpretation of the Supreme People's Court on the Application of the Special Maritime Procedure Law of the People's Republic of China 2003, Article 69, which was adopted at the 1259th meeting of the Adjudication Committee of the Supreme People's Court on 3 December 2002 and came into force on 1 February 2003. See Article 69, '[t]he maritime court, at the request of the insurer of oil pollution damages or any other party providing financial security for such damages, may notify the ship owner to take part in the litigation as a third party without independent right of claim.'
50 Lixin Han, *Legal System of Compensation for Oil Pollution Damage Caused by Ships* (Law Press, China, 2007), pp.393–395.
51 Ibid.
52 Ibid.
53 Article 325(4) of the Merchant Shipping Code of Russian Federation, 'The defendant shall in any event be entitled to require the vessel's owner to be joined in the proceedings as a co-defendant.'

co-defendants. This provision is useful for reference in improving the legislative provisions surrounding the direct action regime in China and also in
perfecting the CLC 1992.

6. The forms of assumed liability

As mentioned above, it is preferable for the court to consider the shipowner
as a co-defendant when he is required to participate in the direct action.
That being the case, the shipowner and the insurer should theoretically
assume joint and several liability so that the victim of the oil pollution will
have the opportunity to obtain adequate compensation from two defendants. By way of example, suppose that a shipowner with poor finances
loses the right to limit its liability because of personal wilful misconduct,
while the entitlement of the insurer to avail itself of the limitation defence
is unaffected. In such circumstances, the victim would choose to bring a
direct action against the insurer; the compensation available will not exceed
an aggregate amount according to the CLC 1992.[54] If the incident is serious, such compensation will not be adequate to cover all the oil pollution
damage. If so, the victim may be able to obtain the remainder from the
shipowner on the basis of joint and several liability. In addition, the victim
could bring litigation against the shipowner and the insurer simultane-
ously which would avoid the lapse of time as a crucial defence against the
claimant.

6.1 Two typical cases

There are two relevant cases from Chinese courts that merit discussion.
The first is the oil pollution case of *M/V Tasman Sea*.[55] This case was the
first claim against a foreign insurer for oil pollution damage based on the
CLC 1992 since China joined that Convention.[56] On 23 November 2002,
the Maltese defendant's tanker, *Tasman Sea*, carrying 80,000 tons of crude
oil collided with another ship. About 200 tons of crude oil were spilled as
a result of the incident. The collision took place in Bohai Bay and also pol-
luted the sea off the port of Tianjin. The event posed a significant threat to
the marine ecological environment.[57]

---

54 Article V(1) of the CLC 1992, 'the owner of a ship shall be entitled to limit his liability
under this Convention in respect of any one incident to an aggregate amount of 2,000
francs for each ton of the ship's tonnage. However, this aggregate amount shall not in any
event exceed 210 million francs.'
55 *Tianjin Oceanic Administration v Infinity Shipping Corp. & The London Steam-ship Owners'
Mutual Insurance Association Ltd* (2003) Tianjin Maritime Court, No.183.
56 Xiaoqin Zhu and Lin Dong, 'Legal Remedies for Marine Ecological Damage in China: As
Illustrated by the Tasman Sea Oil Spills Case' (2009) 2(2) *Marine Ecological Damage in
China* 391 at 394.
57 Ibid.

After the collision, the plaintiff brought an action against the shipowner and his insurer. After six trials, the Tianjin Maritime Court issued its judgment holding that Infinity Shipping Corporation, owners of the *Tasman Sea*, and its insurer, London Steam-Ship Owners Mutual Insurance Association Ltd, should bear joint and several liability for the plaintiff's damage caused by the oil pollution. The case was appealed to the Tianjin Higher People's Court; however, the judgment of that Court only reduced the sum of the compensation without affecting the basis of the liability.

The other case is the *PRC Yantai Maritime Safety Administration v Yun Sung Marine Corporation & Japan Ship Owners' Mutual Protection & Indemnity Association.*[58] The Korean bulk cargo ship the *Golden Rose*, belonging to the defendant shipowner, collided with another ship. As a result of the collision, the *Golden Rose* began sinking and leaking oil. The surrounding waters were affected by oil pollution.

The shipowner of the *Golden Rose* and its insurer, the Japan P&I Club, were both defendants. The plaintiff claimed that the shipowner and the insurer should assume joint and several liability. The court rejected the claim, holding that it had no legal basis.

Although these two cases had similar facts and claims, different courts came to different conclusions. To victims, the judgment in the *Tasman Sea* is clearly preferable. Nevertheless, there is a problem with that judgment. The litigation fell within the scope of application of the CLC 1992 and the defendants are from Malta and the UK, both parties to the Convention, so the applicable law should be the CLC 1992. However, there is no provision in the CLC 1992 stipulating that the shipowner and its insurer should assume joint and several liability in a direct action. As a result, the judgment in the *Tasman Sea* is not well founded on legal authority, as discerned by the court in the second case, causing it to arrive at the opposite conclusion.

6.2 Need for reform

In conclusion, a lacuna in the law with respect to the basis of liability is not only a problem for the domestic law of China but also to the CLC 1992 in improving the legal foundations for direct action. A resolution to this problem would provide express legal authority to the courts when confronted with this type of action. The Chinese courts, operating as they do within a statute law system, do not follow the doctrine of precedent. Accordingly, a provision should be introduced into domestic law as legislative support for joint and several liability on the part of the shipowner and the insurer in the context of direct actions.

58 (2008) Qingdao Maritime Court, No.15.

7. Pay-to-be-paid principle

The marine insurance provided by P&I Clubs is different from the insurance provided by regular insurance companies.[59] The well-known pay-to-be-paid principle entails that the shipowner cannot recover expenses or costs from the P&I Club unless he has paid the victim first. If, therefore, the shipowner is insolvent and unable to pay the victim in advance, the victim cannot recover compensation from the insurer. This principle is unhelpful in the context of direct action, giving rise to problems when the victim sues the P&I Club directly: should the pay-to-be-paid principle be disregarded in such circumstances? The question must be answered in the positive for two main reasons.

The first is the public interest. It is recognised that the pay-to-be-paid principle is a foundational rule of P&I Club insurance, and is one of the preconditions for the operation of P&I Clubs as insurers of a mutual nature. However, the direct action regime provides effective protection to vulnerable victims. By means of the direct action, the victim can obtain full compensation even if the liable shipowner is bankrupt. It ensures that the public benefit has a higher priority than the interest of the P&I Clubs.

Secondly, the legal validity of the right of direct action and the pay-to-be-paid principle are different.[60] The former is granted by legislation in the form of international conventions or national law. The latter, on the other hand, is agreed between the contractual parties. As a basic rule of P&I Clubs, it is effective only when the shipowner chooses to purchase insurance cover from the mutual association. As a result, the pay-to-be-paid principle is a contractual right of the P&I Club. Such a contractual right cannot be contrary to rights under the law, and as a result the pay-to-be-paid principle must be held to be invalid when the victim sues the P&I Club directly. Any other result would render the direct action regime meaningless.

In conclusion, the direct action regime must inevitably trump the pay-to-be-paid principle. The purpose of the direct action regime is to protect vulnerable victims of oil pollution damage. This outcome cannot be achieved if the direct action regime is restricted by the pay-to-be-paid principle.

8. Conclusion

In this chapter we have briefly discussed current issues arising in connection with direct action related to oil pollution damage in China. We have discussed the existence of mandatory liability insurance in respect of oil pollution damage; outlined the significance of the direct action framework

---

59 Robert Merkin et al., *Marine Insurance Legislation* (5th edn, Informa Law from Routledge, 2014).

60 Haitao Zhou and Tiansheng Li, 'On Direct Action of Marine Compulsory Insurance' (2011) 1 *Law Science Magazine* 98 at 101.

and its status quo; explained the deficiency of the relevant provisions of procedural law; and provided improvement suggestions. We have also examined the problem of the direct action regime which is the lack of supporting legal rules and discussed the order of priority between the pay-to-be-paid principle and direct action.

In conclusion, rules permitting direct action under the marine mandatory liability insurance do, to some extent, exist in China. However, due to the lack of supporting substantive legal provisions, the direct action regime is currently toothless and inefficient in judicial practice. Therefore, a special body of legislation underpinning rights to compensation for ship-source oil pollution damage should be added as a new chapter in the Chinese Maritime Code,[61] which should contain defined and detailed provisions that grant and define the rights of direct action to the victim, and should set out the complete defences available to the insurer. At the same time, it should define the litigation status of the shipowner, deeming it to be a co-defendant when joined to litigation. Moreover, the basis of liability between the insurer and the liable shipowner should be joint and several liability. Last, but not least, the direct action regime should supersede the pay-to-be-paid principle for the sake of the vulnerable victims. Reformed accordingly, the direct action regime would work effectively and provide better protection to ship source oil pollution victims and create an appropriate equilibrium with the interests of the insurer.

---

61 Weili Song, 'Comments on the Direct Action by the Claimant against the Insurer for the Owner's Liability for Pollution Damage – Comments on the Legislative Perfection of Article 97 of Special Maritime Procedure Law of the People's Republic of China' (2009) 4 *Annual of China Maritime Law* 69 at 73.

9 Flexibility versus certainty: on classical contract formation and modern methods of trading

Johanna Hjalmarsson and *Keren Wu**

1. Introduction

This chapter considers the approach of Chinese law to modern forms of contract making, exploring what systemic risks might arise from the current system of law. Our chosen example is the spot markets – contracts not least for the sale of commodities made between parties who are likely to be doing business with each other for the first time and who operate in a well-established and fast-trading market. Once the contract is made, the parties must take such risky actions as to charter a ship for thousands of dollars in daily rates, deliver the goods onto an unknown ship or arrange for onward sale of the goods. If there is uncertainty as to the status of the contract, or as to the complete, legally enforceable terms thereof, the parties incur risks arising from the law, rather from the transaction itself. Such risks may be capable of mitigation or dilution, not least by onward sales, and may therefore lie dormant. The risks will materialise where there is a precipitous drop in the market or an export ban, causing one of the parties to find that it would have been better off by not concluding the contract, and to look for ways to escape enforcement thereof. While the vast majority of trades are resolved by resorting to insurance cover, dilution of losses by spreading, writing off or even insolvency, others will end up in dispute resolution or court with one party defending the claim on the basis that the bargain that both parties thought themselves bound by never existed in the first place. This chapter seeks to define those risks in relation to Chinese law and identify the potential pitfalls inherent in the current position.

1.1 Spot market contracts

The spot market, boosted by modern electronic means of communication and contract formation, represents a practical challenge to the traditional,

* The authors wish to thank Professor James Davey, University of Southampton, Dr Ozlem Gurses, University of Southampton, Professor Andrea Lista, Associate Professor in Commercial Law, University of Exeter and Lijie Song, University of Southampton for helpful comments on draft versions. Any errors are attributable to the authors alone.

simple and elegant, but in the modern world occasionally quite fictional model of contract formation that is offer and acceptance. Contracts in the spot markets are made constantly and in large numbers every day. Several industries trade in spot markets, including commodities trades and charterparties. These trades represent values of billions of dollars and if we were to create contract law from scratch today, their sheer value might even mean that we would use such contracts as a model, instead of a basic model of offer and acceptance. The latter may be considered an excessively simple model, rooted in the historically prevailing type of transactions and better adapted to the sale of a horse or a piece of farming equipment.

In the spot markets, the contracting parties typically do not know each other or anything about each other, they have not done business before, they are negotiating very quickly with time at a premium and negotiations are conducted not in person, but via email. There is no concluding handshake. In a complex exchange of partial written communications, a particular term may have been mentioned once but not again thereafter, causing one party to think that there was agreement, and the other party to think that the term was not insisted upon. Indeed, the parties to the type of contract at issue are fairly likely to purposely neglect to mention a contract term that they anticipate to be difficult to negotiate, in the hope that the contingency where that contract term needs to be applied will not arise. Because of the criss-crossing of communications between the parties and the need to preserve an agreed position on the price, there is a need to acknowledge receipt of communications and send holding responses to permit consideration of the other party's offer. Such holding communications, if only ever so slightly ambiguous, may justifiably be interpreted by the receiving party as an acceptance of the offer. It is typically the case in spot transactions that the main contract terms are agreed and much of the contract is left for later determination between the parties (not as with Lloyd's Open Form salvage where the terms of service are well known and the price is deliberately left to an arbitrator; but by the parties themselves, albeit with a dispute resolution mechanism included).

Once a party considers that a contract has been formed, it may need to act immediately by undertaking expensive measures; for instance an FOB terms buyer[1] may need to charter a vessel to which the goods can be delivered.[2] Unless something goes wrong in the performance of the transaction, there is typically no need to agree or even discuss the further and more detailed particulars, some of which would in the context of a different type of contract be considered utterly essential. Needless to say, linguistic confusion alone may

---

1 FOB stands for Free On Board and means the buyer makes the transport arrangements. The seller simply transports the goods to the port and places them on board the vessel.
2 Some such subsequent measures, such as the buyer taking delivery of goods bought FOB on board a vessel it has chartered, may amount to acceptance of the agreement by conduct. But that aspect aside, costly consequent performance measures represent a risk in the transaction for as long as any contract uncertainty prevails.

mean that the parties do not always succeed in staying on the right side of the line between confirmation of receipt and acceptance. The use of brokers may confuse matters further in altering the meaning of communications and in creating delays between one communication and the next, perhaps changing the order in which a revised offer and an acceptance were conveyed.

The challenge of this new type of factual matrix is addressed differently by Chinese and English law. The question to be answered by the law becomes precisely how cautious the parties are required to be in their communications. This is a question that may be answered differently in different jurisdictions – with no concept of the law having any claim to being more correct than any other.

1.2 Illustrating the problem

English courts have addressed spot market contracts on a few recent occasions, and the facts of those cases may serve as illustrations of the issue. *Pagnan SpA v Feed Products Ltd*[3] was a case where a contract for the sale of a quantity of corn feed pellets was said to have been concluded by telex. Having exchanged several telexes, the sellers arrived no less than twice at the belief that the only points of difference had been agreed. Mr Justice Bingham at first instance as well as the Court of Appeal decided that a contract had been concluded on the first pleaded occasion, at a stage when the parties had (in the words of the judge) mutually intended to bind themselves on the terms agreed on 1 February, leaving certain subsidiary and legally inessential terms to be settled later.[4]

In a second case, *Glencore Energy UK Ltd v Cirrus Oil Services Ltd*,[5] the claimant *Glencore* sought damages from the defendant, Cirrus Oil, for repudiation of a contract for the sale of crude oil alleged to have been made on 4 April 2012.[6] Glencore's argument was that the contract was concluded when a 'firm offer' made in an email of 3 April 2012 was accepted by a 'good news' email from Cirrus Oil on the morning of 4 April 2012. The parties were negotiating via email and there was a clearly determined purchase price. The judge decided in favour of Glencore that a contract had been concluded with the intention of finalising further terms.

The third specimen case is *Proton v Orlen Lietuva*.[7] Here, the parties were

---

3 See [1987] 2 Lloyd's Rep. 601 for both Bingham J and CA.

4 Ibid at 613.

5 [2014] EWHC 87 (Comm).

6 At a price of DTD + $0.15 per barrel CFR Tema (Cost and Freight, Tema). DTD was industry shorthand for the index price of Brent crude oil on the relevant specified dates, which in this case were the five days following the bill of lading date.

7 [2013] EWHC 334 (Comm) (summary judgment application) followed by [2013] EWHC 2872 (Comm) (judgment). For this case, see also Johanna Hjalmarsson and Mateusz Bek (2013) 'Deal or no Deal? Proton Energy Group SA v Orlen Lietuva [2013] EWHC 2872 (Comm)' (2013) 13(9) *Shipping and Trade Law* 6–8.

again negotiating the sale of oil via email. By an email sent on 14 June 2012 Proton made what was described as a 'firm offer' to sell to Orlen some crude oil mix on CIF terms. Email correspondence continued between the parties on the same day, culminating in a one-word email from Orlen stating: 'Confirmed'. On 20 June 2012 Proton sent Orlen a draft detailed written contract for the sale. The draft terms of this written contract provoked further email exchanges and ultimately a revised draft which Proton sent to Orlen on 27 June 2012. At this stage, there was at least one issue on which the parties had not agreed: the documents which Proton would be required to present for payment under a proposed documentary letter of credit. On 29 June 2012 Orlen wrote to Proton to say that it was withdrawing from the negotiations. It did not open any letter of credit and it did not accept the cargo.[8] On 2 July 2012 Proton notified Orlen that it was accepting Orlen's failures to open a letter of credit or to take delivery of the cargo as repudiatory breaches of contract and was thereby bringing the sale contract to an end.

One of the issues discussed in the case was the various market practices in the oil trade.[9] Orlen Lietuva had argued that in trades where both parties were spot traders and the priority was on locking in the price of the commodity, a recap with a firm offer would be considered binding.[10] In such trades, the parties were not contemplating physical delivery because the commodity was going to be sold again before delivery in any case. On the other hand, in a trade where one of the parties was a refinery, it was more important to determine further the details as to quality, quantity and delivery, and the price was not as important a term. Based on such differences in market practices, Orlen Lietuva successfully argued against summary judgment, allowing it to bring evidence as to whether a contract had been made according to the practice in the trade.

Having heard that evidence, a second judge held[11] that Proton's claim succeeded – the parties had entered into a binding agreement. A contract had come into existence between the parties and had been repudiated by

---

8 Such inaction amounted to a breach of contract, if concluded. If the judge had been in doubt as to whether a contract had been concluded, evidence that the party had taken such actions might have persuaded the judge that there had been subsequent acceptance, acceptance by conduct or waiver of the right to argue that there was no contract, as in *Percy Trentham Ltd v Archital Luxfer Ltd & Ors* [1993] 1 Lloyd's Rep. 25 where the contract was held to have come into existence during performance. This illustrates the position of a party required to act under a contract, where there is uncertainty as to whether it has been concluded in the first place. To act, or not to act?

9 The discussion was recapped in the judgment of HHJ Mackie QC in *Proton v Orlen Lietuva* [2013] EWHC 2872 (Comm) at [27] *et seq.*

10 Charterparty recaps are valid and binding contracts. The earliest example in case-law appears to be *The Olympic Pride* [1980] 2 Lloyd's Rep. 67; see also *The Mercedes Envoy* [1995] 2 Lloyd's Rep. 559 and most recently *Caresse Navigation Ltd v Zurich Assurances Maroc and others* (the *Channel Ranger*) [2014] EWCA Civ 1366, [2015] 1 Lloyd's Rep. 256.

11 HHJ Mackie QC in [2013] EWHC 2872 (Comm).

Orlen, which was liable in damages. First, the evidence pointed to there being a single contract formation mechanism in the oil trading market, and not a segmented market where contract formation depended on the nature and identity of the parties. The effect of the judge's consideration of market practices was arguably that the meaning of 'offer' and 'acceptance' were specific to what they were understood to mean in that market.[12] Secondly, a contract had come into existence on 14 June. In the words of the judge:

> 'This was a classic spot deal where the speed of the market requires that the parties agree the main terms and leave the details, some of which may be important, to be discussed and agreed later. Lay business people from different jurisdictions will not always conduct all aspects of their dealings to fit the conventions of English contract law . . . the fact that Orlen also saw itself as committed means that both sides did.'[13]

English contract law generally permits partial agreement with terms to be negotiated later.[14] A contract may be void for uncertainty, but that was not the case here.[15] Instead, the judge factored in the speed of transactions in the particular market in question as an indicator of incompleteness of the contract being forgivable, where the overall picture indicated that both parties had seen themselves as committed at the time.

2. Contract formation – the law and its sources

A quick overview of the sources of law and basic concepts of the English and Chinese systems is warranted. First, English law on contract formation takes offer and acceptance as its starting point[16] – but there is remarkable judicial flexibility in the approach to those concepts. Put at its simplest, the parties will have made a contract when there is agreement on all essential terms, even if some terms are left for later negotiation.[17] The fluid nature of the assessment of contract negotiations nevertheless has a binary result: there was either a contract, or there was not.[18] On an objective theory of contract interpretation, subsequent conduct is not of direct assistance to

12 Giving rise to the obvious subsequent question of what would be the effect of an offer or an acceptance where market practice is not well understood, or where there is no joint assumption as to market practices – and what role may be played by objective expert evidence in such a case.

13 *Proton* at [39].

14 See Beale (gen. ed.), *Chitty on Contracts*, 31st edn (London: Sweet & Maxwell, 2012), 2-114 to 2-115.

15 See below.

16 See *Chitty*, 2-003 *et seq* and 2-027 *et seq*, respectively.

17 On generally similar facts involving a negotiation, the court may find that the parties continued to negotiate because they had not yet come to any agreement; or that agreement had been accomplished but the parties continued to negotiate to agree the final terms (see *Chitty*, 2-029).

18 Cf. below on *culpa in contrahendo*.

the process of ascertaining whether the parties thought on a specific date that a contract was in place, and on what terms – subsequent judicial scrutiny is likely to involve a component of hindsight. English law employs the tool of estoppel by convention to take into account evidence of subsequent events to show what contract the parties thought had been made.[19] Judicial scrutiny will always take into account the commercial circumstances such as trade or market practices; characteristics of contract formation such as speed or level of detail of the negotiations; and will conclude accordingly.[20]

As for Chinese contract law, in considering how to apply traditional offer-and-acceptance theory under Chinese contract law to the spot market, the analysis will depend on the statutes, judicial interpretations supporting their application and the express language of international conventions, and on how such principles have been put into practice. The law derives authority from three sources: (a) the relevant statutes including the Contract Law of the People's Republic of China (PRC)[21] and the General Principles of Civil Law of the PRC;[22] (b) judicial interpretations of the application of these statutes made by the Supreme People's Court;[23] and (c) international conventions to which China is a party; for this purpose notably the United Nations Convention on Contracts for the International Sale of Goods 1980 (CISG).[24] If the language of these sources is inapt to address the challenge, there will arguably be if not a vacuum at least some legal uncertainty as to the position. It will be seen that set against the comparatively fluid and adaptable principles of English law, Chinese law operates with a distinct set of explicitly established factors in determining whether a contract is at hand. It will be argued that while the clearly established principles and criteria enable the parties to personally negotiated, longer-term contracts to know when and how a contract has been put in place, spot markets are unlikely to fit neatly into the criteria. As a result of the precise formal grounds of validity, Chinese law to a greater extent than English law allows a party who

19 See further, Gerard McMeel, 'Prior Negotiations and Subsequent Conduct – the Next Step Forward for Contractual Interpretation' (2003) 119 LQR 272. In practice, the subsequent actions of a party in the performance of the contract, as soon as evidence thereof is admissible, may exert a powerful influence on the mind of the judge.

20 The assumption that context-based construction is always better should not be uncritically adopted, as explained by Bernstein in an empirical analysis of the US Uniform Commercial Code; Lisa Bernstein, 'Merchant Law in a Modern Economy', Chapter 13 in G. Klass et al. (eds), *Philosophical Foundations of Contract Law* (Oxford: OUP, 2014).

21 Adopted and promulgated at the 2nd session of the Ninth National People's Congress on 15 March 1999, in force on 1 October 1999.

22 Adopted and promulgated at the 4th session of the Sixth National People's Congress on 12 April 1986, in force on 1 January 1987.

23 For the purposes of this chapter, mainly Interpretation No.2 on Several Issues Concerning the Application of the People's Republic of China Contract Law, which was issued by the Supreme People's Court of PRC on 24 April 1999, in force on 13 May 2009.

24 The Convention is an international treaty which attempted to unify rules for the international sale of goods. It was signed in Vienna in 1980, in force on 1 January 1988.

is unhappy with the bargain made greater opportunities to wriggle out of a contract that, at the time, both parties may well have considered concluded.

3. At the peri-contractual stage

While Chinese law therefore arguably offers greater wriggle room to a party wishing to exit an unprofitable contract, Chinese law along with other civil law systems also offers compensation to the party suffering a loss where the contract has been negated. Thus, some civil law systems operate a concept of *culpa in contrahendo*.[25] The negotiating parties are under a duty to behave carefully in negotiating and may become liable for losses incurred by the other party.[26] Article 42 of the Chinese Contracts Law 1999 stipulates damages in case a negotiating party causes loss to the other party by pretending to conclude a contract, and negotiating in bad faith; or by deliberately concealing important facts relating to the conclusion of the contract or providing false information; or by performing other acts in violation of the principle of good faith. In addition, Article 43 prescribes that disclosing trade secrets will give rise to liability regardless of whether a contract is ultimately concluded. These provisions operate at the pre-contractual stage and fulfil the purpose of mitigating the effect of the simple binary issue of the existence of a contract, in circumstances where one party has somehow acted in such a way as to cause the other party to incur expenses or liabilities.

Without reinventing the concept of *culpa in contrahendo*, English law has found a way to mitigate the binary effect while adhering to its central principle of the contract on/off switch. In *RTS Flexible Systems Ltd v Molkerei Alois Muller GmbH & Co KG*,[27] the parties had entered into negotiations to supply and install automated packaging machinery for the defendant, a producer of dairy products. The parties had agreed a letter of intent so that they could begin works, but the letter of intent expired and no further formal contract was made, although the parties carried on with the work. All negotiations were said to be subject to contract.

Although the Supreme Court laconically noted that 'The moral of the story to is to agree first and to start work later',[28] it upheld the bargain of the parties, such as it was. The Supreme Court held that although the parties had negotiated contract terms 'subject to contract' but work had begun before the terms were finalised, there was a contract on the terms

25 See also Regulation (EC) 864/2007 of the European Parliament and of the Council of 11 July 2007 on the law applicable to non-contractual obligations (Rome II) especially Recitals 29 and 30 and Article 12.
26 This concept is present in German law and Scandinavian law and represents a shade of grey or a half-way house in response to the pure, binary question of whether a contract has been found.
27 [2010] UKSC 14.
28 Ibid at [1].

that had been agreed.[29] Lord Clarke's speech in *RTS* held the parties to the following standard:

> 'It depends not upon their subjective state of mind, but upon a consideration of what was communicated between them by words or conduct, and whether that leads objectively to a conclusion that they intended to create legal relations and had agreed upon all the terms which they regarded or the law requires as essential for the formation of legally binding relations.' At [45].

In the absence of a clear-cut offer and acceptance, the successful claimant's argument and the reasoning of the judge focused on the language employed by the parties. Both parties understood that not all contractual terms had been agreed. This was not fatal since under English law a contract will be binding upon the parties as long as they intended to enter into contractual relations and agreed on the essential terms.[30]

However, the concept of *culpa in contrahendo* is not particularly apposite in the spot market context; and *RTS* is not the best precedent, for related reasons. Spot negotiations are almost instantaneous and there is no perceptible progression through a negotiating stage to conclusion. Communications may well be ambiguous without being in the least culpable. The concept has a more natural home in construction contracts or other partnership-type contracts that evolve over time and are renewed, altered and confirmed as work progresses. If *culpa in contrahendo* is therefore not a workable solution to mitigate errors arising from faulty contract-making processes, we are left with a truly binary contract-making procedure. We must look for the defined preconditions of the law for a contract to arise, in circumstances where by nature those will not be found or are hard to distinguish.

---

29 In *RTS*, the Supreme Court considered that it was not really an option to hold, as the Court of Appeal had done, that the parties had not concluded any contract at all. This was principally because in the letter of intent the parties had agreed the entire contract sum and not just the contract sum. Although at that stage the agreement was expressly stated to be subject to contract, the Supreme Court held that it was not an option to hold that no contract at all had been concluded – there had obviously been agreement on the price, and the question was just the extent of that agreement. The Supreme Court also found that the term 'subject to contract' had been waived – it did not consider that the waiver had to be express, but held that by a certain date that term had been waived so that a contract had come into existence. That being the case, there followed much debate about what set of contract terms had been incorporated and represented the content of the contract. Following *RTS*, it is clear that the requirement for certainty as to terms and conditions and as to essential terms is not the sharp requirement it once was. It should be noted that while spot market contracts involve speedily concluded sale contracts, *RTS* concerned a long-term business relationship carried out in stages. The conclusions from the latter may be less apposite to a spot sale for that reason.

30 *Rossiter v Miller* (1878) 3 App. Cas. 1124.

4. Conditions for contract making

As noted above, Chinese law operates with a distinct set of explicitly established factors in determining whether a contract is at hand. Although the range of types of contracts is legion and the conditions to be satisfied in each may vary greatly, the law operates a finite set of conditions, common to all types of contracts. In Chinese contract theory, there are several doctrines of what are the conditions for the successful formation of a contract. However, the most generally accepted ones are that, first, there must be two or more parties to be bound in a contract.[31] Secondly, there must be mutual assent as to the 'main essential terms' between parties in a contract.[32] Third, there must be a discernible offer and acceptance.[33] These three points are all reminiscent of the English doctrine of contract formation.

4.1 Identified parties to the contract

According to Article 2 of the Chinese Contract Law, a contract is defined as an agreement among natural persons, legal persons or other organisations as equal parties. Accordingly, irrespective of the characteristics of each party, they must be equal and existent when involved in a contract. The parties to a contract may be different from the persons concluding the contract.[34] Also, there must be two or more parties having no mutual benefit involved in a contract, otherwise the contract cannot be regarded as 'formed'. Chinese contract law thus operates a broad brush with clear distinctions; but statute law does not provide fine guidance on the identification of the parties in an individual case, which must ultimately be a matter of fact in context.

As might be expected, the issue of the identity of parties to a contract also arises under English law. The issue falls under the doctrine of mistake and the basic rule, arising from cases of fraud against a seller, is that the contract is void for mistake so that the goods can be recovered from a third party under the *nemo dat* rule.[35] Much like under Chinese law, this will ultimately be a question of facts in context. The *Glencore* case above raised an identity issue, with an argument put forward that if no buyer was identified, there could be no contract. The buyer was referred to in the 'firm offer' as 'Cirrus . . . (Full trading name)', which could have referred to either of two companies; but at the time of the negotiation of the particular crude oil transaction

---

31 Article 2 of the Chinese Contract Law.
32 Article 12 of the Chinese Contract Law.
33 Article 2 of the Chinese Contract Law.
34 Much like in other legal systems, the persons actually making the contract may be the agents or brokers of the parties and are not strictly regarded as real parties involved in a contract; the parties to the contract are persons who in fact have contractual rights and shoulder contractual obligations.
35 As in *Cundy v Lindsay* [1878] 3 App. Cas. 459, and see *Chitty*, 5-089.

at issue, there was only one company in existence whose name began with 'Cirrus', namely the same company with which Glencore had traded previously.[36] Before coming to this conclusion, the judge noted that 'The actual identity of the buyer was not of huge importance to Glencore if payment was to be by letter of credit'.[37] Equally, in *Proton*, the defendant's argument in the decision on summary judgment was that whether a contract had been concluded depended on the character of the parties, so that retail and wholesale traders would be treated differently. This was rejected by the judge who emphasised the spot nature of the trading market – an unspoken idea may well have been that one may or may not have the full picture of who the contracting party is in such a market. While in some business sectors the nature and identity of the contractual party is essential,[38] that is not necessarily the case in other trades.

There are additional elements of complexity in the context of the practice of formation of contracts at a distance in the spot market, in immediate *ad hoc* relationships and with perhaps only superficial information directly available as to the identity of the other party. Chinese law requires as a component of contract formation that the identification of the virtual parties as shown on the electronic device should be real and cannot be made up; failing which the contract cannot be regarded as concluded for want of defined parties.[39] In the spot market, the contracting parties are usually businesses, companies or enterprises rather than individuals, and to assist the identification of such legal persons, the Ministry of Commerce of China has allocated a unique and standardised certification of business code to each enterprise which operates as formal authentication of the trading parties, thus making the determination of the identity of parties in an electronic business a safer and more definite process. Whether negotiating parties will make the most of this tool is another matter, as demonstrated by the facts of *Glencore*.[40]

4.2 Offer and acceptance

Chinese contract law requires a process of offer and acceptance to conclude a contract. This is made explicit by Article 13 of the Chinese Contract Law.

---

36 *Glencore* at [32].
37 *Glencore* at [28].
38 Insurance is such a sector.
39 See Article 55 of the General Principles of Civil Law of the PRC, which provides that one of the requirements to be met for a legal act is that the party's intention must be genuinely expressed. Therefore, there should be a reasonable presumption that the untrue intention expressed by a fake virtual party cannot be regarded as a genuine intention.
40 In which case, uncertainty as to the identity of the party in question persisted, or was discovered, after the conclusion of the contract. Sometimes an identity issue will be conveniently discovered by a party who wishes to argue in legal proceedings that the contract is not enforceable against it.

Accordingly, the two stages of offer and acceptance are essential for to the formation of a contract.[41] This is a state of considerably reduced flexibility compared to English law, which regards offer and acceptance merely as a technical starting point. The judicial starting point under English law is referred to as 'the objective test': the leading text states that 'once the parties have to all outward appearances agreed in the same terms on the same subject-matter, then neither can, generally, rely on some unexpressed qualification or reservation to show that he had not in fact agreed to the terms to which he had appeared to agree'.[42] Indeed, the apparent bargain made, or not made, by the process of offer and acceptance is subject to an overall evaluation according, not least, to the factors mentioned in the following.[43] The language by which the contract was held to be made in two of the specimen cases above was contractual in character: 'firm offer' and 'good news' (*Glencore*); and 'firm offer' and 'confirmed' (*Proton*).[44] However, it is noteworthy that in all three specimen cases continuous negotiations were held to have crystallised into a contract, with each judge taking into account surrounding factors to identify the offer and acceptance, including the specific words used by the parties, trade practices in the particular market place and the apparent mutual intentions of the parties.

In *Glencore*,[45] the judge concluded that it was clear that the parties intended to conclude a binding contract before the extended deadline of 11.00 on 4 April. There was no room for any suggestion that the deal remained 'subject to contract'. The 'firm offer' email was intended to be capable of acceptance with a binding contract thereby concluded, with a deadline for acceptance. The email set out all the main terms necessary for a contract to be concluded and also general terms and conditions which were to be the 2007 BP General Terms and Conditions for CFR sales. The 'good news' email was a clear acceptance of the 'firm offer' and could only mean that there was acceptance of the main terms set out in the firm offer with intention to revert on fine tuning of contract terms. Instead, in *Glencore* the determining factor was that the parties had used the language of 'firm offer' and 'good news'.

As pointed out by counsel for the claimant in *Proton*, its offer was said to be a 'firm offer'. This was 'language requesting a binding commitment – a

---

41 On the obverse side, Chinese law operates two distinct concepts of withdrawal and revocation: an offer or acceptance can always be withdrawn before an offer becomes effective whereas the question of whether or not it may be revoked arises only after that moment. Under Chinese law, withdrawal of an offer or an acceptance can only happen before it arrives at the offeree or the offeror.

42 *Chitty*, 2-002.

43 See section 4.3 *et seq* below.

44 In *The Junior K* [1988] 2 Lloyd's Rep. 583, the word 'confirmed' was immediately followed by a qualification that the confirmation was subject to the details of the Gencon Charterparty form; a form requiring express choices between the options. There was no contract.

45 See above.

definite acceptance or rejection – in reply'.[46] The offer was said to be 'valid till 14.06.2012 COB'. As the judge put it, 'This *firm*, time-limited offer *did not admit of languid negotiation*'. It demanded an immediate, binding commitment. In addition, the transaction contemplated was spot business and of an immediate nature.

The judge also noted the parties' use of language, calling it 'the language is that of commitment'.[47] He noted that the parties to a spot deal in a hectic market situation, coming from a spectrum of cultural, commercial, legal and linguistic backgrounds cannot be expected to 'conduct all aspects of their dealings to fit the conventions of English contract law'.[48] However, the parties could, and should be expected to correctly utilise the language of commitment. A 'firm offer' meeting with the response 'confirmed' looks and smells like a contract, and it is only right that it should, in fact, be a contract.[49]

In China, on the other hand, a crucial question is always whether the offer-and-acceptance mode of formation of contract has been strictly followed. If so, the contract will be regarded as formed, provided that the necessary elements are present, with the offer-and-acceptance process being one of the conditions. While modern methods of making the offer and acceptance can still be subsumed under traditional theory so that the words exchanged can be interpreted as an offer and an acceptance, the law is perfectly capable of operating in the modern context. But a tick box approach to the existence of a contract may – perhaps ironically – create uncertainty: where both parties originally thought themselves bound by a mutually beneficial agreement, but subsequent events have caused one party to wish to exit or avoid the contract, does a tick box approach create a window of opportunity for an opportunistic party to do so? If English law held the parties strictly to the words exchanged without taking into account the surrounding circumstances such as features of the specific trade, and if English judges did not have the tools and flexibility to take into account subsequent actions by the parties as evidence of a bargain, opportunities would be created to exit the contract by a party who has found the bargain less beneficial than it originally thought. It is submitted that Chinese law needs to be equally flexible in this regard, and that a pro forma requirement of offer and acceptance, while offering certainty, may in fact be offering uncertainty in the longer term ostensibly.

46　*Proton* at [32].
47　Ibid at [39].
48　Ibid.
49　It is worth noting the very subtle deviation from the standard established in *RTS Flexible Systems* above, which refers to both 'words and conduct'.

4.3 Incomplete offers and partial bargains – on what terms is the contract made?

English law in principle requires that an offer cannot be ambiguous or incomplete if a contract is to result.[50] However, if the offer is incomplete, there are various ways in which the law may fill it out by using statutorily implied terms[51] or by stipulating that some terms are essential so that a contract made without them is not viable. This already is a form of certainty permitting the parties – and the courts – to say with certainty that a contract was or was not at hand. However, if the offer is ambiguous, the burden on the courts is heavier as they must then infer a contract from the parties' intentions and a variable set of circumstances. While the traditional stance is to require clarity and specificity so that it is clear what intentions the parties had and how to give effect to them, there is today 'an established reluctance to strike down what were obviously intended to be legally enforceable commercial agreements'.[52] In other words, if the parties have obvious commercial intentions and have negotiated an agreement which later proves ambiguous and difficult to enforce, English courts will not nullify the entire bargain on a technicality or because in hindsight the drafting proves not to be up to the challenge.

The Court of Appeal in *Pagnan*[53] held that although certain terms of economic significance to the parties were not agreed, neither party intended agreement of those terms to be a precondition to a concluded agreement. The parties had continued negotiating even after the contract had been made, because they had made an interim agreement that required further terms to be agreed. In some cases, therefore, a partially agreed contract will be upheld by the courts, in other cases it will be insufficiently precise to be enforceable. Lord Justice Lloyd summarised the relevant principles:

'(1) In order to determine whether a contract has been concluded in the course of correspondence, one must first look to the correspondence as a whole . . .

(2) Even if the parties have reached agreement on all the terms of the proposed contract, nevertheless they may intend that the contract shall not become binding until some further condition has been fulfilled. That is the ordinary *"subject to contract"* case.

(3) Alternatively, they may intend that the contract shall not become binding until some *further term or terms have been agreed* . . .

(4) Conversely, the parties may intend to be *bound right away* even

---

50 Although as ever there is flexibility – a party that carries on as if it had agreed to a bargain is unlikely to be able to persuade the court that there was no agreement.
51 Not least, in this context, under the Sale of Goods Act 1979.
52 *Durham Tees Valley Airport v BMI Baby* [2010] EWCA Civ 485, [2011] 1 Lloyd's Rep. 68 at [54].
53 [1987] 2 Lloyd's Rep. 601.

though there are *further terms still to be agreed* or some further formality to be fulfilled . . .

(5) If the parties *fail to reach agreement* on such further terms, the existing contract is not invalidated unless the failure to reach agreement on such further terms renders the contract as a whole *unworkable or void for uncertainty.*'[54]

In *Proton*, the offer explicitly contemplated that further contractual terms should be negotiated.[55] The reasoning of the judge is instructive. He noted that negotiations took place in a fast-moving market where deals were concluded with details to be determined at a later (but not much later) stage. In the spot commodities markets, the detailed terms are arguably less important than in other contracts – what matters is to sell the cargo by its best before date and agree payment by a secure method, and conversely to secure cargo of contractual quality and quantity. It would be unreasonable to expect parties operating in such a fast-paced environment to set out all the terms of the agreement between them in a written contract. It makes much more commercial sense to allow them more flexibility in conducting their business. The leading text notes that there are 'many examples of judicial awareness of the danger that too strict an application of the requirement of certainty could result in the striking down of agreements intended by the parties to have binding force'.[56] Commercial acuity is, for better or worse, the key to English law.

The question on what terms the contract was made is conceptually subsequent in the view of English law – that is, first, the contract is made by offer or acceptance, and only when that dust has settled should it be determined on what terms the contract has been made. However, that is a purely conceptual approach, because the terms are clearly an intrinsic part of the process of formation. In the spot trades, contracts are made by fragmented communications sometimes recapped. Where there is such fragmentation, with reference to other documents and external sets of standard terms, how does one determine with sufficient certainty if a contract is at hand? The issue of the contractual content is determined for the purpose of English law by *Butler Machine Tool Co Ltd v Ex-Cell-O Corp (England) Ltd*[57] wherein an inconclusive battle of the forms involving directly contradictory terms did not prevent a contract from coming into being – the task of the judge will be closely to consider the details of the various proposed contract terms and decide on what terms the contract was in fact made.[58] That said,

54 Pagnan at 619.
55 Proton at [17].
56 *Chitty*, 2-140.
57 *Butler Machine Tool Co Ltd v Ex-Cell-O Corp (England) Ltd* [1979] 1 W.L.R. 401.
58 More recently, in *Tekdata Interconnections Ltd v Amphenol Ltd* [2009] EWCA Civ 1209, [2010] 1 Lloyd's Rep. 357, the Court of Appeal applied a traditional offer-and-acceptance analysis saying that unless there was a clear course of dealing between the parties, the

in terms of the bare, binary formation question, a contract may be formed already when there is agreement upon the essential terms – this is generally expressed as the idea of certainty and enforceability. In *Pagnan*, following the quote from Lord Lloyd's speech above, he went on to say:

> '(6) It is sometimes said that the parties must agree on the *essential terms* and it is only matters of detail which can be left over. This may be misleading, since the word "essential" in that context is ambiguous. If by "essential" one means a term without which the contract cannot be enforced then the statement is true: the law cannot enforce an incomplete contract. If by "essential" one means a term which the parties have agreed to be essential for the formation of a binding contract, then the statement is tautologous. If by "essential" one means only a term which the court regards as important as opposed to a term which the court regards as less important or a matter of detail, the statement is untrue. *It is for the parties to decide whether they wish to be bound and if so, by what terms, whether important or unimportant.* It is the parties who are, in the memorable phrase coined by the judge with "the masters of their contractual fate". Of course the more important the term is the less likely it is that the parties will have left it for future decision. But there is no legal obstacle which stands in the way of the parties agreeing to be bound now while deferring important matters to be agreed later. It happens every day when parties enter into so-called "heads of agreement".'[59]

Chinese law equally operates a concept of 'main essential terms', but on a more formalised footing. Article 12 of Chinese Contract Law lists eight items, namely the titles or names and domiciles of the parties, the subject-matter, the quantity of subject-matter, the quality of subject-matter, the price or remuneration for the subject-matter, the time-limit and place and method of performance, any liability for breach of contract and the chosen dispute settlement method. These eight types of terms are said to be 'generally contained' as distinct from 'must-be-contained' in a contract under Article 12, which means that the terms listed in this article are not compulsorily or necessarily concluded in each specific contract. Interpreting this point of law, the People's Supreme Court enacted the Judicial Interpretation of the Application of Contract Law No.2 in February 2009, Article 1 of which provides that the inclusion of definite parties, subject-matter and the quantity of subject-matter in a contract can be regarded as the 'most

---

traditional analysis was difficult to displace. The parties had been doing business for many years, buying components by purchase order and acknowledgement. The purchase orders and acknowledgements each referred to the issuing party's terms.

59 *Pagnan* at 619.

main essential terms'. Accordingly, the Judicial Interpretation has narrowed down the types of terms that must be contained in every contract and only the three types of terms noted in Article 1 are compulsorily required.

The reasons for maintaining the first two types of terms are obvious: the existence of two or more parties to a contract is one of the conditions to assess whether the contract is formed and therefore it is necessary to specify definite parties to every contract. As for the subject-matter, it is the main object of a contract and although the subject-matter can be of almost infinite variety, the contract cannot be performed without a definite subject-matter. For example, in a contract for the sale of goods, the subject-matter is the goods to be sold by the seller to the buyer. If a term specifying the subject-matter is not included in such a sale contract, the performance of transferring the goods and documents (in some situations) will not be fulfilled and thus the aim of the contract cannot be realised.[60] However, the reason for inclusion of a term of quantity in every type of contract is arguably not as straightforward. Although in a sale of goods contract, a quantity term is fundamental to the decision to what extent the parties have fulfilled their contractual duties, in other types of contracts, such as employment contracts, the quantity term does not seem to be of such importance and the non-inclusion of a quantity term will not affect the performance of such a contract. Therefore, it is arguably open to doubt whether a quantity term can be regarded as a 'main essential term' in every contract.

It will be noted that English law shares some common essential terms with Chinese law. For example, in *Glencore*, the intention to 'revert on the fine tuning of the contract terms so that it was back-to-back' was not making the acceptance subject to such agreement, but giving notice of the likelihood of a wish to negotiate the detailed terms to be found in the BP General Terms and Conditions. There could be no going back on the main terms which, in a spot contract of this kind, were clearly and sufficiently set out and agreed.

The judge in this case did not emphasise the fact that the purchase price had been agreed, like the Supreme Court did in *RTS*, so that there must be a contract in place. Indeed, the factual situation was quite different – the purchase price in *RTS* was agreed at the outset but for the entirety of the contract works. In *Glencore*, the purchase price was for the specified amount of commodity only – it was a classic spot sale. Although the Supreme Court in *RTS* emphasised the purchase price, it is not possible to say that once the price has been agreed the court is more likely to find that there was a contract in place. It has to be said, in a spot sale it would often make a lot

---

60 This issue might come before the court in the shape of arguments on one side that the contract was invalid for vagueness, and on the other that a contract was made but that there was no breach because the vague description of the goods was met by the seller.

of sense to take agreement upon the price as agreement as to the whole. Other terms may vary, but the price is the paramount term to a spot sale.[61]

The essence of Chinese law on this point is that once the main essential terms are agreed, and there is agreement in principle to any other terms, there is recognition by the law that it might be inefficient to make clear every specific term in detail.

4.4 Signature requirement

Besides the three conditions to be satisfied on which contract formation are contingent, there is also a requirement of signature for traditional contracts in written form under Chinese law.[62] English contracts for the most part are not required to take written form or display an authenticated signature; although negotiations that are 'subject to contract' may occasionally cause subsequent signature to be necessary. The facts of *Oceanografia SA de CV v DSND Subsea AS (The Botnica)*[63] serve as a good example from the context of a charterparty dispute. A charterparty was 'subject to the signing of mutually agreeable contract terms and conditions'. All the essential terms had been agreed. As a result of the subject to contract proviso, the signature by one party, and verbal agreement by the other party, did not give rise to a valid contract. This was not fatal, however: one party's conduct in going ahead with the charterparty gave rise to a waiver by that party of the right to insist on signatures.[64]

Chinese law does operate a signature requirement. Article 32 of the Chinese Contract Law provides that the contract is formed when it is signed or sealed by the parties if the contract is concluded in written form. This means that it is only when the contract in written form is equipped with the signature of all the parties that the acceptance can be seen as effective and the contract becomes formed. This requirement for a signature raises issues not just of electronic signature, which for the purpose of Chinese contract law have been resolved by statute, but also of how to provide evidence for the modern contract.[65]

The requirement for a signature has led to an indirect but helpful contribution from legal developments designed to adapt the law to cope with electronic commerce. According to Article 4 of the Electronic Signature

---

61 Section 8(2) of the Sale of Goods Act 1979 provides that where the price is not determined, the buyer must pay a reasonable price. See further, *Chitty*, 2-114.
62 Article 32 of the Chinese Contract Law.
63 [2007] 1 Lloyd's Rep. 37.
64 In the alternative, the judge found an estoppel by convention: both parties had assumed that the *Botnica* was operating on the terms of the 28 August charterparty. This assumption was common between the parties as a result of the numerous communications between them with references to the '28 August Charter Agreement'. Ibid at [109]–[111].
65 See below.

Law of the PRC,[66] electronic contracts are deemed concluded in written form, conforming to the requirements of general contract laws and regulations, because they are capable of providing tangible expression to the contents carried and can readily be picked up for reference.[67] As a result, it is common practice for the parties to sign the confirmation letter of the contract to confirm the contractual contents. Although in paperless trading a signature is not a requirement necessary to the formation of a contract, it is still prudent for the parties to underpin their contract certainty by determining the electronic signatures of their contractual counterparts. A signature on a confirmation letter through an electronic message (or a series thereof) is not a compulsory stage, but by not avoiding this step, the negotiating parties can make sure of the certainty and safety of their electronic contracts. Is dispute resolution a panacea to address these issues?

4.5 Dispute resolution

Inspiration might be sought from other fields of practice: the salvage industry operates a similar contract model with the benefit of perhaps more tradition than the spot trades. Salvage situations are in some ways similar to spot market fixtures. The parties have been forced together in an awkward (perhaps even life threatening) situation and may know nothing about each other except that they do not wish to deal as volunteers at the mercy of the common law. They form an agreement – something less than a contract – containing the bare essentials of contract terms and whereby disputes and even the most essential term, the remuneration of the salvor, are referred to a trusted third party.

Something very similar happens in the commodities trades, where standard terms refer the parties in case of disputes to GAFTA[68] or FOSFA[69] arbitration. Is this the way forward for markets where a large number of fairly standardised agreements are being concluded at speed? Would it be possible to refer all traders within a service or commodity segment to a dispute resolution body? The problem with this suggestion is that in salvage the situation to be resolved is exceptional, not the rule. Moreover, the parties are deliberately opting for later arbitration or mediation, over precision in the agreed contract terms. Unlike in salvage agreements, in the spot trades the absence of precision in the contract-making process is not an indication that the parties wish to be tied together in a dispute resolution procedure – on the contrary, they wish to resolve the trading relationship

---

66 Adopted and promulgated at the 11th meeting of the Standing Committee of the Tenth National People's Congress on 28 August 2004, in force on 1 April 2005.
67 Article 4 of the Electronic Signature Law of the PRC.
68 Grain and Feed Trade Association; the association provides standard contract terms and a dispute resolution service.
69 Federation of Oils Seeds and Fats Association; again, it provides standard contract terms and a dispute resolution service.

as quickly as it came about by shipping the goods and converting the FOB purchase to a CIF sale. The solution is therefore probably not external dispute resolution such as GAFTA or FOSFA arbitration, at least not by default.

5. Conclusion: Reflections on the future of trading

The process of contractual formation in the twenty-first century is becoming increasingly rapid, automatic and simplified between parties who may habitually conduct one-off transactions in fluid markets, where it is the rule not to know the other contracting party when making contracts through email or otherwise at a distance. The parties will not have previously met or done business and will be in a hurry to fix the deal, while happy to dispense with lawyers and detailed consideration of agreements. While such contract-making practices may increase business efficacy and facilitate the making of contracts between parties in a truly globalised marketplace, there are also peculiar issues involved. The identity of the parties may be of little importance to the trade transaction; whereas of course it is crucial in legal terms. The binary question of the existence of a contract is of particular importance in these trades because the negotiation process is rapid and the opportunities for mitigation slight. The verifiable terms may or may not be complete, by normal contractual standards.

In this context, it may or may not be agreed that the common law's flexibility in judicial consideration of contract-making, where there are essentially no fixed criteria, but where the offer and acceptance are merely the beginning and not a precondition for the conclusion of a contract, has the edge over more prescriptive systems of law. As has been demonstrated above, Chinese law prefers the approach that, in order to determine whether a contract has been formed in the modern market, regardless of whether the means of its conclusion are modern or traditional, the conditions to be satisfied should always fulfil first requirements: identity of the parties, established identified offer and acceptance, certainty of terms. Once those conditions are satisfied, the contract is formed. That is all well and good, but the precision in prescriptive rules entails an increased risk that if the transaction goes wrong, because of an unexpected export ban or a precipitous fall in market prices, a party who later finds that it did not benefit from the trade will have increased opportunities to argue that the transaction was flawed from the start and the contract never existed in the first place. A spotlight is also placed on the importance of the parties' choice of law – where the parties have omitted to specify their choice of law, subtle differences between English and Chinese law may translate into vast sums of money under dispute.

10 Globalised maritime commerce and challenges for PRC choice of law rules in defining 'party autonomy'

Professor Jason C.T. Chuah

1. Introduction

In the transnational world of commercial shipping, matters of private international law, especially as regards the choice of law in contracts, are of immense significance. It is also a matter of law which many in the developed countries take for granted. Whether the legal system in western Europe is left or right in the political economy spectrum there is due recognition that for transnational commerce to work successfully contractual choice of law rules not only need to be clear and certain, but, to a large extent, be rooted in a policy of trade promotion and the principle of civil justice. The EU's Rome I Regulation[1] which harmonises the contractual choice of law rules amongst the Member States, for instance, makes that plain in recital 6 of its Preamble:

> 'The proper functioning of the internal market creates a need, in order to improve the predictability of the outcome of litigation, certainty as to the law applicable and the free movement of judgments, for the conflict-of-law rules in the Member States to designate the same national law irrespective of the country of the court in which an action is brought.'

This objective is predicated on the larger paradigm set out in recital 1 of the Preamble, namely, that of maintaining and developing an area of freedom, security and justice which in turn requires 'judicial cooperation in civil matters with a cross-border impact to the extent necessary for the proper functioning of the internal market'.[2]

The objectives behind such a law are especially important where we are

---

1 Regulation (EC) 593/2008 of the European Parliament and of the Council of 17 June 2008 on the law applicable to contractual obligations (Rome I) OJ L 177, 4.7.2008, pp.6–16; it should of course be remembered that this is not 'new' law. The Regulation's predecessor, the Rome Convention Law Applicable to Contractual Obligations 1980, had applied to the then Member States of the EU.
2 Ibid.

to adopt a functional analysis to assess and measure that law's successes and deficiencies. Those objectives also have a private dimension – that is, the recognition of the right of parties to select their applicable law. As recital 11 of Rome I states plainly: 'The parties' freedom to choose the applicable law should be one of the cornerstones of the system of conflict-of-law rules in matters of contractual obligations'. The concept of party autonomy does not however have the same connotation, context or construction in other legal systems, and that is, it is argued, particularly so in the PRC.

It is this backdrop which lends weight to this chapter's evaluation[3] of the much more recent Chinese law on choice of law – the Law on the Application of Laws over Foreign-Related Civil Relations of the People's Republic of China (hereafter referred to as the Conflicts Law). The Law was adopted at the 17th session of the Standing Committee of the 11th National People's Congress of the People's Republic of China on 28 October 2010 and came into force on 1 April 2011. This is notably China's 'codification' of conflict rules (introducing both new rules and consolidating past norms) although there are also some conflict rules provided for in the Maritime Code.[4]

This chapter examines the scope and limits of the contractual choice of law provisions in the new Conflicts Law and the Chinese Maritime Code in the context of globalised maritime commerce. Maritime commerce is of special interest because of the intersection or conflict between what is covered by the Maritime Code and what is to be covered by the Conflicts Law; in certain quarters that *might* conceivably be seen as the appropriate delineation in law for wet and dry shipping. This modest work immediately faces a methodological challenge as regards philosophical hermeneutics. Chinese legal methodology differs from western methodologies of legal

---

3 It is not an exercise of comparative law which is being proposed here – the author is aware of the challenges in comparing western systems of law with non-western systems (see, for example, Riles, 'Wigmore's Treasure Box: Comparative Law in the Era of Information' (1999) 40 Harv. Int. L.J. 221 at 244 (note that the so-called 'Categories School' of comparative law tends to see non-Western systems as 'too different for meaningful comparison') and at p.245 where it is observed that a similar conclusion is reached by the so-called 'Context School' which sees context as all-important making 'meaningful comparison . . . increasingly problematic'. What is being attempted here is modest – namely, a legally syllogistic analysis of how Chinese contractual choice of law rules and precepts are being shaped as a result of its socio-economic change and the increasing inter-dependent commercial and maritime 'world'. The EU backdrop serves as a useful contrast given that EU private international law (as against the private international law rules of its constituent Member States) is relatively recent and had been established amid the rise of globalised commerce in the late twentieth century.

4 Which was adopted at the 28th meeting of the Standing Committee of the Seventh National People's Congress on 7 November 1992, promulgated by Order No.64 of the President of the People's Republic of China on 7 November 1992, and effective as of 1 July 1993. For a summary of the genesis and legislative history of the Law, see Weidong Zhu, 'China's Codification of the Conflict of Laws: Publication of a Draft Text' (2007) 3 J. Priv. Inr. L. 283.

inquiry.[5] The approach in this chapter shall highlight these differences in its inquiry but shall essentially rely on the idea of legal functionalism to argue that the rapid developments in Chinese private international law require legal institutions in the PRC to recognise not only the pragmatism of the international shipping and trade sector, but also the notion of 'party autonomy' itself and the importance of judicial creativity in giving effect to any evolving legal and commercial norms.

The Conflicts Law is laid out in 52 articles which are classified into eight chapters.[6] What is perhaps noteworthy is that the Law will apply chiefly to 'foreign-related civil relations of the PRC'. There is no definition provided in the Law as to what the phrase means, as is usually consistent with PRC statutory law where an interpretation document/instrument (often simply called an 'Interpretation') explaining the terminology in the primary statute might occasionally be published some time later. The Conflicts Law is as yet without a companion interpretation instrument. We remain thus left with the question as to what is covered by the Conflicts Law.

For one thing, it should be noted that 'foreign' would extend beyond China's relations with other independent states to its relations with its own special administrative regions, namely, Hong Kong and Macau. Another observation to be made is that the term 'foreign' is preferred instead of 'international'. That is indicative as to what is envisaged by the Law – namely, the emphasis on civil relations instead of any international relations.[7] Perhaps a comparison and contrast might be had to the Conflicts Law with the private international law provisions in the Maritime Code. In the Maritime Code, the relevant chapter dealing with private international law is Chapter XIV (Articles 268–276). In that chapter, the Code specifically refers to matters governed by an international treaty[8] *and* foreign law. It might thus be ventured that in the Maritime Code 'foreign'[9] is more capacious than the Conflicts Law. Despite the new Conflicts Law, it should not be ignored that international law, or at least treaty law, has always had a degree of prominence in the question of choice of law. For example, Article 260 of the Civil Procedure Code unequivocally states that where an international treaty to which China is a party contains provisions different from those found in this law, the provisions of such international treaty shall apply.[10]

---

5 P. Keller, 'Sources of Order in Chinese Law' (1994) 42 Am. J. Comp. L. 711.

6 Covering respectively general rules, civil subjects, succession, real rights, obligations, intellectual property and supplementary provisions.

7 It is interesting to note that PRC laws in general are quite precise in making the distinction between foreign and international; the increasing literature in western legal thinking on international and transnational commerce reflects this (rough) divide between civil and public, and might make for a useful analogy.

8 For example, Article 268.

9 Chapter XIV is entitled 'Application of Law in Relation to Foreign-Related Matters'.

10 The Civil Procedure Law has recently been amended, including in 2013, but the

A further comparison might be made. In the area of arbitration law, PRC Laws make explicit distinctions between arbitrations that are 'domestic' (i.e. between Chinese parties, with a seat in mainland China), 'foreign-related' (e.g. involving one foreign party or between two Chinese parties where the subject-matter of the dispute is outside mainland China and with a seat in mainland China) and 'foreign' ('foreign-related' arbitrations with a seat outside mainland China).[11] It is submitted that although the new Conflicts Law is silent as to the definition of 'foreign-related', for consistency and systemic unity in the application of the law, these distinctions should as far as possible be followed.

There is further support for this proposition in the 1988 Interpretation of the General Principles of Civil Law;[12] noting of course that the General Principles of Civil Law[13] do not also contain a definition of 'foreign-related'. Part 7 of the 1988 Interpretation provides in paragraph 178:

> 'Foreign-related civil legal relationships are those civil legal relationships in which one or both parties are foreign, a stateless person or a foreign legal person; or the subject matter of the concerned civil legal relationship is located outside the territory of the PRC; or any legal fact that caused the formation, alteration or extinguishment of the concerned legal relationship occurred outside the territory of the PRC.'

It is useful to note that there only needs to be one foreign element present – namely, one of the parties' nationality, the location of the subject-matter or the location of the relevant legal event.

As regards the foreignness of the party in question, that is dependent on nationality, not on other indicators such as domicile or residence. It has been pointed out that that is inconsistent with other modern private

amendments do not affect this provision. A version of the Civil Procedure Law (unofficial translation) is available at <http://www.inchinalaw.com/wp-content/uploads/2013/09/PRC-Civil-Procedure-Law-2012.pdf> accessed 24 February 2015.

11 See China Disputes E-Bulletin (May 2013) by Herbert Smith Freehills LLP, <http://www.herbertsmithfreehills.com/insights/legal-briefings?area=ab9ffab9-6a9d-405c-bc28-5b932ec78229&location=0f5f0ff3-61d6-448c-8f92-a13d44d67b8b> accessed 24 February 2015.

12 The 1988 Interpretation of the General Principles of Civil Law is the short title for the Opinions of the Supreme People's Court on Several Issues concerning the Implementation of the General Principles of the Civil Law of the People's Republic of China (For Trial Implementation), adopted at the Judicial Committee of the Supreme People's Court on 26 January 1988, No.6 [1988] of the Supreme People's Court and issued on 2 April 1988. Due to the conflict with the PRC Property Law in 2007, the interpretation becomes partially valid, in which paragraph 178 remains intact.

13 The General Principles of the Civil Law of the People's Republic of China, adopted at the 4th session of the Sixth National People's Congress, and promulgated on 12 April 1986, further amended on 27 August 2009.

international law regimes.[14] The Rome I regime, for example, largely places the emphasis on residence or habitual residence.[15] In the case of jurisdiction, the Brussels I regime places emphasis on domicile.[16] As a matter of fact, Article 4(1) of the Brussels I Recast Regulation explicitly provides that 'persons domiciled in a Member State shall, whatever their nationality, be sued in the courts of that Member State'.

Three observations might be made. The first is that this says much about the PRC's [new] political economy. However much liberalisation we have seen in recent times, its characterisation of personal law remains one rooted in the historical Chinese thinking of 'citizens' or 'subjects' especially across the twentieth and into the twenty-first century. China has had a chequered history of discomfort with 'subjects', 'citizens' and, perhaps more so now, autonomous 'legal and commercial entities'. It is largely incontrovertible to assert that equally it has had a long history of subordination of private commercial interests to the national interest. Whether there has been the creation of a civil society in commerce and business is cause for many debates.[17] For our purposes, it might be ventured that there is still much rhetorical belief in the notion that what is good for a Chinese business is good for the PRC. The separation between the business interest and the national interest is not properly recognised in this law. That rhetorical line is also to some extent subscribed to by enterprises, both partly privatised and fully private, which are keen to preserve their newly embedded status in the emerging Chinese socio-political terrain. The second observation is that the express admission of non-nationals (both natural and legal persons) into the realm of conflict of laws implies that foreign law could potentially always be a relevant factor with a non-national resident or domiciled in the PRC. That raises the legal conundrum for the non-national resident – which aspects of their day-to-day relationships and transactions will be subject to the Law and thus, potentially, foreign law, and which aspects are subject to local PRC law? That lack of certainty makes it imperative for non-nationals conducting business in China always to ensure that proper contractual choice of law is provided for. The third is that it is not appropriate to give the impression that the Chinese developments in private international law are entirely pragmatic.[18] There are some ideological foundational norms from which it

---

14 G. Tu, 'China's New Conflicts Code: General Issues and Selected Topics' (2011) 59 Am. J. Comp. L. 563 at 565
15 See Articles 4(2), 5–8 and 19 for example.
16 For example, Article 2 of Council Regulation (EC) No. 44/2001 and Article 4 of its Recast, EU Regulation No. 1215/2012.
17 For a general account of Chinese communism and the business interest, see B.R. Dickson, *Red Capitalists in China – The Party, Private Entrepreneurs, and Prospects for Political Change* (Cambridge University Press, 2003).
18 It has often been suggested that Chinese economic and legal modernisation is driven by sheer pragmatism rather than being motivated by ideology. See S. Zhao, 'The China

would not be easily derogated. So the Chinese popular saying that, 'a cat, whether it is white or black, is a good one as long as it is able to catch mice' is perhaps not redolent of the whole truth.

The subordination of the business or personal interest to the national interest is also seen in the words 'relations of the PRC' in the title of the Law. Although the Law refers to 'civil entities'[19] as the natural subjects of the Law, the overarching title does not shy away from stressing that in the final analysis, although it is civil entities who are engaged in the operations of commercial transactions, the state is ultimately engaged in that relationship with the foreign participant. It might even be said that there is no private relationship – the Chinese civil entity is simply making a commercial transaction as proxy of the state. It is perhaps this point which is particularly challenging for tribunals and courts attempting to give effect to the Law.

2. 'Party autonomy' or state's proxy

As is similar to the Rome I system in the EU, the starting premise of the PRC Law is expressed to be 'party autonomy'. Article 3 of the Conflicts Law provides that the parties may explicitly choose the law applicable to their foreign-related civil relation in accordance with the provisions of this Law. As for contracts of carriage, charterparties[20] and other maritime transport service contracts,[21] the relevant law as has been pointed out is the Maritime Code. Article 269 of the Code provides in like manner that the parties to a contract may choose the law applicable to such contract, unless the law provides otherwise.[22]

In both cases, there is expressed a notion of party autonomy. That freedom, however, is not absolute. There are doctrinal boundaries as well as practical considerations. In the Law, the condition is that the choice must be consistent with the provisions of the Law. In the Maritime Code, the choice could be restricted by the other provisions of the Code. Article 3 of the Conflicts Law uses the word 'explicitly', whilst there is no such reference in Article 269 of the Maritime Code. It is unlikely that, for practical purposes, 'explicitly' means express terms to the exclusion of any inference to be drawn from the contract and other circumstances. The wording in Article 269 is probably preferable in that it is more consistent with the selection being both express and tacit.

There is some debate in common law circles as to whether there is a difference between an implied choice of law and a choice of law which is

---

Model: Can it Replace the Western Model of Modernization?' (2010) 19(65) *Journal of Contemporary China* 419 at 423.
19 Chapter II of the Conflicts Law.
20 Namely, time charters, voyage charterparties and bareboat charters.
21 Including towage, salvage, marine insurance, ship mortgages and, to a limited extent, multimodal transport contracts.
22 The first sentence of Article 269.

to be inferred from the circumstances surrounding the contract.[23] Whilst it is unlikely that the PRC drafters had in contemplation this somewhat fine distinction,[24] the matter is important to the extent that it injects an element of uncertainty in the choice of law process. It has been opined that 'the expansion of the doctrine of party autonomy without recognizing implicit choices will amplify the tension between the law and reality'.[25] There is a need to ensure thus that implied selection is properly recognised.[26] However, the challenge is how will gaps be filled? This raises significant challenges for any PRC court or tribunal having to decide whether it could be inferred from the circumstances or whether, from the terms of the contract, that a certain selection of the applicable law had been made. One thing is for sure and it is that when it comes to preserving the relationship,[27] it is very likely that public morality or policy and the need to preserve public morality or policy would be largely considered by the court. This is borne out by Article 276 of the Maritime Code which provides that 'the application of foreign laws or international practices pursuant to the provisions of this Chapter shall not jeopardize the public interests of the People's Republic of China'. The new PRC Law is similar in tenor but uses the EU terminology of mandatory rules to achieve that end. It states in Article 4 of the Conflicts Law that where a mandatory provision of the law of the PRC exists with respect to a foreign-related civil relation, that mandatory provision shall be applied directly. It does not say that the parties are disallowed from derogating from these mandatory provisions, simply that they will apply regardless. It follows on in Article 5 of the Conflicts Law that 'where the application of a

23 See Dicey, Morris and Collins, *The Conflict of Laws* (14th edition, Sweet & Maxwell, 2006), pp.1573–1574.
24 In the light of the developing jurisprudence on construction of terms in cases such as *Mediterranean Salvage & Towage Ltd v Seamar Trading & Commerce Inc (The 'Reborn')* [2009] EWCA Civ 531, *Attorney-General of Belize v Belize Telecom Ltd* [2009] UKPC 10, *Barclays Bank plc v HHY Luxembourg SARL* [2010] EWCA Civ 1248, and significantly, *Rainy Sky SA v Kookmin Bank* [2011] UKSC 50. Also, in *The Reborn*, Lord Clarke had observed, '. . . as I read Lord Hoffmann's analysis [in *Belize Telecom*], . . . he is emphasising that the process of implication is part of the process of construction of the contract . . .' (at [15]).
25 See G. Tu, 'China's New Conflicts Code: General Issues and Selected Topics' (2011) 58 *American Journal of Comparative Law* 563 at 568.
26 The English courts have made it quite plain that caution must be exercised when implying the applicable law so as not to find party agreement when none was ever present. In *Sapporo Breweries Ltd (A Company incorporated under the Laws of Japan) v Lupofresh Ltd* [2012] EWHC 2013 (QB), the High Court held that the use of English language and the reference to CIF were not enough to suggest that there was an implied choice of English law. Under the Rome I Regulation not much guidance is offered; except for recital 12 of the Preamble which states: 'An agreement between the parties to confer on one or more courts or tribunals of a Member State exclusive jurisdiction to determine disputes under the contract should be one of the factors to be taken into account in determining whether a choice of law has been clearly demonstrated.'
27 Sometimes called 'guanxi' (see note 39 below).

foreign law will be prejudicial to the social and public interest of the PRC, the PRC law shall be applied'. It is quite clear that no court or tribunal would be in a position to disregard the social and public interest of the PRC in its application and interpretation of the new Conflicts Law.

What is less clear is that whilst the public or state interest will prevail over the private interest, the question is how will interpretive discretion be exercised by the administrative or judicial authorities when there are gaps in the contract. As was pointed out above, the idea of a contract extends beyond its four corners. Quite in contradistinction to the western conception of the contract, the contract in the Chinese normative environment is a less formalistic and more distended creature.[28] There is evidence showing, for example, that in the PRC the commercial contract is seldom considered as the formal distillation of the terms of the agreement. It is important to note that, in the PRC, the written contract is often seen by the Chinese party merely as evidence of the (contractual) *relationship*.[29] That said, it is undeniable that with the large volumes of law being rewritten to suit the international trading needs of the PRC, more and more of the western concept of an exclusively relevant contract in writing is being accommodated. It might perhaps be said that PRC international commercial law is at a cross-roads. Where it will lead, one can only conjecture – perhaps, western with Chinese characteristics?

Another important facet to this discussion is the fact that although Chinese/PRC civil laws have been borrowed from civilian systems of law, such as the German and Japanese codes from as early as the turn of the twentieth century, certain concepts continued to be subject to pre-PRC traditions[30] and emerging policies of the PRC. It was probably not the best kind of legal transplantation. The notion of party autonomy which was borrowed from civilian systems was gradually reformed by government or policy;[31] starting with the freedom to contract as understood in the German Civil Code but arriving at a narrower concept - the voluntariness or competence to make a contract.[32]

In the early reform of Contract Law in 1999,[33] the legislators decided

---

28 C. Leonhard, 'Beyond the Four Corners of a Written Contract: A Global Challenge to U.S. Contract Law' (2009) XXI(1) *Pace International Law Review* 15.

29 See B. Kwock, M. James, and A. Tsui, 'Doing Business in China: What is the Use of Having a Contract? The Rule of Law and Guanxi when Doing Business in China' (2013) 4(4) *Journal of Business Studies Quarterly* 56.

30 Including, for example, Confucius's thinking. See A.S. Cua, 'Confucianism: Ethics', in A.S. Cau (ed), *Encyclopedia of Chinese Philosophy* (Routledge, 2003), pp.72–78.

31 It is understandable why some would conclude that until the liberalisation of its market, the PRC was governed in substance by policy rather than law. See J. Fu, 'Freedom of Contract in the EU and China' (2003) 8(4) *Journal of International Commercial Law and Technology* 274.

32 Ibid.

33 Contract Law of the People's Republic of China, adopted at the 2nd session of the Ninth National People's Congress on 15 March 1999.

not to define freedom of contract and no steps were taken to introduce the notion of party autonomy to the modern PRC Contract Law despite some rhetorical concessions to the principles of equality[34] and *pacta sunt servanda*.[35] A commentator observed:

> 'Freedom of contract in most countries is circumscribed by the law, and that most Chinese enterprises have not developed appropriate self-discipline to engage freely in commercial activities on a free market. Warnings were voiced that freedom of contract is only good for large and monopolistic enterprises, that it can only induce the strong to bully the weak and engage in unfair competition, and that it would lead to more rampant illegal business conduct that would disrupt social and economic order.'[36]

Voluntariness or competence continues to be a cornerstone of the 1999 Contract Law. Article 4 of the Contract Law provides that a 'party is entitled to enter into a contract voluntarily under the law, and no entity or individual may unlawfully interfere with such right'. That provision on voluntariness must further be subject to the ever prevailing Article 1 which provides that the Contract Law 'is formulated in order to protect the lawful rights and interests of contracting parties, to safeguard social and economic order, and to promote socialist modernization'.

Until the *present* flood of modernising commercial and civil laws, the central question remained thus not whether an individual is free to choose the content of his or her promise but whether the state has allowed or ordained them to make contracts. Hence, we have a question of status or capacity rather than party autonomy, as understood in western jurisprudence. It is not surprising, therefore, that some of the most important changes to PRC civil law since economic modernisation have been in relation to the notion of legal persons.[37] It would be unrealistic to imagine that PRC law and practice would settle for party autonomy without continuing to pay some deference to the state's role in the socialist legal order. That said, given that it is indeed the country's policy to liberalise trade and commerce, the institutions in the legal system should actively seek to give proper effect to party autonomy, rather than restrain it. Formal legal institutions will thus need to make a positive deference to commerce for economic liberalisation to succeed.[38]

It is submitted that at least for these early years of implementation, a

---

34 See Article 3 of the PRC Contract Law 1999.
35 See Article 8 of the PRC Contract Law 1999.
36 B Ling, *Contract Law in China* (Sweet & Maxwell Asia, 2002), pp.42–43.
37 H.R. Zheng, 'China's New Civil Law' (1986) 34 Am. J. Comp. L. 669.
38 D. Clarke, et al., 'The Role of Law in China's Economic Development' in T. Rawski and L. Brandt (eds), *China's Great Economic Transformation* (Cambridge University Press, 2008), pp.375–428.

way of understanding or deconstructing the idea of party autonomy in PRC jurisprudence is to consider certain practical problems which are likely to impact on judicial creativity. How judicial creativity is developed in response to these challenges will dictate how a workable hybrid idea of party autonomy might be properly established in the PRC system.

The first problem or challenge is that the contract is not often perceived by formal institutions in the PRC as the be all and end all. Notably, notions of a moral relationship long held to reflect Chinese perception of business relationships or, '*guanxi*',[39] for some commentators, such as good faith, long-termism, compromise and cooperation would become relevant to the process of interpretation. The circumstances the courts can refer to when interpreting the applicable law agreement or when seeking to infer what the applicable law is in the absence of an agreement must be properly understood. Therein perhaps lies the biggest challenge to the PRC system of private international law in seeking to uphold 'party autonomy' when its contract legal system had not been entirely at ease with the concept commonly accepted in the west.

The second is perhaps less about the interpretation process than the issue of whether a selection had been properly incorporated in the contract. This is an acute problem in the English process of finding the choice of law agreement; English law is highly formalised and structured as regards the formation of the agreement. There is usually to be insisted a discrete moment in time where an offer was made and another where the acceptance was made. Hence, in one shipping case a general incorporation clause[40] in a bill of lading was said not to have incorporated the jurisdiction clause in the master charterparty in the bill of lading,[41] and in another concerning reinsurance, a 'follow the leader' clause in a reinsurance contract was held not to have incorporated the jurisdiction clause found in the main insurance contract.[42]

The Court of Justice of the EU (CJEU) would always ascertain whether there is *consensus ad idem* before finding that a contractual clause (such as an applicable law clause, a jurisdiction clause or an arbitration clause) had

---

39 In Kwock (note 29 above) the researchers argue and demonstrate that guanxi is more than the four corners of the contract. It is also submitted here that it is not merely the factual matrix English common law judges rely on to interpret the contract. It imports elements of mutual trust, stability of the relationship, long-termism (including, for example, the duty to renegotiate the terms when circumstances change materially), compromise, and controversially, a duty to protect public morality. See also E.A. Buttery, 'The difference Between Chinese and Western Negotiations' (1998) 32 *European Journal of Marketing* 374 and also Leonhard (note 28 above). However, the use of the word 'guanxi' is fraught with controversy and sensitivities. Some construe it as bordering on corruption – a form of 'you scratch my back, I scratch yours'. See, for example, <http://www.bbc.co.uk/news/business-29538125> accessed 24 February 2016.

40 A general incorporation clause usually would state: 'all terms and conditions to follow charterparty'.

41 *Siboti K/S v BP France* [2003] EWHC 1278 (Comm).

42 *Dornoch v Mauritius Union Assurance* [2006] EWCA Civ 389.

been properly incorporated. In *Refcomp SpA v AXA Corporate Solutions*,[43] the CJEU refused to extend a jurisdiction clause in the original contract of sale to bind a sub-buyer several links down the sale chain. That was despite the fact that under French law which applied to the case (from France) the sub-buyer would have been deemed to have a contractual situation with the original seller. The Court said:

> 'Since, the sub-buyer and the manufacturer cannot be regarded . . . as being bound by a contractual link, it must be concluded that they cannot be regarded as having "agreed" . . . to the court designated as having jurisdiction in the initial contract concluded between the manufacturer and the first buyer.'[44]

The CJEU, like the English courts, is not averse to finding 'agreement' in usage and established customs. In *Refcomp SpA*, for example, the CJEU acknowledged that it is a legally accepted norm in many EU states that, through trade usage, a bill of lading (unlike a sale contract) is capable of transferring rights and obligations to third parties.[45] The reference to trade practice is important and it is reasoned that a similar approach by tribunals in the PRC would not clash with the PRC's desire to mould the concept of party autonomy after its own political economic leanings.

In the PRC Contract Law[46] there is no explicit requirement for any agreement to be in writing; indeed, in the Maritime Code and the Conflicts Law the provisions are silent as to any writing requirement for the applicable law agreement. Unlike in English law, there is no requirement for consideration – Article 2 of the PRC Contract Law simply provides that a contract is 'an agreement between natural persons, legal persons or other organizations with equal standing, for the purpose of establishing, altering or discharging a relationship of civil rights and obligations'.

In modern shipping and commercial practice where there is often the battle of the forms or the sustained and febrile exchange of electronic communications and paper correspondence, it is not unexpected for one party to allege that a choice of law had been agreed with the other asserting otherwise. The PRC Contract law sets out in Article 30 that only where the acceptance materially alters the terms of the offer is the acceptance to be regarded as a counter offer. Where the changes to the offer are not material,[47] Article 31 states that the acceptance would remain valid and

---

43 Case C-543/10 [2013] English report reference: Case C-543/10, reported at [2013] 1 Lloyd's Rep 449.

44 Paragraph 33 of the judgment.

45 See also related cases such as Case 71/83 *Russ* [1984] ECR 2417, para.24; Case C-159/97 *Trasporti Castelletti Spedizioni Internazionali SpA v Hugo Trumpy SpA* [1999] ECR. I-1597, para.41; and Case C-387/98 *Coreck* [2000] ECR I-9337, paras 23–27.

46 Notably the 1999 Law.

47 There are naturally issues around what constitutes 'material', but for the purposes of choice of law, a different applicable law or a clear non-selection would be clearly material.

the terms of the acceptance will prevail, unless the offeror objects to such changes without delay, or if the offer indicates that no changes to the terms could be made in the acceptance.

In the case of standard form contracts,[48] there is a general duty of good faith requiring the party whose standard form it is to warn the other party about any provision which limits or excludes its liability.[49] The duty to notify also entails the duty to explain, especially when a request is made by the other party.[50] Other factors which would be considered include how unbalanced the provision is, the language used and the frailty of the other party.[51] Therein lies the challenge for contracting parties – is a choice of law clause one such provision requiring express notification? That is a vexed question and has reared its head in different guises[52] before the CJEU.[53] It is reasoned that PRC administrative and judicial institutions should take account of the conventional wisdom that in pure commercial transactions it is better to take a *laissez-faire* approach. The conventional reasons are well known to most readers, but it is worth stressing how an interventionist approach could increase the transaction costs rendering the economy as a whole less competitive.

Making clear the policy agenda early is important, given the complexities in the so-called process of an unconscionability review[54] and any potential for fraud and corruption. That would deter spurious and vexatious challenges to the agreed choice of law.

In sum, with a largely blank canvas, the PRC legal institutions would do well to avoid an over-technical approach to the matter of incorporation and to encourage greater party autonomy in the sense of the commercial participants taking responsibility for their business relations. It is important for these institutions to see choice of law not as a matter of constitutionalism but commercial pragmatism, the facilitation of commerce, rather a strictly construed allocation of which legal system has sovereignty over the contractual terms.

---

48 Defined by Article 39(2) of the Contract Law as 'contract provisions which were prepared in advance by a party for repeated use, and which are not negotiated with the other party in the course of concluding the contract'.

49 Article 39 of the Contract Law.

50 See Ling (note 36 above), p.111.

51 See Article 6 of the Contract Law on good faith.

52 Including the choice of a perceived less advantageous jurisdiction, or arbitration venue.

53 See, for example, Case C-168/05 *Mostaza Claro v Centro Móvil Milenium SL* [2006] ECR I-10421; Joined Cases C-240/98–C-244/98 *Océano Grupo Editorial and Salvat Editores* [2000] ECR I-4941; Case C-40/08 *Asturcom Telecomunicaciones SL v Cristina Rodríguez Nogueira* [2009] ECR I-9579; Case C-243/08 *Pannon GSM Zrt v Erzsébet Sustikné Gyo"rfi* [2009] ECR I-4713; Case C-137/08 *Pénzügyi Lízing Zrt v Ferenc Schneider* OJ C [2010] ECR I-10847.

54 The right to have the agreement reviewed on the grounds of conscience is provided for in Article 54 of the 1999 Contract Law. See also Ling (note 36 above), p.192.

3. Challenges and risks

The recourse to those notions outside the four corners of the contract clearly runs the risk of creating uncertainty, or even arbitrariness. It is often concerning for a new and developing jurisprudence as to how much uncertainty the system and, indeed, the commercial participants can bear. There is perhaps no silver bullet here, but whilst not advocating some kind of practice of *stare decisis*, it would not be remiss for PRC tribunals to consult the decisions of their 'brethren' as they seek to develop the corpus of principles. This is not inconsistent with the civilian tradition; indeed, it is the practice of EU and western European judges (not subscribed to the common law tradition) to draw on the wisdom of past and present case law in the resolution of disputes. The publication of those judgments has also offered much guidance to judges and arbitrators in other jurisdictions.[55]

Legal history may not be entirely helpful *if* the policy is to evolve a concept of party autonomy in the likeness of the EU system.[56] That is because PRC legal history is not one which yielded to an ideology of freedom (whereas party autonomy is largely a construct of the ideology of freedom); the PRC's policy of 'Emphasise Agriculture whilst restraining Commerce' had been prevalent for a long time.[57] Even now, the emphasis is more on industrial policy than commercial policy.[58] Be that as it may, there is no doubting that China is a fully paid-up member of the world trading community and there is clearly a shift to some convergence of its legal norms with those in transnational commercial law. The recognition of these transnational norms would be helpful to PRC judges and lawyers seeking to grow new or enhance current jurisprudence.[59]

---

55 For example, an important resource for tribunals dealing with disputes involving the UN Convention on Contracts for the International Sale of Goods 1978 (CISG) is surely the CISG website (<http://www.cisg.law.pace.edu/> accessed 24 February 2015) maintained by Pace University.

56 It is difficult to conjecture what the policy is – in the legislative history to the new PRC Law, for example, several suggestions by academics and policy makers to adopt more EU/western approaches (not confined to party autonomy, it has to be said) have been rejected with few reasons given. See Tu (note 25 above). From a PRC perspective, the Supreme People's Court does publish various Interpretations and Opinions to guide the lower courts.

57 J. Fu, *Modern European and Chinese Contract Law: A Comparative Study of Party Autonomy* (Kluwer, 2011), p.67.

58 See OECD Report, <http://www.oecd.org/china/WP-2013_1.pdf> accessed 24 February 2015.

59 We are not considering here legal transplants *per se* but the evolution of a concept which has some resonance in PRC law though not in the manner and nature adopted elsewhere. Also, the issue is not so much about the adoption of foreign law or rules, but normative principles (perhaps even ideological principles) applied elsewhere in the transnational commercial community. As to whether Chinese contract laws and other civil laws are legal transplants, much has been written (see generally J. Fu, 'Freedom of Contract in the EU and China' (2013) 8(4) *Journal of International Commercial Law and Technology* 274 at 274–275).

The second is that of language. In the matter of transnational contracts which are more likely to be expressed in a foreign language (mostly in English) and contained in a foreign boilerplate (again predominantly English forms in the case of shipping), the question of construction of the contract would be more than simply a matter of translation. If it is a mere matter of translation, there are several concerns:

(a) It departs from the multi-textured approach[60] to contract construction, the deference of which to a relationship (guanxi) is vital.
(b) It risks passing too much control and power to the translator or interpreter who may not be legally trained or commercially aware.
(c) The accuracy of the translation to the derogation of other evidence of agreement becomes all important.
(d) Translations are not foolproof evidence of the facts or 'truth'.

The matter is highly relevant because the PRC regime is an inquisitorial system like many civil law countries. That means that in theory it is for the court to produce the relevant translation for its consumption; in practice, it is not unknown for the judge and parties to work collaboratively in some instances. However, there is no deference to the adversarial system's approach which is for either side to find the best evidence 'money could buy'.

The third is doctrinal integrity. It has to be said that the new modernising laws,[61] including those on private international law, have been produced in the last two decades at a steady rate. For legal certainty, those new laws need to be read, interpreted and applied in a manner which causes the least friction between them. Perhaps a lesson might be drawn from the English common law tradition in this regard. English judges have long been comfortable with 'judicial law making'. Whilst not advocating a sudden shift from the civilian juridical norm to a case law system, the gradual development of doctrine (or principles, if the term doctrine causes discomfort) by examining how the interpretation of a new problem in law could cause tension elsewhere in the spanking new body of commercial laws should go some distance towards managing the worst effects of resolving legal disputes on the hoof.

4. Mandatory provisions

It is not inappropriate, in received wisdom, to ensure that the parties' choice of law does not avoid the application of rules of an interested country which

---

60 To the common law reader, this approach may evoke the same concerns which Lord Hoffmann's 'absolutely anything' approach to the construction of contracts in *Investors Compensation Scheme v West Bromwich Building Society* [1998] 1 All ER 98 caused.
61 Including Laws and Interpretations on Contracts, Companies, Securities, Foreign Civil Relations, Agency, Trusts, etc.

are of mandatory effect. That is true in the case of the Rome I Regulation[62] as for the Chinese new Conflicts Law. The Conflicts Law provides in Article 4 that 'where a mandatory provision of the law of PRC exists with respect to a foreign-related civil relation, that mandatory provision shall be applied directly'. In contrast, the Maritime Code does not have such a provision. Instead, it simply provides in Article 276 that 'the application of foreign laws or international practices . . . shall not jeopardize the public interests'.

Party autonomy is clearly not therefore absolute, both in the EU and the PRC. However, the EU system is quite specific as to what types of mandatory rules could not be derogated from. They are:

(a)   mandatory rules of the country with the closest connection to the contract, disregarding the foreign law clause (Article 3(3) of the Rome I Regulation);
(b)   mandatory rules of the EU (Article 3(4) of the Rome I Regulation);
(c)   mandatory rules of the forum (Article 9(2) of the Rome I Regulation);
(d)   mandatory rules of the place of performance which would have rendered performance of the contract (as against the contract itself) illegal (Article 9(3) of the Rome I Regulation).

In the case of (d), there is discretion for the forum not to give effect to those mandatory rules.[63]

The PRC system is concerned largely only with its own mandatory rules.[64] It is clear that where it is the forum, there can be no derogation from its mandatory rules. The PRC system has the advantage of not imposing the burden on its judges and tribunals (in an inquisitorial system) to protect the interests of other countries. Although the Rome I Regulation does not make a distinction between EU and non-EU countries for the purposes of Article 3(3), it might be said that it does have the advantage of managing the good relations between its Member States. Such an objective would naturally not be relevant to the PRC which does not belong to any supranational grouping. At an economic level, it might be suggested that deference to the mandatory rules of a country with the closest connection is beneficial in that frequently that is the country where the judgment would be sought to be recognised and enforced. The acknowledgment of those mandatory provisions early on reduces the risk of a resulting judgment being rejected. That said, it can be costly and inconvenient to attempt to show: (a) that there is another country to which all the relevant connecting factors point;

---

62   See Articles 3(3), (4) and 9.
63   Article 9(3) of the Rome I Regulation uses the wording 'effect *may* be given to the overriding mandatory provisions' (emphasis added).
64   This is entirely consistent with the PRC's foreign policy of non-intervention or non-interference (see A.J. Nathan and R.S. Ross, *The Great Wall and the Empty Fortress: China's Search for Security* (New York: W.W. Norton, 1997); indeed, there is a common Chinese saying that 'water from the well does not intrude into river water'.

(b) that that country has certain mandatory provisions which are likely to conflict with the applicable law if applied to the dispute; and (c) what those mandatory provisions are.

It is of some interest to note that the concept of 'mandatory' has not been properly defined in the many PRC modernising laws, unlike the Rome I Regulation which stipulates explicitly that:

> 'overriding mandatory provisions are provisions the respect for which is regarded as crucial by a country for safeguarding its public interests, such as its political, social or economic organisation, to such an extent that they are applicable to any situation falling within their scope, irrespective of the law otherwise applicable to the contract under this Regulation.'

Whether 'overriding' adds anything to 'mandatory' is not especially clear but it is pellucid that there is a link between mandatory provisions and the state's public interests. As if that is not enough, Article 21 of the Rome I Regulation provides that 'the application of a provision of the law of any country specified by this Regulation may be refused only if such application is manifestly incompatible with the public policy (*ordre public*) of the forum'.

In both the EU and PRC systems, it is clear that the public interest or policy should not be allowed to be damaged by the parties' contract. That said, in practice, in the EU the exceptional provisions have been applied *primarily* to constrain choice of law or jurisdiction agreements which attempt to avoid mandatory rules intended to protect one or more of the parties.[65] There has been no reported case on an applicable law clause being struck down because it offended a matter of the state's larger political or economic interest. It might thus be said that, as regards the EU, mandatory rules are perceived principally (and in practical terms) as measures to protect the private interest of a vulnerable party instead of the so-called national interest.

It is of course also a trite proposition that the wider the 'public interest or policy' exception is interpreted, the less effective a system of choice of law becomes. How the PRC institutions respond to the paternalistic tendency to defend the 'public interest' would be interesting to observe.

5. Conclusion

It is not the intention in this chapter to explore the issue of whether or to what degree PRC private international law is converging with EU norms, merely whether the concept of party autonomy which is central in global

---

65 See, for example, Case 381/98 *Ingmar GB Ltd v Eaton Leonard Technologies Inc* [2000] ECR 263; also the EU Green Paper on the conversion of the Rome Convention of 1980 on the law applicable to contractual obligations into a Community instrument and its modernisation (COM/2002/0654 final), paras 38–39.

shipping and trade law should not be misperceived in the context of examining PRC laws on private international law and maritime law. What has been demonstrated is the need to recognise that concepts such as 'party autonomy' in private international law do not necessarily have the same connotation as adopted in the EU and elsewhere, such as the PRC. In short, from a functional perspective, the concept of 'party autonomy' does not command a universal, transnational understanding or interpretation.

There will be significant challenges for PRC institutions to consider what scope and importance they wish to give the western (EU) idea of party autonomy in the ever-closer world of shipping and international trade, given the PRC's legal history and emerging economic policies. The (dis-) advantage the PRC has is the fact that it does not need to be shackled by unwieldy legal doctrines in commercial contract law. It is also argued, perhaps somewhat controversially, that PRC judicial institutions do not need to fear adopting that function of common law judges in developing and growing a set of principles for the country. To do so is not to discard their civilian traditions; indeed, as we have seen, the CJEU (and a number of civil law countries in the EU) have already taken on with some enthusiasm a new-found freedom to refer to previous judicial decisions to help develop jurisprudence.

The extent to which the new jurisprudence in the PRC should continue to take into account the public good or collective interest is controlled and managed by the government, as to be expected in a system of government as that prevailing in the PRC. However, it would not be a mistake to adopt a stakeholders' approach to the development of commercial law norms. That means the involvement of all participants in the market. For the modernising laws, including those dealing with private international law in the maritime and commercial sector, to succeed in attracting foreign investment, increasing competition in the PRC and enhancing the respectability the PRC so craves for its economic laws, institutions and policies, the PRC's legal and administrative institutions would be wise to rise to the challenge and be cognisant of pragmatic commercial interests.[66]

In the context of enforcing party autonomy in choice of law, it is undeniable that many transnational commercial disputes would end up not before a court but an arbitration tribunal. The involvement of these non-state institutions in helping develop the jurisprudence in private international law is essential given their proximity to the market place and players. Their access to market participants gives them special insights not only on how transnational commerce should and could be supported by the PRC

---

66 There is research showing that in certain parts of the PRC and within a discrete time frame, economic development and growth had not been influenced by the functioning of judicial institutions – in other words, economic development had flourished regardless. X. He, 'Enforcing Commercial Judgments in the Pearl River Delta of China' (2009) 57 Am. J. Comp. L. 419 at 453.

modernising laws, but also on the practical challenges and difficulties of all business stakeholders and participants. Their involvement at a public level is also important in ensuring that these insights are, in turn, communicated to the legal and administrative institutions.[67]

It is certainly welcome that the PRC now has a set of conflicts rules applicable not only to shipping and trade but wider areas (including family matters, etc). However, legislating new laws is only the first step; for those commercial and maritime laws to succeed, legal and judicial institutions in the PRC must not only develop in legal expertise and competence but also become more commercially aware from a transnational point of view.

---

67 Naturally, the issue of education and training cannot be far from the agenda. So too is the need for legal professionals in the PRC to share with, and learn from, their counterparts elsewhere in the world.

11 An English jurisdiction clause in a bill of lading: construction and consequences of breach

Professor Yvonne Baatz[*]

1. Introduction

The choice of English court jurisdiction in bills of lading is popular even in bills of lading which have no connection with England. England is a highly regarded neutral venue for the resolution of such disputes principally because the English court system is efficient and not corrupt. Furthermore, the choice of jurisdiction will usually go hand in hand with an express choice of English law. Such a choice of law is also popular not only in Europe,[1] but also in Asia,[2] as English law is well developed and sophisticated. Traditionally, the English courts have recognised party autonomy at common law and, more recently, as a result of European legislation giving

[*] My thanks go to Robert Veal, Senior Assistant at The Institute of Maritime Law, University of Southampton, for all his help. Any errors remain my own.

1 S. Vogenauer and S. Weatherill, 'The European Community's Competence to Pursue the Harmonisation of Contract Law – An Empirical Contribution to the Debate', in S. Vogenauer and S. Weatherill (eds), *Harmonisation of European Contract Law: Implications for European Private Laws, Business and Practice* (Hart Publishing, 2006), p.105; S. Vogenauer, 'Perceptions of Civil Justice Systems in Europe and their Implications for Choice of Forum and Choice of Contract Law: an Empirical Analysis', in S. Vogenauer and C. Hodges (eds), *Civil Justice Systems in Europe: Implications for Choice of Forum and Choice of Contract Law* (forthcoming April 2017), p.1.

2 G. Cuniberti, 'The Laws of Asian International Business Transactions', forthcoming in the *Washington International Law Journal* and posted in draft on Conflict of Laws.net on 28 June 2015. The latter contains a study based on unpublished data provided by the four main arbitral institutions active in Asia (outside mainland China) for 2011 and 2012, which finds that 'English law is chosen in transactions between parties of all nationalities, in the context of arbitration under the aegis of all institutions, in proceedings with their seat anywhere in Asia. Where Asian international transactions are not governed by the law of one of the parties (which often means that none of them had a sufficiently strong bargaining power to impose it), they are typically governed by English law. English law dominates completely the Asian market for neutral laws ... English law appears to be the only law to be considered as attractive to international commercial parties operating in Asia and seeking an option other than the laws of one of the parties' (p.4). See also G. Cuniberti, 'The International Market for Contract – The Most Attractive Contract Laws' 34 Northwestern J. Int'l & Business 455 (2014) on the choice of law in ICC arbitration where the choice of English law is also popular.

effect to that principle both where there is a choice of court jurisdiction[3] or a choice of governing law.[4] The principle of party autonomy has also been adopted internationally in the 2005 Hague Convention on Choice of Court Agreements[5] and is well recognised in the field of arbitration by the New York Convention on the Recognition and Enforcement of Foreign Arbitral Awards 1958, which has been ratified by numerous States worldwide, including China and the UK.[6]

This chapter will consider the recent decision of the English Court of Appeal in *Compania Sud Americana De Vapores SA v Hin-Pro International Logistics Ltd*,[7] a decision on an English court jurisdiction clause in bills of lading which had no connection with England on the facts but which contained an express choice of English jurisdiction and English law. The case considered the construction of the English jurisdiction clause in a standard form bill of lading and whether it was an exclusive choice of jurisdiction or whether it merely gave the parties an option to sue in England. The case illustrates the application of the principle of party autonomy at English common law and the clash between that approach and the approach of the Chinese courts which disregard agreed jurisdiction clauses where the circumstances of the case have little or nothing to do with the agreed jurisdiction. That clash resulted in multiple proceedings in various courts in China, Hong Kong and England with inconsistent judgments on jurisdiction and possibly in the future on the merits of the dispute.[8]

This chapter will also explore the remedies the English court granted in the case in order to try to avoid such a clash: both an anti-suit injunction

---

3 Council Regulation (EC) 44/2001 of 22 December 2000 on Jurisdiction and the Recognition and Enforcement of Judgments in Civil and Commercial Matters ('the EC Jurisdiction Regulation'); and Regulation (EU)1215/2012 of the European Parliament and of the Council of 12 December 2012 on jurisdiction and the recognition and enforcement of judgments in civil and commercial matters (recast) (the Recast Regulation) which applies to legal proceedings instituted on or after 10 January 2015 (Article 66). The Recast Regulation applies to all Member States of the European Union, including Denmark according to the Agreement between the European Community and the Kingdom of Denmark on jurisdiction and the recognition and enforcement of judgments in civil and commercial matters (OJ L 79/4, 21.3.2013).

4 Regulation (EC) 593/2008 on the law applicable to contractual obligations (Rome I), particularly Article 3, and Regulation (EC) 864/2007 on the law applicable to non-contractual obligations (Rome II), particularly Articles 12 and 14 on party choice. See Jason Chuah, Chapter 10 of this book, and particularly at p. 191.

5 The Convention entered into force on 1 October 2015 as the two ratifications or accessions required by Article 31 have been given by Mexico and the EU. No further State have ratified as at 18 April 2016. However, the convention does not apply to the carriage of goods – see Article 2(2)(f) and (g).

6 As at 18 April 2016 over 150 states are party to the New York Convention.

7 [2015] EWCA Civ 401, [2015] 2 Lloyd's Rep 1; [2014] EWHC 3632 (Comm), [2015] 1 Lloyd's Rep 301.

8 The English court did not make any determination on the substance of the dispute – [2014] EWHC 3632 (Comm), [2015] 1 Lloyd's Rep 301 at [5].

and damages for breach of an English jurisdiction clause, and will consider their effectiveness. It will also consider the changes introduced by the Recast Regulation where there is an English jurisdiction clause in proceedings instituted on or after 10 January 2015[9] which strengthens the principle of party autonomy in the Member States of the EU and compels the English courts to give effect to an English jurisdiction clause even where neither party is domiciled in the EU and the dispute has no connection with England, or indeed the EU.

The author will argue that a jurisdiction clause should be upheld as it is part of the parties' contractual bargain and serves a useful purpose in carriage of goods by sea to define one court to determine all the disputes which could arise out of one carriage by sea, rather than having, as in the *Hin-Pro* case, proceedings in numerous different courts, with the risk of having to call complex evidence in relation to fraud in several different courts with the consequent risk of conflicting judgments and unnecessary legal costs.

2. The facts

Compania Sud Americana De Vapores SA (CSAV) is an international shipping corporation with a worldwide business. The other party to the litigation, Hin-Pro International Logistics Ltd (Hin-Pro), was a freight forwarder registered in Hong Kong. CSAV bills of lading were issued for shipment from China to Venezuela naming Raselca Consolidadores CA (Raselca) as consignee. Some of the bills of lading named Hin-Pro as shipper but others did not. Nevertheless, Hin-Pro claimed to be an original party to the contract of carriage contained in the bills of lading and alleged that CSAV wrongly delivered cargo without production of original bills of lading in various ports in Venezuela. Hin-Pro claimed for the alleged value of the cargo carried under the bills at approximately US$24 million, the freight which Hin-Pro claims it was entitled to receive of US$1.8 million and exchange rate loss, port and other charges and attorney's fees.

Clause 23 of the bills of lading provided:

> 'Law and jurisdiction
> This Bill of Lading and any claim or dispute arising hereunder shall be subject to English law and the jurisdiction of the English High Court of Justice in London. If, notwithstanding the foregoing, any proceedings are commenced in another jurisdiction, such proceedings shall be referred to ordinary courts of law. In the case of Chile, arbitrators shall not be competent to deal with any such disputes and proceedings shall be referred to the Chilean Ordinary Courts.'

9 See note 4 above.

The bills of lading further contained a clause paramount which provided for the application of the Hague Rules[10] except in three situations: first, where as a matter of English law and the English Carriage of Goods by Sea Act 1971 the Hague-Visby Rules[11] are compulsorily applicable, those rules apply; secondly, where there are shipments to and from the USA, the US Carriage of Goods by Sea Act 1936[12] applies; and, thirdly, where the bill of lading is subject to legislation which makes the Hamburg Rules[13] compulsorily applicable, then those rules apply 'Which shall nullify any stipulation derogating therefrom to the detriment of shipper or consignee'.

In 2012 Hin-Pro commenced proceedings against CSAV under five bills of lading in the Wuhan Maritime Court in China, despite CSAV having informed them that this would be a breach of the jurisdiction clause in the bills of lading. The bills of lading covered carriage of goods from Nanjing, China to Puerto Caballo in Venezuela.

CSAV's position in the Chinese proceedings was that no misdelivery took place because Venezuelan law required that the cargo should be delivered to the storage provider authorised by the Venezuelan Government (except in two cases which were not applicable to this case) and that the bills of lading specifically provided for this. Furthermore, CSAV alleged that delivery was so made and all the goods were in fact then delivered to Raselca, the named consignee in the bills of lading and CSAV's agents in Venezuela,[14] but were then and were then delivered by them to the buyers of the cargo. Furthermore, CSAV alleged that the Chinese sellers, who sold on a C&F basis, had been fully paid for the goods and Hin-Pro had not suffered any loss, so that the claim in China was dishonest.

In November 2012 CSAV commenced proceedings in England seeking an anti-suit injunction. Burton J granted an *ex parte* interim anti-suit injunction restraining Hin-Pro from pursuing or taking any further steps in the Wuhan proceedings and Andrew Smith J continued that injunction at an *inter partes* hearing at the end of November. Hin-Pro did not attend that hearing or comply with the order but continued with the proceedings in Wuhan. As a result in March 2013 the English court held that Hin-Pro and their director, Miss Sui Wei, were in contempt of court. Miss Wei was sentenced to imprisonment for three months and permission was given for writs of sequestration to be issued against Hin-Pro.

Between May and July 2013 Hin-Pro commenced a further 23 sets of

---

10 The International Convention for the Unification of Certain Rules of Law Relating to Bills of Lading (Brussels, 25 August 1924).

11 The International Convention for the Unification of Certain Rules of Law Relating to Bills of Lading (Brussels, 25 August 1924) as amended by the Protocol signed at Brussels on 23 February 1968 and by the Protocol signed at Brussels on 21 December 1979.

12 Which gives effect to the Hague Rules.

13 UN Convention on the Carriage of Goods by Sea 1978 (the Hamburg Rules). Neither China nor the UK is a party to the Hamburg Rules.

14 In the judgment of the Court of Appeal it states that Raselca were the agents of Hin-Pro, at [8].

proceedings in the Guangzhou, Qingdao, Tianjin, Ningbo and Shanghai Maritime Courts in respect of a further 70 bills of lading. CSAV challenged the jurisdiction of the court in China but its challenges were dismissed on the ground that Chinese courts disregard agreed jurisdiction clauses where the circumstances of the case have little or nothing to do with the agreed jurisdiction.[15]

CSAV commenced proceedings in England for declarations that Hin-Pro were obliged by clause 23 to litigate claims under the bills of lading in England, damages and a permanent injunction. Permission to serve out of the jurisdiction was granted by Eder J in October 2013. The claim form was served on Hin-Pro at their offices in Hong Kong on 10 October. Hin-Pro did not acknowledge service within time but did so some ten months late. Permission was granted to do so late and to make submissions at the trial provided Hin-Pro satisfied certain conditions, only one of which was met.

In November 2013 Blair J granted an *inter partes* anti-suit injunction in relation to the proceedings commenced in China in 2013, which again was ignored.

On 27 May 2014 the Ningbo Court gave judgment in one of the cases before it. CSAV considered the documents provided to the court shortly before judgment fraudulent[16] but had no opportunity to deal with that. The judgment was for the value of the cargo of US$360,000 and legal costs, but not freight on the basis that Hin-Pro were sellers on C & F terms. CSAV paid the judgment sum. The decision, and that of an appeal court, was subject to challenge in the Chinese courts.

On 13 June 2014 Walker J granted an *ex parte* worldwide freezing order for US$27,835,500 and disclosure of assets against Hin-Pro. He was satisfied that there was:

> 'good reason for concern that Hin-Pro's activities in China involve a fraudulent bringing of proceedings and there are good grounds to fear that they may result in execution in China so as to force CSAV to pay a sum which, when combined with costs in this country, would total something in the region of US$27,845,000.'[17]

Hin-Pro did not appear on the date fixed for the *inter partes* hearing. Eder J continued that order at the end of that month. Hin-Pro did not file an affidavit as to assets until 8 October 2014.

A *Mareva* injunction[18] was also sought and obtained *ex parte* in Hong Kong against Hin-Pro on 16 June 2014 from Deputy Judge Saunders. Again, Hin-Pro did not appear at the *inter partes* hearing. On 17 July Deputy

---

15 [2014] EWHC 3632 (Comm), [2015] 1 Lloyd's Rep 301 at [9]. See V. Bath, 'overlapping jurisdiction adn the Chinese Courts' (2016) JIBFL 174A for the position under Chinese law.
16 Ibid at [21]–[22].
17 Ibid at [13].
18 The name given to a freezing order in Hong Kong.

Judge Saunders granted a receivership order in respect of Hin-Pro ancillary to the Hong Kong *Mareva* injunction. On 18 July the same judge extended the Hong Kong *Mareva* to cover the assets of Soar International Logistics Ltd (Soar)[19] on the basis that Soar were holding assets which Hin-Pro had some right to, control over or other right of access to[20] and on 30 July he appointed a receiver in respect of Soar. Hin-Pro and Soar appealed against the appointment of receivers and the Hong Kong *Mareva* injunctions. On 5 August, some six weeks late, Hin-Pro served an affidavit of assets, which was incomplete and deficient.

In September 2014 the Ningbo court gave a further judgment for US$652,936 in respect of cargo value and in addition legal costs, but not freight. CSAV appealed. The judgment was not paid. CSAV alleged that Hin-Pro's claims in China were fraudulent and based on forged documents.

On 25 September 2014 Hin-Pro applied to adjourn the trial listed for 14 October 2014 in England. On 29 September Hin-Pro filed an acknowledgment of service some ten months out of time. On 3 October Flaux J dismissed Hin-Pro's application to adjourn. He permitted Hin-Pro to file their acknowledgment of service late provided that six conditions were complied with, including the discontinuance of all proceedings in China and cooperation with the Hong Kong receivers, failing which Hin-Pro should not be entitled to participate in the trial. Hin-Pro finally served an affidavit of assets on 8 October 2014 stating that their only assets were the sums paid by CSAV in respect of a judgment in China, and various rights in other Chinese actions against CSAV. Five of the conditions were not complied with and Hin-Pro did not attend the trial.

3. The judgment of Cooke J

3.1 Construction of the clause

Cooke J held that clause 23, the law and jurisdiction clause, was an exclusive English jurisdiction clause. He considered the first sentence of clause 23 and reviewed the authorities. In *Svendborg v Wansa*[21] the clause provided:

> 'Wherever the Carriage of Goods by Sea Act 1936 (COGSA) of the United States of America applies . . . this contract is to be governed by United States law and the United States Federal Court Southern District of New York is to have exclusive jurisdiction to hear all disputes hereunder. In all other cases, this Bill of Lading is subject to English law and jurisdiction.'

---

19 An affiliated company of Hin-Pro. Both companies have the same registered office in Hong Kong and Miss Wei is the sole director of both companies. For the role of Soar, see the judgment of Cooke J [2014] EWHC 3632 (Comm), [2015] 1 Lloyd's Rep 301 at [22].
20 Pursuant to the third limb in *TSB Private Bank National SA v Chabra* [1992] 1 WLR 23.
21 [1997] 2 Lloyd's Rep 183.

He quoted from the judgment of Staughton LJ in that case with whom the other members of the Court of Appeal agreed:

> 'It can be argued that the express mention of exclusive jurisdiction in the first part of the clause excludes any implication that the second part provides for exclusive jurisdiction. On the other hand it can be argued that the author wished to provide for exclusive jurisdiction throughout, and did not think it necessary to repeat the word "exclusive" in the second part . . . I conclude that the clause does confer exclusive jurisdiction on the English courts. My reasons are in substance, first those which I stated in *Sohio Supply Co v. Gatoil (USA) Inc* (1989) 1 Ll R 588 at pp. 591–2, and in particular that I could think of no reason why businessmen should choose to go to the trouble of saying that the English Courts should have non-exclusive jurisdiction. My second reason is that the parties in the second part of the clause were plainly saying that English *law* was to be mandatory if the American Carriage of Goods by Sea Act did not apply; it seems to me that they must have intended English *jurisdiction* likewise to be mandatory in that event.'

Cooke J did not find the first reason given 'entirely persuasive because parties may wish to provide for a neutral court to have agreed jurisdiction, where they wish to be able to institute proceedings, whilst accepting that other courts may also exercise jurisdiction by reference to their own connection to the dispute and their own procedural rules'.[22] However, the second reason was 'more compelling'[23] as English courts would be seen by the parties as best able to apply the law agreed, English law.

Furthermore, in the later case of *British Aerospace v Dee Howard*[24] Waller J, as he then was, considered a clause which provided:

> 'This agreement shall be governed by and construed and take effect according to English law and the parties hereto agree that the courts of law in England shall have jurisdiction to entertain any action in respect hereof . . .'

He also referred to the first reason given by Staughton LJ that this was an exclusive jurisdiction agreement. As the parties had agreed English law he said that the English court would in any event have jurisdiction and by expressly agreeing to English jurisdiction they must be seeking to add something, ie that the English court had exclusive jurisdiction. However, as Cooke J pointed out where the English court applies Part 6 of the Civil

---

22 [2014] EWHC 3632 (Comm), [2015] 1 Lloyd's Rep 301 at [24].
23 Ibid.
24 [1993] 1 Ll R 368.

Procedure Rules[25] the fact that the parties have agreed English law is a ground on which the English court can grant permission to serve English proceedings out of the jurisdiction,[26] but it will not always do so.[27] He thought that the English jurisdiction provision added something.[28]

An agreement to English law and jurisdiction is generally an agreement to the exclusive jurisdiction of the English court, if there is no other provision in the contract. Therefore, had the clause only consisted of the first sentence even though that sentence did not spell out that the jurisdiction of the English court was exclusive, it would clearly have been exclusive on the English authorities.[29] This principle is not only applicable to bills of lading but to any other commercial contract. So, for example, in *Austrian Steamship Co v Gresham Life Assurance Society*[30] where a life insurance contract provided:

'24. For all disputes which may arise out of the contract of insurance, all the parties interested expressly agree to submit to the jurisdiction of the Courts of Budapest having jurisdiction in such matters'

that was not simply an option for either party to commence proceedings in Budapest but an obligation on both parties to commence proceedings there. However, clause 23 also had a further two sentences and the issue was

---

25 Proceedings in this case were instituted before 10 January 2015 and therefore the EC Jurisdiction Regulation applied and, in particular, Articles 4 and 23(3) as both parties were not domiciled in an EU Member State. Therefore, the English court applied its own national law in the Civil Procedure Rules. For the changed position where proceedings are instituted on or after 10 January 2015 and the parties have agreed on English jurisdiction see Article 25 of the Recast Regulation and the discussion at section 6.3 below.

26 Part 6 Practice Direction 6B para.3.1 ground 6(c).

27 For recent examples see *Star Reefers Pool Inc v JFC Group Co Ltd* [2012] EWCA Civ 14, [2012] 2 All ER (Comm) 225; *Navig8 Pte Ltd v Al-Riyadh Co for Vegetable Oil Industry (The Lucky Lady)* [2013] EWHC 328 (Comm), [2013] 2 All ER (Comm) 145 applied in *Golden Endurance Shipping SA v RMA Watanya SA (The Golden Endurance)* [2014] EWHC 3917 (Comm), [2015] 1 Lloyd's Rep 266.

28 Although the English court would usually grant permission to serve out of the jurisdiction where there was an English jurisdiction clause under Part 6 Practice Direction 6B para.3.1 ground 6(d), the court still had a discretion even if there was both an English law and jurisdiction clause and could refuse jurisdiction even in those circumstances if there were strong grounds not to give effect to an English jurisdiction agreement, usually if there were multiple proceedings between multiple parties some of whom were not bound by the English jurisdiction agreement – see eg *Donohue v Armco* [2001] UKHL 64, [2002] 1 Lloyd's Rep 425. There is no longer such a discretion in proceedings instituted on or after 10 January 2015 where there is a jurisdiction clause in favour of the courts of an EU Member State – see note 26 and section 6.43.

29 *Svendborg v Wansa* [1997] 2 Lloyd's Rep 183; *Sohio Supply Co v Gatoil* [1989] 1 Lloyd's Rep 588 and *British Aerospace v Dee Howard* [1993] 1 Ll R 368.

30 [1903] 1 KB 249. Special provisions of the Recast Regulation relating to life insurance policies would now apply to this case.

whether those sentences effectively provided for different courts to have different jurisdiction in different circumstances as in *Svendborg v Wansa*.

Cooke J considered the judgment in *Import Export Metro Ltd v CSAV*[31] where the parties and the court proceeded on the basis that clause 24 of the CSAV bills of lading, which was in similar terms to clause 23 in the current case, provided for the non-exclusive jurisdiction of the English courts. There Metro had commenced proceedings in England under 11 bills of lading. However, as it had missed the one-year time-bar applicable to the bills of lading if the Hague Rules applied, it commenced proceedings under 14 bills of lading in Chile, which applies the Hamburg Rules which have a two-year time-bar. CSAV applied for a stay of the English proceedings. Neither party had any interest in arguing that the English court had exclusive jurisdiction; the cargo interests because of the longer time-bar; and CSAV because of provisions of the law of Chile relating to the discharge of performance there. It was common ground that claims for loss of, or damage to, cargo in Chile were subject to mandatory arbitration, so that the last sentence of the jurisdiction clause was void. Furthermore, the provision for English law and English jurisdiction would be void and the Metro Chile claims would be determined in accordance with Chilean law. If CSAV obtained a stay from the English court then, if Metro so chose, its claims under all the bills of lading could be heard by the same arbitrator. Even though the jurisdiction clause was treated as if it were non-exclusive, Gross J refused CSAV's application to stay the English court proceedings and held it to its choice of jurisdiction.

CSAV's counsel argued in *Hin-Pro* that Gross J was wrong in *Import Export* to state that the jurisdiction clause provided for non-exclusive English jurisdiction. The second and third sentences of clause 23 clearly envisaged the situation where proceedings were brought elsewhere than in England. The third sentence specifically covered proceedings in Chile, where CSAV is incorporated and which gives effect to the Hamburg Rules. Under Article 21 of those rules the claimant has an option as to where to bring court proceedings and the choice of jurisdiction by the parties in the bill of lading is reduced to just one of the places that it may choose. It was common ground that as a matter of Chilean law the third sentence of the bill of lading was void.

Cooke J construed clause 23 as an exclusive English jurisdiction clause so that if proceedings were commenced elsewhere than in England that would be in breach of the clause. The second and third sentences had to be read in light of the clause paramount, which meant that in some cases US COGSA or the Hamburg Rules might apply and in the latter case the English choice of jurisdiction might be ignored. The inconsistent stance of CSAV in the earlier *Import Export* case treating the choice of English jurisdiction as

---

31 [2003] 1 Lloyd's Rep 405.

non-exclusive was irrelevant. Thus proceedings brought in China in the present case were a breach of clause 23.

3.2 Anti-suit injunction

Applying the principles set out in *The Angelic Grace*[32] that an anti-suit injunction will be granted where there is a breach of an exclusive jurisdiction or arbitration clause unless there are strong reasons not to do so, CSAV were entitled to an anti-suit injunction to restrain Hin-Pro from pursuing the claims in China. In this case there were no strong grounds to refuse an anti-suit injunction and, indeed, every good reason to grant one. Although the court was not determining the substance of the dispute, it was satisfied that there was a good arguable case that fraud was being perpetrated in China.

Hin-Pro were now out of time to commence proceedings in England in accordance with Article III rule 6 of the Hague Rules, but they had deliberately chosen to commence proceedings in China and not in England, despite knowing the English court's view before the one-year time-bar expired.

3.3 Damages

Hin-Pro's breach was to bring proceedings in China. Therefore CSAV's loss and damage arising from that breach amounted to all the sums awarded to Hin-Pro in China, including costs incurred in China, sums paid, sums for which it had been found liable to pay and sums which might yet be awarded against it in China. Cooke J refused to consider the hypothetical question of what might be the result if Hin-Pro had brought a claim in England. If Hin-Pro had complied with its obligation not to bring proceedings other than in England there would be no judgment in China. This approach was that of the Court of Appeal in *Starlight Shipping Co v Allianz Marine & Aviation Versicherungs AG (The Alexandros T)*.[33] Even if he had considered any hypothetical liability in England, that would not avail Hin-Pro as their claim was time-barred both as a result of Article III rule 6 of the Hague Rules and also an express contractual time-bar in clause 18.

3.4 Freezing injunction

Cooke J also continued the freezing injunction.

---

32 [1995] 1 Lloyd's Rep 87.
33 [2014] EWCA Civ 1010, [2014] 2 Lloyd's Rep 544 at [19] and [20].

4. The Hong Kong proceedings

On 15 October 2014, the day after the hearing before Cooke J, Deputy High Court Judge Wilson Chan discharged the *Mareva* injunctions and the receivership orders granted by Deputy High Court Judge Saunders against Hin-Pro and Soar. This was primarily on the ground that as there was a judicial conflict between the English court and the Chinese courts, the courts in Hong Kong should not exercise their jurisdiction under section 21M of the High Court Ordinance in favour of one side. Furthermore, Hin-Pro had offered not to take any step to enforce any Chinese judgment against CSAV without first obtaining the prior consent of CSAV or the leave of the Hong Kong court and the English court and this provided sufficient protection to CSAV. CSAV obtained leave to appeal on 26 November 2014 but the judge refused to stay his decision pending the appeal. Hin-Pro undertook to pay into court the sum of US$2,916,522.80 and to abide by further orders of the court as to its disposal as protection for the interests of CSAV. Instead, the judge granted a short stay to preserve the position pending a stay application to the Hong Kong Court of Appeal. That court also refused a stay pending the appeal but directed that the appeal be expedited.[34] Although the appeal was arguable, it was not so strong that a stay should be granted on the basis of strong prospects of success alone. The court also dismissed CSAV's argument that without a stay the appeal would be rendered nugatory. Although Hin-Pro had shunned the English court this was not evidence of its likelihood to disobey the orders of, or the undertaking given to, the Hong Kong court as Hin-Pro and its director were present in Hong Kong. More fundamentally, CSAV would only suffer any loss if the Chinese judgments were enforced, apart from costs incurred.[35]

The Hong Kong Court of Appeal upheld the decision of Deputy High Court Judge Wilson Chan discharging the *Mareva* order and receivership order on the ground of judicial conflicts. Although the hearing took place on 21 January 2015, judgment had not been given at the time of the Court of Appeal hearing in England.

5. The judgment of the Court of Appeal

Hin-Pro sought permission to appeal, out of time, the order of Flaux J dated 3 October 2014. They also sought permission to appeal the judgment of Cooke J. Tomlinson LJ refused permission in respect of the former but granted permission for the latter. He did not grant a stay but expedited the appeal. CSAV applied under rule 52.9 of the Civil Procedure Rules to set aside Tomlinson LJ's order granting permission to appeal the order of

---

34   *Compania Sud Americana de Vapores SA v Hin Pro International Logistics Ltd* [2014] HKCA 631, CACV 243/2014 (18 December 2014).

35   Costs of £286,036.50 had been granted by the English court.

Cooke J. The Court of Appeal heard that application immediately before it heard the appeal by Hin-Pro.

5.1 Contempt of court

First, the Court of Appeal considered whether it should hear Hin-Pro's appeal in view of the fact that it was in contempt of orders of the Commercial Court. The court has a discretion not to hear a contemnor until its contempt is purged. However, here Christopher Clarke LJ, with whom Elias and Beatson LJJ agreed, held that:

'since the appeal (a) concerns a clause which is the foundation of all the orders which Hin-Pro and Miss Wei have disobeyed; (b) is, in effect, an appeal against one of *the very [orders] disobedience of which [has] put the person concerned in contempt*; (c) raises matters of some general importance; and (d) is an appeal for which Tomlinson LJ has already given leave, subject to the provision of security for costs (which has been given) we should entertain it. I am also conscious of the fact that our knowledge of exactly what orders have been made in Hong Kong is incomplete. The Receivership and Receiving Orders are said to have been set aside and replaced by undertakings, which, again, we have not seen.'[36]

5.2 Refusal to set aside the permission to appeal

The Court of Appeal has jurisdiction to set aside a permission given to appeal if there is a compelling reason to do so under rule 52.9 of the Civil Procedure Rules. CSAV argued that there was such a compelling reason because Hin-Pro ignored the proceedings for ten months and had never served a valid acknowledgment of service. The court held that there is nothing in the rules which provides that failure to file an acknowledgment of service prevents an appeal. It was not an abuse of process for Hin-Pro to seek permission. Christopher Clarke LJ stated:

'The point in respect of which permission was given is a short point of construction with which Cooke J said that he had "*struggled*" and arises in relation to CSAV's standard form. It goes to the jurisdiction of the court to make the orders that it did. If the clause was not an exclusive jurisdiction clause neither the declarations, nor the injunctions, nor the award of damages can stand, since on that hypothesis there was no breach on Hin-Pro's part in suing outside England. It was within Tomlinson LJ's discretion, having decided that there was a real point to be considered, to give permission to allow Hin-Pro to argue that the

---

36 [2015] EWCA Civ 401; [2015] 2 Lloyds Rep at [31] (original emphasis).

clause was non-exclusive. The alternative, which would be to let the matter go by default, is not attractive. It would leave Hin-Pro subject to a permanent injunction, enforceable by penal sanction, when arguably the order should not have been made at all. The fact that Hin-Pro was in breach of the rules in not filing an [acknowledgment of service] in time was a factor weighing against the grant of permission but by no means a conclusive one.'[37]

The court also found that Tomlinson LJ had not been misled.

Hin-Pro submitted that clause 23 did not provide for exclusive English jurisdiction for the following reasons. First the clause does not say so. It does not refer to exclusive jurisdiction; nor does it say that only the English court has jurisdiction or that no other court shall have it. Indeed, the second and third sentences recognise that proceedings may not be brought in England and make provision for that eventuality. This shows that the English courts were not intended to have exclusive jurisdiction as rather than prohibiting proceedings elsewhere the clause seeks to regulate them. Second, the clause is in a set of standard terms which would be read by many whose first language was not English. A reasonable person reading the clause would think that both parties could commence proceedings either in England or the ordinary courts of some other jurisdiction. Third, at the lowest the wording leaves room for doubt as to whether CSAV should have the benefit of exclusivity and it should be construed *contra proferentem*.

Hin-Pro observed that the reasoning in *Svendborg v Wansa*[38] derived from *Sohio v Gatoil*.[39] However, the circumstances in the two cases were different as in *Sohio* the jurisdiction clause was specifically negotiated by sophisticated businessmen, whereas in *Svendborg* the clause was in a standard form intended for use by many parties, who might well wish to sue elsewhere than in England. If CSAV had intended English jurisdiction to be exclusive they would have said so expressly. One reason for preferring a non-exclusive jurisdiction clause is that in some cases (eg where CSAV is suing for freight or other liabilities) it may be quicker and cheaper to sue the shipper in its place of domicile rather than sue in England and enforce abroad. It may also be highly desirable for CSAV not to sue in England if

---

37 [2015] EWCA Civ 401 at [38].
38 [1997] 2 Lloyd's Rep 183 followed by Flaux J in *A/S D/S Svendborg v Akar* [2003] EWHC 797 (Comm) at [36] where proceedings had been commenced in Hong Kong and Guinea in breach of the English jurisdiction clause in Maersk's standard form bill of lading. Maersk's solicitor gave evidence as to fraudulent theft of cargo by the cargo interests which was accepted by Flaux J. He awarded damages for breach of the jurisdiction clause for the costs of the proceedings in Guinea and Hong Kong together with interest thereon, and also a declaration that the claimants were entitled to an indemnity in respect of any future costs and expenses incurred as a consequence of the proceedings commenced by the defendants in Guinea and Hong Kong.
39 [1989] 1 Lloyd's Rep 588.

an English judgment could not be enforced in the place(s) where the paying party's assets are situated.

Hin-Pro also submitted that it was wrong to argue that an agreement for non-exclusive jurisdiction was otiose where there is an English law provision as it would strengthen the case for the English court to exercise its jurisdiction. Christopher Clarke LJ could see a reason for a non-exclusive jurisdiction agreement, and he thought such a clause could have additional benefit where there was an English law provision, as was illustrated in *Import Export Metro Ltd* which had been decided on the basis that the jurisdiction provision was non-exclusive.

The clause in this case was in a contract of adhesion, a standard form prepared by CSAV which was not the subject of separate negotiation. It would apply to a wide range of shipments by many different shippers from and to many different ports as in *Wansa*, but this did not cast much light on the interpretation of the clause. This was a contract between corporations in international trade and not a consumer contract.[40]

This bill of lading, like all commercial contracts, was to be interpreted in light of the facts known to the original parties to it or which were reasonably available to them in the situation in which they were at the time of the contract in accordance with *Rainy Sky v Kookmin Bank*.[41] The first fact in that category was knowledge of the English language. The Court of Appeal did not accept Hin-Pro's submission that the fact that the bills of lading were likely to be issued to companies staffed by those whose first language is not English should affect the way in which they are to be interpreted, or that the court should endeavour to determine what the words would mean to a person in that category. By agreeing in English to an English law contract the parties must be taken to have agreed that it would be interpreted with all the nuances of the English language and in the way that a speaker whose first or only language was English would do.[42]

It seemed 'somewhat unrealistic'[43] to regard the knowledge of both parties as extending to the provisions of the Civil Procedure Rules about service out of the jurisdiction, but even if it should be so regarded, this did not resolve the question of whether or not the clause was exclusive.

The Court of Appeal held that clause 23 did provide for exclusive English jurisdiction for the following reasons. First the words 'shall be subject to' were imperative and directory and were not apt simply to provide an

---

40 See J. Chuah in Chapter 10 of this book p. 193.

41 [2011] UKSC 2900 at [14] applying *ICS v West Bromwich Building Society* [1998] 1 WLR 896. See also *Arnold v Britton* [2015] UKSC 36.

42 Cf *Xia Zhengyan v Geng Changging* [2015] SGCA 22 at [46]–[53] and in particular at [48]. The Singapore Court of Appeal took into account the fact that the parties were laypersons whose first language was not English where the agreement was not originally drafted in English and was drafted by laypersons and not lawyers. See J. Chuah in Chapter 10 of this book pp. 194 and 195.

43 [2015] EWCA Civ 401; [2015] 2 Lloyd's Rep 1 at [59].

option. That would be the case in relation to the applicable law and the same should apply to jurisdiction.

Secondly, whilst Christopher Clarke LJ accepted that a non-exclusive jurisdiction clause is not worthless even where there is express provision of English law and that there can, generally speaking, be only one law governing the contract although there can be more than one court having jurisdiction over disputes, the natural commercial purpose of a clause such as the present is to stipulate what law will govern and which court will be the court having jurisdiction over any dispute. The judge said:

> 'In a case such as the present, there is only limited benefit in specifying England as an optional jurisdiction without any obligation on either party to litigate here. The number of courts that might have jurisdiction over a dispute between the bill of lading holder and the owners is at least as large as the range of countries in which (in this and other cases) cargo may be loaded, transshipped, or discharged, and might include the country where the bill of lading contract was made or that of the ship's flag. Some of these countries are likely not to apply English law, despite clause 23, if their jurisdiction is invoked. Some might apply it in an idiosyncratic way. Which court a claimant might select could not, itself be predicted with any certainty. In those circumstances it makes little commercial sense to add England as an optional additional court, but without any obligation on either party to litigate there; and there was every reason to think, as the judge did, that when the parties were agreed that claims and disputes should be determined by the English High Court, by necessary inference they were agreeing that they should not be determined elsewhere. That would make good commercial sense.
>
> What I have said in the previous paragraph takes some account of the fact that the terms of the bill of lading will apply not only to the bills of lading in suit, but to the many other bills which CSAV will issue to other shippers. I regard that as a relevant consideration. A reasonable person would realise that the clause was intended for widespread use by CSAV for many different shipments.'[44]

Thirdly, there is obvious sense in making both English law and English jurisdiction mandatory as England is the best forum for the application of English law.

Fourthly, the use of the words 'If notwithstanding the foregoing, any proceedings are commenced in another jurisdiction' in the second sentence of clause 23, recognised that the first sentence requires litigation in England as a matter of contract. Such words would not be necessary if the first sentence made English jurisdiction optional.

44 [2015] EWCA Civ 401 at [64] and [65].

Fifthly, the second and third sentences cover a situation where the first sentence is ineffective, for example because of the application of the Hamburg Rules, as for example in Chile or where the country whose jurisdiction is invoked does not recognise the intended effect of an exclusive jurisdiction clause as in China.

Sixthly, little assistance could be derived from the *contra proferentem* rule,[45] first because the clause was not ambiguous. If that was too strong a view, it would be necessary to assess whether, when the contract was made, a requirement of English jurisdiction was more favourable to the owner than a non-exclusive clause. Hin-Pro submitted that CSAV, which introduced the clause, must have thought that it would be for its benefit. However, it was unlikely to be of benefit to CSAV's customers unless they were based in England, and for small-size customers litigation in England would be a very real, and, quite possibly major inconvenience, particularly if the claim was a modest one. Most claims would be likely to be against CSAV, which would probably not need to resort to litigation since freight would either be prepaid, or, if it was not, they would have a lien for it. Christopher Clark LJ concluded that the clause bound and benefited both parties in the same way – 'The benefit of the clause is that it provides certainty and the selection of a court which will be neutral and which will be applying its own law.'[46]

Seventhly, although authorities in relation to different provisions in different contracts are at best a guide; and the result in other cases is of no binding force in relation to a different clause; and that the question is one of construction; the tenor of English authorities is that an English law and jurisdiction clause in this form is likely to be interpreted as involving both the mandatory application of English law and the exclusive jurisdiction of the English court. He referred to *The Alexandros T*[47] and the authorities cited therein. This tendency to construe clauses as exclusive provided some confirmation of what view the reasonable businessman would take.

Finally, the Court of Appeal interpreted Article 21(1)(d) of the Hamburg Rules which provides that the plaintiff may institute an action in a court situated within the jurisdiction of which is situated any of the following

---

45 In *K/S Victoria Street v House of Fraser (Stores Management) Ltd* [2011] EWCA Civ 904, [2012] Ch 497 at [68] Lord Neuberger said that 'such rules are rarely if ever of any assistance when it comes to construing commercial contracts'. This case concerned a negotiated contract. However, in cases of a standard form contract the principle may be helpful – *Taylor v River Droite Music Ltd* [2005] EWCA Civ 1300; [2006] per Neuberger LJ at [142] and *SAS Institute Inc v World Programming Ltd* [2013] EWCA Civ 1482, [2014] RPC 8 per Lewison LJ at [108].

46 [2015] EWCA Civ 401; [2015] 2 Lloyd's Rep 1 EMLR 4 [76].

47 [2011] EWHC 3381 (Comm), [2012] 1 Lloyd's Rep 162 at [19]–[23]. This case concerned insurance policies, which expressly provided for exclusive English jurisdiction, and settlement agreements, one of which provided for English law and exclusive English jurisdiction but the other provided for English law and English jurisdiction. Burton J held that this latter settlement agreement should be construed as providing for exclusive English jurisdiction. This part of his judgment was not subject to appeal.

places: 'any additional place designated for that purpose in the contract of carriage by sea'. These words referred to a place designated for the institution of proceedings and not to an additional place designated as a port of loading or discharge. Hin-Pro submitted that this analysis supported its case that the jurisdiction clause was non-exclusive. The Court of Appeal rejected that argument as the effect of the Hamburg Rules was to render clause 23 void in so far as it provides for exclusive jurisdiction. Even if it were to render the clause wholly void that could not affect the proper construction of clause 23 in accordance with English law.

The Court of Appeal refused *Hin-Pro's* application for leave to appeal to the Supreme Court.

6. Comment

The English court went to great lengths to give Hin-Pro the right to be heard despite its recalcitrance in taking part in the English court proceedings and failure to comply with the English court orders.

The benefits of an exclusive jurisdiction clause are certainty for the parties and consolidation of proceedings, so that there are not multiple proceedings in numerous jurisdictions on numerous bills of lading all on the same terms, as there were in *CSAV v Hin-Pro*. It is sensible that all proceedings should be consolidated in one court where they arise on the same contractual terms rather than being scattered throughout the courts of China with complex evidence as to fraudulent claims having to be called in numerous courts with the consequent risk of conflicting decisions and additional legal costs. This is especially so for a carrier such as CSAV which may otherwise face litigation anywhere that it trades to.

One could argue that if a carrier chooses to trade to a particular place it takes the risk that it is subject to the jurisdiction of the courts of that place. However, it is to avoid that situation that the carrier inserts a jurisdiction clause in its bill of lading. It is to the benefit of both parties that all proceedings can be heard in one court so as to avoid duplicating the costs of litigation. The cargo interests already have the advantage that they can arrest the carrier's ship or ships[48] in order to obtain security for their claims, usually by means of a P&I Club letter of undertaking. Thus enforcement of any judgment subsequently obtained is a straightforward matter of complying with the trigger for payment in the letter of undertaking, for example presentation of an English court judgment in favour of the cargo interests.[49]

---

48 The place of arrest is a further place where the cargo interests may institute an action under Article 21(2)(a) of the Hamburg Rules, unless the defendant requests the removal of the action to one of the jurisdictions in Article 21(1), at the cargo interests' choice.

49 Zheng Sophia Tang, 'Effectiveness of Exclusive Jurisdiction Clauses in the Chinese Courts – a Pragmatic Study' [2012] ICLQ 459 argues that Chinese law needs to be reformed as to recognition and enforcement of judgments as the fact that the Chinese court could not recognise and enforce a judgment of, eg, an English court, would prevent

There is a clear trend in the English court towards a generous interpretation of English jurisdiction clauses. The authorities discussed by both Cooke J and Christopher Clarke LJ indicate that where the parties have chosen English law and jurisdiction this is likely to be construed as exclusive English jurisdiction, unless there is some indication that non-exclusive jurisdiction was intended. This is in line with the wording of Article 23(1) of the EC Jurisdiction Regulation which provides that where at least one of the parties is domiciled in an EU Member State and the parties have chosen the courts of an EU Member State that court shall have jurisdiction and that jurisdiction shall be exclusive unless the parties have agreed otherwise.[50] Nevertheless, where parties are drafting a contract it would be wise to state that the jurisdiction is exclusive if that is what is required.

That trend is not limited to the construction of whether a jurisdiction clause is exclusive or non-exclusive but is part of a wider trend which is also evident in the recent case law on issues such as the scope of the disputes covered by the clause;[51] the persons who may benefit from such a clause;[52] and whether words of incorporation in one contract are effective to incorporate a jurisdiction clause from, for example, a charterparty into a bill of lading contract.[53]

The position was less complicated in *CSAV v Hin-Pro* than it often is in bill of lading cases as the bill of lading set out all the terms including the jurisdiction clause. Furthermore, Hin-Pro alleged that they were the original party to the bill of lading contract.

The position may often be more complex for a number of reasons. The

---

it from giving effect to the parties' choice of the English court. In shipping disputes there may be no difficulty of enforcing the judgment of the chosen court against the carrier where it has already provided security to prevent arrest of its ship or to release the ship from arrest.

50 See also Article 25(1) of the Recast Regulation discussed at section 6.3 above which is wider in that it applies regardless of the parties' domicile where they have chosen the court of an EU Member State. Such jurisdiction shall also be exclusive unless the parties have agreed otherwise.

51 *Fiona Trust & Holding Corp v Privalov* [2007] UKHL 40, [2007] 4 All ER 951 applied in *Starlight Shipping Co v Allianz Marine & Aviation Versicherungs AG (The Alexandros T)* [2014] EWCA Civ 1010, [2014] 2 Lloyd's Rep 544; *Starlight Shipping Co v Allianz Marine and Aviation Versicherungs AG* [2014] EWHC 3068 (Comm), [2014] 2 Lloyd's Rep 579 noted in <http://www.stonechambers.com/news-pages/15.10.14--judgment--the-alexandros-t---the-final-(english)-word----james-smithdale.asp> accessed 2 September 2015. See also on a bill of lading *People's Insurance Company of China, Hebei Branch v Vysanthi Shipping Co Ltd (The Joanna V)* [2003] 2 Lloyd's Rep 617 and on a charterparty *The Front Comor* [2005] EWHC 454 (Comm).

52 *Starlight Shipping Co v Allianz Marine & Aviation Versicherungs AG (The Alexandros T)* [2014] EWCA Civ 1010, [2014] 2 Lloyd's Rep 544 and the decision of Flaux J in the same litigation at [2014] EWHC 3068 (Comm).

53 *Caresse Navigation Ltd v Office National de L'Electricite (The Channel Ranger)* [2014] EWCA Civ 1366, [2015] 1 Lloyd's Rep 256; [2013] EWHC 3081 (Comm); [2014] 1 Lloyd's Rep 337.

bill of lading may incorporate the terms and conditions of a charterparty. In that event issues may arise, for example, as to which charterparty has been incorporated; whether the charterparty is sufficiently clearly recorded in writing where it has never been drawn up and signed; and whether the words of incorporation are effective to incorporate the jurisdiction clause in the charterparty.[54]

Whether or not the jurisdiction clause is incorporated from a charterparty or is contained in the bill of lading, the cargo claimant may be a third party. It will be necessary to consider whether any third parties are bound by the clause as the claim may be brought on the bill of lading by the party to whom the bill of lading has been transferred, usually in order to obtain payment for the goods, such as the consignee named in a straight bill of lading or the bill of lading holder to whom the bill of lading has been transferred and endorsed in the case of a negotiable bill of lading. Under English law the named consignee under a straight bill of lading or the lawful holder of a transferable or negotiable bill of lading will be bound by the jurisdiction clause in the bill of lading if it chooses to sue on it as a result of the Carriage of Goods by Sea Act 1992.[55]

Usually where cargo is damaged, lost or misdelivered, the cargo interests will claim against their subrogated insurers who once the claim is paid will exercise their subrogated rights and pursue the carrier under the bill of lading. Under English law the subrogated insurer would also be bound by any jurisdiction or arbitration clause in the bill of lading.[56]

On each of these issues English law may reach a different result from the

---

54 For consideration of these issues in relation to arbitration clauses, see Y. Baatz, 'Should Third Parties be Bound by Arbitration Clauses in Bills of Lading?' [2015] LMCLQ 85. Similar principles apply to jurisdiction agreements.

55 See eg *Welex AG v Rosa Maritime Ltd (The Epsilon Rosa) (No.2)* [2003] EWCA Civ 938, [2003] 2 Lloyd's Rep 509 where the Court of Appeal held that the consignee of the bill of lading was bound by the arbitration clause incorporated in the bill of lading from the charterparty evidenced by the fixture recap telex and *Caresse Navigation Ltd v Office National de L'Electricite (The Channel Ranger)* [2014] EWCA Civ 1366, [2015] 1 Lloyd's Rep 256; [2013] EWHC 3081 (Comm); [2014] 1 Lloyd's Rep 337. See J. Chuah, in Chapter 10 p.191 of this book.

56 *Schiffahrtsgesellschaft Detlev von Appen GmbH v Voest Alpine Intertrading GmbH (The Jay Bola)* [1997] 2 Lloyd's Rep 279; *The Ivan Zagubanski* [2002] 1 Lloyd's Rep 106 at [52] and [54]; *People's Insurance Company of China, Hebei Branch v Vysanthi Shipping Co Ltd (The Joanna V)* [2003] 2 Lloyd's Rep 617; *Welex AG v Rosa Maritime Ltd (The Epsilon Rosa) (No.2)* [2003] EWCA Civ 938, [2003] 2 Lloyd's Rep 509; *Kallang Shipping SA v Axa Assurances Senegal (The Kallang)* [2006] EWHC 2825 (Comm), [2007] 1 Lloyd's Rep 160; *The Front Comor* [2005] EWHC 454 (Comm), [2005] 2 Lloyd's Rep 257 at [32] and [33]; *Starlight Shipping Co v Tai Ping Insurance Co Ltd* [2007] EWHC 1893 (Comm), [2008] 1 Lloyd's Rep 230; *Niagara Maritime SA v Tianjin Iron & Steel Group Co Ltd* [2011] EWHC 3035 (Comm); *Caresse Navigation Ltd v Office National de L'Electricite (The Channel Ranger)* [2014] EWCA Civ 1366; [2013] EWHC 3081 (Comm); [2014] 1 Lloyd's Rep 337; *London Steam Ship Owners Mutual Insurance Association Ltd v Spain (The Prestige)* [2015] EWCA Civ 333, [2014] 1 Lloyd's Rep 137.

law of another State, thereby giving rise to the risk of different decisions as to whether there is a valid jurisdiction or arbitration clause.

6.1 Enforcement

It is extremely unlikely that Hin-Pro would wish to enforce any Chinese judgments obtained in their favour in England. They would seek to enforce such judgments by applying commercial pressure on CSAV who would not wish to have their vessels arrested due to the commercial damage this would do to their reputation and the disruption and cost this would cause.[57] CSAV had already paid one judgment. However, in the Hong Kong proceedings Hin-Pro had offered not to enforce any of the Chinese judgments without the permission of CSAV and the English court.

Even had Hin-Pro wished to enforce a Chinese judgment in England, the recognition and enforcement of any judgment of the Chinese court in England in the circumstances of *Hin-Pro* would be very unlikely. There is no treaty between the UK and China on the recognition and enforcement of each other's judgments. Nevertheless, the English court would apply its common law rules[58] to the recognition and enforcement of a Chinese judgment. There would be grounds on which that court judgment would be refused recognition and enforcement in England. The most relevant grounds for such refusal in the *Hin-Pro* litigation include the ground that the Chinese court gave judgment in breach of a valid dispute resolution agreement;[59] provided that the defendant in the Chinese court has not submitted to the jurisdiction of that court;[60] the foreign judgment was obtained by fraud; recognition of the foreign judgment would be contrary to English public policy as it was in breach of an English court order, ie an anti-suit injunction;[61] or the foreign judgment is inconsistent with a prior judgment.[62]

6.2 Remedies for breach

6.2.1 Anti-suit injunction

The English courts have sought to strengthen the effectiveness of an exclusive jurisdiction agreement by the remedies which it can grant for its

---

57 [2014] EWHC 3632 (Comm), [2015] 1 Lloyd's Rep 301 at [37].

58 See A. Briggs, *Civil Jurisdiction and Judgments* (6th edn, 2015, Informa Law from Routledge), paras [7.46]–[7.84].

59 Section 32 of the Civil Jurisdiction and Judgments Act 1982.

60 See V. Bath, 'Overlapping jurisdiction and the Chinese courts', (2016) 3 JIBFL 174A and footnote 74 on the position as to recognition and enforcement of foreign judgments in China.

61 *Phillip Alexander Securities & Futures Ltd v Bamberger* [1997] ILPr 73 at 104.

62 See eg *People's Insurance Company of China, Hebei Branch v Vysanthi Shipping Co Ltd (The Joanna V)* [2003] 2 Lloyd's Rep 617.

breach. Thus if the shipper, consignee, indorsee or their subrogated insurer commences or threatens to commence proceedings elsewhere in breach of the jurisdiction agreement[63] or arbitration agreement,[64] the other party to the agreement may apply to the English court for an anti-suit injunction to restrain the first party from commencing or pursuing the proceedings elsewhere, provided the proceedings are in a court of a State which is neither an EU Member State nor a Lugano Contracting State.[65]

An anti-suit injunction will only be effective if it prevents the cargo interests from enforcing their judgments obtained in breach of the English jurisdiction agreement,[66] which will depend on the method of enforcement and where the carrier's assets are, or whether there is some other sanction which affects the directors of the cargo interests. In *Hin-Pro* we have already seen that Hin-Pro would have sought to enforce the Chinese judgments by arresting CSAV's vessels or threatening to do so. However, it appears that the effect of the proceedings in Hong Kong to wind up the company was to get Hin-Pro to offer not to enforce the Chinese judgments without the permission of CSAV and the English court.[67] Where the cargo interests are

63 *YM Mars Tankers Ltd v Shield Petroleum Co Nigeria Ltd (The YM Saturn)* [2012] EWHC 2652 (Comm); *Caresse Navigation Ltd v Office National de L'Electricite (The Channel Ranger)* [2014] EWCA Civ 1366, [2015] 1 Lloyd's Rep 256; [2013] EWHC 3081 (Comm), [2014] 1 Lloyd's Rep 337 and *Compania Sud Americana de Vapores SA v Hin-Pro Logistics International Ltd* [2015] EWCA Civ 401 [2015] 2 Lloyd's Rep 1; [2014] EWHC 3632 (Comm), [2015] 1 Lloyd's Rep 301.

64 *AES Ust-Kamenogorsk Hydropower Plant LLP v Ust-Kamenogorsk Hydropower Plant JSC* [2013] UKSC 35, [2013] 1 WLR 1889 (Kazakhstan); *Kallang Shipping SA v Axa Assurances Senegal (The Kallang)* [2006] EWHC 2825 (Comm), [2007] 1 Lloyd's Rep 160 (Senegal); *Sotrade Denizcilik Sanayi Ve Ticaret AS v Amadou LO (The Duden)* [2008] EWHC 2762 (Comm), [2009] 1 Lloyd's Rep 145 (Senegal); *Noble Assurance Co v Gerling-Konzern General Insurance Co* [2007] EWHC 253 (Comm), [2007] 1 CLC 85; *Markel International Co Ltd v Craft (The Norseman)* [2006] EWHC 3150 (Comm), [2007] Lloyd's Rep IR 403; *Starlight Shipping Co v Tai Ping Insurance Co Ltd* [2007] EWHC 1893 (Comm), [2008] 1 Lloyd's Rep 230 (China); *Midgulf International Ltd v Groupe Chimiche Tunisien* [2010] EWCA Civ 66, [2010] 2 Lloyd's Rep 411 (Tunisia); *Niagara Maritime SA v Tianjin Iron & Steel Group Co Ltd* [2011] EWHC 3035 (Comm) (China); *Golden Endurance Shipping SA v RMA Watanya SA* [2014] EWHC 3917 (Comm), [2015] 1 Lloyd's Rep 266.

65 For the position where the proceedings are in the court of an EU Member State or a Lugano Contracting State the European Court of Justice held in Case C-185/07 *Allianz SpA (formerly Riunione Adriatica di Sicurta SpA) v West Tankers Inc (The Front Comor)* [2009] ECR I-00663 that it was inconsistent with the EC Jurisdiction Regulation for the English court to grant an anti-suit injunction. Although doubt was thrown on that decision by Advocate General Wathelet in his Opinion in Case C-536/13 *Gazprom OAO v Lietuvos dujos AB* (not yet published) and Advocate General Jaaskinen in his Opinion in Case C-352/13 *CDC Cartel Damage Claims Hydrogen Peroxide SA* (not yet published), the CJEU in its judgment in *Gazprom* in May 2015 upheld its earlier decision in *The Front Comor* and did not comment on the Advocate General's Opinion. The position under the Recast Regulation may raise new arguments.

66 See note 61 above.

67 The Court of Appeal in *Hin-Pro* was not aware of the terms of any such undertakings by Hin-Pro.

in breach of the anti-suit injunction the company and its directors will be in contempt of court. Their director was given a three-month prison sentence but this is not likely to have any effect unless Miss Wei, the director, chose to come to England.[68]

6.2.2 Damages for breach of an exclusive jurisdiction or arbitration clause

Furthermore, in all situations, no matter where the other proceedings are brought, where they are in breach of an English jurisdiction agreement or London arbitration agreement, the English courts will grant damages for the breach of contract[69] or for the tort of procuring a breach of contract.[70]

6.3 The Recast Regulation

The English proceedings in *CSAV v Hin-Pro* were commenced before the Recast Regulation[71] started to apply. They are therefore dealt with under the English national law on jurisdiction clauses because, as neither party was domiciled in an EU Member State or a Lugano Contracting State, Article 23(1) of the EC Jurisdiction Regulation[72] did not apply, but Article 23(3) did, which means that the English court still has a discretion as to whether to exercise jurisdiction.

---

68 See also *Kallang Shipping SA v Axa Assurances Senegal (The Kallang)* [2006] EWHC 2825 (Comm), [2007] 1 Lloyd's Rep 160 where an anti-suit injunction was sought against the receivers; their cargo insurers, Axa Senegal; and Axa France.

69 In relation to court jurisdiction clauses, see *Donohue v Armco* [2001] UKHL 64, [2002] 1 Lloyd's Rep 425; *Horn Linie GmbH & Co v Panamericana Formas E Impresos SA, Ace Seguros SA (The Hornbay)* [2006] EWHC 373 (Comm), [2006] 2 Lloyd's Rep 44 at [26]; *Starlight Shipping Co v Allianz Marine & Aviation Versicherungs AG (The Alexandros T)* [2014] EWCA Civ 1010, [2014] 2 Lloyd's Rep 544; [2014] EWHC 3068 (Comm), [2014] 2 Lloyd's Rep 579 (exclusive English court jurisdiction agreement where the other proceedings are in an EU Member State. For criticism of this decision, see A. Dickinson, 'Once Bitten – Mutual Distrust in European Private International Law' [2015] LQR 186; *Compania Sud Americana de Vapores SA v Hin-Pro Logistics International Ltd* [2015] EWCA Civ 401;[2015] 2 Lloyd's Rep 1; [2014] EWHC 3632 (Comm), [2015] 1 Lloyd's Rep 301; and *Swissmarine Services SA v Gupta Coal India Pt Ltd* [2015] EWHC 265 (Comm); [2015] 1 Lloyd's Rep 453. In relation to arbitration clauses, see *West Tankers Inc v Allianz SpA* [2012] EWHC 854 (Comm), [2012] 2 All ER (Comm) 395, [2012] 2 Lloyd's Rep 103. For a history of this litigation, see paras [4]–[16]. The right to damages for breach of an arbitration clause has also been approved by Advocate General Wathelet in his Opinion in Case C-536/13 *Gazprom OAO v Lietuvos dujos AB* (not yet published), but in its judgment the CJEU made no comment.

70 See Morison J in *Horn Linie GmbH & Co v Panamericana Formas E Impresos SA, Ace Seguros SA (The Hornbay)* [2006] EWHC 373 (Comm), [2006] 2 Lloyd's Rep 44 at [26] (court jurisdiction) and *Kallang Shipping SA Panama v Axa Assurances Senegal and Comptoir Commercial Mandiaye Ndiaye (The Kallang)* [2008] EWHC 2761 (Comm), [2009] 1 Lloyd's Rep 124 (arbitration).

71 See note 3 above.

72 Ibid.

In the future where proceedings are commenced on or after 10 January 2015 and the Recast Regulation applies, Article 25 of that Regulation makes no distinction according to where the parties to a jurisdiction clause choosing the court of an EU Member State are domiciled. Even if neither party is domiciled in an EU Member State, the court of an EU Member State chosen must take jurisdiction, provided that the jurisdiction agreement satisfies the formalities set out in Article 25(1) of the Recast Regulation. As a result it has been necessary to amend the Civil Procedure Rules, which as we have seen above previously required a claimant to obtain the permission of the court to serve a defendant domiciled outside the EU Member States or Lugano Contracting States. This will no longer be the case where such a defendant has agreed to a jurisdiction agreement for the court of an EU Member State which satisfies the formalities of Article 25(1) of the Recast Regulation. Therefore, rule 6.33(2)(b) of the Civil Procedure Rules provides for situations where permission of the court is not required for service of the claim form out of the UK and rule 6.33(2)(b)(v) has a new situation where 'the defendant is a party to an agreement conferring jurisdiction within article 25 of the [Recast] Regulation'.

6.4 The Rotterdam Rules

The 2005 Hague Convention on Choice of Court Agreements,[73] which adopts the principle of party autonomy, does not apply to bills of lading as it was hoped that negotiations which culminated in the Convention on Contracts for the International Carriage of Goods Wholly or Partly by Sea and signed in Rotterdam in September 2009 (the Rotterdam Rules)[74] would provide their own solution to jurisdiction in bills of lading. In fact the provisions in those Rules on jurisdiction and arbitration were so controversial that they are contained in two Chapters which States can choose whether to opt in to if they ratify the Rotterdam Rules, or they can ratify the Rules without opting in to either or both of those Chapters.[75] Even

---

73 See fn 5 above.
74 The Rotterdam Rules are not in force as at 18 April 2016. As at that date only Congo, Spain, and Togo have ratified the Rules.
75 This author is not in favour of the solution in Chapters 14 and 15 of the Rotterdam Rules for the reasons set out in Y. Baatz et al., *The Rotterdam Rules: A Practical Annotation* (Informa, 2009), pp.221–223 in relation to jurisdiction clauses and pp.237–239 in relation to arbitration clauses. See also F. Berlingieri, *A Review of Some Recent Analyses of the Rotterdam Rules* (Il Diritto Marittimo, 2009), pp.1028 and 1029 agreeing with those criticisms and Y. Baatz, 'Should Third Parties be Bound by Arbitration Clauses in Bills of Lading?' [2015] LMCLQ 85. It is considered that the principle of party autonomy is not given sufficient recognition in the Rotterdam Rules. For a different view, see N. Gaskell, 'Australian Recognition and Enforcement of Foreign Charterparty Arbitration Clauses' [2014] LMCLQ 174 at 182 where he states, 'One suspects that the claimant-friendly jurisdiction and arbitration provisions in the Rotterdam Rules would be attractive for Australia, but that the volume contract provisions may be less acceptable.'

those Rules adopt the principle of party autonomy in certain circumstances and it is permissible to have a binding court jurisdiction agreement for the courts of a Contracting State to the Rules if it is in a volume contract and is between the original parties to the bill of lading. A neutral choice cannot bind a third party but that situation did not arise in *Hin-Pro*.

7. Conclusion

At the heart of the *Hin-Pro* litigation is the principle of party autonomy. That principle is of great significance in the UK and indeed in any Member State of the EU. The principle has been strengthened in the Recast Regulation which applies to any proceedings commenced on or after 10 January 2015, so that any jurisdiction agreement choosing the court of any EU Member State is binding no matter where the parties are domiciled, provided certain formalities are fulfilled. The 2005 Hague Convention on Choice of Court Agreements[76] also adopts that principle, although bills of lading are not covered by that Convention and even the Rotterdam Rules adopt that principle to a limited extent for volume contracts. However, the principle is not recognised by all States around the world as is clearly illustrated in the *Hin-Pro* case.[77] This may lead to multiple proceedings in one State[78] and in several other States, involving jurisdiction, the merits of the dispute, anti-suit injunctions, damages for breach of the jurisdiction agreement, freezing orders and receivership orders, with the risk of conflicting judgments and massive costs. There is a crying need for an international solution to this issue. The attempt made to find a solution in the Rotterdam Rules, which in this author's view does not give sufficient weight to party autonomy, although it does give some, has not come into force, and may never do so. This author would advocate that the parties' choice of jurisdiction and governing law is an important part of their contractual bargain for which a price is negotiated, so that there is certainty and predictability for both parties. If that part of their bargain is ignored the uncertainty, waste of legal costs and potential for commercial chaos is not an appealing outcome.

---

76 See note 5 above.

77 Zheng Sophia Tang, 'Effectiveness of Exclusive Jurisdiction Clauses in the Chinese Courts – A Pragmatic Study' [2012] ICLQ 459.

78 *Hin-Pro* obtained 19 judgments from the Chinese courts against CSAV. See *Compania Sud Americana de Vapores SA v Hin Pro International Logistics Ltd* [2015] HKDC 1339, [7] and [28]. CSAV successfully appealed 18 of these judgments - ibid [45].

Editors' notes

The English translation that follows of the Maritime Code of the People's Republic of China is provided by the National People's Congress of the People's Republic of China.[1] The editors wish to add a few words of a technical nature regarding our annotation of the translation.

The language of codified law requires a high degree of standardisation and precision, which is not always possible or desirable in the target language. The main purpose of adding the English translation of the Chinese Maritime Code as an appendix is to provide an overall picture to the English reader, while the annotation to the translation aims to assist readers with a background of English common law to digest the translated text.

In the editors' view, the most significant issue is that the Code uses a single word '解除' to cover the remedies of termination, cancellation and rescission. A few words to explain '解除' are therefore in order here.

Among the possible translations, the word 'cancellation' is most frequently used in the English translation that follows. This use of a single word means that the Code will also specify the remedy in each case. We have as a result occasionally felt a need to note the closest English common law equivalent.

'Cancellation' is at hand in two types of circumstances: (1) when the party has an option to cancel the contract based on certain conduct, whether performance or non-performance, of the other contracting party, such as in Articles 89 and 131; and (2) when the contract cannot be performed due to *force majeure* or other causes which are not attributable to any party's fault, such as in Articles 90 and 158.

As for 'termination' of a contract, that might be the result if one party has breached the contract and that breach is also within those provisions of the Code which confer upon the other party a right to bring the contract to an end, such as in Articles 96, 100 and 134.

---

1 The full text is available at <http://www.npc.gov.cn/englishnpc/Law/2007-12/12/content_1383863.htm> accessed 2 November 2015. The original Chinese language text is available at <http://www.npc.gov.cn/wxzl/gongbao/1992-11/07/content_1479260.htm> accessed 17 December 2015.

Distinction should also be drawn between 'rescission' of a contract *ab initio* and 'termination' of the contract for subsequent breach. Rescission has retrospective effect, while termination usually brings the contract to an end with prospective effect only. Therefore, rescission would be applied in the event of misrepresentation, as exemplified by Article 223. Once the contract is rescinded, it is void *ab initio*.

There may be other controversial choices evident in the translation. We welcome observations and comments and hope the annotated translation will be a useful tool in stimulating research and discussion of the Chinese Maritime Code.

The editors particularly wish to thank Ms Chenxuan Li, Research Fellow in the Institute of Maritime Law at Southampton Law School, for her valuable assistance with the annotations.

Dr Jingbo Zhang and Johanna Hjalmarsson

Appendix: Maritime Code of the People's Republic of China[1]

(Adopted at the 28th Meeting of the Standing Committee of the Seventh National People's Congress on November 7, 1992 and promulgated by Order No.64 of the President of the People's Republic of China on November 7, 1992)

CONTENTS

---

1 Maritime Code of the People's Republic of China <http://www.npc.gov.cn/englishnpc/Law/2007-12/12/content_1383863.htm> accessed 2 November 2015. The English translation of the Maritime Code of the People's Republic of China is provided by the National People's Congress of the People's Republic of China. Readers are strongly advised to refer to the official text of the Code in Chinese whenever necessary. The editors are not responsible for errors or liabilities that may arise from the use of this translation for whatsoever purpose.

Chapter I General Provisions

Article 1
This Code is enacted with a view to regulating the relations arising from maritime transport and those pertaining to ships, to securing and protecting the legitimate rights and interests of the parties concerned, and to promoting the development of maritime transport, economy and trade.

Article 2
'Maritime transport' as referred to in this Code means the carriage of goods and passengers by sea, including the sea-river and river-sea direct transport.

The provisions concerning contracts of carriage of goods by sea as contained in Chapter IV of this Code shall not be applicable to the maritime transport of goods between the ports of the People's Republic of China.

Article 3
'Ship' as referred to in this Code means sea-going ships and er mobile units, but does not include ships or craft to be used for military or public service purposes, nor small ships of less than 20 tons gross tonnage.

The term 'ship' as referred to in the preceding paragraph shall also include ship's apparel.

Article 4

Maritime transport and towage services between the ports of the People's Republic of China shall be undertaken by ships flying the national flag of the People's Republic of China, except as otherwise provided for by laws or administrative rules and regulations.

No foreign ships may engage in the maritime transport or towage services between the ports of the People's Republic of China unless permitted by the competent authorities of transport and communications under the State Council.

Article 5

Ships are allowed to sail under the national flag of the People's Republic of China after being registered, as required by law, and granted the nationality of the People's Republic of China.

Ships illegally flying the national flag of the People's Republic of China shall be prohibited and fined by the authorities concerned.[2]

Article 6

All matters pertaining to maritime transport shall be administered by the competent authorities of transport and communications under the State Council. The specific measures governing such administration shall be worked out by such authorities and implemented after being submitted to and approved by the State Council.

Chapter II Ships

Section 1 Ownership of Ships

Article 7

The ownership of a ship means the shipowner's rights to lawfully possess, utilize, profit from and dispose of the ship in his ownership.

Article 8

With respect to a state-owned ship operated by an enterprise owned by the whole people[3] having a legal person status granted by the State, the provisions of this Code regarding the shipowner shall apply to that legal person.

---

2 A better translation would be: 'Unauthorised flying of the flag of the People's Republic of China shall be prohibited and offenders shall be fined by the competent authorities.' Ed. note.

3 'An enterprise owned by the whole people' refers to a form of state-owned enterprise through which the public shares in socialist ownership.

Article 9

The acquisition, transference or extinction of the ownership of a ship shall be registered at the ship registration authorities; no acquisition, transference or extinction of the ship's ownership shall act against a third party unless registered.

The transference of the ownership of a ship shall be made by a contract in writing.

Article 10

Where a ship is jointly owned by two or more legal persons or individuals, the joint ownership thereof shall be registered at the ship registration authorities. The joint ownership of the ship shall not act against a third party unless registered.

Section 2 Mortgage of Ships

Article 11

The right of mortgage with respect to a ship is the right of preferred compensation enjoyed by the mortgagee of that ship from the proceeds of the auction sale made in accordance with law[4] where and when the mortgagor fails to pay his debt to the mortgagee secured by the mortgage of that ship.

Article 12

The owner of a ship or those authorized thereby may establish the mortgage of the ship.

The mortgage of a ship shall be established by a contract in writing.

Article 13

The mortgage of a ship shall be established by registering the mortgage of the ship with the ship registration authorities jointly by the mortgagee and the mortgagor. No mortgage may act against a third party unless registered.

The main items for the registration of the mortgage of a ship shall be:

(1) Name or designation and address of the mortgagee and the name or designation and address of the mortgagor of the ship;
(2) Name and nationality of the mortgaged ship and the authorities that issued the certificate of ownership and the certificate number thereof;
(3) Amount of debt secured, the interest rate and the period for the repayment of the debt.

---

4 This refers to judicial sale.

Information about the registration of mortgage of ships shall be accessible to the public for enquiry.

Article 14

Mortgage may be established on a ship under construction.

In registering the mortgage of a ship under construction, the building contract of the ship shall as well be submitted to the ship registration authorities.

Article 15

The mortgaged ship shall be insured by the mortgagor unless the contract provides otherwise. In case the ship is not insured, the mortgagee has the right to place the ship under insurance coverage and the mortgagor shall pay for the premium thereof.

Article 16

The establishment of mortgage by the joint owners of a ship shall, unless otherwise agreed upon among the joint owners, be subject to the agreement of those joint owners who have more than two thirds of the shares thereof.

The mortgage established by the joint owners of a ship shall not be affected by virtue of the division of ownership thereof.

Article 17

Once a mortgage is established on a ship, the ownership of the mortgaged ship shall not be transferred without the consent of the mortgagee.

Article 18

In case the mortgagee has transferred all or part of his right to debt secured by the mortgaged ship to another person, the mortgage shall be transferred accordingly.

Article 19

Two or more mortgages may be established on the same ship. The ranking of the mortgages shall be determined according to the dates of their respective registrations.

In case two or more mortgages are established, the mortgagees shall be paid out of the proceeds of the auction sale of the ship in the order of registration of their respective mortgages. The mortgages registered on the same date shall rank equally for payment.

Article 20

The mortgages shall be extinguished when the mortgaged ship is lost.[5] With respect to the compensation paid from the insurance coverage on account of the loss of the ship, the mortgagee shall be entitled to enjoy priority in compensation over other creditors.

Section 3 Maritime Liens

Article 21

A maritime lien is the right of the claimant, subject to the provisions of Article 22 of this Code, to take priority in compensation against shipowners, bareboat charterers or ship operators with respect to the ship which gave rise to the said claim.

Article 22

The following maritime claims shall be entitled to maritime liens:

(1) Payment claims for wages, other remuneration, crew repatriation and social insurance costs made by the Master, crew members and other members of the complement in accordance with the relevant labour laws, administrative rules and regulations or labour contracts;
(2) Claims in respect of loss of life or personal injury occurred in the operation of the ship;
(3) Payment claims for ship's tonnage dues, pilotage dues, harbour dues and other port charges;
(4) Payment claims for salvage payment; and
(5) Compensation claims for loss of or damage to property resulting from tortious act in the course of the operation of the ship.

Compensation claims for oil pollution damage caused by a ship carrying more than 2,000 tons of oil in bulk as cargo that has a valid certificate attesting that the ship has oil pollution liability insurance coverage or other appropriate financial security are not within the scope of sub-paragraph(5) of the preceding paragraph.

Article 23

The maritime claims set out in paragraph 1 of Article 22 shall be satisfied in the order listed. However, any of the maritime claims set out in sub-paragraph(4) arising later than those under sub-paragraph (1) through (3) shall have priority over those under sub-paragraph (1) through (3). In case there are more than two maritime claims under sub-paragraphs (1), (2), (3) or (5) of paragraph 1 of Article 22, they shall be satisfied at the same time regardless of their respective occurrences; where they could not be paid in

---

5 The original text also includes the situation when the mortgaged ship is destroyed.

full, they shall be paid in proportion. Should there be more than two maritime claims under sub-paragraph (4), those arising later shall be satisfied first.

Article 24

The legal costs for enforcing the maritime liens, the expenses for preserving and selling the ship, the expenses for distribution of the proceeds of sale and other expenses incurred for the common interests of the claimants, shall be deducted and paid first from the proceeds of the auction sale of the ship.

Article 25

A maritime lien shall have priority over a possessory lien, and a possessory lien shall have priority over ship mortgage.

The possessory lien referred to in the preceding paragraph means the right of the ship builder or repairer to secure the building or repairing cost of the ship by means of detaining the ship in his possession when the other party to the contract fails in the performance thereof. The possessory lien shall be extinguished when the ship builder or repairer no longer possesses the ship he has built or repaired.

Article 26

Maritime liens shall not be extinguished by virtue of the transfer of the ownership of the ship, except those that have not been enforced within 60 days of a public notice on the transfer of the ownership of the ship made by a court at the request of the transferee when the transfer was effected.

Article 27

In case the maritime claims provided for in Article 22 of this Code are transferred, the maritime liens attached thereto shall be transferred accordingly.

Article 28

A maritime lien shall be enforced by the court by arresting the ship that gave rise to the said maritime lien.

Article 29

A maritime lien shall, except as provided for in Article 26 of this Code, be extinguished under one of the following circumstances:

(1) The maritime claim attached by a maritime lien has not been enforced within one year of the existence of such maritime lien;
(2) The ship in question has been the subject of a forced sale by the court; or
(3) The ship has been lost.[6]

---

6 Add 'or destroyed' based on the original text.

The period of one year specified in sub-paragraph (1) of the preceding paragraph shall not be suspended or interrupted.

Article 30
The provisions of this Section shall not affect the implementation of the limitation of liability for maritime claims provided for in Chapter XI of this Code.

Chapter III Crew

Section 1 Basic Principles

Article 31
The term 'crew' means the entire complement of the ship, including the Master.

Article 32
The Master, deck officers, chief engineer, engineers, electrical engineer and radio operator must be those in possession of appropriate certificates of competency.

Article 33
Chinese 'crew' engaged in international voyages must possess Seaman's Book and other relevant certificates issued by the harbour superintendency authorities of the People's Republic of China.

Article 34
In the absence of specific stipulations in this Code as regards the employment of the crew as well as their labour-related rights and obligations, the provisions of the relevant laws and administrative rules and regulations shall apply.

Section 2 The Master

Article 35
The Master shall be responsible for the management and navigation of the ship.

Orders given by the Master within the scope of his functions and powers must be carried out by other members of the crew, the passengers and all persons on board.

The Master shall take necessary measures to protect the ship and all persons on board, the documents, postal matters, the goods as well as other property carried.

Article 36

To ensure the safety of the ship and all persons on board, the Master shall be entitled to confine or take other necessary measures against those who have committed crimes or violated laws or regulations on board, and to guard against their concealment, destruction or forging of evidence.

The Master, having taken actions as referred to in the preceding paragraph of this Article, shall make a written report of the case, which shall bear the signature of the Master himself and those of two or more others on board, and shall be handed over, together with the offender, to the authorities concerned for disposition.

Article 37

The Master shall make entries in the log book of any occurrence of birth or death on board and shall issue a certificate to that effect in the presence of two witnesses. The death certificate shall be attached with a list of personal belongings of the deceased, and attestation shall be given by the Master to the will, if any, of the deceased. Both the death certificate and the will shall be taken into safe keeping by the Master and handed over to the family members of the deceased or the organizations concerned.

Article 38

Where a sea casualty has occurred to a ship and the life and property on board have thus been threatened, the Master shall, with crew members and other persons on board under his command, make best efforts to run to the rescue. Should the foundering and loss of the ship have become inevitable, the Master may decide to abandon the ship. However, such abandonment shall be reported to the shipowner for approval except in case of emergency.[7]

Upon abandoning the ship, the Master must take all measures first to evacuate the passengers safely from the ship in an orderly way,[8] then make arrangements for crew members to evacuate, while the Master shall be the last to evacuate. Before leaving the ship, the Master shall direct the crew members to do their utmost[9] to rescue the deck log book, the engine log book, the oil record book, the radio log book, the charts, documents and papers used in the current voyage, as well as valuables, postal matters and cash money.

---

7   A better translation would be: 'Where a maritime casualty involving a ship endangers the personal and property safety on board her, the Master shall command crew members and other persons on board to rescue the ship using their best efforts. The Master may decide to abandon ship when the sinking or destruction of the ship becomes inevitable. However, such a decision shall be reported to the shipowner for approval except in case of emergency.' Ed. note.

8   Add 'and' here.

9   These words refer to the crew's 'best endeavours'.

Article 39
The duty of the Master in the management and navigation of the ship shall not be absolved even with the presence of a pilot piloting the ship.

Article 40
Should death occur to the Master or the Master be unable to perform his duties for whatever reason, the deck officer with the highest rank shall act as the Master; before the ship sails from its next port of call, the shipowner shall appoint a new Master to take command.

Chapter IV Contract of Carriage of Goods by Sea

Section 1 Basic Principles

Article 41
A contract of carriage of goods by sea is a contract under which the carrier, against payment of freight, undertakes to carry by sea the goods contracted for shipment by the shipper from one port to another.[10]

Article 42
For the purposes of this Chapter:

(1) 'Carrier' means the person by whom or in whose name a contract of carriage of goods by sea has been concluded with a shipper;
(2) 'Actual carrier' means the person to whom the performance of carriage of goods, or of part of the carriage, has been entrusted by the carrier, and includes any other person to whom such performance has been entrusted under a sub-contract;
(3) 'Shipper' means:

   a) The person by whom or in whose name or on whose behalf a contract of carriage of goods by sea has been concluded with a carrier;
   b) The person by whom or in whose name or on whose behalf the goods have been delivered to the carrier involved in the contract of carriage of goods by sea;

(4) 'Consignee' means the person who is entitled to take delivery of the goods;
(5) 'Goods' includes live animals and containers, pallets or similar articles of transport supplied by the shipper for consolidating the goods.

---

10 A better translation would be: 'A contract for the carriage of goods by sea is a contract under which the carrier is responsible for carrying the shipper's goods from one port to another by sea in exchange for freight.' Ed. note.

Article 43

The carrier or the shipper may demand confirmation of the contract of carriage of goods by sea in writing. However, voyage charter shall be done in writing. Telegrams, telexes and telefaxes have the effect of written documents.

Article 44

Any stipulation in a contract of carriage of goods by sea or a bill of lading or other similar documents evidencing such contract that derogates from the provisions of this Chapter shall be null and void. However, [the invalidity of such a provision] shall not affect the validity of other provisions of the contract or the bill of lading or other similar documents. A clause assigning the benefit of insurance of the goods in favour of the carrier or any similar clause shall be null and void.

Article 45

The provisions of Article 44 of this Code shall not prejudice the increase of duties and obligations by the carrier besides those set out in this Chapter.

Section 2   Carrier's Responsibilities[11]

Article 46

The responsibilities of the carrier with regard to the goods carried in containers covers the entire period during which the carrier is in charge of the goods, starting from the time the carrier has taken over the goods at the port of loading, until the goods have been delivered at the port of discharge. The responsibility of the carrier with respect to non-containerized goods covers the period during which the carrier is in charge of the goods, starting from the time of loading of the goods onto the ship until the time the goods are discharged therefrom. During the period the carrier is in charge of the goods, the carrier shall be liable for the loss of or damage to the goods, except as otherwise provided for in this Section.

The provisions of the preceding paragraph shall not prevent the carrier from entering into any agreement concerning carrier's responsibilities with regard to non-containerized goods prior to loading onto and after discharging from the ship.

Article 47

The carrier shall, before and at the beginning of the voyage, exercise due diligence to make the ship seaworthy, properly man, equip and supply the ship and to make the holds, refrigerating and cool chambers and all other

---

11 A better translation would be 'Carrier's Liabilities'.

parts of the ship in which goods are carried, fit and safe for their reception, carriage and preservation.[12]

Article 48

The carrier shall properly and carefully load, handle, stow, carry, keep, care for and discharge the goods carried.

Article 49

The carrier shall carry the goods to the port of discharge on the agreed or customary or geographically direct route.

Any deviation in saving or attempting to save life or property at sea or any reasonable deviation shall not be deemed to be an act deviating from the provisions of the preceding paragraph.

Article 50

Delay in delivery occurs when the goods have not been delivered at the designated port of discharge within the time expressly agreed upon.[13]

The carrier shall be liable for the loss of or damage to the goods caused by delay in delivery due to the fault of the carrier, except those arising or resulting from causes for which the carrier is not liable as provided for in the relevant Articles of this Chapter.

The carrier shall be liable for the economic losses caused by delay in delivery of the goods due to the fault of the carrier, even if no loss of or damage to the goods had actually occurred, unless such economic losses had occurred from causes for which the carrier is not liable as provided for in the relevant Articles of this Chapter.

The person entitled to make a claim for the loss of goods may treat the goods as lost when the carrier has not delivered the goods within 60 days from the expiry of the time for delivery specified in paragraph 1 of this Article.

Article 51

The carrier shall not be liable for the loss of or damage to the goods occurred during the period of carrier's responsibility arising or resulting from any of the following causes:

12 A better translation would be: 'The carrier should, prior to and at the commencement of the voyage, exercise due diligence to make the ship seaworthy, properly manned, equipped and supplied, and to make the goods holds, refrigerating cabins, cool chambers and all other stowage parts fit for safely receiving, carrying and preserving the goods.' Ed. note.
13 A better translation would be: 'Failure to deliver the goods within the expressly stipulated time at the agreed port constitutes late delivery.' Ed. note.

(1) Fault of the Master, crew members, pilot or servant of the carrier in the navigation or management of the ship;
(2) Fire, unless caused by the actual fault of the carrier;
(3) *Force majeure* and perils, dangers and accidents of the sea or other navigable waters;
(4) War or armed conflict;
(5) Act of the government or competent authorities, quarantine restrictions or seizure under legal process;
(6) Strikes, stoppages or restraint of labour;
(7) Saving or attempting to save life or property at sea;
(8) Act of the shipper, owner of the goods or their agents;
(9) Nature or inherent vice of the goods;
(10) Inadequacy of packing or insufficiency or illegibility of marks;
(11) Latent defect of the ship not discoverable by due diligence; and
(12) Any other cause arising without the fault of the carrier or his servant or agent.

The carrier who is entitled to exoneration from the liability for compensation as provided for in the preceding paragraph shall, with the exception of the causes given in sub-paragraph (2), bear the burden of proof.[14]

Article 52
The carrier shall not be liable for the loss of or damage to the live animals arising or resulting from the special risks inherent in the carriage thereof. However, the carrier shall be bound to prove that he has fulfilled the special requirements of the shipper with regard to the carriage of the live animals and that under the circumstances of the sea carriage, the loss or damage has occurred due to the special risks inherent therein.

Article 53
In case the carrier intends to ship the goods on deck, he shall come into an agreement with the shipper or comply with the custom of the trade or the relevant laws or administrative rules and regulations.

When the goods have been shipped on deck in accordance with the provisions of the preceding paragraph, the carrier shall not be liable for the loss of or damage to the goods caused by the special risks involved in such carriage.

If the carrier, in breach of the provisions of the first paragraph of this Article, has shipped the goods on deck and the goods have consequently suffered loss or damage, the carrier shall be liable therefore.

---

14 A better translation would be: 'With the exception of sub-paragraph (2) above, a carrier has the burden of proof for demonstrating that it is entitled to exclude liability in accordance with the preceding provisions of this Article.' Ed. note.

Article 54

Where loss or damage or delay in delivery has occurred from causes from which the carrier or his servant or agent is not entitled to exoneration from liability, together with another cause, the carrier shall be liable only to the extent that the loss, damage or delay in delivery is attributable to the causes from which the carrier is not entitled to exoneration from liability; however, the carrier shall bear the burden of proof with respect to the loss, damage or delay in delivery resulting from the other cause.

Article 55

The amount of indemnity for the loss of the goods shall be calculated on the basis of the actual value of the goods so lost, while that for the damage to the goods shall be calculated on the basis of the difference between the values of the goods before and after the damage, or on the basis of the expenses for the repair.

The actual value shall be the value of the goods at the time of shipment plus insurance and freight.

From the actual value referred to in the preceding paragraph, deduction shall be made, at the time of compensation, of the expenses that had been reduced or avoided as a result of the loss or damage occurred.

Article 56

The carrier's liability for the loss of or damage to the goods shall be limited to an amount equivalent to 666.67 Units of Account per package or other shipping unit, or 2 Units of Account per kilogramme of the gross weight of the goods lost or damaged, whichever is the higher, except where the nature and value of the goods had been declared by the shipper before shipment and inserted in the bill of lading, or where a higher amount than the amount of limitation of liability set out in this Article had been agreed upon between the carrier and the shipper.

Where a container, pallet or similar article of transport is used to consolidate goods, the number of packages or other shipping units enumerated in the bill of lading as packed in such article of transport shall be deemed to be the number of packages or shipping units. If not so enumerated, the goods in such article of transport shall be deemed to be one package or one shipping unit.

Where the article of transport is not owned or furnished by the carrier, such article of transport shall be deemed to be one package or one shipping unit.

Article 57

The liability of the carrier for the economic losses resulting from delay in delivery of the goods shall be limited to an amount equivalent to the freight payable for the goods so delayed. Where the loss of or damage to the goods has occurred concurrently with the delay in delivery thereof, the limitation of liability of the carrier shall be that as provided for in paragraph 1 of Article 56 of this Code.

Article 58

The defence and limitation of liability provided for in this Chapter shall apply to any legal action brought against the carrier with regard to the loss of or damage to or delay in delivery of the goods covered by the contract of carriage of goods by sea, whether the claimant is a party to the contract or whether the action is founded in contract or in tort.

The provisions of the preceding paragraph shall apply if the action referred to in the preceding paragraph is brought against the carrier's servant or agent, and the carrier's servant or agent proves that his action was within the scope of his employment or agency.

Article 59

The carrier shall not be entitled to the benefit of the limitation of liability provided for in Article 56 or 57 of this Code if it is proved that the loss, damage or delay in delivery of the goods resulted from an act or omission of the carrier done with the intent to cause such loss, damage or delay or recklessly and with knowledge that such loss, damage or delay would probably result.

The servant or agent of the carrier shall not be entitled to the benefit of limitation of liability provided for in Article 56 or 57 of this Code, if it is proved that the loss, damage or delay in delivery resulted from an act or omission of the servant or agent of the carrier done with the intent to cause such loss, damage or delay or recklessly and with knowledge that such loss, damage or delay would probably result.

Article 60

Where the performance of the carriage or part thereof has been entrusted to an actual carrier, the carrier shall nevertheless remain responsible for the entire carriage according to the provisions of this Chapter. The carrier shall be responsible, in relation to the carriage performed by the actual carrier, for the act or omission of the actual carrier and of his servant or agent acting within the scope of his employment or agency.

Notwithstanding the provisions of the preceding paragraph, where a contract of carriage by sea provides explicitly that a specified part of the carriage covered by the said contract is to be performed by a named actual carrier other than the carrier, the contract may nevertheless provide that the carrier shall not be liable for the loss, damage or delay in delivery arising from an occurrence which takes place while the goods are in the charge of the actual carrier during such part of the carriage.

Article 61

The provisions with respect to the responsibility of the carrier contained in this Chapter shall be applicable to the actual carrier. Where an action is brought against the servant or agent of the actual carrier, the provisions contained in paragraph 2 of Article 58 and paragraph 2 of Article 59 of this Code shall apply.

Article 62

Any special agreement under which the carrier assumes obligations not provided for in this Chapter or waives rights conferred by this Chapter shall be binding upon the actual carrier when the actual carrier has agreed in writing to the contents thereof. The provisions of such special agreement shall be binding upon the carrier whether the actual carrier has agreed to the contents or not.

Article 63

Where both the carrier and the actual carrier are liable for compensation, they shall jointly and severally be liable within the scope of such liability.

Article 64

If claims for compensation have been separately made against the carrier, the actual carrier and their servants or agents with regard to the loss of or damage to the goods, the aggregate amount of compensation shall not be in excess of the limitation provided for in Article 56 of this Code.

Article 65

The provisions of Article 60 through 64 of this Code shall not affect the recourse between the carrier and the actual carrier.

Section 3 Shipper's Responsibilities

Article 66

The shipper shall have the goods properly packed and shall guarantee the accuracy of the description, mark, number of packages or pieces, weight or quantity of the goods at the time of shipment and shall indemnify the carrier against any loss resulting from inadequacy of packing or inaccuracies in the above-mentioned information.

The carrier's right to indemnification as provided for in the preceding paragraph shall not affect the obligation of the carrier under the contract of carriage of goods towards those other than the shipper.

Article 67

The shipper shall perform all necessary procedures[15] at the port, customs, quarantine, inspection or other competent authorities with respect to the shipment of the goods and shall furnish to the carrier all relevant documents concerning the procedures the shipper has gone through. The shipper shall be liable for any damage to the interest of the carrier resulting from the inadequacy or inaccuracy or delay in delivery of such documents.

Article 68

At the time of shipment of dangerous goods, the shipper shall, in compliance with the regulations governing the carriage of such goods, have them properly packed, distinctly marked and labelled and notify the carrier in writing of their proper description, nature and the precautions to be taken. In case the shipper fails to notify the carrier or notified him inaccurately, the carrier may have such goods landed, destroyed or rendered innocuous when and where circumstances so require, without compensation. The shipper shall be liable to the carrier for any loss, damage or expense resulting from such shipment.

Notwithstanding the carrier's knowledge of the nature of the dangerous goods and his consent to carry, he may still have such goods landed, destroyed or rendered innocuous, without compensation, when they become an actual danger to the ship, the crew and other persons on board or to other goods. However, the provisions of this paragraph shall not prejudice the contribution in general average, if any.

Article 69

The shipper shall pay the freight to the carrier as agreed.

The shipper and the carrier may reach an agreement that the freight shall be paid by the consignee. However, such an agreement shall be noted in the transport documents.

Article 70

The shipper shall not be liable for the loss sustained by the carrier or the actual carrier, or for the damage sustained by the ship, unless such loss or damage was caused by the fault of the shipper, his servant or agent.

The servant or agent of the shipper shall not be liable for the loss sustained by the carrier or the actual carrier, or for the damage sustained by the ship, unless the loss or damage was caused by the fault of the servant or agent of the shipper.

---

15 The original Chinese text contains the words 'without delay' here.

Section 4 Transport Documents

Article 71

A bill of lading is a document which serves as an evidence of the contract of carriage of goods by sea and the taking over or loading of the goods by the carrier, and based on which the carrier undertakes to deliver the goods against surrendering the same. A provision in the document stating that the goods are to be delivered to the order of a named person, or to order, or to bearer, constitutes such an undertaking.[16]

Article 72

When the goods have been taken over by the carrier or have been loaded on board, the carrier shall, on demand of the shipper, issue to the shipper a bill of lading.

The bill of lading may be signed by a person authorized by the carrier. A bill of lading signed by the Master of the ship carrying the goods is deemed to have been signed on behalf of the carrier.

Article 73

A bill of lading shall contain the following particulars:

(1) Description of the goods, mark, number of packages or pieces, weight or quantity, and a statement, if applicable, as to the dangerous nature of the goods;
(2) Name and principal place of business of the carrier;
(3) Name of the ship;
(4) Name of the shipper;
(5) Name of the consignee;
(6) Port of loading and the date on which the goods were taken over by the carrier at the port of loading;
(7) Port of discharge;
(8) Place where the goods were taken over and the place where the goods are to be delivered in case of a multimodal transport bill of lading;
(9) Date and place of issue of the bill of lading and the number of originals issued;
(10) Payment of freight;
(11) Signature of the carrier or of a person acting on his behalf.

---

16 A better translation would be 'A bill of lading is a document which not only evidences the contract of carriage of goods by sea, but also proves the fact that the carrier has either received or loaded the goods concerned on board, and based on which the carrier undertakes to deliver the goods against surrender of the bill of lading. The clause in the bill of lading which indicates that the cargo should be delivered to a named consignee, at the instruction of a nominated person, or to the holder of the bill of lading, constitutes the carrier's undertaking to deliver the cargo accordingly.' Ed. note.

In a bill of lading, the lack of one or more particulars referred to in the preceding paragraph does not affect the function of the bill of lading as such, provided that it nevertheless meets the requirements set forth in Article 71 of this Code.

Article 74

If the carrier has issued, on demand of the shipper, a received-for-shipment bill of lading or other similar documents before the goods are loaded on board, the shipper may surrender the same to the carrier as against a shipped bill of lading when the goods have been loaded on board. The carrier may also note on the received-for-shipment bill of lading or other similar documents with the name of the carrying ship and the date of loading, and, when so noted, the received-for-shipment bill of lading or other similar documents shall be deemed to constitute a shipped bill of lading.

Article 75

If the bill of lading contains particulars concerning the description, mark, number of packages or pieces, weight or quantity of the goods with respect to which the carrier or the other person issuing the bill of lading on his behalf has the knowledge or reasonable grounds to suspect that such particulars do not accurately represent the goods actually received, or, where a shipped bill of lading is issued, loaded, or if he has had no reasonable means of checking, the carrier or such other person may make a note in the bill of lading specifying those inaccuracies, the grounds for suspicion or the lack of reasonable means of checking.

Article 76

If the carrier or the other person issuing the bill of lading on his behalf made no note in the bill of lading regarding the apparent order and condition of the goods, the goods shall be deemed to be in apparent good order and condition.

Article 77

Except for the note made in accordance with the provisions of Article 75 of this Code, the bill of lading issued by the carrier or the other person acting on his behalf is *prima facie* evidence of the taking over or loading by the carrier of the goods as described therein. Proof to the contrary by the carrier shall not be admissible if the bill of lading has been transferred to a third party, including a consignee, who has acted in good faith in reliance on the description of the goods contained therein.

Article 78

The relationship between the carrier and the holder of the bill of lading with respect to their rights and obligations shall be defined by the clauses of the bill of lading.

Neither the consignee nor the holder of the bill of lading shall be liable for the demurrage, dead freight and all other expenses in respect of loading occurred at the loading port unless the bill of lading clearly states that the aforesaid demurrage, dead freight and all other expenses shall be borne by the consignee and the holder of the bill of lading.

Article 79

The negotiability of a bill of lading shall be governed by the following provisions:

(1) A straight bill of lading is not negotiable;
(2) An order bill of lading may be negotiated with endorsement to order or endorsement in blank;
(3) A bearer bill of lading is negotiable without endorsement.

Article 80

Where a carrier has issued a document other than a bill of lading as an evidence of the receipt of the goods to be carried, such a document is *prima facie* evidence of the conclusion of the contract of carriage of goods by sea and the taking over by the carrier of the goods as described therein.

Such documents that are issued by the carrier shall not be negotiable.

Section 5 Delivery of Goods

Article 81

Unless notice of loss or damage is given in writing by the consignee to the carrier at the time of delivery of the goods by the carrier to the consignee, such delivery shall be deemed to be *prima facie* evidence of the delivery of the goods by the carrier as described in the transport documents and of the apparent good order and condition of such goods.

Where the loss of or damage to the goods is not apparent, the provisions of the preceding paragraph shall apply if the consignee has not given the notice in writing within 7 consecutive days from the next day of the delivery of the goods, or, in the case of containerized goods, within 15 days from the next day of the delivery thereof.

The notice in writing regarding the loss or damage need not be given if the state of the goods has, at the time of delivery, been the subject of a joint survey or inspection by the carrier and the consignee.

Article 82

The carrier shall not be liable for compensation if no notice on the economic losses resulting from delay in delivery of the goods has been received from the consignee within 60 consecutive days from the next day on which the goods had been delivered by the carrier to the consignee.

Article 83

The consignee may, before taking delivery of the goods at the port of destination, and the carrier may, before delivering the goods at the port of destination, request the cargo inspection agency to have the goods inspected. The party requesting such inspection shall bear the cost thereof but is entitled to recover the same from the party causing the damage.

Article 84

The carrier and the consignee shall mutually provide reasonable facilities for the survey and inspection stipulated in Articles 81 and 83 of this Code.

Article 85

Where the goods have been delivered by the actual carrier, the notice in writing given by the consignee to the actual carrier under Article 81 of this Code shall have the same effect as that given to the carrier, and that given to the carrier shall have the same effect as that given to the actual carrier.

Article 86

If the goods were not taken delivery of at the port of discharge or if the consignee has delayed or refused the taking delivery of the goods, the Master may discharge the goods into warehouses or other appropriate places, and any expenses or risks arising therefrom shall be borne by the consignee.

Article 87

If the freight, contribution in general average, demurrage to be paid to the carrier and other necessary charges paid by the carrier on behalf of the owner of the goods as well as other charges to be paid to the carrier have not been paid in full, nor has appropriate security been given, the carrier may have a lien, to a reasonable extent, on the goods.

Article 88

If the goods under lien in accordance with the provisions of Article 87 of this Code have not been taken delivery of within 60 days from the next day of the ship's arrival at the port of discharge, the carrier may apply to the court for an order on selling the goods by auction; where the goods are perishable or the expenses for keeping such goods would exceed their value, the carrier may apply for an earlier sale by auction.

The proceeds from the auction sale shall be used to pay off the expenses for the storage and auction sale of the goods, the freight and other related charges to be paid to the carrier. If the proceeds fall short of such expenses, the carrier is entitled to claim the difference from the shipper, whereas any amount in surplus shall be refunded to the shipper. If there is no way to make the refund and such surplus amount has not been claimed at the end of one full year after the auction sale, it shall go to the State Treasury.

Section 6 Cancellation of Contract[17]

Article 89

The shipper may request the cancellation of the contract of carriage of goods by sea before the ship sails from the port of loading. However, except as otherwise provided for in the contract, the shipper shall in this case pay half of the agreed amount of freight; if the goods have already been loaded on board, the shipper shall bear the expenses for the loading and discharge and other related charges.

Article 90

Either the carrier or the shipper may request the cancellation of the contract and neither shall be liable to the other if, due to *force majeure* or other causes not attributable to the fault of the carrier or the shipper, the contract could not be performed prior to the ship's sailing from its port of loading. If the freight has already been paid, it shall be refunded to the shipper, and, if the goods have already been loaded on board, the loading/discharge expenses shall be borne by the shipper. If a bill of lading has already been issued, it shall be returned by the shipper to the carrier.

Article 91

If, due to *force majeure* or any other causes not attributable to the fault of the carrier or the shipper, the ship could not discharge its goods at the port of destination as provided for in the contract of carriage, unless the contract provides otherwise, the Master shall be entitled to discharge the goods at a safe port or place near the port of destination and the contract of carriage shall be deemed to have been fulfilled.

In deciding the discharge of the goods, the Master shall inform the shipper or the consignee and shall take the interests of the shipper or the consignee into consideration.

Section 7 Special Provisions Regarding Voyage Charter Party

Article 92

A voyage charter party is a charter party under which the shipowner charters out and the charterer charters in the whole or part of the ship's space for the carriage by sea of the intended goods from one port to another and the charterer pays the agreed amount of freight.

---

17 'Cancellation' here has two levels of meaning: one is the shipper's option to cancel the carriage contract before sailing, and the other is cancellation of the contract due to *force majeure* and other causes not arising as a result of the fault of the parties.

Article 93

A voyage charter party shall mainly contain, *inter alia*, name of the shipowner, name of the charterer, name and nationality of the ship, its bale or grain capacity, description of the goods to be loaded, port of loading, port of destination, laydays, time for loading and discharge, payment of freight, demurrage, dispatch and other relevant matters.

Article 94

The provisions in Article 47 and Article 49 of this Code shall apply to the shipowner under voyage charter party.

The other provisions in this Chapter regarding the rights and obligations of the parties to the contract shall apply to the shipowner and the charterer under voyage charter only in the absence of relevant provisions or in the absence of provisions differing therefrom in the voyage charter.

Article 95

Where the holder of the bill of lading is not the charterer in the case of a bill of lading issued under a voyage charter, the rights and obligations of the carrier and the holder of the bill of lading shall be governed by the clauses of the bill of lading. However, if the clauses of the voyage charter party are incorporated into the bill of lading, the relevant clauses of the voyage charter party shall apply.

Article 96

The shipowner shall provide the intended ship. The intended ship may be substituted with the consent of the charterer. However, if the ship substituted does not meet the requirements of the charter party, the charterer may reject the ship or cancel[18] the charter. Should any damage or loss occur to the charterer as a result of the shipowner's failure in providing the intended ship due to his fault, the shipowner shall be liable for compensation.

Article 97

If the shipowner has failed to provide the ship within the laydays fixed in the charter, the charterer is entitled to cancel the charter party. However, if the shipowner had notified the charterer of the delay of the ship and the expected date of its arrival at the port of loading, the charterer shall notify the shipowner whether to cancel the charter within 48 hours of the receipt of the shipowner's notification.

Where the charterer has suffered losses as a result of the delay in providing the ship due to the fault of the shipowner, the shipowner shall be liable for compensation.

---

18 In the editors' opinion, the appropriate English translation here would be 'terminate', as the charterparty will come to an end because of the shipowner's breach.

Article 98

Under a voyage charter, the time for loading and discharge and the way of calculation thereof, as well as the rate of demurrage that would incur after the expiration of the laytime and the rate of dispatch money to be paid as a result of the completion of loading or discharge ahead of schedule, shall be fixed by the shipowner and the charterer upon mutual agreement.

Article 99

The charterer may sublet the ship he chartered, but the rights and obligations under the head charter shall not be affected.

Article 100

The charterer shall provide the intended goods, but he may replace the goods with the consent of the shipowner. However, if the goods replaced are detrimental to the interests of the shipowner, the shipowner shall be entitled to reject such goods and cancel[19] the charter.

Where the shipowner has suffered losses as a result of the failure of the charterer in providing the intended goods, the charterer shall be liable for compensation.

Article 101

The shipowner shall discharge the goods at the port of discharge specified in the charter party. Where the charter party contains a clause allowing the choice of the port of discharge by the charterer, the Master may choose one from among the agreed picked ports to discharge the goods, in case the charterer did not, as agreed in the charter, instruct in time as to the port chosen for discharging the goods. Where the charterer did not instruct in time as to the chosen port of discharge, as agreed in the charter, and the shipowner suffered losses thereby, the charterer shall be liable for compensation; where the charterer has suffered losses as a result of the shipowner's arbitrary choice of a port to discharge the goods, in disregard of the provisions in the relevant charter, the shipowner shall be liable for compensation.

Section 8 *Special Provisions Regarding Multimodal Transport Contract*

Article 102

A multimodal transport contract as referred to in this Code means a contract under which the multimodal transport operator undertakes to transport the goods, against the payment of freight for the entire transport, from the place where the goods were received in his charge to the destination

---

19 'Cancel' here would be best translated by 'terminate', as the discharge of the contract is caused by the charterer's breach.

and to deliver them to the consignee by two or more different modes of transport, one of which being sea carriage.

The multimodal transport operator as referred to in the preceding paragraph means the person who has entered into a multimodal transport contract with the shipper either by himself or by another person acting on his behalf.

Article 103
The responsibility of the multimodal transport operator with respect to the goods under multimodal transport contract covers the period from the time he takes the goods in his charge to the time of their delivery.

Article 104
The multimodal transport operator shall be responsible for the performance of the multimodal transport contract or the procurement of the performance therefore, and shall be responsible for the entire transport.

The multimodal transport operator may enter into separate contracts with the carriers of the different modes defining their responsibilities with regard to the different sections of the transport under the multimodal transport contracts. However, such separate contracts shall not affect the responsibility of the multimodal transport operator with respect to the entire transport.

Article 105
If loss of or damage to the goods has occurred in a certain section of the transport, the provisions of the relevant laws and regulations governing that specific section of the multimodal transport shall be applicable to matters concerning the liability of the multimodal transport operator and the limitation thereof.

Article 106
If the section of transport in which the loss of or damage to the goods occurred could not be ascertained, the multimodal transport operator shall be liable for compensation in accordance with the stipulations regarding the carrier's liability and the limitation thereof as set out in this Chapter.

Chapter V Contract of Carriage of Passengers by Sea

Article 107
A contract of carriage of passengers by sea is a contract whereby the carrier undertakes to carry passengers and their luggage by sea from one port to another by ships suitable for that purpose against payment of [a] fare by the passengers.

Article 108
For the purposes of this Chapter:

(1) 'Carrier' means the person by whom or in whose name a contract of carriage of passengers by sea has been entered into with the passengers;
(2) 'Actual carrier' means the person by whom the whole or part of the carriage of passengers has been performed as entrusted by the carrier, including those engaged in such carriage under a sub-contract;
(3) 'Passenger' means a person carried under a contract of carriage of passengers by sea. With the consent of the carrier, a person supervising the carriage of goods aboard a ship covered by a contract of carriage of goods is regarded as a passenger;
(4) 'Luggage' means any article or vehicle shipped by the carrier under the contract of carriage of passengers by sea, with the exception of live animals;
(5) 'Cabin luggage' means the luggage which the passenger has in his cabin or is otherwise in his possession, custody or control.

Article 109
The provisions regarding the responsibilities of the carrier as contained in this Chapter shall be applicable to the actual carrier, and the provisions regarding the responsibilities of the servant or agent of the carrier as contained in this Chapter shall be applicable to the servant or agent of the actual carrier.

Article 110
The passage ticket serves as an evidence that a contract of carriage of passengers by sea has been entered into.[20]

Article 111
The period of carriage for the carriage of passengers by sea commences from the time of embarkation of the passengers and terminates at the time of their disembarkation, including the period during which the passengers are transported by water from land to the ship or vice versa, if such cost of transport is included in the fare. However, the period of carriage does not include the time when the passengers are at a marine terminal or station or on a quay or in or on any other port installations.

The period of carriage for the cabin luggage of the passengers shall be the same as that stipulated in the preceding paragraph. The period of carriage for luggage other than the cabin luggage commences from the time when the carrier or his servant or agent receives it into his charge and terminates

---

20 A better translation would be 'The passenger's ticket serves as evidence of the contract of carriage of the passenger by sea.' Ed. note.

at the time when the carrier or his servant or agent redelivers it to the passengers.

Article 112

A passenger travelling without a ticket or taking a higher class berth than booked or going beyond the distance paid for shall pay for the fare or the excess fare as required by relevant regulations, and the carrier may, according to the relevant regulations, charge additional fare. Should any passenger refuse to pay, the Master is entitled to order him to disembark at a suitable place and the carrier has the right of recourse against him.

Article 113

No passenger may take on board or pack in their luggage contraband goods or any article of an inflammable, explosive, poisonous, corrosive or radioactive nature or other dangerous goods that would endanger the safety of life and property on board.

The carrier may have the contraband or dangerous goods brought on board by the passenger or packed in his luggage in breach of the provisions of the preceding paragraph discharged, destroyed or rendered innocuous at any time and at any place or sent over to the appropriate authorities, without being liable for compensation.

The passenger shall be liable for compensation if any loss or damage occurs as a result of his breach of the provisions of paragraph 1 of this Article.

Article 114

During the period of carriage of the passengers and their luggage as provided for in Article 111 of this Code, the carrier shall be liable for the death of or personal injury to passengers or the loss of or damage to their luggage resulting from accidents caused by the fault of the carrier or his servant or agent committed within the scope of his employment or agency.

The claimant shall bear the burden of proof regarding the fault of the carrier or his servant or agent, with the exception, however, of the circumstances specified in paragraphs 3 and 4 of this Article.

If the death of or personal injury to the passengers or loss of or damage to the passengers' cabin luggage occurred as a result of shipwreck, collision, stranding, explosion, fire or the defect of the ship, it shall be presumed that the carrier or his servant or agent has committed a fault, unless proof to the contrary has been given by the carrier or his servant or agent.

As to any loss of or damage to the luggage other than the passenger's cabin luggage, unless the carrier or his servant or agent proves to the contrary, it shall be presumed that the carrier or his servant or agent has committed a fault, no matter how the loss or damage was caused.

Article 115

If it is proved by the carrier that the death of or personal injury to the passenger or the loss of or damage to his luggage was caused by the fault of the passenger himself or the faults of the carrier and the passenger combined, the carrier's liability may be exonerated or appropriately mitigated.

If it is proved by the carrier that the death of or personal injury to the passenger or the loss of or damage to the passenger's luggage was intentionally caused by the passenger himself, or the death or personal injury was due to the health condition of his, the carrier shall not be liable therefore.

Article 116

The carrier shall not be liable for any loss of or damage to the monies, gold, silver, jewellery, negotiable securities or other valuables of the passengers.

If the passenger has entrusted the above-mentioned valuables to the safe-keeping of the carrier under an agreement for that purpose, the carrier shall be liable for compensation in accordance with the provisions of Article 117 of this Code. Where the limitation of liability agreed upon between the carrier and the passenger in writing is higher than that set out in Article 117 of this Code, the carrier shall make the compensation in accordance with that higher amount.

Article 117

Except the circumstances specified in paragraph 4 of this Article, the limitation of liability of the carrier under each carriage of passengers by sea shall be governed by the following:

(1) For death of or personal injury to the passenger: not exceeding 46,666 Units of Account per passenger;
(2) For loss of or damage to the passengers' cabin luggage: not exceeding 833 Units of Account per passenger;
(3) For loss of or damage to the passengers' vehicles including the luggage carried therein: not exceeding 3,333 Units of Account per vehicle;
(4) For loss of or damage to luggage other than those described in sub-paragraphs (2) and (3) above: not exceeding 1,200 Units of Account per passenger.

An agreement may be reached between the carrier and the passengers with respect to the deductibles applicable to the compensation for loss of or damage to the passengers' vehicles and luggage other than their vehicles. However, the deductible with respect to the loss of or damage to the passengers' vehicles shall not exceed 117 Units of Account per vehicle, whereas the deductible for the loss of or damage to the luggage other than the vehicle shall not exceed 13 Units of Account per piece of luggage per passenger. In calculating the amount of compensation for the loss of or damage to the passenger's vehicle or the luggage other than the vehicle, deduction shall be made of the agreed deductibles the carrier is entitled to.

A higher limitation of liability than that set out in sub-paragraph (1) above may be agreed upon between the carrier and the passenger in writing.

The limitation of liability of the carrier with respect to the carriage of passengers by sea between the ports of the People's Republic of China shall be fixed by the competent authorities of transport and communications under the State Council and implemented after its being submitted to and approved by the State Council.

Article 118
If it is proved that the death of or personal injury to the passenger or the loss of or damage to the passenger's luggage resulted from an act or omission of the carrier done with the intent to cause such loss or damage or recklessly and with knowledge that such death or personal injury or such loss or damage would probably result, the carrier shall not invoke the provisions regarding the limitation of liability contained in Articles 116 and 117 of this Code.

If it is proved that the death of or personal injury to the passenger or the loss of or damage to the passenger's luggage resulted from an act or omission of the servant or agent of the carrier done with the intent to cause such loss or damage or recklessly and with knowledge that such death or personal injury or such loss or damage would probably result, the servant or agent of the carrier shall not invoke the provisions regarding the limitation of liability contained in Articles 116 and 117 of this Code.

Article 119
In case of apparent damage to the luggage, the passenger shall notify the carrier or his servant or agent in writing according to the following:

(1) Notice with respect to cabin luggage shall be made before or at the time of his embarkation;
(2) Notice regarding luggage other than cabin luggage shall be made before or at the time of redelivery thereof.

If the damage to the luggage is not apparent and it is difficult for the passenger to discover such damage at the time of his disembarkation or of the redelivery of the luggage, or if the luggage has been lost, the passenger shall notify the carrier or his servant or agent in writing within 15 days from the next day of disembarkation of the passenger or of the redelivery of the luggage.

If the passenger fails to send in the notice in writing in time in accordance with the provisions of sub-paragraphs (1) and (2) of this Article, it shall be presumed that the luggage has been received undamaged, unless proof to the contrary is made.

Where the luggage has been jointly surveyed or inspected by the passenger and the carrier at the time of redelivery thereof, the above-mentioned notice need not be given.

Article 120

With regard to the claims made to the carrier's servant or agent, such servant or agent shall be entitled to invoke the provisions regarding defence and limitation of liability contained in Articles 115, 116 and 117 of this Code if such servant or agent proves that his act or omission was within the scope of his employment or agency.

Article 121

Where the performance of the carriage of passengers or part thereof has been entrusted by the carrier to an actual carrier, the carrier shall, as stipulated in this Chapter, remain liable for the entire carriage. Where the carriage is performed by the actual carrier, the carrier shall be liable for the act or omission of the actual carrier or the act or omission of his servant or agent within the scope of his employment or agency.

Article 122

Any special agreement under which the carrier assumes obligations not provided for in this Chapter or waives the rights conferred by this Chapter shall be binding upon the actual carrier where the actual carrier has expressly agreed in writing to the contents thereof. Such a special agreement shall be binding upon the carrier whether the actual carrier has agreed to its contents or not.

Article 123

Where both the carrier and the actual carrier are liable for compensation, they shall be liable jointly and severally within the scope of such liability.

Article 124

Where separate claims have been brought against the carrier, the actual carrier and their servants or agents with respect to the death of or personal injury to the passengers or the loss of or damage to their luggage, the aggregate amount of compensation shall not be in excess of the limitation prescribed in Article 117 of this Code.

Article 125

The provisions of Articles 121 through 124 of this Code shall not affect the right of recourse between the carrier and the actual carrier.

Article 126
Any of the following clauses contained in a contract of carriage of passengers by sea shall be null and void:[21]

(1) Any clause that exonerates the statutory responsibility of the carrier in respect of the passenger;
(2) Any clause that reduces the limitation of liability of the carrier as contained in this Chapter;
(3) Any clause that contains provisions contrary to those of this Chapter concerning burden of proof; and
(4) Any clause that restricts the right of claim of the passenger.

The nullity and voidness[22] of the clauses set out in the preceding paragraph shall not prejudice the validity of the other clauses of the contract.

Chapter VI Charter Parties

Section 1 Basic Principles

Article 127
The provisions concerning the rights and obligations of the shipowner and the charterer in this Chapter shall apply only when there are no stipulations or no different stipulations[23] in this regard in the charter party.

Article 128
Charter parties including time charter parties and bareboat charter parties shall be concluded in writing.

Section 2 Time Charter Party

Article 129
A time charter party is a contract under which the shipowner provides a designated manned ship to the charterer, and the charterer employs the ship during the contractual period for the agreed service against payment of hire.

Article 130
A time charter party mainly contains the name of the shipowner, the name of the charterer; the name, nationality, class, tonnage, capacity, speed and fuel consumption of the ship; the trading area; the agreed service, the contractual period, the time, place and conditions of delivery and redelivery of the ship; the hire and the way of its payment and other relevant matters.

---

21 The original text states '无效' which means 'invalid' in English.
22 The noun of '无效' is 'invalidity'.
23 These words refer to 'stipulations to the contrary'.

Article 131

The shipowner shall deliver the ship within the time agreed upon in the charter party.

Where the shipowner acts against the provisions of the preceding paragraph, the charterer is entitled to cancel the charter. However, if the shipowner has notified the charterer of the anticipated delay in delivery and has given an estimated time of arrival of the ship at the port of delivery, the charterer shall notify the shipowner, within 48 hours of the receipt of such notice from the shipowner, of his decision whether to cancel the charter or not.

The shipowner shall be liable for the charterer's loss resulting from the delay in delivery of the ship due to the shipowner's fault.

Article 132

At the time of delivery, the shipowner shall exercise due diligence to make the ship seaworthy. The ship delivered shall be fit for the intended service.

Where the shipowner acts against the provisions in the preceding paragraph, the charterer shall be entitled to cancel the charter and claim any losses resulting therefrom.

Article 133

During the charter period, if the ship is found at variance with the seaworthiness or the other conditions agreed upon in the charter, the shipowner shall take all reasonable measures to have them restored as soon as possible.

Where the ship has not been operated normally for 24 consecutive hours due to its failure to maintain the seaworthiness or the other conditions as agreed upon, the charterer shall not pay the hire for the operating time so lost, unless such failure was caused by the charterer.

Article 134

The charterer shall guarantee that the ship shall be employed in the agreed maritime transport between the safe ports or places within the trading area agreed upon.

If the charterer acts against the provisions of the preceding paragraph, the shipowner is entitled to cancel[24] the charter and claim any losses resulting therefrom.

Article 135

The charterer shall guarantee that the ship shall be employed to carry the lawful merchandise agreed.

---

24 'Cancel' is here used in the sense of 'terminate', as the shipowner brings the charterparty to an end as a result of the charterer's breach.

Where the ship is to be employed by the charterer to carry live animals or dangerous goods, a prior consent of the shipowner is required.

The charterer shall be liable for any loss of the shipowner resulting from the charterer's violation of the provisions of paragraph 1 or paragraph 2 of this Article.

Article 136
The charterer shall be entitled to give the Master instructions with respect to the operation of the ship. However, such instructions shall not be inconsistent with the stipulations of the time charter.

Article 137
The charterer may sublet the ship under charter, but he shall notify the shipowner of the sublet in time. The rights and obligations agreed upon in the head charter shall not be affected by the sub-charter.

Article 138
Where the ownership of the ship under charter has been transferred by the shipowner, the rights and obligations agreed upon under the original charter shall not be affected. However, the shipowner shall inform the charterer thereof in time. After such transfer, the transferee and the charterer shall continue to perform the original charter.

Article 139
Should the ship be engaged in salvage operations during the charter period, the charterer shall be entitled to half of the amount of the payment for salvage operations after deducting therefrom the salvage expenses, compensation for damage, the portion due to crew members and other relevant costs.

Article 140
The charterer shall pay the hire as agreed upon in the charter. Where the charterer fails to pay the hire as agreed upon, the shipowner shall be entitled to cancel the charter party and claim any losses resulting therefrom.

Article 141
In case the charterer fails to pay the hire or other sums of money as agreed upon in the charter, the shipowner shall have a lien on the charterer's goods, other property on board and earnings from the sub-charter.

Article 142
When the charterer redelivers the ship to the shipowner, the ship shall be in the same good order and condition as it was at the time of delivery, fair wear and tear excepted.

Where, upon redelivery, the ship fails to remain in the same good order and condition as it was at the time of delivery, the charterer shall be responsible for rehabilitation or for compensation.

Article 143

If, on the basis of a reasonable calculation, a ship may be able to complete its last voyage at around the time of redelivery specified in the charter and probably thereafter, the charterer is entitled to continue to use the ship in order to complete that voyage even if its time of redelivery will be overdue. During the extended period, the charterer shall pay the hire at the rate fixed by the charter, and, if the current market rate of hire is higher than that specified in the charter, the charterer shall pay the hire at the current market rate.

Section 3 Bareboat Charter Party

Article 144

A bareboat charter party is a charter party under which the shipowner provides the charterer with an unmanned ship which the charterer shall possess, employ and operate within an agreed period and for which the charterer shall pay the shipowner the hire.

Article 145

A bareboat charter party mainly contains the name of the shipowner and the name of the charterer; the name, nationality, class, tonnage and capacity of the ship; the trading area, the employment of the ship and the charter period; the time, place and condition of delivery and redelivery; the survey, maintenance and repair of the ship; the hire and its payment; the insurance of the ship; the time and condition for the termination of the charter and other relevant matters.

Article 146

The shipowner shall deliver the ship and its certificates to the charterer at the port or place and time as stipulated in the charter party. At the time of delivery, the shipowner shall exercise due diligence to make the ship seaworthy. The ship delivered shall be fit for the agreed service.

Where the shipowner acts against the provisions of the preceding paragraph, the charterer shall be entitled to cancel[25] the charter and claim any losses resulting therefrom.

---

25 'Cancel' is here used in the sense of 'terminate'.

Article 147

The charterer shall be responsible for the maintenance and repair of the ship during the bareboat charter period.

Article 148

During the bareboat charter period, the ship shall be insured, at the value agreed upon in the charter and in the way consented to by the shipowner, by the charterer at his expense.

Article 149

During the bareboat charter period, if the charterer's possession, employment or operation of the ship has affected the interests of the shipowner or caused any losses thereto, the charterer shall be liable for eliminating the harmful effect or compensating for the losses.

Should the ship be arrested due to any disputes over its ownership or debts owed by the shipowner, the shipowner shall guarantee that the interest of the charterer is not affected. The shipowner shall be liable for compensation for any losses suffered by the charterer thereby.

Article 150

During the bareboat charter period, the charterer shall not assign the rights and obligations stipulated in the charter or sublet the ship under bareboat charter without the shipowners's consent in writing.

Article 151

The shipowner shall not establish any mortgage of the ship during the bareboat charter period without the prior consent in writing by the charterer.

Where the shipowner acts against the provisions of the preceding paragraph and thereby causes losses to the charterer, the shipowner shall be liable for compensation.

Article 152

The charterer shall pay the hire as stipulated in the charter. In default of payment by the charterer for seven consecutive days or more after the time as agreed in the charter for such payment, the shipowner is entitled to cancel[26] the charter without prejudice to any claim for the loss arising from the charterer's default.

Should the ship be lost or missing, payment of hire shall cease from the day when the ship was lost or last heard of. Any hire paid in advance shall be refunded in proportion.

---

26 'Cancel' is here used in the sense of 'terminate'.

Article 153

The provisions of Article 134, paragraph 1 of Article 135, Article 142 and Article 143 of this Code shall be applicable to bareboat charter parties.

Article 154

The ownership of a ship under bareboat charter containing a lease-purchase[27] clause shall be transferred to the charterer when the charterer has paid off the lease-purchase[28] price to the shipowner as stipulated in the charter.

Chapter VII Contract of Sea Towage

Article 155

A contract of sea towage is a contract whereby the tugowner undertakes to tow an object by sea with a tug from one place to another and the tow party pays the towage.

The provisions of this Chapter shall not be applicable to the towage service rendered to ships within the port area.

Article 156

A contract of sea towage shall be made in writing. Its contents shall mainly include name and address of the tugowner, name and address of the tow party, name and main particulars of the tug and name and main particulars of the object to be towed, horse power of the tug, place of commencement of the towage and the destination, the date of commencement of the towage, towage price and the way of payment thereof, as well as other relevant matters.

Article 157

The tugowner shall, before and at the beginning of the towage, exercise due diligence to make the tug seaworthy and towworthy and to properly man the tug and equip it with gears and tow lines and to provide all other necessary supplies and appliances for the intended voyage.

The tow party shall, before and at the beginning of the towage, make all necessary preparations therefore and shall exercise due diligence to make the object to be towed towworthy and shall give a true account of the object to be towed and provide the certificate of towworthiness and other documents issued by the relevant survey and inspection organizations.

---

27 'Hire purchase' is a more precise translation here.
28 Ibid.

Article 158

If before the commencement of the towage service, due to *force majeure* or other causes not attributable to the fault of either party, the towage contract could not be performed, either party may cancel the contract and neither shall be liable to the other. In such event, the towage price that had already been paid shall be returned to the tow party by the tugowner, unless otherwise agreed upon in the towage contract.

Article 159

If after the commencement of the towage service, due to *force majeure* or other causes not attributable to the fault of either party, the towage contract could not be performed, either party may cancel the towage contract and neither shall be liable to the other.

Article 160

Where the object towed could not reach its destination due to *force majeure* or other causes not attributable to the fault of either party, unless the towage contract provides otherwise, the tugowner may deliver the object towed to the tow party or its agent at a place near the destination or at a safe port or an anchorage chosen by the Master of the tug, and the contract of towage shall be deemed to have been fulfilled.

Article 161

Where the tow party fails to pay the towage price or other reasonable expenses as agreed, the tugowner shall have a lien on the object towed.

Article 162

In the course of the sea towage, if the damage suffered by the tugowner or the tow party was caused by the fault of one of the parties, the party in fault shall be liable for compensation. If the damage was caused by the faults of both parties, both parties shall be liable for compensation in proportion to the extent of their respective faults.

Notwithstanding the provisions of the preceding paragraph, the tugowner shall not be liable if he proves that the damage suffered by the tow party is due to one of the following causes:

(1) Fault of the Master or other crew members of the tug or the pilot or other servants or agents of the tugowner in the navigation and management of the tug;
(2) Fault of the tug in saving or attempting to save life or property at sea.

The provisions of this Article shall only apply if and when there are no provisions or no different provisions in this regard in the sea towage contract.

Article 163

If death of or personal injury to a third party or damage to property thereof has occurred during the sea towage due to the fault of the tugowner or the tow party, the tugowner and the tow party shall be liable jointly and severally to that third party. Except as otherwise provided for in the towage contract, the party that has jointly and severally paid a compensation in an amount exceeding the proportion for which it is liable shall have the right of recourse against the other party.

Article 164

Where a tugowner towing a barge owned or operated by him to transport goods by sea from one port to another, it shall be deemed as an act of carriage of goods by sea.

Chapter VIII Collision of Ships

Article 165

Collision of ships means an accident arising from the touching of ships at sea or in other navigable waters adjacent thereto.

Ships referred to in the preceding paragraph shall include those non-military or public service ships or craft that collide with the ships mentioned in Article 3 of this Code.

Article 166

After a collision, the Master of each of the ships in collision is bound, so far as he can do so without serious danger to his ship and persons on board to render assistance to the other ship and persons on board.

The Master of each of the ships in collision is likewise bound so far as possible to make known to the other ship the name of his ship, its port of registry, port of departure and port of destination.

Article 167

Neither of the parties shall be liable to the other if the collision is caused by *force majeure* or other causes not attributable to the fault of either party or if the cause thereof is left in doubt.

Article 168

If the collision is caused by the fault of one of the ships, the one in fault shall be liable therefore.

Article 169

If the colliding ships are all in fault, each ship shall be liable in proportion to the extent of its fault; if the respective faults are equal in proportion or it is impossible to determine the extent of the proportion of the respective faults, the liability of the colliding ships shall be apportioned equally.

The ships in fault shall be liable for the damage to the ship, the goods and other property on board pursuant to the proportions prescribed in the preceding paragraph. Where damage is caused to the property of a third party, the liability for compensation of any of the colliding ships shall not exceed the proportion it shall bear.

If the ships in fault have caused loss of life or personal injury to a third party, they shall be jointly and severally liable therefore. If a ship has paid an amount of compensation in excess of the proportion prescribed in paragraph 1 of this Article, it shall have the right of recourse against the other ship(s) in fault.

Article 170
Where a ship has caused damage to another ship and persons, goods or other property on board that ship, either by the execution or non-execution of a manoeuvre[29] or by the non-observance of navigation regulations, even if no collision has actually occurred, the provisions of this Chapter shall apply.

Chapter IX Salvage at Sea

Article 171
The provisions of this Chapter shall apply to salvage operations rendered at sea or any other navigable waters adjacent thereto to ships and other property in distress.

Article 172
For the purposes of this Chapter:

(1) 'Ship' means any ship referred to in Article 3 of this Code and any other non-military, public service ship or craft that has been involved in a salvage operation therewith;
(2) 'Property' means any property not permanently and intentionally attached to the shoreline and includes freight at risk;
(3) 'Payment' means any reward, remuneration or compensation for salvage operations to be paid by the salved party to the salvor pursuant to the provisions of this Chapter.

Article 173
The provisions of this Chapter shall not apply to fixed or floating platforms or mobile offshore drilling units when such platforms or units are on

---

29 A better translation would be '... either by the improper manoeuvring of the ship ...'
    Ed. note.

location engaged in the exploration, exploitation or production of sea-bed mineral resources.

Article 174
Every Master is bound, so far as he can do so without serious danger to his ship and persons on board, to render assistance to any person in danger of being lost at sea.

Article 175
A contract for salvage operations at sea is concluded when an agreement has been reached between the salvor and the salved party regarding the salvage operations to be undertaken.

The Master of the ship in distress shall have the authority to conclude a contract for salvage operations on behalf of the shipowner. The Master of the ship in distress or its owner shall have the authority to conclude a contract for salvage operations on behalf of the owner of the property on board.

Article 176
The salvage contract may be modified by a judgment of the court which has entertained the suit brought by either party, or modified by an award of the arbitration organization to which the dispute has been submitted for arbitration upon the agreement of the parties, under any of the following circumstances:

(1) The contract has been entered into under undue influence or the influence of danger and its terms are obviously inequitable;
(2) The payment under the contract is in an excessive degree too large or too small for the services actually rendered.

Article 177
During the salvage operation, the salvor shall owe a duty to the salved party to:

(1) carry out the salvage operation with due care;
(2) exercise due care to prevent or minimize the pollution damage to the environment;
(3) seek the assistance of other salvors where reasonably necessary;
(4) accept the reasonable request of the salved party to seek the participation in the salvage operation of other salvors. However, if the request is not well-founded, the amount of payment due to the original salvor shall not be affected.

Article 178
During the salvage operation, the party salved is under an obligation to the salvor to:

(1) cooperate fully with the salvor;
(2) exercise due care to prevent or minimize the pollution damage to the environment;
(3) promptly accept the request of the salvor to take delivery of the ship or property salved when such ship or property has been brought to a place of safety.

Article 179
Where the salvage operations rendered to the distressed ship and other property have had a useful result, the salvor shall be entitled to a reward. Except as otherwise provided for by Article 182 of this Code or by other laws or the salvage contract, the salvor shall not be entitled to the payment if the salvage operations have had no useful result.

Article 180
The reward shall be fixed with a view to encouraging salvage operations, taking into full account the following criteria:

(1) Value of the ship and other property salved;
(2) Skill and efforts of the salvors in preventing or minimizing the pollution damage to the environment;
(3) Measure of success obtained by the salvors;
(4) Nature and extent of the danger;
(5) Skill and efforts of the salvors in salving the ship, other property and life;
(6) Time used and expenses and losses incurred by the salvors;
(7) Risk of liability and other risks run by the salvors or their equipment;
(8) Promptness of the salvage services rendered by the salvors;
(9) Availability and use of ships or other equipment intended for salvage operations;
(10) State of readiness and efficiency of the salvor's equipment and the value thereof.

The reward shall not exceed the value of the ship and other property salved.

Article 181
The salved value of the ship and other property means the assessed value of the ship and other property salved or the proceeds of the sale thereof, after deduction of the relevant taxes and customs dues, quarantine expenses, inspection charges as well as expenses incurred in connection with the discharge, storage, assessment of the value and the sale thereof.

The value prescribed in the preceding paragraph does not include the value of the salved personal belongings of the crew and that of the cabin luggage of the passengers.

Article 182

If the salvor has carried out the salvage operations in respect of a ship which by itself or its goods threatened pollution damage to the environment and has failed to earn a reward under Article 180 of this Code at least equivalent to the special compensation assessable in accordance with this Article, he shall be entitled to special compensation from the owner of that ship equivalent to his expenses as herein defined.

If the salvor has carried out the salvage operations prescribed in the preceding paragraph and has prevented or minimized pollution damage to the environment, the special compensation payable by the owner to the salvor under paragraph 1 of this Article may be increased by an amount up to a maximum of 30% of the expenses incurred by the salvor. The court which has entertained the suit or the arbitration organization may, if it deems fair and just and taking into consideration the provisions of paragraph 1 of Article 180 of this Code, render a judgment or an award further increasing the amount of such special compensation, but in no event shall the total increase be more than 100% of the expenses incurred by the salvor.

The salvor's expenses referred to in this Article means the salvor's out-of-pocket expenses reasonably incurred in the salvage operation and the reasonable expenses for the equipment and personnel actually used in the salvage operation. In determining the salvor's expenses, the provisions of sub-paragraphs (8), (9) and (10) of paragraph 1 of Article 180 of this Code shall be taken into consideration.

Under all circumstances, the total special compensation provided for in this Article shall be paid only if such compensation is greater than the reward recoverable by the salvor under Article 180 of this Code, and the amount to be paid shall be the difference between the special compensation and the reward.

If the salvor has been negligent and has thereby failed to prevent or minimize the pollution damage to the environment, the salvor may be totally or partly deprived of the right to the special compensation.

Nothing in this Article shall affect the right of recourse on the part of the shipowner against any other parties salved.

Article 183

The salvage reward shall be paid by the owners of the salved ship and other property in accordance with the respective proportions which the salved values of the ship and other property bear to the total salved value.

Article 184

The distribution of salvage reward among the salvors taking part in the same salvage operation shall be made by agreement among such salvors on the basis of the criteria set out in Article 180 of this Code; failing such agreement, the matter may be brought before the court hearing the case for judgment, or, upon the agreement of the parties, submitted to the arbitration organization for an award.

Article 185

The salvors of human life may not demand any remuneration from those whose lives are saved. However, salvors of human life are entitled to a fair share of the payment awarded to the salvor for salving the ship or other property or for preventing or minimizing the pollution damage to the environment.

Article 186

The following salvage operations shall not be entitled to remuneration:

(1) The salvage operation is carried out as a duty to normally perform a towage contract or other service contract, with the exception, however, of providing special services beyond the performance of the above said duty.
(2) The salvage operation is carried out in spite of the express and reasonable prohibition on the part of the Master of the ship in distress, the owner of the ship in question and the owner of the other property.

Article 187

Where the salvage operations have become necessary or more difficult due to the fault of the salvor or where the salvor has committed fraud or other dishonest conduct, the salvor shall be deprived of the whole or part of the payment payable to him.

Article 188

After the completion of the salvage operation, the party salved shall, at the request of the salvor, provide satisfactory security for salvage reward and other charges.

Without prejudice to the provisions of the preceding paragraph, the owner of the ship salved shall, before the release of the goods, make best endeavours to cause the owners of the property salved to provide satisfactory security for the share of the payment that they ought to bear.

Without the consent of the salvor, the ship or other property salved shall not be removed from the port or place at which they first arrived after the completion of the salvage operation, until satisfactory security has been provided with respect to the ship or other property salved, as demanded by the salvor.

Article 189

The court or the arbitration organization handling the salvor's claim for payment may, in light of the specific circumstances and under fair and just terms, decide or make an award ordering the party salved to pay on account an appropriate amount to the salvor.

On the basis of the payment on account made by the party salved in accordance with the provisions of the preceding paragraph, the security provided under Article 188 of this Code shall be reduced accordingly.

Article 190

If the party salved has neither made the payment nor provided satisfactory security for the ship and other property salved after 90 days of the salvage, the salvor may apply to the court for an order on forced sale by auction. With respect to the ship or the property salved that cannot be kept or cannot be properly kept, or the storage charge to be incurred may exceed its value, the salvor may apply for an earlier forced sale by auction.

The proceeds of the sale shall, after deduction of the expenses incurred for the storage and sale, be used for the payment in accordance with the provisions of this Code. The remainder, if any, shall be returned to the party salved, and, if there is no way to return the remainder or if the remainder has not been claimed after one year of the forced sale, it shall go to the State treasury. In case of any deficiency, the salvor has the right of recourse against the party salved.

Article 191

The provisions of this Chapter shall apply to the salvor's right to the payment for the salvage operations carried out between the ships of the same owner.

Article 192

With respect to the salvage operations performed or controlled by the relevant competent authorities of the State, the salvors shall be entitled to avail themselves of the rights and remedies provided for in this Chapter in respect of salvage operations.

Chapter X General Average

Article 193

General average means the extraordinary sacrifice or expenditure intentionally and reasonably made or incurred for the common safety for the purpose of preserving from peril the ship, goods or other property involved in a common maritime adventure.

Loss or damage sustained by the ship or goods through delay, whether on the voyage or subsequently, such as demurrage and loss of market as well as other indirect losses, shall not be admitted as general average.

Article 194

When a ship, after having been damaged in consequence of accident, sacrifice or other extraordinary circumstances, shall have entered a port or place of refuge or returned to its port or place of loading to effect repairs which are necessary for the safe prosecution of the voyage, then the port charges paid, the wages and maintenance of the crew incurred and the fuel and stores consumed during the extra period of detention in such port or place, as well as the loss or damage and charges arising from the discharge, storage, reloading and handling of the goods, fuel, stores and other property on board in order to have the repairs done shall be allowed as general average.

Article 195

Any extra expense incurred in place of another expense which would have been allowed as general average shall be deemed to be general average and so allowed, but the amount of such expense incurred shall not be in excess of the general average expense avoided.

Article 196

The onus of proof shall be upon the party claiming in general average to show that the loss or expense claimed is properly allowable as general average.

Article 197

Rights to contribution in general average shall not be affected, though the event which gave rise to the sacrifice or expenditure may have been due to the fault of one of the parties to the adventure. However, this shall not prejudice any remedies or defences which may be open against or to that party in respect of such fault.

Article 198

The amounts of sacrifice of the ship, the goods and the freight shall be respectively determined as follows:

(1) The amount of sacrifice of the ship shall be calculated on the basis of the repair cost of the ship actually paid, from which any reasonable deduction in respect of 'new for old' being made. Where the ship has not been repaired after the sacrifice, the amount of sacrifice thereof shall be calculated on the basis of the reasonable reduced value of ship after the general average sacrifice. Such amount shall not exceed the estimated cost of repair.

Where the ship is an actual total loss or where the cost of repair would exceed the value of the ship after the repair, the amount of sacrifice of the ship shall be calculated on the basis of the estimated sound value of the ship, less the estimated cost of repair not allowable as general average, as well as the value of the ship after the damage.

(2) The amount of sacrifice of the goods already lost shall be calculated on the basis of the value of the goods at the time of shipment plus insurance and freight, from which the freight that need not be paid due to the sacrifice made being deducted. For the damaged goods that had already been sold before an agreement was reached on the extent of the damage sustained, the amount of sacrifice thereof shall be calculated on the basis of the difference between the value of the goods at the time of shipment plus insurance and freight, and the net proceeds of the goods so sold.

(3) The amount of sacrifice of the freight shall be calculated on the basis of the amount of loss of freight on account of the sacrifice of the goods, from which the operating expenses that ought to be paid in order to earn such freight but need not be paid because of the sacrifice shall be deducted.

Article 199

The contribution in general average shall be made in proportion to the contributory values of the respective beneficiaries.

The contributory value in general average by the ship, goods and freight shall be determined as follows:

(1) The contributory value of the ship shall be calculated on the basis of the sound value of the ship at the place where the voyage ends, from which any damage that does not come under general average sacrifice being deducted; alternately, the actual value of the ship at the place where the voyage ends, plus the amount of general average sacrifice.

(2) The contributory value of the goods shall be calculated on the basis of the value of the goods at the time of shipment plus insurance and freight, from which the damage that does not come under the general average sacrifice and the carrier's freight at risk being deducted. Where the goods had been sold before arriving at the port of destination, their value for contribution shall be the net proceeds plus the amount of general average sacrifice.

Passenger's luggage and personal belongings shall not be included in the value for contribution.

(3) The Contributory value of freight shall be calculated on the basis of the amount of freight at the risk of the carrier and which the carrier is entitled to collect at the end of the voyage, less any expense incurred for the prosecution of the voyage after the general average, in order to earn the freight, plus the amount of general average sacrifice.

Article 200

Goods undeclared or wrongfully declared shall be liable for the contribution to general average, but the special sacrifice sustained by such goods shall not be allowed as general average.

Where the value of the goods has been improperly declared at a value below [their] actual value, the contribution to general average shall be made on the basis of their actual value and, where a general average sacrifice has occurred, the amount of sacrifice shall be calculated on the basis of the declared value.

Article 201

Interest shall be allowed on general average sacrifice and general average expenses paid on account. A commission shall be allowed for the general average expenses paid on account, except those for the wages and maintenance of the crew and fuel and store consumed.

Article 202

The contributing parties shall provide security for general average contribution at the request of the parties that have an interest therein.

Where the security has been provided in the form of cash deposits, such deposits shall be put in a bank by an average adjuster in the name of a trustee.

The provision, use and refund of the deposits shall be without prejudice to the ultimate liability of the contributing parties.

Article 203

The adjustment of general average shall be governed by the average adjustment rules agreed upon in the relevant contract. In the absence of such an agreement in the contract, the relevant provisions contained in this Chapter shall apply.

Chapter XI Limitation of Liability for Maritime Claims

Article 204

Shipowners and salvors may limit their liability in accordance with the provisions of this Chapter for claims set out in Article 207 of this Code.

The shipowners referred to in the preceding paragraph shall include the charterer and the operator of a ship.

Article 205

If the claims set out in Article 207 of this Code are not made against shipowners or salvors themselves but against persons for whose act, neglect or default the shipowners or salvors are responsible, such persons may limit their liability in accordance with the provisions of this Chapter.

Article 206
Where the assured may limit his liability in accordance with the provisions of this Chapter, the insurer liable for the maritime claims shall be entitled to the limitation of liability under this Chapter to the same extent as the assured.

Article 207
Except as provided otherwise in Articles 208 and 209 of this Code, with respect to the following maritime claims, the person liable may limit his liability in accordance with the provisions of this Chapter, whatever the basis of liability may be:

(1) Claims in respect of loss of life or personal injury or loss of or damage to property including damage to harbour works, basins and waterways and aids to navigation occurring on board or in direct connection with the operation of the ship or with salvage operations, as well as consequential damages resulting therefrom;
(2) Claims in respect of loss resulting from delay in delivery in the carriage of goods by sea or from delay in the arrival of passengers or their luggage;
(3) Claims in respect of other loss resulting from infringement of rights other than contractual rights occurring in direct connection with the operation of the ship or salvage operations;
(4) Claims of a person other than the person liable in respect of measures taken to avert or minimize loss for which the person liable may limit his liability in accordance with the provisions of this Chapter, and further loss caused by such measures.

All the claims set out in the preceding paragraph, whatever the way they are lodged, may be entitled to limitation of liability. However, with respect to the remuneration set out in sub-paragraph (4) for which the person liable pays as agreed upon in the contract, in relation to the obligation for payment, the person liable may not invoke the provisions on limitation of liability of this Article.

Article 208
The provisions of this Chapter shall not be applicable to the following claims:

(1) Claims for salvage payment or contribution in general average;
(2) Claims for oil pollution damage under the International Convention on Civil Liability for Oil Pollution Damage to which the People's Republic of China is a party;
(3) Claims for nuclear damage under the International Convention on Limitation of Liability for Nuclear Damage to which the People's Republic of China is a party;

(4) Claims against the shipowner of a nuclear ship for nuclear damage;

(5) Claims by the servants of the shipowner or salvor, if under the law governing the contract of employment, the shipowner or salvor is not entitled to limit his liability or if he is by such law only permitted to limit his liability to an amount greater than that provided for in this Chapter.

Article 209

A person liable shall not be entitled to limit his liability in accordance with the provisions of this Chapter, if it is proved that the loss resulted from his act or omission done with the intent to cause such loss or recklessly and with knowledge that such loss would probably result.

Article 210

The limitation of liability for maritime claims, except as otherwise provided for in Article 211 of this Code, shall be calculated as follows:

(1) In respect of claims for loss of life or personal injury:

    a) 333,000 Units of Account for a ship with a gross tonnage ranging from 300 to 500 tons;

    b) For a ship with a gross tonnage in excess of 500 tons, the limitation under a) above shall be applicable to the first 500 tons and the following amounts in addition to that set out under a) shall be applicable to the gross tonnage in excess of 500 tons:

> For each ton from 501 to 3,000 tons: 500 Units of Account;
> For each ton from 3,001 to 30,000 tons: 333 Units of Account;
> For each ton from 30,001 to 70,000 tons: 250 Units of Account;
> For each ton in excess of 70,000 tons: 167 Units of Account;

(2) In respect of claims other than that for loss of life or personal injury:

    a) 167,000 Units of Account for a ship with a gross tonnage ranging from 300 to 500 tons;

    b) For a ship with a gross tonnage in excess of 500 tons, the limitation under a) above shall be applicable to the first 500 tons, and the following amounts in addition to that under a) shall be applicable to the part in excess of 500 tons:

> For each ton from 501 to 30,000 tons: 167 Units of Account;
> For each ton from 30,001 to 70,000 tons: 125 Units of Account;
> For each ton in excess of 70,000 tons: 83 Units of Account.

(3) Where the amount calculated in accordance with sub-paragraph (1) above is insufficient for payment of claims for loss of life or personal

injury set out therein in full, the amount calculated in accordance with sub-paragraph (2) shall be available for payment of the unpaid balance of claims under sub-paragraph (1), and such unpaid balance shall rank rateably with claims set out under sub-paragraph (2).

(4) However, without prejudice to the right of claims for loss of life or personal injury under sub-paragraph (3), claims in respect of damage to harbour works, basins and waterways and aids to navigation shall have priority over other claims under sub-paragraph (2).

(5) The limitation of liability for any salvor not operating from any ship or for any salvor operating solely on the ship to, or in respect of which, he is rendering salvage services, shall be calculated according to a gross tonnage of 1,500 tons.

The limitation of liability for ships with a gross tonnage not exceeding 300 tons and those engaging in transport services between the ports of the People's Republic of China as well as those for other coastal works shall be worked out by the competent authorities of transport and communications under the State Council and implemented after its being submitted to and approved by the State Council.

Article 211

In respect of claims for loss of life or personal injury to passengers carried by sea, the limitation of liability of the shipowner thereof shall be an amount of 46,666 Units of Account multiplied by the number of passengers which the ship is authorized to carry according to the ship's relevant certificate, but the maximum amount of compensation shall not exceed 25,000,000 Units of Account.

The limitation of liability for claims for loss of life or personal injury to passengers carried by sea between the ports of the People's Republic of China shall be worked out by the competent authorities of transport and communications under the State Council and implemented after its being submitted to and approved by the State Council.

Article 212

The limitation of liability under Articles 210 and 211 of this Code shall apply to the aggregate of all claims that may arise on any given occasion against shipowners and salvors themselves, and any person for whose act, neglect or fault the shipowners and the salvors are responsible.

Article 213

Any person liable claiming the limitation of liability under this Code may constitute a limitation fund with a court having jurisdiction. The fund shall be constituted in the sum of such an amount set out respectively in Articles 210 and 211, together with the interest thereon from the date of the occurrence giving rise to the liability until the date of the constitution of the fund.

Article 214
Where a limitation fund has been constituted by a person liable, any person having made a claim against the person liable may not exercise any right against any assets of the person liable. Where any ship or other property belonging to the person constituting the fund has been arrested or attached, or, where a security has been provided by such person, the court shall order without delay the release of the ship arrested or the property attached or the return of the security provided.

Article 215
Where a person entitled to limitation of liability under the provisions of this Chapter has a counter-claim against the claimant arising out of the same occurrence, their respective claims shall be set off against each other and the provisions of this Chapter shall only apply to the balance, if any.

Chapter XII Contract of Marine Insurance

Section 1 Basic Principles
Article 216
A contract of marine insurance is a contract whereby the insurer under-takes, as agreed, to indemnify the loss to the subject matter insured and the liability of the insured caused by perils covered by the insurance against the payment of an insurance premium by the insured.

The covered perils referred to in the preceding paragraph mean any maritime perils agreed upon between the insurer and the insured, including perils occurring in inland rivers or on land which is related to a maritime adventure.

Article 217
A contract of marine insurance mainly includes:

(1) Name of the insurer;
(2) Name of the insured;
(3) Subject matter insured;
(4) Insured value;
(5) Insured amount;
(6) Perils insured against and perils excepted;[30]
(7) Duration of insurance coverage;
(8) Insurance premium.

---

30 Or 'Insured perils and excluded perils'.

Article 218
The following items may come under the subject matter of marine insurance:

(1) Ship;
(2) Cargo;
(3) Income from the operation of the ship including freight, charter hire and passenger's fare;
(4) Expected profit on cargo;
(5) Crew's wages and other remuneration;
(6) Liabilities to a third person;
(7) Other property which may sustain loss from a maritime peril and the liability and expenses arising therefrom.

The insurer may reinsure the insurance of the subject matter enumerated in the preceding paragraph. Unless otherwise agreed in the contract, the original insured shall not be entitled to the benefit of the reinsurance.

Article 219
The insurable value of the subject matter insured shall be agreed upon between the insurer and the insured.

Where no insurable value has been agreed upon between the insurer and the insured, the insurable value shall be calculated as follows:

(1) The insurable value of the ship shall be the value of the ship at the time when the insurance liability commences, being the total value of the ship's hull, machinery, equipment, fuel, stores, gear, provisions and fresh water on board as well as the insurance premium;
(2) The insurable value of the cargo shall be the aggregate of the invoice value of the cargo or the actual value of the non-trade commodity at the place of shipment, plus freight and insurance premium when the insurance liability commences;
(3) The insurable value of the freight shall be the aggregate of the total amount of freight payable to the carrier and the insurance premium when the insurance liability commences;
(4) The insurable value of other subject matter insured shall be the aggregate of the actual value of the subject matter insured and the insurance premium when the insurance liability commences.

Article 220
The insured amount shall be agreed upon between the insurer and the insured. The insured amount shall not exceed the insured value. Where the insured amount exceeds the insured value, the portion in excess shall be null and void.

Section 2 Conclusion, Termination and Assignment of Contract

Article 221

A contract of marine insurance comes into being after the insured puts forth a proposal for insurance and the insurer agrees to accept the proposal and the insurer and the insured agree on the terms and conditions of the insurance. The insurer shall issue to the insured an insurance policy or other certificate of insurance in time, and the contents of the contract shall be contained therein.

Article 222

Before the contract is concluded, the insured shall truthfully inform the insurer of the material circumstances which the insured has knowledge of or ought to have knowledge of in his ordinary business practice and which may have a bearing on the insurer in deciding the premium or whether be agrees to insure or not.

The insured need not inform the insurer of the facts which the insurer has known of or the insurer ought to have knowledge of in his ordinary business practice if about which the insurer made no inquiry.

Article 223

Upon failure of the insured to truthfully inform the insurer of the material circumstances set forth in paragraph 1 of Article 222 of this Code due to his intentional act, the insurer has the right to terminate the contract without refunding the premium. The insurer shall not be liable for any loss arising from the perils insured against before the contract is terminated.

If, not due to the insured's intentional act, the insured did not truthfully inform the insurer of the material circumstances set out in paragraph 1 of Article 222 of this Code, the insurer has the right to terminate the contract or to demand a corresponding increase in the premium. In case the contract is terminated by the insurer, the insurer shall be liable for the loss arising from the perils insured against which occurred prior to the termination of the contract, except where the material circumstances uninformed or wrongly informed of have an impact on the occurrence of such perils.

Article 224

Where the insured was aware or ought to be aware that the subject matter insured had suffered a loss due to the incidence of a peril insured against when the contract was concluded, the insurer shall not be liable for indemnification but shall have the right to the premium. Where the insurer was aware or ought to be aware that the occurrence of a loss to the subject matter insured due to a peril insured against was impossible, the insured shall have the right to recover the premium paid.

Article 225

Where the insured concludes contracts with several insurers for the same subject matter insured and against the same risk, and the insured amount of the said subject matter insured thereby exceeds the insured value, then, unless otherwise agreed in the contract, the insured may demand indemnification from any of the insurers and the aggregate amount to be indemnified shall not exceed the loss value of the subject matter insured. The liability of each insurer shall be in proportion to that which the amount he insured bears to the total of the amounts insured by all insurers. Any insurer who has paid an indemnification in an amount greater than that for which he is liable, shall have the right of recourse against those who have not paid their indemnification in the amounts for which they are liable.

Article 226

Prior to the commencement of the insurance liability, the insured may demand the termination of the insurance contract but shall pay the handling fees to the insurer, and the insurer shall refund the premium.

Article 227

Unless otherwise agreed in the contract, neither the insurer nor the insured may terminate the contract after the commencement of the insurance liability.

Where the insurance contract provides that the contract may be terminated after the commencement of the liability, and the insured demands the termination of the contract, the insurer shall have the right to the premium payable from the day of the commencement of the insurance liability to the day of termination of the contract and refund the remaining portion. If it is the insurer who demands the termination of the contract, the unexpired premium from the day of the termination of the contract to the day of the expiration of the period of insurance shall be refunded to the insured.

Article 228

Notwithstanding the stipulations in Article 227 of this Code, the insured may not demand termination of the contract for cargo insurance and voyage insurance on ship after the commencement of the insurance liability.

Article 229

A contract of marine insurance for the carriage of goods by sea may be assigned by the insured by endorsement or otherwise, and the rights and obligations under the contract are assigned accordingly. The insured and the assignee shall be jointly and severally liable for the payment of the premium if such premium remains unpaid up to the time of the assignment of the contract.

Article 230

The consent of the insurer shall be obtained where the insurance contract is assigned in consequence of the transfer of the ownership of the ship insured. In the absence of such consent, the contract shall be terminated from the time of the transfer of the ownership of the ship. Where the transfer takes place during the voyage, the contract shall be terminated when the voyage ends.

Upon termination of the contract, the insurer shall refund the unexpired premium to the insured calculated from the day of the termination of the contract to the day of its expiration.

Article 231

The insured may conclude an open cover with the insurer for the goods to be shipped or received in batches within a given period. The open cover shall be evidenced by an open policy to be issued by the insurer.

Article 232

The insurer shall, at the request of the insured, issue insurance certificates separately for the cargo shipped in batches according to the open cover.

Where the contents of the insurance certificates issued by the insurer separately differ from those of the open policy, the insurance certificates issued separately shall prevail.

Article 233

The insured shall notify the insurer immediately on learning that the cargo insured under the open cover has been shipped or has arrived. The items to be notified of shall include the name of the carrying ship, the voyage, the value of the cargo and the insured amount.

Section 3 Obligation of the Insured

Article 234

Unless otherwise agreed in the insurance contract, the insured shall pay the premium immediately upon conclusion of the contract. The insurer may refuse to issue the insurance policy or other insurance certificate before the premium is paid by the insured.

Article 235

The insured shall notify the insurer in writing immediately where the insured has not complied with the warranties under the contract. The insurer may, upon receipt of the notice, terminate the contract or demand an amendment to the terms and conditions of the insurance coverage or an increase in the premium.

Article 236
Upon the occurrence of the peril insured against, the insured shall notify the insurer immediately and shall take necessary and reasonable measures to avoid or minimize the loss. Where special instructions for the adoption of reasonable measures to avoid or minimize the loss are received from the insurer, the insured shall act according to such instructions.

The insurer shall not be liable for the extended loss caused by the insured's breach of the provisions of the preceding paragraph.

Section 4 Liability[31] of the Insurer

Article 237
The insurer shall indemnify the insured promptly after the loss from a peril insured against has occurred.

Article 238
The insurer's indemnification for the loss from the peril insured against shall be limited to the insured amount. Where the insured amount is lower than the insured value, the insurer shall indemnify in the proportion that the insured amount bears to the insured value.

Article 239
The insurer shall be liable for the loss to the subject matter insured arising from several perils insured against during the period of the insurance even though the aggregate of the amounts of loss exceeds the insured amount. However, the insurer shall only be liable for the total loss where the total loss occurs after the partial loss which has not been repaired.

Article 240
The insurer shall pay, in addition to the indemnification to be paid with regard to the subject matter insured, the necessary and reasonable expenses incurred by the insured for avoiding or minimizing the loss recoverable under the contract, the reasonable expenses for survey and assessment of the value for the purpose of ascertaining the nature and extent of the peril insured against and the expenses incurred for acting on the special instructions of the insurer.

The payment by the insurer of the expenses referred to in the preceding paragraph shall be limited to that equivalent to the insured amount.

Where the insured amount is lower than the insured value, the insurer shall be liable for the expenses referred to in this Article in the proportion that the insured amount bears to the insured value, unless the contract provides otherwise.

31 'Duties' seems to be a more precise translation.

Article 241

Where the insured amount is lower than the value for contribution under the general average, the insurer shall be liable for the general average contribution in the proportion that the insured amount bears to the value for contribution.

Article 242

The insurer shall not be liable for the loss caused by the intentional act of the insured.

Article 243

Unless otherwise agreed in the insurance contract, the insurer shall not be liable for the loss of or damage to the insured cargo arising from any of the following causes:

(1) Delay in the voyage or in the delivery of cargo or change of market price;
(2) Fair wear and tear, inherent vice or nature of the cargo; and
(3) Improper packing.

Article 244

Unless otherwise agreed in the insurance contract, the insurer shall not be liable for the loss of or damage to the insured ship arising from any of the following causes:

(1) Unseaworthiness of the ship at the time of the commencement of the voyage, unless where under a time policy the insured has no knowledge thereof;
(2) Wear and tear or corrosion of the ship.

The provisions of this Article shall apply *mutatis mutandis* to the insurance of freight.

Section 5 Loss of or Damage to the Subject Matter Insured and Abandonment

Article 245

Where after the occurrence of a peril insured against the subject matter insured is lost or is so seriously damaged that it is completely deprived of its original structure and usage or the insured is deprived of the possession thereof, it shall constitute an actual total loss.

Article 246

Where a ship's total loss is considered to be unavoidable after the occurrence of a peril insured against or the expenses necessary for avoiding the occurrence of an actual total loss would exceed the insured value, it shall constitute a constructive total loss.

Where an actual total loss is considered to be unavoidable after the cargo has suffered a peril insured against, or the expenses to be incurred for avoiding the total actual loss plus that for forwarding the cargo to its destination would exceed its insured value, it shall constitute a constructive total loss.

Article 247
Any loss other than an actual total loss or a constructive total loss is a partial loss.

Article 248
Where a ship fails to arrive at its destination within a reasonable time from the place where it was last heard of, unless the contract provides otherwise, if it remains unheard of upon the expiry of two months, it shall constitute missing. Such missing shall be deemed to be an actual total loss.

Article 249
Where the subject matter insured has become a constructive total loss and the insured demands indemnification from the insurer on the basis of a total loss, the subject matter insured shall be abandoned to the insurer. The insurer may accept the abandonment or choose not to, but shall inform the insured of his decision whether to accept the abandonment within a reasonable time.

The abandonment shall not be attached with any conditions. Once the abandonment is accepted by the insurer, it shall not be withdrawn.

Article 250
Where the insurer has accepted the abandonment, all rights and obligations relating to the property abandoned are transferred to the insurer.

Section 6 Payment of Indemnity

Article 251
After the occurrence of a peril insured against and before the payment of indemnity, the insurer may demand that the insured submit evidence and materials related to the ascertainment of the nature of the peril and the extent of the loss.

Article 252
Where the loss of or damage to the subject matter insured within the insurance coverage is caused by a third person, the right of the insured to demand compensation from the third person shall be subrogated to the insurer from the time the indemnity is paid.

The insured shall furnish the insurer with necessary documents and information that should come to his knowledge and shall endeavour to assist the insurer in pursuing recovery from the third person.

Article 253
Where the insured waives his right of claim against the third person without the consent of the insurer or the insurer is unable to exercise the right of recourse due to the fault of the insured, the insurer may make a corresponding reduction from the amount of indemnity.

Article 254
In effecting payment of indemnity to the insured, the insurer may make a corresponding reduction therefrom of the amount already paid by a third person to the insured.

Where the compensation obtained by the insurer from the third person exceeds the amount of indemnity paid by the insurer, the part in excess shall be returned to the insured.

Article 255
After the occurrence of a peril insured against, the insurer is entitled to waive his right to the subject matter insured and pay the insured the amount in full to relieve himself of the obligations under the contract.

In exercising the right prescribed in the preceding paragraph, the insurer shall notify the insured thereof within seven days from the day of the receipt of the notice from the insured regarding the indemnity. The insurer shall remain liable for the necessary and reasonable expenses paid by the insured for avoiding or minimizing the loss prior to his receipt of the said notice.

Article 256
Except as stipulated in Article 255 of this Code, where a total loss occurs to the subject matter insured and the full insured amount is paid, the insurer shall acquire the full right to the subject matter insured. In the case of under-insurance, the insurer shall acquire the right to the subject matter insured in the proportion that the insured amount bears to the insured value.

Chapter XIII Limitation of Time

Article 257
The limitation period for claims against the carrier with regard to the carriage of goods by sea is one year, counting from the day on which the goods were delivered or should have been delivered by the carrier. Within the limitation period or after the expiration thereof, if the person allegedly liable has brought up a claim of recourse against a third person, that claim

is time-barred at the expiration of 90 days, counting from the day on which the person claiming for the recourse settled the claim, or was served with a copy of the process by the court handling the claim against him.

The limitation period for claims against the carrier with regard to voyage charter party is two years, counting from the day on which the claimant knew or should have known that his right had been infringed.

Article 258
The limitation period for claims against the carrier with regard to the carriage of passengers by sea is two years, counting respectively as follows:

(1) Claims for personal injury: Counting from the day on which the passenger disembarked or should have disembarked;
(2) Claims for death of passengers that occurred during the period of carriage: Counting from the day on which the passenger should have disembarked; whereas those for the death of passengers that occurred after the disembarkation but resulted from an injury during the period of carriage by sea, counting from the day of the death of the passenger concerned, provided that this period does not exceed three years from the time of disembarkation.
(3) Claims for loss of or damage to the luggage: Counting from the day of disembarkation or the day on which the passenger should have disembarked.

Article 259
The limitation period for claims with regard to charter parties is two years, counting from the day on which the claimant knew or should have known that his right had been infringed.

Article 260
The limitation period for claims with regard to sea towage is one year, counting from the day on which the claimant knew or should have known that his right had been infringed.

Article 261
The limitation period for claims with regard to collision of ships is two years, counting from the day on which the collision occurred. The limitation period for claims with regard to the right of recourse as provided for in paragraph 3 of Article 169 of this Code is one year, counting from the day on which the parties concerned jointly and severally paid the amount of compensation for the damage occurred.

Article 262
The limitation period for claims with regard to salvage at sea is two years, counting from the day on which the salvage operation was completed.

Article 263
The limitation period for claims with regard to contribution in general average is one year, counting from the day on which the adjustment was finished.

Article 264
The limitation period for claims with regard to contracts of marine insurance is two years, counting from the day on which the peril insured against occurred.

Article 265
The limitation period for claims with regard to compensation for oil pollution damage from ships is three years, counting from the day on which the pollution damage occurred. However, in no case shall the limitation period exceed six years, counting from the day on which the accident causing the pollution occurred.

Article 266
Within the last six months of the limitation period if, on account of *force majeure* or other causes preventing the claims from being made, the limitation period shall be suspended. The counting of the limitation period shall be resumed when the cause of suspension no longer exists.

Article 267
The limitation of time shall be discontinued as a result of bringing an action or submitting the case for arbitration by the claimant or the admission to fulfill obligations by the person against whom the claim was brought up. However, the limitation of time shall not be discontinued if the claimant withdraws his action or his submission for arbitration, or his action has been rejected by a decision of the court.

Where the claimant makes a claim for the arrest of a ship, the limitation of time shall be discontinued from the day on which the claim is made.

The limitation period shall be counted anew from the time of discontinuance.

Chapter XIV Application of Law in Relation to Foreign-related Matters

Article 268
If any international treaty concluded or acceded to by the People's Republic of China contains provisions differing from those contained in this Code,

the provisions of the relevant international treaty shall apply, unless the provisions are those on which the People's Republic of China has announced reservations.

International practice may be applied to matters for which neither the relevant laws of the People's Republic of China nor any international treaty concluded or acceded to by the People's Republic of China contain any relevant provisions

Article 269
The parties to a contract may choose the law applicable to such contract, unless the law provides otherwise. Where the parties to a contract have not made a choice, the law of the country having the closest connection with the contract shall apply.

Article 270
The law of the flag State of the ship shall apply to the acquisition, transfer and extinction of the ownership of the ship.

Article 271
The law of the flag State of the ship shall apply to the mortgage of the ship.

The law of the original country of registry of a ship shall apply to the mortgage of the ship if its mortgage is established before or during its bareboat charter period.

Article 272
The law of the place where the court hearing the case is located shall apply to matters pertaining to maritime liens.

Article 273
The law of the place where the infringing act is committed shall apply to claims for damages arising from collision of ships.

The law of the place where the court hearing the case is located shall apply to claims for damages arising from collision of ships on the high sea.

If the colliding ships belong to the same country, no matter where the collision occurs, the law of the flag State shall apply to claims against one another for damages arising from such collision.

Article 274
The law where the adjustment of general average is made shall apply to the adjustment of general average.

Article 275

The law of the place where the court hearing the case is located shall apply to the limitation of liability for maritime claims.

Article 276

The application of foreign laws or international practices pursuant to the provisions of this Chapter shall not jeopardize the public interests of the People's Republic of China.

Chapter XV Supplementary Provisions

Article 277

The Unit of Account referred to in this Code is the Special Drawing Right as defined by the International Monetary Fund; the amount of the Chinese currency (RMB) in terms of the Special Drawing Right shall be that computed on the basis of the method of conversion established by the authorities in charge of foreign exchange control of this country on the date of the judgment by the court or the date of the award by the arbitration organization or the date mutually agreed upon by the parties.

Article 278

This Code shall come into force as of July 1, 1993.

Index